GOOD HOUSEKEEPING

400 HEALTHY RECIPES

GOOD HOUSEKEEPING

400 HEALTHY RECIPES

EASY • DELICIOUS • LOW-CALORIE

HEARST
books

HEARSTBOOKS

An Imprint of Sterling Publishing Co., Inc.
1166 Avenue of the Americas
New York, NY 10036

ISBN 978-1-4351-6705-6

The Good Housekeeping Cookbook Seal guarantees that the recipes in this publication
meet the strict standards of the Good Housekeeping Research Institute.
The Institute has been a source of reliable information and a consumer advocate
since 1900, and established its seal of approval in 1909. Every recipe in this publication
has been triple-tested for ease, reliability, and great taste by the Institute.

Distributed in Canada by Sterling Publishing Co., Inc.
c/o Canadian Manda Group, 664 Annette Street
Toronto, Ontario, Canada M6S 2C8
Distributed in Australia by NewSouth Books
45 Beach Street, Coogee, NSW 2034, Australia

For information about custom editions, special sales, and premium and corporate purchases,
please contact Sterling Special Sales at 800-805-5489 or specialsales@sterlingpublishing.com.

Manufactured in China

2 4 6 8 10 9 7 5 3 1

sterlingpublishing.com
Book design by Memo Production

FOREWORD

400 Healthy Recipes puts together three of our favorite cookbooks to bring you hundreds of recipes for healthy meals to cook at home. The book is divided into three sections—Grains, Vegetarian, and Light & Healthy—to give you nutritious, delicious options for everything from a quick breakfast to a full sit-down dinner.

We've all heard about the health benefits of whole grains—how eating three servings a day of these "good carbs" can help reduce our chances of stroke, heart disease, and type 2 diabetes. But how do you incorporate their heart-healthy goodness into your family's daily meals? We teach you how to identify, prepare, and enjoy any whole grain that comes your way.

Vegetarian cooking is becoming increasingly popular, and our recipes provide real food for real families—even if you have only 30 minutes to make dinner for picky eaters. This collection will give you family-friendly weeknight choices that require no mysterious ingredients or complicated techniques, and there are also tips, shortcuts, and suggestions for rounding out the meal.

Everyone wants to eat nutritious meals, but sometimes it's hard to find easy, healthy recipes that everyone in your family love. We'll show you that cooking with an eye toward good health doesn't mean sacrificing taste or familiar foods you know your family will eat. Standbys like roasted chicken, lasagna, and even chocolate mousse can be light and nutritious.

Happy, healthy cooking for you and your family!

—SUSAN WESTMORELAND
Food Director, *Good Housekeeping*

CONTENTS

VEGETARIAN

LIGHT & HEALTHY

Couscous Paella (page 97)

GRAINS

INTRODUCTION

What's so great about grains? Why is it that everywhere you turn, someone is saying that we should all be eating more grains, specifically, more whole grains?

Here's the great, good news about whole grains. By consuming three servings of grains–which are rich in dietary fiber, protein, vitamins, and other nutrients–a day (and some studies say just one serving a day can have an impact), you can significantly, positively affect your health. Here are the numbers:

- You can reduce your chance of stroke 30% to 36%
- You can reduce your chance of developing type 2 diabetes 21% to 30%
- You can decrease your chance of heart disease 25% to 28%

In addition to that, enjoying several servings of grains a day in their many forms can:

- Reduce the risk of asthma
- Lower blood pressure
- Promote better dental health
- Help with weight maintenance
- Lower the risk of colorectal cancer
- Help maintain good health of carotid arteries

DIETARY GUIDELINES FOR GRAINS

According to the USDA, for optimum dietary health Americans should eat three or more 1-ounce servings of whole grains per day. How much is a 1-ounce serving? It's equivalent to:
- ½ cup cooked brown rice, oatmeal, or other whole grain
- ½ cup cooked 100% whole-grain pasta
- 1 slice 100% whole-grain bread
- 1 cup ready-to-eat 100% whole-grain cereal

Grains and Dietary Fiber

Whole grains are an excellent source of fiber. But what is dietary fiber? It consists of the indigestible components of plant food—basically, the material that travels right through you. There are two types of fiber: insoluble fiber, which promotes good digestion and can be an aid in weight loss, as the consumption of insoluble fiber can give you a feeling of fullness, quelling hunger; and soluble fiber. This type of fiber dissolves in water to form a gel-like substance and has been shown in studies to be effective in lowering blood cholesterol and glucose levels. Some studies show that eating just 3 grams of soluable fiber a day (the equivalent of a bowl of oatmeal) can lower the cholesterol level of those suffering from high cholesterol anywhere from 8% to 23%.

What's a Grain? What's a Whole Grain?

Grains are the seeds or fruit of grasses (there are a couple exceptions—more on that later). A grain consists of three components: the bran, which is the tough outer layer of the grain; the germ or embryo, which, if it were fertilized, would sprout into a new plant; and the endosperm, which comprises the bulk of the grain. The bran contains a wealth of antioxidants, vitamins, and dietary fiber; the germ, B vitamins, protein, minerals, and healthy fats; and the endosperm is comprised of starchy carbohydrates, proteins, and some vitamins and minerals. When the germ and bran are removed (which happens to different extents with different grains in the process known as milling or polishing), up to 25 percent of the grain's protein is lost as well as a host of nutrients, though some of that gets added back in (that's what has happened when you see on a label that a grain has been "enriched"). A "whole grain" is one that still possesses all three parts (bran, germ, and endosperm) in their natural proportions.

How Do You Know It's Whole Grain?

Searching your supermarket for whole-grain foods can be confusing—an oat waffle may be packed with whole grains, but a slice of 100 percent wheat bread isn't. Here are some tips for separating the wheat from the chaff when it comes to shopping for whole-grain foods.

- **SEEK OUT THE WHOLE-GRAIN COUNCIL STAMP.** This bright-yellow stamp was launched by the WGC in 2005 and states exactly how many grams of whole grains are contained in a serving of the product. Found on more than 600 packaged items, the stamp isn't an official standard and isn't endorsed by the FDA. But it's a clear, legitimate indicator of just how much whole grain you're getting.

Beef-Barley and Root Vegetable Stew (page 64)

EASY WAYS TO ADD GRAINS EVERY DAY

- Choose whole-wheat or whole-grain pasta instead of pasta made from more refined semolina flour.
- Use a combination of wild and brown rice in place of white rice in your favorite pilaf or rice-salad recipes, making sure to adjust the rice's cooking time (soak brown rice in cold water overnight in fridge to cut cooking time in half).
- Slice whole-wheat or multigrain bread into ½-inch cubes; toss with olive oil and bake until golden for tasty and healthy croutons.
- For a new twist, stir some plain vanilla yogurt and fruit jam into hot oatmeal before serving.
- When making a wrap or burrito, use whole-wheat or whole-kernel corn tortillas.
- Slice precooked polenta logs into rounds. Place on a cookie sheet and top with spaghetti sauce and cheese; bake until hot and bubbly for an easy vegetarian entrée.
- Sprinkle a spoonful of toasted wheat germ on your breakfast cereal (choose a cereal that lists whole grains at the top of the list of ingredients).
- Toss cooked bulgur, chopped parsley, and finely chopped celery, carrots, and red onion with your favorite vinaigrette for a tasty side dish.
- For a power-packed accompaniment to meat, mix a combination of cooked wheat berries and brown rice with sautéed onions, dried fruit, olive oil, and a pinch of ground cinnamon.
- For a quick dinner from the pantry, toss cooked whole-wheat couscous with drained and flaked tuna, diced jarred roasted red peppers, capers, chopped basil, olive oil, and red wine vinegar.
- Stir in cooked barley to turn your favorite canned or home-made vegetable soup into a hearty main dish.
- Mix cooked quinoa with canned corn, butter, and chopped basil for a new side dish.

- **BEWARE OF BUZZWORDS.** Even though breads and crackers may be labeled as multigrain, 9-grain, and 12-grain, there's no guarantee that any of them are whole grain. These foods may contain highly processed grains—stripped of much of their fiber and nutrients—rather than whole grains. The best way to verify that a product has whole grains is to scrutinize the ingredients panel carefully. If an item is whole grain, the word *whole* will typically precede the grain's name, i.e., whole rye or whole cornmeal. That's why a loaf that's labeled 100% wheat bread, or that lists wheat flour in the ingredients, falls short.

- **GO EASY ON THE SWEET STUFF.** Manufacturers are slapping the words whole grains on newly reformulated foods that are marginally nutritious at best. Yes, some cookies, for instance, contain whole-grain flour, but that doesn't offset all the sugar, fat, and calories. Remember: Whole-grain junk food is still junk food.

Grains Glossary

What follows is a rundown on the grains you'll find recipes for in this book, which are the grains most commonly found. But the grain world extends beyond what's covered here, so explore!

BARLEY: Barley is one of the oldest grains in cultivation. The fiber in barley may be even more effective than the fiber in oats at lowering cholesterol. **PEARL BARLEY** has been polished (milled) to remove its outer hull, which removes some of the bran. It has a creamy, chewy texture. **HULLED BARLEY** has had only the hull removed; it's chewier and more nutritious than pearl barley because it contains all the bran but takes longer to cook.

BUCKWHEAT: Native to Russia, buckwheat, botanically speaking, isn't a grain but rather the seed of a plant that is a cousin of rhubarb. It's a hearty, earthy tasting grain that is high in magnesium and manganese, and a good source of phosphorus and copper. It's usually found in the forms of **BUCKWHEAT GROATS,** which are the whole kernels, **KASHA** (the toasted kernels), and **BUCKWHEAT FLOUR** (Japanese udon noodles are made from a combination of buckwheat and whole-wheat flours).

CORN: Corn has the highest level of antioxidants of any grain or vegetable. **HOMINY,** available dried or canned, are corn kernels that

Bulgur (parboiled cracked wheat)

Wheat berries (whole-wheat kernels)

Barley

Kasha (toasted buckwheat kernels)

have been treated with lime to remove the germ and bran, which results in the loss of nutrients. However, the lime treatment activates the niacin in the corn kernel, which is essential in the healthy function of the nervous system.

CORNMEAL is ground hulled yellow or white corn kernels. Coarse-ground cornmeal or ground hominy is used for making grits, medium-grind cornmeal for polenta. When buying cornmeal, if possible choose one that is water-ground or stone-ground; both processes leave more of the bran and germ intact.

GLUTEN-FREE GRAINS

If you're on a gluten-free diet or cooking for family or friends with celiac disease, explore these gluten-free grains:

- **BUCKWHEAT**
- **CORN**
- **MILLET**
- **OATS** (look for an organic brand that specifies "wheat-free" on its label)
- **QUINOA**
- **RICE**
- **SORGHUM**
- **TEFF**
- **WILD RICE**

FARRO (FAHR-OH): This ancient grain related to wheat (and also known as emmer wheat) contains starch that is similar to the starch found in short-grain rices; try it instead of Arborio rice the next time you make risotto. A good source of fiber and protein, farro has a nutty wheat flavor and chewy texture.

OATS: Native to central Asia and Russia, oats contain a type of fiber, beta-glucan, that studies have shown to be effective in reducing cholesterol levels. Oats are also a good source of thiamin and protein, and their regular inclusion in a diet can help regulate blood sugar. **STEEL-CUT OATS** are the whole-grain oat kernels, with only the inedible outer chaff removed, cut into pieces. They are very chewy but have a wonderful nutty sweet flavor. **ROLLED OATS** are whole oats that have been toasted, hulled, steamed, and flattened with rollers.

MILLET: Although we typically cultivate this cereal grass for birdseed and fodder, it is a staple in Asia and Africa. It's best toasted, then prepared like rice by boiling it in water to make hot cereal or seasoned pilafs. Millet flour can be used for puddings, breads, and cakes.

Cornmeal

Quinoa

Couscous

Grits (coarse-ground cornmeal)

Soba Noodles with Shrimp,
Snow Peas, and Carrots (page 94)

QUINOA (KEEN-WAH): This is another grain that, botanically speaking, isn't a grain; rather, quinoa is a relative of Swiss chard and beets. A native of the high altitudes of the Andes in South America, quinoa is a complete protein, containing all the essential amino acids the body can't produce for itself. It's also a good source of riboflavin and is high in iron, manganese, and magnesium. Shaped a lot like a sesame seed, quinoa has a simultaneous crunchy-melting quality. It is coated with a natural pesticide substance called saponin that is very bitter; quinoa goes through a process to remove the saponin but you still need to wash it well (rub the grains under cold running water, then rinse until the water is clear) to remove any remaining traces of it.

RICE: In this book, when we talk of rice, we mean brown rice. Because it's been stripped of its bran and germ, white rice has a shadow of the nutritive value of brown rice, even though it's often enriched. Brown rice is processed to remove only its inedible outer husk. It is an excellent source of manganese (a mineral that help produce energy from protein and carbohydrates), and a good source of magnesium (helps build bones) and selenium (key to a healthy immune system). Brown rice can be long-, medium-, or short-grain.

WHEAT: Wheat is a nutrition powerhouse, containing 13 B vitamins, vitamin E, protein, and essential fatty acids. **WHEAT BERRIES,** the unmilled kernels of wheat, are nutty tasting and very chewy. The coarsely crushed kernels are sold as **CRACKED WHEAT;** because the kernels have been split open, the grain cooks faster. **BULGUR** is cracked wheat that has been parboiled and dried and cooks fastest of all. You can also enjoy the whole-grain goodness of wheat in the form of **WHOLE-WHEAT FLOUR,** which is made from whole hard wheat berries, and **WHEAT GERM.** Wheat germ is sold both raw and toasted. Toasted is tastier than raw and has a longer shelf life. Although not technically a whole grain, wheat germ is a great source of vitamin E, protein, and folic acid.

WILD RICE: Wild rice isn't really a rice; it's the seed of a marsh grass native to the Great Lakes region of the U.S. Wild rice contains twice the protein and fiber of brown rice but less iron and calcium. The rice grains vary in both length and color and have a slightly smoky, earthy flavor and chewy texture. Because of its high cost, wild rice is often cooked in tandem with rice.

Grains Storage

In addition to fiber and nutrients, the bran and germ of whole grains contain oils that can turn rancid quickly if not stored properly. Store uncooked grains in an airtight container in a cool dark place, in the refrigerator for up to one month, or in the freezer for up to three months.

Cooking Grains

RINSING: Whole grains (especially those bought in bulk bins) benefit from being washed in cold water to remove any dust and chaff. Quinoa has a natural coating that could impart a bitter taste, so it is best rinsed if you are not toasting the grain. Place the grains in a sieve, then place in a bowl of cold water and swish the sieve back and forth. Lift out the sieve, pour off the water, and repeat until the water looks clear. Give the grains a final rinse, then drain.

SOAKING: Whole wheat berries and brown rice cook more quickly if presoaked. At least eight or up to 24 hours before cooking, place the rinsed grain in a large bowl of cold water and let stand at room temperature. (In hot weather, let stand in the refrigerator.) Drain well before cooking.

TOASTING: Some grains, such as farro and wheat berries, are toasted before cooking to enhance their flavor. To toast whole grains, place them in a heavy dry skillet over medium heat. Cook, stirring almost constantly, until the grains are fragrant but not colored, 3 to 5 minutes.

COOKING: The general rule of thumb when cooking grains is 2 cups of liquid to 1 cup of grain. If the cooking liquid is absorbed before the grain is tender, simply add more hot liquid, cover, and let continue to cook. Or, if the grain is tender and some liquid remains, simply drain it off. Follow the instructions on the package for exact liquid measurements and estimated cooking time.

A HEALTHY START

There's no need to wait till dinner to start adding grains to your diet. And breakfast allows you to do it in such a delicious and satisfying way. Who can say no to a steaming hot bowl of oatmeal? Make it with steel-cut oats, with the entire bran and germ left intact, and the health benefits are even greater. Gild the grain lily and add a tablespoon of toasted wheat germ on top for some crunchy goodness.

Granola is another great grains breakfast choice. Make it with toasted oats, then add nutrient-packed dried fruit and nuts and you've got healthy jet fuel for breakfast or a midafternoon energy booster.

Morning baked goods are also a tasty vehicle for grains—muffins made with bran or stone-ground cornmeal, and oats in scones. You can also add oatmeal (or buckwheat) to pancakes, top polenta with a baked egg and vegetable sauce, or throw some leftover brown rice into a frittata. And when buying breakfast cereal, make sure it's 100% whole grain.

5-Minute Multigrain Cereal (page 23)

STEEL-CUT OATMEAL

If you haven't tried steel-cut oats, you're in for a deliciously chewy, full-flavored treat. We've included several topping choices so you can customize your oatmeal the way you like. Enjoy your breakfast knowing that you're getting twice the fiber of regular rolled oats.

ACTIVE TIME: 5 MIN · **TOTAL TIME:** 30 MIN
MAKES: 4 SERVINGS

3 CUPS WATER
1 CUP STEEL-CUT OATS
PINCH SALT

In medium saucepan, combine water, oats, and salt. Bring to boiling over high heat. Reduce heat and cover. Simmer until water is absorbed and oats are tender but still chewy, 20 to 25 minutes, stirring occasionally.

EACH SERVING: ABOUT 75 CALORIES | 3G PROTEIN | 14G CARBOHYDRATE | 1G TOTAL FAT (0G SATURATED) | 2G FIBER | 0MG CHOLESTEROL | 35MG SODIUM

BLUEBERRY-ALMOND OATMEAL

In small bowl, mix **¼ cup fresh blueberries, 1 tablespoon toasted, chopped almonds**, and **1 teaspoon honey**. Divide topping among 4 bowls of oatmeal.

EACH SERVING: ABOUT 95 CALORIES | 3G PROTEIN | 17G CARBOHYDRATE | 2G TOTAL FAT (0G SATURATED) | 2G FIBER | 0MG CHOLESTEROL | 35MG SODIUM

CRANBERRY-WALNUT OATMEAL

In small bowl, mix **¼ cup dried cranberries, ¼ cup chopped walnuts**, and **4 teaspoons maple syrup**. Divide topping among 4 bowls of oatmeal.

EACH SERVING: ABOUT 165 CALORIES | 4G PROTEIN | 25G CARBOHYDRATE | 6G TOTAL FAT (1G SATURATED) | 3G FIBER | 0MG CHOLESTEROL | 36MG SODIUM

APPLE-CINNAMON OATMEAL

Melt **1 tablespoon butter** in medium skillet over medium-high heat. Add **2 peeled, cored, and diced apples**. Reduce heat to medium; cook apples until tender, about 8 minutes, stirring a few times. Stir in **¼ teaspoon ground cinnamon**. Divide apples between 4 bowls of oatmeal and sprinkle each bowl with **1 tablespoon brown sugar**.

EACH SERVING: ABOUT 190 CALORIES │ 3G PROTEIN │ 37G CARBOHYDRATE │ 4G TOTAL FAT (2G SATURATED) │ 3G FIBER │ 8MG CHOLESTEROL │ 59MG SODIUM

5-MINUTE MULTIGRAIN CEREAL

Get a great grains start to your day with a hot, flavorful serving of three kinds of grains in five minutes. (For photo, see page 20.)

ACTIVE TIME: 5 MIN · **TOTAL TIME: 10 MIN**

MAKES: 1 SERVING

2 TABLESPOONS QUICK-COOKING BARLEY

2 TABLESPOONS BULGUR

2 TABLESPOONS OLD-FASHIONED OATS, UNCOOKED

⅔ CUP WATER

2 TABLESPOONS RAISINS

PINCH GROUND CINNAMON

1 TABLESPOON CHOPPED WALNUTS OR PECANS

LOW-FAT MILK (OPTIONAL)

In microwave-safe 1-quart bowl, combine barley, bulgur, oats, and water. Microwave on High 2 minutes. Stir in raisins and cinnamon; microwave 3 minutes longer. Stir, then top with walnuts. Serve with milk, if desired.

EACH SERVING: ABOUT 265 CALORIES │ 8G PROTEIN │ 50G CARBOHYDRATE │ 6G TOTAL FAT (1G SATURATED) │ 7G FIBER │ 0MG CHOLESTEROL │ 5MG SODIUM

PECAN-OATMEAL PANCAKES

Everyone's talking "back to basics." What could be more down-home than fluffy hot pancakes with warm maple syrup? We think we've done "back to basics" one better by adding whole-grain oats and toasted pecans to the batter, and cooking the pancakes in a nonstick skillet lightly brushed with oil.

ACTIVE TIME: 25 MIN · **TOTAL TIME:** 25 MIN

MAKES: 16 PANCAKES OR 8 SERVINGS

---

1   CAN (3 OUNCES) PECANS

2   CUPS BUTTERMILK

1½ CUPS QUICK-COOKING OATS

½   CUP ALL-PURPOSE FLOUR

1   TEASPOON BAKING SODA

½   TEASPOON SALT

2   LARGE EGGS

2   TABLESPOONS CONFECTIONERS' SUGAR

1   TABLESPOON VEGETABLE OIL

1   CUP MAPLE OR MAPLE-FLAVOR SYRUP

¼   TEASPOON GROUND CINNAMON, OR MORE, TO TASTE

GRAPES AND STRAWBERRIES FOR GARNISH

1 In nonstick 12-inch skillet over medium-high heat, toast pecans until golden brown, 3 to 4 minutes. Cool pecans slightly; coarsely chop.

2 In large bowl, combine buttermilk, oats, flour, baking soda, salt, eggs, and 1 tablespoon confectioners' sugar, and stir just until flour is moistened; stir in toasted pecans.

3 Over medium heat, heat same skillet until hot; brush lightly with oil. Pour batter by ¼ cups into hot skillet, making 2 or 3 pancakes at a time. Cook until tops are bubbly and bubbles burst, 2 to 3 minutes; edges will look dry. With pancake turner, turn and cook until undersides are golden, 1 to 2 minutes. Place on warm platter; keep warm. Repeat until all batter is used, brushing skillet with more oil if necessary.

4 In small saucepan over medium heat, heat maple syrup until very warm. In cup, mix cinnamon with remaining 1 tablespoon confectioners' sugar. Sprinkle pancakes with cinnamon-sugar; serve with warm maple syrup. Garnish platter with fruit.

EACH SERVING: ABOUT 330 CALORIES | 8G PROTEIN | 50G CARBOHYDRATE | 13G TOTAL FAT (1.5G SATURATED FAT) | 3G FIBER | 56MG CHOLESTEROL | 388MG SODIUM

BUCKWHEAT PANCAKES

The buckwheat flour adds a wonderful nutty flavor to these buttermilk pancakes. Look for buckwheat flour in natural and whole food stores. Because it contains more of the whole grain, keep buckwheat flour stored, tightly covered, in the refrigerator to keep it from going rancid.

ACTIVE TIME: 30 MIN · **TOTAL TIME:** 30 MIN

MAKES: 14 PANCAKES OR 7 SERVINGS

½ CUP ALL-PURPOSE FLOUR

½ CUP BUCKWHEAT FLOUR

1 TABLESPOON SUGAR

2 TEASPOONS BAKING POWDER

½ TEASPOON BAKING SODA

¼ TEASPOON SALT

1¼ CUPS BUTTERMILK, OR 1 CUP PLAIN YOGURT PLUS ¼ CUP MILK

3 TABLESPOONS BUTTER OR MARGARINE, MELTED

1 LARGE EGG, LIGHTLY BEATEN

VEGETABLE OIL FOR BRUSHING PAN

1 In large bowl, combine all-purpose flour, buckwheat flour, sugar, baking powder, baking soda, and salt. Add buttermilk, butter, and egg; stir just until flour is moistened.

2 Heat griddle or 12-inch skillet over medium heat until drop of water sizzles; brush lightly with oil. Pour batter by scant ¼ cups onto hot griddle, making a few pancakes at a time. Cook until tops are bubbly and edges look dry, 2 to 3 minutes. With a wide spatula, turn pancakes and cook until underside is browned. Transfer to platter; keep warm.

3 Repeat with remaining batter, brushing griddle with more oil as necessary.

EACH SERVING: ABOUT 150 CALORIES | 4G PROTEIN | 16G CARBOHYDRATE | 8G TOTAL FAT (4G SATURATED) | 2G FIBER | 46MG CHOLESTEROL | 420MG SODIUM

BUCKWHEAT BLINIS

Prepare Buckwheat Pancakes as directed but use only **1 teaspoon sugar.** Drop batter by teaspoonfuls onto hot griddle. Meanwhile, cut 4 ounces smoked salmon into 1-inch pieces. Arrange **1 piece of salmon** on top of each blini with **1/2 teaspoon sour cream** and a **sprig of dill.** Makes 30 blinis.

EACH BLINI: ABOUT 45 CALORIES | 2G PROTEIN | 3G CARBOHYDRATE | 2G TOTAL FAT (1G SATURATED) | 0G FIBER | 12MG CHOLESTEROL | 130MG SODIUM

BAKED EGGS AND POLENTA WITH CHUNKY VEGETABLE SAUCE

Polenta makes a tasty—and unexpected—base for this saucy baked-egg casserole.

ACTIVE TIME: 30 MIN · **TOTAL TIME:** 42 MIN

MAKES: 4 SERVINGS

---

1   CUP BOILING WATER

1   CUP LOW-FAT MILK (1%)

½   CUP YELLOW CORNMEAL

½   TEASPOON SALT

½   CUP FRESHLY GRATED PARMESAN CHEESE

1   TABLESPOON OLIVE OIL

1   MEDIUM CARROT, PEELED AND CHOPPED

1   SMALL ONION, CHOPPED

1   SMALL ZUCCHINI (6 OUNCES), CHOPPED

1   CAN (14½ OUNCES) TOMATOES, CHOPPED

1   CAN (8 OUNCES) TOMATO SAUCE

¼   TEASPOON COARSELY GROUND BLACK PEPPER

4   LARGE EGGS

1 Prepare polenta: In deep 2½-quart microwave-safe bowl or casserole, stir boiling water, milk, cornmeal, and salt. Cook, uncovered, in microwave on High 3 minutes. Remove bowl from microwave and whisk cornmeal mixture vigorously until smooth (mixture may be lumpy at first). Microwave 2 to 3 minutes longer or until thickened; whisk once after cooking is done. Stir in Parmesan. Spread polenta in greased 8-inch square glass baking dish.

2 Meanwhile, preheat oven to 400°F.

3 Prepare sauce: In 12-inch skillet, heat oil over medium heat until hot. Add carrot and onion, and cook until tender and beginning to brown, about 10 minutes. Stir in zucchini and cook just until zucchini is tender, about 5 minutes. Add tomatoes with their juice, tomato sauce, and pepper; heat to boiling over medium-high heat. Reduce heat to medium and cook 5 minutes, stirring occasionally. Spread tomato mixture over polenta in baking dish.

4 With large spoon, make 4 indentations in tomato mixture. Crack eggs into custard cup, one at a time, and slip into each indentation. Bake until eggs are set, 12 to 14 minutes.

EACH SERVING: ABOUT 290 CALORIES | 16G PROTEIN | 29G CARBOHYDRATE | 13G TOTAL FAT (4G SATURATED) | 4G FIBER | 223MG CHOLESTEROL | 1,325MG SODIUM

CHEESY SOUTHWESTERN CORN FRITTATA

Frittatas are a great choice for breakfast or brunch, served up hot out of the pan or at room temperature. Here we used packaged precooked brown rice but next time you make brown rice for dinner, cook up some extra and you're halfway to a delicious breakfast the next morning.

ACTIVE TIME: 25 MIN · TOTAL TIME: 48 MIN

MAKES: 6 SERVINGS

---

1   PACKAGE (8.8 OUNCES) PRECOOKED BROWN RICE (SCANT 2 CUPS)

4   TEASPOONS OLIVE OIL

1   SMALL ONION, CHOPPED

1   JALAPEÑO CHILE, SEEDED AND FINELY CHOPPED

1   GARLIC CLOVE, FINELY CHOPPED

1   CUP FROZEN CORN KERNELS

8   LARGE EGGS

¼   CUP MILK

¼   CUP LOOSELY PACKED FRESH CILANTRO LEAVES, CHOPPED

½   TEASPOON SALT

½   CUP SHREDDED MEXICAN CHEESE BLEND

PREPARED SALSA (OPTIONAL)

1 Heat brown rice as label directs.

2 Meanwhile, preheat oven to 400°F.

3 In nonstick 10-inch skillet with oven-safe handle (or with handle wrapped in double thickness of foil for baking in oven later), heat 2 teaspoons olive oil over medium-high heat until hot. Add onion and cook until lightly browned, 2 to 3 minutes, stirring occasionally. Stir in jalapeño and garlic; cook 30 seconds, stirring. Add frozen corn and cook until thawed, about 1 minute, stirring a few times. Transfer corn mixture to bowl.

4 In large bowl, with wire whisk, beat eggs, milk, cilantro, and salt until well blended. Stir in rice, corn mixture, and cheese.

5 In same skillet, heat remaining 2 teaspoons oil over medium heat until hot. Pour in egg mixture; cover and cook until egg mixture starts to set around the edge, about 3 minutes.

6 Remove cover and place skillet in oven; bake until knife inserted 2 inches from edge comes out clean, about 20 minutes. Remove frittata from oven; let stand 5 minutes.

7 To serve, loosen frittata from skillet; slide onto warm platter. Cut into wedges; serve with salsa, if you like.

EACH SERVING: ABOUT 245 CALORIES, | 13G PROTEIN | 19G CARBOHYDRATE | 14G TOTAL FAT (5G SATURATED) | 2G FIBER | 293MG CHOLESTEROL | 355MG SODIUM

OATMEAL SCONES

These nutritious scones are hearty and just slightly sweet.

ACTIVE TIME: 15 MIN · TOTAL TIME: 35 MIN
MAKES: 8 SCONES

1   CUP OLD-FASHIONED OR QUICK-
    COOKING OATS

1¾ CUPS ALL-PURPOSE FLOUR

3   TABLESPOONS SUGAR

2   TEASPOONS BAKING POWDER

½   TEASPOON BAKING SODA

¼   TEASPOON SALT

6   TABLESPOONS COLD BUTTER OR
    MARGARINE, CUT UP

½   CUP PECANS, TOASTED (SEE TIP)
    AND COARSELY CHOPPED

⅔   CUP BUTTERMILK

1   LARGE EGG, SEPARATED

2   TEASPOONS WATER

1 Preheat oven to 400°F. On a jelly-roll pan, toast oats until lightly browned, 5 to 7 minutes. Cool. Grease large cookie sheet; dust with flour.

2 In large bowl, stir together flour, 2 tablespoons sugar, baking powder, baking soda, salt, and oats. With pastry blender or two knives used scissor-fashion, cut in butter until mixture resembles coarse crumbs. Stir in pecans. In small bowl, with fork, mix buttermilk and egg yolk. Stir buttermilk mixture into flour mixture until combined. Lightly knead in bowl until dough just holds together.

3 Transfer dough to prepared cookie sheet. Shape into 7½-inch round. With floured knife, score into 8 wedges. In small bowl, stir egg white and water. Brush over top of round. Sprinkle with remaining 1 tablespoon sugar.

4 Bake until toothpick inserted in center comes out clean, 20 to 25 minutes. Separate scones and serve warm, or transfer to wire rack to cool.

TIP To toast nuts, preheat the oven to 350°F. Spread the shelled nuts in a single layer on a cookie sheet. Bake, stirring occasionally, until lightly browned and fragrant, about 10 minutes.

EACH SCONE: ABOUT 305 CALORIES | 7G PROTEIN | 36G CARBOHYDRATE | 15G TOTAL FAT (6G SATURATED) | 2G FIBER | 51MG CHOLESTEROL | 390MG SODIUM

CORN MUFFINS

These tender muffins are a versatile base for sweet or savory additions.

ACTIVE TIME: 15 MIN · **TOTAL TIME:** 33 MIN
MAKES: 12 MUFFINS

---

1   CUP YELLOW CORNMEAL

1   CUP ALL-PURPOSE FLOUR

¼   CUP SUGAR

2   TEASPOONS BAKING POWDER

½   TEASPOON SALT

¼   TEASPOON BAKING SODA

1   CUP BUTTERMILK (SEE TIP)

6   TABLESPOONS BUTTER OR MARGARINE, MELTED

1   LARGE EGG

1 Preheat oven to 400°F. Grease twelve 2½" by 1¼" muffin-pan cups.

2 In large bowl, combine cornmeal, flour, sugar, baking powder, salt, and baking soda.

3 In small bowl, with fork, beat buttermilk, melted butter, and egg until well blended. Add liquid mixture to flour mixture; stir just until flour is evenly moistened. Spoon batter into prepared muffin-pan cups.

4 Bake muffins until toothpick inserted in centers comes out clean, 18 to 20 minutes. Immediately remove muffins from pan. Serve warm, or cool on wire rack to serve later.

TIP If you don't have buttermilk, in glass measuring cup, place **1 tablespoon distilled white vinegar or fresh lemon juice**, then pour in enough **milk** to equal 1 cup. Stir; let stand 5 minutes to thicken before using.

EACH MUFFIN: ABOUT 160 CALORIES | 3G PROTEIN | 22G CARBOHYDRATE | 7G TOTAL FAT (1G SATURATED) | 1G FIBER | 18MG CHOLESTEROL | 290MG SODIUM

BLUEBERRY CORN MUFFINS

Prepare Corn Muffins as directed but fold **½ pint blueberries** into batter before spooning into muffin cups.

EACH MUFFIN: ABOUT 170 CALORIES | 3G PROTEIN | 24G CARBOHYDRATE | 7G TOTAL FAT (1G SATURATED) | 2G FIBER | 18MG CHOLESTEROL | 295MG SODIUM

MOLASSES CORN MUFFINS

Prepare Corn Muffins as directed but use only **¾ cup buttermilk** and add **¼ cup light (mild) molasses** to buttermilk mixture.

EACH MUFFIN: ABOUT 175 CALORIES | 3G PROTEIN | 27G CARBOHYDRATE | 7G TOTAL FAT (1G SATURATED) | 1G FIBER | 18MG CHOLESTEROL | 290MG SODIUM

JALAPEÑO-CHEESE CORN MUFFINS

Prepare Corn Muffins as directed but fold **¾ cup frozen whole-kernel corn,** thawed, and **3 ounces Monterey Jack cheese with jalapeño peppers**, shredded (¾ cup), into batter before spooning into muffin cups.

EACH MUFFIN: ABOUT 195 CALORIES | 5G PROTEIN | 24G CARBOHYDRATE | 9G TOTAL FAT (3G SATURATED) | 1G FIBER | 26MG CHOLESTEROL | 340MG SODIUM

BACON-PEPPER CORN MUFFINS

Prepare Corn Muffins as directed but stir **3 strips bacon**, cooked and crumbled, and **¼ teaspoon coarsely ground black pepper** into batter before spooning into muffin cups.

EACH MUFFIN: ABOUT 170 CALORIES | 4G PROTEIN | 22G CARBOHYDRATE | 7G TOTAL FAT (2G SATURATED) | 1G FIBER | 20MG CHOLESTEROL | 315MG SODIUM

SUPER
SALADS

Grains in salads? Absolutely! Think of the classic Middle Eastern tabbouleh—it's a wonderful combination of chewy nutty bulgur and the herby green freshness of tons of chopped parsley and mint. You'll find variations on the tabbouleh theme in this tasty collection of side- and main-dish salads, as well as other satisfying salads made with wheat berries, barley, quinoa, farro, brown rice, and whole-wheat couscous.

Building a salad around grains gives you a delicious contrast of textures and flavors, as well as providing fantastic health benefits. Grain salads make a lot a sense when you're looking for a hearty meatless choice for dinner—the grain provides a good measure of protein and you can complete it with a host of fresh vegetables, greens, and/or fruit for a rainbow-colored main course bursting with antioxidant goodness. Use these recipes as a jumping-off point, adding whatever's fresh or looking good in your refrigerator. And remember, you can add whole grains to your favorite pasta salad just by making it with 100% whole-wheat pasta instead of the regular semolina.

Warm Quinoa Salad with Toasted Almonds (page 44)

WHEAT BERRY SALAD WITH DRIED CHERRIES

This salad is a wonderful mix of textures and flavors—the chewy nutty taste of the wheat berries, combined with the pucker of tart dried cherries and lemon juice, the crunch of celery, and the hot-sweetness of Dijon and honey.

ACTIVE TIME: 15 MIN · **TOTAL TIME:** 1 HR 45 MIN

MAKES: 12 SIDE-DISH SERVINGS

2   CUPS WHEAT BERRIES (WHOLE-WHEAT KERNELS)

1   LARGE SHALLOT, MINCED

3   TABLESPOONS FRESH LEMON JUICE

1   TABLESPOON DIJON MUSTARD

1   TABLESPOON OLIVE OIL

2   TEASPOONS HONEY

1½ TEASPOONS SALT

½   TEASPOON COARSELY GROUND BLACK PEPPER

3   MEDIUM STALKS CELERY, EACH CUT LENGTHWISE IN HALF, THEN CUT CROSSWISE INTO ¼-INCH-THICK SLICES

¾   CUP DRIED TART CHERRIES, CHOPPED

½   CUP CHOPPED FRESH FLAT-LEAF PARSLEY

FLAT-LEAF PARSLEY SPRIGS FOR GARNISH

1   In 4-quart saucepan, heat wheat berries and **8 cups water** to boiling over high heat. Reduce heat to low; cover and simmer until wheat berries are just tender but still firm to the bite, about 1½ hours.

2   Meanwhile, in large bowl, with wire whisk or fork, mix shallot, lemon juice, mustard, oil, honey, salt, and pepper.

3   When wheat berries are cooked, drain well. Add warm wheat berries to dressing with celery, cherries, and chopped parsley; toss well. Serve salad at room temperature, or cover and refrigerate until ready to serve. Garnish with parsley sprigs.

EACH SERVING: ABOUT 130 CALORIES | 4G PROTEIN | 26G CARBOHYDRATE | 2G TOTAL FAT (0G SATURATED) | 6G FIBER | 0MG CHOLESTEROL | 310MG SODIUM

WHEAT BERRY SALAD WITH SPINACH AND TOMATOES

This delightfully satisfying salad gets a double dose of tomatoes—fresh from the garden and sun-dried—and a wonderful contrast of textures.

ACTIVE TIME: 15 MIN · **TOTAL TIME:** 1 HR 30 MIN
MAKES: 4 MAIN-DISH SERVINGS

1½ CUPS WHEAT BERRIES (WHOLE-WHEAT KERNELS)

1 BUNCH SPINACH (10 TO 12 OUNCES), TOUGH STEMS TRIMMED

1 RIPE MEDIUM TOMATO

10 SUN-DRIED TOMATO HALVES

3 TABLESPOONS OLIVE OIL

2 TABLESPOONS RED WINE VINEGAR

½ TEASPOON DIJON MUSTARD

1 TEASPOON SALT

½ TEASPOON SUGAR

¼ TEASPOON COARSELY GROUND BLACK PEPPER

1 CUP GOLDEN RAISINS

1 In large bowl, soak wheat berries overnight in enough water to cover by 2 inches.

2 Drain wheat berries. In 4-quart saucepan, heat **7 cups water** to boiling over high heat. Add soaked wheat berries; heat to boiling. Reduce heat to low; cover and simmer until wheat berries are tender, about 1 hour. Drain.

3 Meanwhile, coarsely chop spinach. Chop tomato. Place dried tomato halves in small bowl; add **1 cup boiling water.** Let stand 5 minutes; drain well. Coarsely chop dried tomatoes.

4 In medium bowl, with wire whisk or fork, mix oil, vinegar, mustard, salt, sugar, and pepper until blended. Add raisins, chopped fresh and dried tomatoes, spinach, and wheat berries; toss well.

EACH SERVING: ABOUT 455 CALORIES | 12G PROTEIN | 82G CARBOHYDRATE | 12G TOTAL FAT (1G SATURATED) | 10G FIBER | 0MG CHOLESTEROL | 625MG SODIUM

FRUIT AND BARLEY SALAD

The simple lime-juice vinaigrette gives this salad its delectable flavor. You can also use mangoes or peaches instead of the nectarines.

ACTIVE TIME: 20 MIN · **TOTAL TIME:** 45 MIN
MAKES: 16 SIDE-DISH SERVINGS

---

6 CUPS WATER

1 PACKAGE (16 OUNCES) PEARL BARLEY

2¾ TEASPOONS SALT

4 MEDIUM LIMES

⅓ CUP OLIVE OIL

1 TABLESPOON SUGAR

¾ TEASPOON COARSELY GROUND BLACK PEPPER

1½ POUNDS NECTARINES (4 MEDIUM), PITTED AND CUT INTO ½-INCH PIECES

1 POUND RIPE TOMATOES (2 LARGE), SEEDED AND CUT INTO ½-INCH PIECES

4 GREEN ONIONS, THINLY SLICED

½ CUP CHOPPED FRESH MINT

1 In 4-quart saucepan, heat water to boiling over high heat. Add barley and 1½ teaspoons salt; heat to boiling. Reduce heat to low; cover and simmer until barley is tender and liquid is absorbed (barley will have a creamy consistency), 35 to 45 minutes.

2 Meanwhile, from limes, grate 1 tablespoon peel and squeeze ½ cup juice. In large nonreactive bowl, with wire whisk or fork, mix lime peel and juice, oil, sugar, pepper, and remaining 1¼ teaspoons salt.

3 Rinse barley with cold running water; drain well. Add barley, nectarines, tomatoes, green onions, and mint to lime dressing; with rubber spatula, stir gently to coat. If not serving right away, cover and refrigerate.

EACH SERVING: ABOUT 170 CALORIES | 4G PROTEIN | 28G CARBOHYDRATE | 5G TOTAL FAT (1G SATURATED) | 0G FIBER | 0MG CHOLESTEROL | 375MG SODIUM

BARLEY, CORN, AND TOMATO SALAD

Here the whole-grain goodness of pearl barley is combined with corn cut from the cob, tomatoes off the vine, and the heady perfume of basil.

ACTIVE TIME: 15 MIN · **TOTAL TIME:** 50 MIN

MAKES: 12 SIDE-DISH SERVINGS

2½ CUPS WATER

1¼ CUPS PEARL BARLEY

5 MEDIUM EARS CORN, HUSKS AND SILK REMOVED

1 SMALL BUNCH FRESH BASIL

¼ CUP RICE VINEGAR

¼ CUP OLIVE OIL

1 TEASPOON SALT

¼ TEASPOON GROUND BLACK PEPPER

2 LARGE RIPE TOMATOES (8 OUNCES EACH), CUT INTO ½-INCH CHUNKS

2 GREEN ONIONS, CHOPPED

1 In 2-quart saucepan, heat water until boiling over high heat. Stir in barley; heat to boiling. Reduce heat to low; cover and simmer until barley is tender, 30 to 35 minutes.

2 Meanwhile, place corn on plate in microwave. Cook on High 4 to 5 minutes, turning and rearranging corn halfway through cooking. Cool slightly until easy to handle. Chop enough basil leaves to equal ⅓ cup; reserve remaining basil for garnish.

3 With sharp knife, cut corn kernels from cobs. In large bowl, with fork, mix vinegar, oil, salt, and pepper; stir in corn, warm barley, tomatoes, green onions, and chopped basil until combined. If not serving right away, cover and refrigerate up to 4 hours. Garnish with basil leaves.

EACH SERVING: ABOUT 155 CALORIES | 4G PROTEIN | 26G CARBOHYDRATE | 5G TOTAL FAT (1G SATURATED) | 5G FIBER | 0MG CHOLESTEROL | 205MG SODIUM

SHRIMP AND BULGUR SALAD WITH ARTICHOKE HEARTS

Light and lemony, this composed salad features golden sautéed shrimp, tender artichoke hearts, and heart-healthy bulgur wheat. Serve as a light main-course or appetizer salad.

ACTIVE TIME: 15 MIN · TOTAL TIME: 45 MIN
MAKES: 4 MAIN-DISH SERVINGS

- 2 LARGE ARTICHOKES (12 OUNCES EACH)
- 2 LARGE LEMONS
- 1½ CUPS CHICKEN BROTH
- ¾ CUP BULGUR
- 1 POUND LARGE SHRIMP, SHELLED AND DEVEINED
- 4 SUN-DRIED TOMATO HALVES
- 1 RIPE MEDIUM TOMATO

- 1 GREEN ONION
- 3 TEASPOONS OLIVE OIL
- ⅛ TEASPOON PLUS ¼ TEASPOON SALT
- 1 CUP FROZEN PEAS, THAWED
- 2 TABLESPOONS SEASONED RICE VINEGAR
- ½ POUND MIXED BABY GREENS OR MIXED SALAD GREENS (6 CUPS LOOSELY PACKED)

1 Cut off stems and 1 inch across top of each artichoke. Pull off any small, loose, or discolored leaves from around bottom of artichokes. With kitchen shears, trim thorny tips from leaves. Rinse artichokes well under cold running water.

2 Squeeze ¼ cup juice from lemons. In 5-quart saucepot over high heat, heat 2 tablespoons lemon juice and **1 inch water** to boiling over high heat. Place artichokes on their stem ends in boiling water; heat to boiling. Reduce heat to low; cover and simmer until a leaf can be pulled off easily, 30 to 40 minutes.

3 Meanwhile, in 2-quart saucepan over high heat, heat chicken broth to boiling over high heat; add bulgur. Reduce heat to low; cover and simmer until bulgur is tender and liquid is absorbed, about 15 minutes. Place bulgur in large bowl.

4 Rinse shrimp with cold running water and pat dry with paper towels. Leave 8 shrimp whole for garnish; cut remaining shrimp into ½-inch pieces.

5 Place dried tomato halves in small bowl; pour **1 cup boiling water** over tomatoes; let stand 15 minutes to soften. Dice fresh tomato. Thinly slice green onion. Drain dried tomato halves; chop.

6 In nonstick 10-inch skillet over medium-high heat, in 1 teaspoon olive oil, cook whole shrimp and ⅛ teaspoon salt, stirring frequently, until shrimp are golden and turn opaque throughout; set aside.

7 In same skillet, in remaining 2 teaspoons olive oil, cook shrimp pieces and remaining ¼ teaspoon salt, stirring frequently, until shrimp are golden and turn opaque throughout; remove to bowl with bulgur. Add peas, fresh tomato, chopped dried tomatoes, green onion, and remaining 2 tablespoons lemon juice; stir to mix well.

8 In medium bowl, toss mixed baby greens with vinegar. When artichokes are done, cut each lengthwise in half. With spoon, scoop out fuzzy choke from center of each half; discard. Arrange mixed baby greens and artichoke halves on 4 dinner plates. Spoon bulgur mixture onto artichoke halves. Garnish each plate with 2 whole shrimp.

EACH SERVING: ABOUT 290 CALORIES | 28G PROTEIN | 39G CARBOHYDRATE | 4G TOTAL FAT (1G SATURATED) | 12G FIBER | 140MG CHOLESTEROL | 765MG SODIUM

CHUNKY VEGETABLE BULGUR SALAD

Reminiscent of tabbouleh, this bulgar salad also contains cherry tomatoes and two kinds of summer squash.

ACTIVE TIME: 20 MIN · **TOTAL TIME:** 20 MIN PLUS STANDING

MAKES: 8 SIDE-DISH SERVINGS

- 2 CUPS BULGUR
- 2½ CUPS BOILING WATER
- 2 LEMONS
- 1 TABLESPOON OLIVE OIL
- 1 SMALL RED ONION, FINELY CHOPPED
- 1 CUP CHERRY TOMATOES, EACH CUT IN HALF
- 1 MEDIUM ZUCCHINI (8 TO 10 OUNCES), CHOPPED
- 1 MEDIUM YELLOW SUMMER SQUASH (8 TO 10 OUNCES), CHOPPED
- ½ CUP LOOSELY PACKED FRESH MINT LEAVES, CHOPPED
- ½ CUP LOOSELY PACKED FRESH PARSLEY LEAVES, CHOPPED
- ½ TEASPOON SALT
- ¼ TEASPOON COARSELY GROUND BLACK PEPPER

1 In large bowl, stir together bulgur and boiling water. Cover and let stand until liquid is absorbed, about 30 minutes.

2 Meanwhile, from lemons, grate 1 teaspoon peel and squeeze ¼ cup juice; set aside.

3 In nonstick 12-inch skillet, heat oil over medium-high heat until hot. Add onion and cook until it begins to soften, 3 to 4 minutes. Add tomatoes, zucchini, and squash, and cook until vegetables are tender, 6 to 8 minutes, stirring occasionally.

4 Stir vegetables into bulgur with lemon peel and juice, mint, parsley, salt, and pepper. If not serving right away, spoon into container with tight-fitting lid and refrigerate up to 1 day.

EACH SERVING: ABOUT 160 CALORIES | 6G PROTEIN | 32G CARBOHYDRATE | 2G TOTAL FAT (0G SATURATED) | 8G FIBER | 0MG CHOLESTEROL | 160MG SODIUM

FETA AND DILL TABBOULEH

Our Greek-style variation of this well-known salad makes a perfect side dish for a light summer meal of grilled fish, meat kabobs, or chicken.

ACTIVE TIME: 25 MIN · **TOTAL TIME:** 25 MIN PLUS STANDING
MAKES: 8 SIDE-DISH SERVINGS

1½ CUPS WATER

1 GARLIC CLOVE, CUT IN HALF

1 CUP BULGUR

2 RIPE MEDIUM TOMATOES (¾ POUND), CHOPPED

2 GREEN ONIONS, THINLY SLICED

2 KIRBY (PICKLING) CUCUMBERS, EACH CUT LENGTHWISE INTO QUARTERS, THEN CROSSWISE INTO ¼-INCH-THICK SLICES

2 OUNCES FETA CHEESE, CRUMBLED (½ CUP)

2 CUPS LOOSELY PACKED FRESH PARSLEY LEAVES, CHOPPED

½ CUP LOOSELY PACKED FRESH DILL SPRIGS, CHOPPED

1 TABLESPOON OLIVE OIL

¾ TEASPOON SALT

¼ TEASPOON COARSELY GROUND BLACK PEPPER

1 In 1-quart saucepan, heat water with garlic to boiling over high heat. Stir in bulgur; cover and remove saucepan from heat. Let stand until liquid is absorbed, about 40 minutes.

2 When bulgur is ready, transfer to large bowl; discard garlic. Stir in tomatoes, green onions, cucumbers, feta, parsley, dill, oil, salt, and pepper. If not serving right away, cover and refrigerate.

EACH SERVING: ABOUT 110 CALORIES | 4G PROTEIN | 17G CARBOHYDRATE | 4G TOTAL FAT (1G SATURATED) | 5G FIBER | 6MG CHOLESTEROL | 310MG SODIUM

COUSCOUS SALAD WITH GRAPES AND THYME

Green and red grapes, toasted pine nuts, and fresh thyme liven up this summery couscous salad.

ACTIVE TIME: 15 MIN · **TOTAL TIME:** 20 MIN

MAKES: 6 SIDE-DISH SERVINGS

---

1 PACKAGE (10 OUNCES) WHOLE-WHEAT COUSCOUS (MOROCCAN PASTA)

1½ TEASPOONS FRESH THYME LEAVES

½ CUP CIDER VINEGAR

2 TABLESPOONS OLIVE OIL

1 TEASPOON SALT

1½ CUPS MIXED GREEN AND RED SEEDLESS GRAPES (½ POUND), EACH CUT INTO QUARTERS

½ CUP PINE NUTS (PIGNOLI), TOASTED (SEE TIP PAGE 29)

THYME SPRIGS FOR GARNISH

1 Prepare couscous as label directs, but do not use salt or butter. Stir thyme into couscous.

2 In large bowl, mix vinegar, oil, and salt. Add grapes, pine nuts, and warm couscous; toss well to coat. Cover and refrigerate if not serving right away. Garnish with thyme sprigs to serve.

EACH SERVING: ABOUT 220 CALORIES | 6G PROTEIN | 34G CARBOHYDRATE | 7G TOTAL FAT (1G SATURATED) | 5G FIBER | 0MG CHOLESTEROL | 270MG SODIUM

WARM QUINOA SALAD WITH TOASTED ALMONDS

Quinoa is often called a super-grain. Because it contains all eight essential amino acids, it is considered a complete protein. Toast it to reduce bitterness and bring out its tasty nutty flavor.

ACTIVE TIME: 5 MIN · **TOTAL TIME:** 30 MIN

MAKES: 5 SIDE-DISH SERVINGS

1½ CUPS QUINOA, THOROUGHLY RINSED AND DRIED

2½ CUPS PLUS 1 TABLESPOON WATER

½ TEASPOON SALT

2 TABLESPOONS REDUCED-SODIUM SOY SAUCE

1 TABLESPOON RICE VINEGAR

1 TEASPOON ASIAN SESAME OIL

1 TEASPOON GRATED, PEELED FRESH GINGER

2 GREEN ONIONS, THINLY SLICED DIAGONALLY

¼ CUP SLICED NATURAL ALMONDS, TOASTED (SEE TIP PAGE 29)

1 In 12-inch skillet, toast quinoa over medium heat until fragrant and golden, about 5 minutes, stirring frequently.

2 Stir 2½ cups water and salt into toasted quinoa; heat to boiling on high. Reduce heat to low; cover and simmer until all water is absorbed, 15 to 17 minutes.

3 Meanwhile, in small bowl, stir together soy sauce, vinegar, oil, ginger, green onions, and remaining 1 tablespoon water.

4 Transfer quinoa to large serving bowl. Stir in soy sauce mixture until quinoa is evenly coated. Sprinkle with toasted almonds to serve.

EACH SERVING: ABOUT 305 CALORIES | 9G PROTEIN | 38G CARBOHYDRATE | 7G TOTAL FAT (1G SATURATED) | 4G FIBER | 0MG CHOLESTEROL | 460MG SODIUM

WARM QUINOA AND BROCCOLI SALAD

With just a few ingredients, this salad is a powerhouse of vitamins A, C, and K, minerals, and cancer- and heart-disease-fighting phytonutrients.

ACTIVE TIME: 12 MIN · **TOTAL TIME:** 32 MIN

MAKES: 6 SIDE-DISH SERVINGS

1½ CUPS QUINOA

3¼ CUPS PLUS 3 TABLESPOONS WATER

¾ TEASPOON SALT

1 BAG (10 OUNCES) BROCCOLI FLOWERETS

⅔ CUP CHOPPED CARROT (1 LARGE)

3 TABLESPOONS FINELY CHOPPED, PEELED FRESH GINGER

3 TABLESPOONS VEGETABLE OIL

2 TABLESPOONS SEASONED RICE VINEGAR

2 TEASPOONS SOY SAUCE

2 TEASPOONS ASIAN SESAME OIL

1 In sieve, rinse quinoa with cold running water, rubbing the grains, until the water runs clear. In 3-quart saucepan, combine quinoa, 3 cups water, and ½ teaspoon salt; heat to boiling over high heat. Reduce heat to low; cover and simmer until water is absorbed, about 20 minutes. Transfer quinoa to large bowl.

2 Meanwhile, place broccoli and remaining ¼ cup water in microwave-safe medium bowl; cover and cook in microwave on High 4 to 5 minutes or until tender-crisp. Drain; add to quinoa in bowl.

3 In blender, combine carrot, ginger, oil, vinegar, soy sauce, sesame oil, remaining 3 tablespoons water, and remaining ¼ teaspoon salt; blend until pureed. Add to quinoa and broccoli and toss to combine. Serve salad warm or at room temperature.

EACH SERVING: ABOUT 265 CALORIES | 7G PROTEIN | 36G CARBOHYDRATE | 11G TOTAL FAT (1G SATURATED) | 5G FIBER | 0MG CHOLESTEROL | 605MG SODIUM

PIZZA, BURGERS, WRAPS & SANDWICHES

Once you get in the right mindset, it's easy to add whole grains to most everything you eat. Pizza? Buy whole-wheat ready-made pizza crusts or refrigerated whole-wheat pizza dough, which is now available in most supermarkets. Or try something totally different and use sliced precooked polenta as the foundation of your pizza, with whatever toppings you like.

Making a wrap or sandwich? Use whole-wheat or corn tortillas instead of flour, whole-wheat lavash or pita bread, or whole-grain or whole-wheat sliced bread. And if you're making a wrap or pita sandwich, consider filling it with one of our super grain salads (see page 32) for a double dose of whole grains.

Homemade veggie burgers are another delicious way to get your grains—we've included two scrumptious recipes, one based on bulgur, the other on brown rice. Enjoy them for a filling lunch or serve them up for dinner with all the fixin's (on whole-wheat hamburger buns, of course!).

Health Club Sandwiches (page 55)

BROCCOLI-CHEESE POLENTA PIZZA

Here's a different flavor take on pizza, made with the toothsome corn goodness of ready-made polenta.

ACTIVE TIME: 20 MIN · **TOTAL TIME:** 28 MIN
MAKES: 4 MAIN-DISH SERVINGS

OLIVE OIL NONSTICK COOKING SPRAY

1 LOG (16 OUNCES) PRECOOKED PLAIN POLENTA, CUT INTO ¼-INCH-THICK SLICES

1 BAG (12 OUNCES) BROCCOLI FLOWERETS

¾ CUP PART-SKIM RICOTTA CHEESE

¼ CUP FRESHLY GRATED PARMESAN CHEESE

1 TEASPOON FRESHLY GRATED LEMON PEEL

⅛ TEASPOON GROUND BLACK PEPPER

1 LARGE RIPE PLUM TOMATO, CHOPPED

1 Preheat broiler.

2 Coat 12-inch pizza pan or large cookie sheet with cooking spray. In center of pizza pan, place 1 slice polenta; arrange remaining slices in two concentric circles around first slice, overlapping slightly, to form a 10-inch round. Generously coat polenta with cooking spray. Place pan in oven about 4 inches from source of heat and broil polenta until heated through, about 5 minutes. Do not turn broiler off.

3 Meanwhile, in microwave-safe medium bowl, combine broccoli and **2 tablespoons water.** Cover with plastic wrap, turning back one section to vent. Heat broccoli in microwave oven on High 3 minutes or just until tender. Drain.

4 In small bowl, combine ricotta, Parmesan, lemon peel, and pepper.

5 Arrange broccoli evenly over polenta. Drop cheese mixture by tablespoons over polenta and broccoli; sprinkle with tomato. Broil pizza until topping is hot, 3 to 5 minutes.

EACH SERVING: ABOUT 200 CALORIES | 12G PROTEIN, | 25G CARBOHYDRATE | 6G TOTAL FAT (3G SATURATED) | 4G FIBER | 18MG CHOLESTEROL | 530MG SODIUM

VEGETARIAN RICE AND BEAN BURGERS

Forget the bun and enjoy these mini "burger" patties wrapped up in a tortilla with a refreshing tahini-lemon yogurt sauce.

TOTAL TIME: 20 MIN

MAKES: 4 MAIN-DISH SERVINGS

---

1   LEMON

1   CONTAINER (6 OUNCES) PLAIN LOW-FAT YOGURT

4   TABLESPOONS WELL-STIRRED TAHINI (SESAME PASTE)

¾   TEASPOON SALT

1   PACKAGE (8.8 OUNCES) PRECOOKED BROWN RICE

1   CAN (15 TO 19 OUNCES) GARBANZO BEANS

1   GARLIC CLOVE, CRUSHED WITH GARLIC PRESS

½   TEASPOON FENNEL SEEDS

NONSTICK COOKING SPRAY

4   BURRITO-SIZE (10-INCH) SPINACH OR SUN-DRIED-TOMATO TORTILLAS

2   MEDIUM CARROTS, PEELED AND SHREDDED

2   RIPE PLUM TOMATOES, THINLY SLICED

1   KIRBY (PICKLING) CUCUMBER, UNPEELED, THINLY SLICED

1   Prepare outdoor grill for direct grilling over medium heat.

2   From lemon, grate 1½ teaspoons peel and squeeze 2 tablespoons juice. In small serving bowl, stir lemon juice, yogurt, 2 tablespoons tahini, and ½ teaspoon salt until blended. Set yogurt sauce aside. Makes about ¾ cup.

3   Heat rice in microwave oven as label directs. Set aside.

4   Reserve ¼ cup liquid from beans. Rinse beans and drain well. In medium bowl, combine beans, lemon peel, garlic, fennel seeds, remaining ¼ teaspoon salt, remaining 2 tablespoons tahini, and reserved bean liquid. With potato masher, coarsely mash bean mixture until well blended but still lumpy. Add rice and continue to mash just until blended.

5   Shape bean mixture into eight 1-inch-thick burgers. Coat both sides of burgers with cooking spray. Place burgers on very hot grill rack. Cook until well browned on the outside, 10 to 12 minutes, turning burgers over once.

6   To serve, place 2 burgers in center of each tortilla; top with sauce, carrots, tomatoes, and cucumber. Fold opposite sides of each tortilla over filling, then fold ends over to form a package.

EACH SERVING: ABOUT 490 CALORIES | 15G PROTEIN | 83G CARBOHYDRATE | 11G TOTAL FAT (2G SATURATED) | 10G FIBER | 3MG CHOLESTEROL | 1,260MG SODIUM

BULGUR BEAN BURGERS

Why buy expensive veggie burgers in the store when they're so easy to make at home? This version gets its "meaty" texture from a combination of bulgur and black beans. Get an extra helping of grains by serving them up on whole-wheat buns.

ACTIVE TIME: 20 MIN · **TOTAL TIME:** 28 MIN
MAKES: 4 BURGERS

1   CUP WATER

¾   TEASPOON SALT

½   CUP BULGUR

1   CAN (15 TO 19 OUNCES) REDUCED-SODIUM BLACK BEANS, RINSED AND DRAINED

1   CONTAINER (6 OUNCES) PLAIN LOW-FAT YOGURT

¼   TEASPOON GROUND ALLSPICE

¼   TEASPOON GROUND CINNAMON

½   TEASPOON GROUND CUMIN

¼   CUP PACKED FRESH MINT LEAVES, CHOPPED

NONSTICK COOKING SPRAY

⅛   TEASPOON GROUND BLACK PEPPER

½   CUP SHREDDED KIRBY (PICKLING) CUCUMBER (1 SMALL)

4   LETTUCE LEAVES

1   RIPE MEDIUM TOMATO, SLICED

4   WHOLE-WHEAT HAMBURGER BUNS

1   In 1-quart saucepan, heat water and ½ teaspoon salt to boiling over high heat. Stir in bulgur. Reduce heat to low; cover and simmer until water is absorbed, 10 to 12 minutes.

2   Meanwhile, in large bowl, with potato masher or fork, mash beans with 2 tablespoons yogurt until almost smooth. Stir in bulgur, allspice, cinnamon, cumin, and half of mint until combined. With lightly floured hands, shape bean mixture into four 3-inch-round patties. Coat both sides of each patty lightly with cooking spray.

3   Heat nonstick 12-inch skillet over medium heat until hot. Add burgers and cook until lightly browned and heated through, about 8 minutes, turning them over once.

4   While burgers are cooking, prepare yogurt sauce: In small bowl, combine remaining yogurt, remaining mint, remaining ¼ teaspoon salt, and pepper. Makes about 1¼ cups.

5   To serve, divide lettuce, tomato slices, and burgers among buns; top with some yogurt sauce. Serve with remaining yogurt sauce on the side.

EACH BURGER: ABOUT 295 CALORIES | 16G PROTEIN | 58G CARBOHYDRATE
3G TOTAL FAT (1G SATURATED) | 14G FIBER | 3MG CHOLESTEROL | 960MG SODIUM

SPICY GUACAMOLE AND CHICKEN ROLL-UPS

Don't miss this zesty guacamole—it's great with tortilla chips too.

ACTIVE TIME: 30 MIN · TOTAL TIME: 42 MIN PLUS COOLING

MAKES: 4 ROLL-UPS

---

2   TEASPOONS OLIVE OIL

4   MEDIUM SKINLESS, BONELESS CHICKEN-BREAST HALVES (1 POUND)

½   TEASPOON SALT

½   TEASPOON COARSELY GROUND PEPPER

2   RIPE MEDIUM AVOCADOS, PEELED AND CUT INTO SMALL CHUNKS

1   RIPE MEDIUM TOMATO, DICED

¼   CUP LOOSELY PACKED FRESH CILANTRO LEAVES, COARSELY CHOPPED

4   TEASPOONS FRESH LIME JUICE

2   TEASPOONS FINELY CHOPPED RED ONION

1   TEASPOON ADOBO SAUCE FROM CANNED CHIPOTLE CHILES OR 2 TABLESPOONS GREEN JALAPEÑO SAUCE

4   BURRITO-SIZE (10-INCH) WHOLE-WHEAT TORTILLAS, WARMED

2   CUPS SLICED ICEBERG LETTUCE

1 In 10-inch skillet, heat oil over medium-high heat until hot. Add chicken and sprinkle with ¼ teaspoon salt and ¼ teaspoon pepper. Cook chicken, turning once, until juices run clear when thickest part is pierced with tip of knife, about 12 minutes. Transfer chicken to plate; cool until easy to handle, about 5 minutes.

2 Meanwhile, in medium bowl, with rubber spatula, gently stir avocados, tomato, cilantro, lime juice, onion, and adobo sauce until blended.

3 Pull chicken into thin shreds using two forks. Place tortillas on work surface; spread with guacamole. Place chicken, then lettuce on top of guacamole. Roll tortillas around filling.

EACH ROLL-UP: ABOUT 510 CALORIES | 34G PROTEIN | 40G CARBOHYDRATE | 25G TOTAL FAT (4G SATURATED) | 10G FIBER | 72MG CHOLESTEROL | 625MG SODIUM

TURKEY MEATBALL PITAS

No one need ever know these meatballs are made with turkey instead of beef.

ACTIVE TIME: 20 MIN · TOTAL TIME: 30 MIN
MAKES: 5 SERVINGS

1   POUND GROUND TURKEY

2   SLICES WHOLE-GRAIN BREAD, CHOPPED

2   TABLESPOONS GRATED ONION

1   LARGE EGG WHITE

1½ TEASPOONS GROUND CUMIN

1¼ TEASPOONS SALT

3   TABLESPOONS WATER

5   (6-INCH) WHOLE-WHEAT PITA BREADS

½   LARGE CUCUMBER, PEELED AND CUT INTO ¾-INCH PIECES

1   CONTAINER (8 OUNCES) PLAIN NONFAT YOGURT

2   TABLESPOONS CHOPPED FRESH CILANTRO OR 1 TEASPOON DRIED MINT

4   CUPS THINLY SLICED ROMAINE LETTUCE

1 Preheat oven to 425°F. Coat 15 ½" by 10½" jelly-roll pan with nonstick cooking spray.

2 In large bowl, with hands, mix turkey, bread, onion, egg white, cumin, ¾ teaspoon salt, and water. Shape turkey mixture into 25 meatballs. (For easier shaping, use wet hands.) Place meatballs in prepared jelly-roll pan and bake until cooked through (meatballs will not brown), 12 to 15 minutes.

3 Cut about 1 inch from top of each pita; reserve cut-off pieces for use another day. Wrap pitas in foil. After meatballs have baked 5 minutes, warm pitas in oven until meatballs are done.

4 Meanwhile, in small bowl, mix cucumber, yogurt, cilantro, and remaining ½ teaspoon salt.

5 To serve, fill pitas with lettuce and meatballs; top with cucumber sauce.

EACH SERVING: ABOUT 380 CALORIES | 28G PROTEIN | 44G CARBOHYDRATE | 11G TOTAL FAT (3G SATURATED) | 5G FIBER | 46MG CHOLESTEROL | 1,020MG SODIUM

FALAFEL SANDWICHES

Serve these small bean patties in whole-wheat pita pockets.

ACTIVE TIME: 10 MIN · TOTAL TIME: 18 MIN

MAKES: 4 SANDWICHES

- 4 GREEN ONIONS, CUT INTO ½-INCH PIECES
- 2 GARLIC CLOVES, EACH CUT IN HALF
- ½ CUP PACKED FRESH FLAT-LEAF PARSLEY LEAVES
- 2 TEASPOONS DRIED MINT
- 1 CAN (15 TO 19 OUNCES) GARBANZO BEANS, RINSED AND DRAINED
- ½ CUP PLAIN DRIED BREAD CRUMBS
- 1 TEASPOON GROUND CORIANDER
- 1 TEASPOON GROUND CUMIN
- 1 TEASPOON BAKING POWDER
- ½ TEASPOON SALT
- ¼ TEASPOON GROUND RED PEPPER (CAYENNE)
- ¼ TEASPOON GROUND ALLSPICE
- OLIVE OIL NONSTICK COOKING SPRAY
- 4 (6- TO 7-INCH) WHOLE-WHEAT PITA BREADS

ACCOMPANIMENTS: SLICED ROMAINE LETTUCE, SLICED RIPE TOMATOES, SLICED CUCUMBER, SLICED RED ONION, PLAIN LOW-FAT YOGURT

1   In food processor with knife blade attached, finely chop green onions, garlic, parsley, and mint. Add beans, bread crumbs, coriander, cumin, baking powder, salt, ground red pepper, and allspice, and blend until a coarse puree forms.

2   Shape mixture, by scant ½ cups, into eight 3-inch patties and place on sheet of waxed paper; coat both sides of patties with cooking spray.

3   Heat nonstick 10-inch skillet over medium-high heat until hot. Add half of patties and cook until dark golden brown, about 8 minutes, turning once. Transfer patties to paper towels to drain. Repeat with remaining patties.

4   Cut off top third of each pita to form a pocket. Place two warm patties in each pita. Serve with choice of accompaniments.

EACH SANDWICH WITHOUT ACCOMPANIMENTS: ABOUT 365 CALORIES | 14G PROTEIN
68G CARBOHYDRATE | 5G TOTAL FAT (1G SATURATED) | 10G FIBER | 0MG CHOLESTEROL
1,015MG SODIUM

HEALTH CLUB SANDWICHES

This carrot, sprout, and bean spread combo will satisfy your palate and ease your conscience. (See photo on page 46.) For an extra wholesome sandwich, serve on our homemade Multigrain Bread (page 142).

TOTAL TIME: 25 MIN

MAKES: 4 SANDWICHES

2 TABLESPOONS OLIVE OIL

2 TEASPOONS PLUS 1 TABLESPOON FRESH LEMON JUICE

1 TEASPOON HONEY

⅛ TEASPOON GROUND BLACK PEPPER

3 CARROTS, PEELED AND SHREDDED (1 CUP)

2 CUPS ALFALFA SPROUTS

1 GARLIC CLOVE, FINELY CHOPPED

½ TEASPOON GROUND CUMIN

PINCH GROUND RED PEPPER (CAYENNE)

1 CAN (15 TO 19 OUNCES) GARBANZO BEANS, RINSED AND DRAINED

1 TABLESPOON WATER

12 SLICES MULTIGRAIN BREAD, LIGHTLY TOASTED

1 LARGE RIPE TOMATO (10 TO 12 OUNCES), THINLY SLICED

1 BUNCH WATERCRESS (4 OUNCES), TOUGH STEMS TRIMMED

1 In medium bowl, stir 1 tablespoon oil, 2 teaspoons lemon juice, honey, and black pepper until mixed. Add carrots and alfalfa sprouts; toss until mixed and evenly coated with dressing.

2 In 2-quart saucepan, heat remaining 1 tablespoon oil over medium heat. Add garlic, cumin, and ground red pepper and cook until very fragrant. Stir in beans and remove from heat. Add remaining 1 tablespoon lemon juice and mash to a coarse puree.

3 Spread garbanzo-bean mixture on 8 toast slices. Place tomato slices and watercress over 4 garbanzo-topped toast slices. Top remaining 4 garbanzo-topped slices with alfalfa-sprout mixture and place on watercress-topped bread. Cover with 4 remaining toast slices. Cut sandwiches in half.

EACH SANDWICH: ABOUT 379 CALORIES | 14G PROTEIN | 57G CARBOHYDRATE | 12G TOTAL FAT (2G SATURATED) | 17G FIBER | 0MG CHOLESTEROL | 545MG SODIUM

SOUPS, STEWS & CHILIS

You can add grains to comforting soups, stews, and chilis in a lot of different ways. For Asian-style soups, drop in cooked brown rice or udon, a Japanese noodle made from a blend of buckwheat and whole-wheat flour. For other soups and stews, depending on how hearty and what else is in it, any kind of cooked grain will be a healthful and tasty addition—barley, wild rice, hominy, wheat berries. A handful of left-over whole-grain pasta (corkscrews, bow-ties, little soup pastas) will make most any soup taste even better.

For chilis, both those with and without meat, cooked grains like wheat berries, bulgur, quinoa, farro, and pearl barley will provide a welcome toothsomeness and added depth of flavor. You don't need to add much to reap a bounty of good health benefits.

Beef and Wheat Berry Chili (page 66)

MUSHROOM AND BROWN RICE SOUP

To make this soup a complete meal, serve with crackers or crusty bread and a mixed green salad with an herb vinaigrette.

ACTIVE TIME: 25 MIN · **TOTAL TIME:** 30 MIN

MAKES: 4 MAIN-DISH SERVINGS

1   TABLESPOON OLIVE OIL

1   MEDIUM ONION, FINELY CHOPPED

1   PACKAGE (10 OUNCES) SLICED WHITE MUSHROOMS

1   PACKAGE (4 OUNCES) ASSORTED SLICED WILD MUSHROOMS

1   CUP BAGGED SHREDDED CARROTS

1   GARLIC CLOVE, CRUSHED WITH GARLIC PRESS

½   TEASPOON SALT

¼   TEASPOON DRIED THYME

⅛   TEASPOON GROUND BLACK PEPPER

1   CONTAINER (32 OUNCES) CHICKEN BROTH

¾   CUP INSTANT (10-MINUTE) BROWN RICE

2   CUPS WATER

1 In 4-quart saucepan, heat oil over medium-high heat. Add onion and cook 5 minutes, stirring occasionally. Add white and wild mushrooms and carrots and cook until mushrooms are golden and tender, 8 to 10 minutes, stirring occasionally. Add garlic, salt, thyme, and pepper, and cook 1 minute, stirring.

2 Add broth, rice, and water; cover and heat to boiling over high heat. Reduce heat to medium; cook, partially covered, until rice is tender, about 5 minutes.

EACH SERVING: ABOUT 170 CALORIES | 8G PROTEIN | 24G CARBOHYDRATE | 6G TOTAL FAT (1G SATURATED) | 4G FIBER | 0MG CHOLESTEROL | 1,260MG SODIUM

BRANDIED SHRIMP AND WILD RICE SOUP

This is such a wonderfully elegant soup to serve as a holiday dinner first course, but don't hesitate to make it for your family, accompanied by a crisp salad.

ACTIVE TIME: 10 MIN · **TOTAL TIME:** 25 MIN

MAKES: 12 FIRST-COURSE OR 6 MAIN-DISH SERVINGS

---

1 BOX (6 OUNCES) LONG-GRAIN AND WILD RICE MIX

⅓ CUP ALL-PURPOSE FLOUR

¾ TEASPOON SALT

¼ TEASPOON GROUND BLACK PEPPER

4 CUPS WHOLE MILK

1 TABLESPOON BUTTER OR MARGARINE

1 SMALL ONION, FINELY CHOPPED

2 BOTTLES (8 OUNCES EACH) CLAM JUICE

1 CUP HEAVY OR WHIPPING CREAM

⅓ CUP BRANDY

1½ POUNDS SHRIMP, SHELLED AND DEVEINED

1 Prepare rice mix as label directs.

2 Meanwhile, in 2-cup liquid measuring cup, with wire whisk, mix flour, salt, and pepper with ½ cup milk until smooth. Set aside.

3 In 5- to 6-quart saucepot, melt butter over medium-low heat. Add onion and cook until tender, about 5 minutes, stirring occasionally. Increase heat to medium-high. Stir in clam juice, cream, brandy, and remaining 3½ cups milk; heat to boiling. Boil 1 minute.

4 Stir in shrimp and rice; cook just until shrimp turn opaque throughout, about 2 minutes.

EACH FIRST-COURSE SERVING: ABOUT 270 CALORIES | 16G PROTEIN | 19G CARBOHYDRATE 13G TOTAL FAT (8G SATURATED) | 1G FIBER | 131MG CHOLESTEROL | 580MG SODIUM

LEMONY ASIAN-STYLE CHICKEN NOODLE SOUP

This is a deliciously different take on traditional chicken noodle soup, with the flavorful addition of fresh ginger, lemongrass, and fish sauce.

ACTIVE TIME: 25 MIN · **TOTAL TIME:** 40 MIN

MAKES: 6 MAIN-DISH SERVINGS

---

8   OUNCES WHOLE-WHEAT SOBA NOODLES (¼ INCH WIDE)

2   TEASPOONS VEGETABLE OIL

1   TABLESPOON MINCED, PEELED FRESH GINGER

1   LARGE GARLIC CLOVE, CRUSHED WITH GARLIC PRESS

2   TEASPOONS GROUND CORIANDER

2   PIECES (3 INCHES EACH) DRIED OR FRESH LEMONGRASS (OPTIONAL)

3   GREEN ONIONS, THINLY SLICED

2   CANS (14½ OUNCES EACH) CHICKEN BROTH

¼   CUP ASIAN FISH SAUCE (SEE TIP PAGE 199)

4   CUPS WATER

1   POUND SKINLESS, BONELESS CHICKEN THIGHS, CUT INTO ½-INCH-THICK SLICES

1   SMALL HEAD NAPA (CHINESE) CABBAGE (1½ POUNDS), CORED AND CUT CROSSWISE INTO ½-INCH STRIPS

½   CUP LOOSELY PACKED FRESH MINT LEAVES, CHOPPED

1   Heat large covered saucepot of **salted water** to boiling on high heat. Add soba and cook as label directs. Drain noodles.

2   Meanwhile, in 4-quart saucepan, heat oil over medium heat. Add ginger and garlic and cook 30 seconds; stir in coriander and lemongrass, if using, and cook 30 seconds, stirring. Add green onions and cook 2 minutes. Stir in broth, fish sauce, and water; cover and heat to boiling over high heat.

3   Stir noodles, chicken, cabbage, and mint into broth mixture; cook until chicken loses its pink color throughout, about 4 minutes. Discard lemongrass. Stir in noodles and heat through.

EACH SERVING: ABOUT 265 CALORIES | 17G PROTEIN | 20G CARBOHYDRATE | 5G TOTAL FAT (1G SATURATED) | 2G FIBER | 63MG CHOLESTEROL | 1,447MG SODIUM

BARLEY MINESTRONE

Top this soup with a dollop of our homemade pesto, which you can make in a mini food processor. No mini processor? Store-bought refrigerated pesto makes an excellent stand-in—although it's not as light as our version.

ACTIVE TIME: 35 MIN · **TOTAL TIME:** 1 HR 25 MIN
MAKES: 6 MAIN-DISH SERVINGS

MINESTRONE

1   CUP PEARL BARLEY

1   TABLESPOON OLIVE OIL

2   CUPS THINLY SLICED GREEN CABBAGE (¼ SMALL HEAD)

2   LARGE CARROTS, PEELED AND EACH CUT LENGTHWISE IN HALF, THEN CROSSWISE INTO ½-INCH-THICK SLICES

2   LARGE STALKS CELERY, CUT INTO ½-INCH DICE

1   MEDIUM ONION, CUT INTO ½-INCH DICE

1   GARLIC CLOVE, FINELY CHOPPED

3   CUPS WATER

2   CANS (14½ OUNCES EACH) VEGETABLE BROTH

1   CAN (14½ OUNCES) DICED TOMATOES

¼   TEASPOON SALT

1   MEDIUM ZUCCHINI (8 TO 10 OUNCES), CUT INTO ½-INCH DICE

¼   POUND GREEN BEANS, TRIMMED AND CUT INTO ½-INCH PIECES (1 CUP)

LIGHT PESTO

1   CUP FIRMLY PACKED FRESH BASIL LEAVES

2   TABLESPOONS OLIVE OIL

2   TABLESPOONS WATER

¼   TEASPOON SALT

¼   CUP FRESHLY GRATED PECORINO-ROMANO CHEESE

1   GARLIC CLOVE, FINELY CHOPPED

1 Prepare Minestrone: Heat 5- to 6-quart Dutch oven over medium-high heat until hot. Add barley and toast until fragrant, 3 to 4 minutes, stirring constantly. Transfer barley to small bowl; set aside.

2 In same Dutch oven, heat oil over medium-high heat until hot. Add cabbage, carrots, celery, and onion; cook until vegetables are tender and lightly browned, 8 to 10 minutes, stirring occasionally. Add garlic and cook until fragrant, 30 seconds. Stir in barley, water, broth, tomatoes, and salt. Cover and heat to boiling over high heat. Reduce heat to low and simmer, covered, 25 minutes.

3 Stir zucchini and green beans into barley mixture; increase heat to medium and cook, covered, until all vegetables and barely are tender, 10 to 15 minutes longer.

4 Meanwhile, prepare Light Pesto: In blender container with narrow base or in mini food processor, combine basil, oil, water, and salt; cover and blend until mixture is pureed. Transfer pesto to small bowl; stir in Pecorino and garlic. Makes about ½ cup pesto.

5 Ladle minestrone into 6 large soup bowls. Top each serving with some pesto.

EACH SERVING SOUP: ABOUT 215 CALORIES | 7G PROTEIN | 42G CARBOHYDRATE | 4G TOTAL FAT (0G SATURATED) | 9G FIBER | 0MG CHOLESTEROL | 690MG SODIUM

EACH TEASPOON PESTO: ABOUT 15 CALORIES | 0G PROTEIN | 0G CARBOHYDRATE | 1G TOTAL FAT (0G SATURATED) | 0G FIBER | 1MG CHOLESTEROL | 35MG SODIUM

BEEF-BARLEY AND ROOT VEGETABLE STEW

This stew is a delicious rib-sticker for a cold winter night. (See photo on page 12.)

ACTIVE TIME: 25 MIN · **TOTAL TIME:** 2 HR 55 MIN

MAKES: 12 MAIN-DISH SERVINGS

---

2   SLICES BACON, CUT INTO ¼-INCH PIECES

3   POUNDS BONE-IN BEEF CHUCK STEAK

2   TEASPOONS PLUS 1 TABLESPOON VEGETABLE OIL

4   LARGE STALKS CELERY (12 OUNCES), CUT INTO ½-INCH-THICK SLICES

2   MEDIUM CARROTS, PEELED AND CUT INTO ½-INCH-THICK SLICES

2   SMALL PARSNIPS, PEELED AND CUT INTO ½-INCH-THICK SLICES

1   LARGE ONION, CHOPPED

1   PACKAGE (10 OUNCES) MUSHROOMS, TRIMMED AND EACH CUT INTO QUARTERS, OR EIGHTHS IF LARGE

3   TABLESPOONS TOMATO PASTE

12 CUPS WATER

2   TABLESPOONS SOY SAUCE

1   TABLESPOON SALT

1   PACKAGE (16 OUNCES) PEARL BARLEY

---

1 In 6- to 8-quart saucepot, cook bacon over medium heat until browned, about 5 minutes, stirring occasionally. With slotted spoon, transfer bacon to medium bowl. Meanwhile, trim and discard fat from beef. Cut beef into 1-inch chunks, reserving bones.

2 Add beef and bones, in 4 batches, to bacon drippings, and cook over medium-high heat until well browned on all sides, 3 to 4 minutes per batch, adding 2 teaspoons oil as necessary. (Reduce heat to medium if drippings begin to smoke.) With slotted spoon, transfer beef as it browns to bowl with bacon.

3 Reduce heat to medium. Add remaining 1 tablespoon oil to saucepot. Add celery, carrots, parsnips, onion, and mushrooms, and cook, covered, until vegetables are tender, 15 minutes, stirring occasionally. Add tomato paste and cook 1 minute, stirring.

4 Return meat with its juices and bacon to saucepot. Stir in water, soy sauce, and salt; heat to boiling over high heat. Reduce to low and simmer, covered, 45 minutes, stirring occasionally.

5 Stir in barley; heat to boiling over high heat. Reduce heat to low; simmer, covered, until beef and barley are tender, 40 minutes longer, stirring.

EACH SERVING: ABOUT 405 CALORIES | 29G PROTEIN | 38G CARBOHYDRATE | 15G TOTAL FAT (5G SATURATED) | 8G FIBER | 69MG CHOLESTEROL | 876MG SODIUM

INDIAN LENTIL STEW WITH SWEET POTATOES AND SPINACH

We love the warm flavor that garam masala brings to our lentil stew. This essential component of Indian and other South Asian cuisines is a sweet aromatic blend of dry-roasted ground spices that may include: coriander, green and black cardamom, cinnamon, cloves, bay leaves, nutmeg or mace, ginger, black pepper, and cumin. Our suggested substitution in the recipe works well, but it isn't quite as authentic.

ACTIVE TIME: 25 MIN · **TOTAL TIME:** 1 HR
MAKES: 6 MAIN-DISH SERVINGS

1½ CUPS BROWN BASMATI RICE

1 TABLESPOON VEGETABLE OIL

1 LARGE ONION, CHOPPED

2 TABLESPOONS MINCED, PEELED FRESH GINGER

1½ TEASPOONS GARAM MASALA (OR 1½ TEASPOONS CURRY POWDER PLUS ¼ TEASPOON GROUND CINNAMON)

1 GARLIC CLOVE, CHOPPED

4 CUPS WATER

2 CUPS GREEN LENTILS, PICKED OVER AND RINSED

1 POUND SWEET POTATOES, PEELED AND CUT INTO ½-INCH CHUNKS

1 CAN (14½ OUNCES) DICED TOMATOES

1 CAN (14½ OUNCES) VEGETABLE BROTH

½ TEASPOON SALT

1 BAG (9 OUNCES) FRESH SPINACH OR 1 PACKAGE (10 OUNCES) FROZEN LEAF SPINACH, THAWED AND SQUEEZED DRY

1 Prepare rice as label directs.

2 Meanwhile, in 6-quart saucepot, heat oil over medium heat until hot. Add onion and cook until tender and lightly browned, 8 to 10 minutes, stirring occasionally. Stir in ginger, garam masala, and garlic, and cook 1 minute. Add water, lentils, sweet potatoes, tomatoes with their juice, broth, and salt; heat to boiling over high heat.

3 Reduce heat to low; cover and simmer until lentils and sweet potatoes are tender, about 25 minutes, stirring occasionally.

4 Add spinach to stew; heat through. Serve stew with brown rice.

EACH SERVING: ABOUT 520 CALORIES | 25G PROTEIN | 97G CARBOHYDRATE | 5G TOTAL FAT (0G SATURATED) | 17G FIBER | 0MG CHOLESTEROL | 675 MG SODIUM

BEEF AND WHEAT BERRY CHILI

Our recipe calls for ground ancho chile pepper. Ancho chile, the dried pod of a chile indigenous to Mexico, has a sweet fruity flavor and a mild heat. It is also called *poblano* when fresh. If you can't find ground ancho chile pepper in your supermarket, substitute Mexican-style chili powder.

ACTIVE TIME: 15 MIN · **TOTAL TIME:** 2 HR 15 MIN
MAKES: 8 MAIN-DISH SERVINGS

4   TEASPOONS VEGETABLE OIL

2   POUNDS BONELESS BEEF BOTTOM ROUND, CUT INTO 1-INCH CUBES

2   MEDIUM ONIONS, CHOPPED

3   GARLIC CLOVES, FINELY CHOPPED

3   TABLESPOONS GROUND ANCHO CHILE PEPPER

2   TEASPOONS GROUND CUMIN

1   TEASPOON SALT

1   CAN (14½ OUNCES) DICED TOMATOES WITH CHILES

1   CAN (14½ OUNCES) LOW-SODIUM BEEF BROTH

1   CUP WHEAT BERRIES (WHOLE-WHEAT KERNELS)

1   BOTTLE (12 OUNCES) DARK BEER

2   SLICES BACON

1   BAY LEAF

SOUR CREAM AND SLICED GREEN ONIONS (OPTIONAL)

1   In nonstick 5- to 6-quart Dutch oven, heat 1 teaspoon oil over medium-high heat until hot. Add half of beef and cook until browned on all sides, 4 to 5 minutes, stirring occasionally. With slotted spoon, transfer beef to large bowl. Repeat with another 1 teaspoon oil and remaining beef.

2   In same Dutch oven, heat remaining 2 teaspoons oil over medium heat until hot. Add onions and cook until golden, about 5 minutes, stirring occasionally. Stir in garlic and cook 30 seconds, stirring constantly. Stir in ground ancho chile, cumin, and ½ teaspoon salt; cook 1 minute. Return beef to Dutch oven; add tomatoes and broth. Heat to boiling over medium-high heat. Reduce heat to low; cover and simmer 1½ hours.

3   Meanwhile, in 3-quart saucepan, combine **2½ cups water**, wheat berries, beer, bacon, bay leaf, and remaining ½ teaspoon salt; cover and heat to boiling over medium-high heat. Reduce heat to low and simmer, covered, 1½ hours. Drain wheat berries, reserving **1 cup cooking water**. Discard bacon and bay leaf.

4 Stir wheat berries and reserved cooking water into Dutch oven with beef mixture. Reduce heat to low and simmer, uncovered, until beef and wheat berries are tender, about 15 minutes.

5 Serve chili with sour cream and green onions, if desired.

EACH SERVING: ABOUT 360 CALORIES | 28G PROTEIN | 23G CARBOHYDRATE | 18G TOTAL FAT (6G SATURATED) | 5G FIBER | 72MG CHOLESTEROL | 530MG SODIUM

EVERYDAY CASSEROLES

When it comes to serving up something bubbling hot from the oven, adding a healthy dose of whole grains is a snap. Next time you make your favorite lasagna, stuffed shell, or mac and cheese recipe, use a whole-grain pasta instead, or try our new take on lasagna, layering tomato sauce, spinach, and ricotta cheese with sliced precooked polenta.

You can engineer a whole-grain meatloaf makeover by trying the two recipes we include here or by adding some cooked brown rice, bulgur, or wheat berries to the meat mixture or substituting fresh whole-wheat or other whole-grain bread crumbs for regular white crumbs to your own meatloaf recipe.

Or try stuffing your favorite vegetable—artichokes, acorn squash, bell peppers—with the whole-grain filling of your choice. You'll see that grains add a substantial meatiness to any dish but also absorb all those wonderful juices.

Bulgur and Beef Stuffed Peppers (page 80)

POLENTA LASAGNA

This stress-free dish is perfect for a last-minute get-together; serve with a salad of mixed baby greens.

ACTIVE TIME: 45 MIN · **TOTAL TIME:** 1 HR 15 MIN
MAKES: 6 MAIN-DISH SERVINGS

1   TABLESPOON OLIVE OIL

1   SMALL ONION, FINELY CHOPPED

1   GARLIC CLOVE, MINCED

1   CAN (28 OUNCES) TOMATOES

2   TABLESPOONS TOMATO PASTE

2   TABLESPOONS CHOPPED FRESH BASIL

1   TEASPOON SALT

1   PACKAGE (10 OUNCES) FROZEN CHOPPED SPINACH, THAWED AND SQUEEZED DRY

1   CUP PART-SKIM RICOTTA CHEESE

2   TABLESPOONS FRESHLY GRATED PARMESAN CHEESE

¼   TEASPOON COARSELY GROUND BLACK PEPPER

1   LOG (24 OUNCES) PRECOOKED PLAIN POLENTA, CUT INTO 16 SLICES

4   OUNCES PART-SKIM MOZZARELLA CHEESE, SHREDDED (1 CUP)

1 In 3-quart saucepan, heat oil over medium heat. Add onion and cook until tender, about 8 minutes, stirring occasionally. Add garlic and cook 30 seconds longer. Stir in tomatoes with their juice, tomato paste, basil, and ½ teaspoon salt, breaking up tomatoes with side of spoon; heat to boiling over high heat. Reduce heat to low and simmer, uncovered, 20 minutes, stirring occasionally. Set sauce aside.

2 Meanwhile, in medium bowl, mix spinach, ricotta, Parmesan, pepper, and remaining ½ teaspoon salt until blended.

3 Preheat oven to 350°F. Grease 8-inch square glass baking dish.

4 Arrange half of polenta slices, overlapping slightly, in baking dish. Drop half of spinach mixture, by rounded tablespoons, on top of polenta (mixture will not completely cover slices). Pour half of sauce over spinach mixture; spread to form an even layer. Sprinkle with half of mozzarella. Repeat layering.

5 Bake casserole until hot and bubbling, about 30 minutes. Let stand 10 minutes for easier serving.

EACH SERVING: ABOUT 270 CALORIES | 16G PROTEIN | 3G CARBOHYDRATE | 15G TOTAL FAT (10G SATURATED) | 4G FIBER | 28MG CHOLESTEROL | 1,210MG SODIUM

HEALTHY MAKEOVER MEATLOAF

In the kingdom of comfort food, meatloaf is royalty. Rich in carbs and fat, it fills you up and makes you feel good—that is, until your waistband becomes too tight. To get the comfort without the calories, try this version. We've cut the fat in half by using 93 percent lean ground turkey, instead of ground beef chuck, and opted for fat-free milk, which still keeps the loaf plenty tender. Whole-wheat bread crumbs complete the healthy makeover.

ACTIVE TIME: 15 MIN · TOTAL TIME: 1 HR 10 MIN
MAKES: 8 MAIN-DISH SERVINGS

1   TABLESPOON OLIVE OIL
2   MEDIUM STALKS CELERY, FINELY CHOPPED
1   SMALL ONION, FINELY CHOPPED
1   GARLIC CLOVE, CRUSHED WITH GARLIC PRESS
2   POUNDS LEAN GROUND TURKEY
¾   CUP FRESH WHOLE-WHEAT BREAD CRUMBS (FROM 1½ SLICES BREAD)

⅓   CUP SKIM MILK
1   TABLESPOON WORCESTERSHIRE SAUCE
2   LARGE EGG WHITES
½   CUP KETCHUP
½   TEASPOON SALT
½   TEASPOON COARSELY GROUND BLACK PEPPER
1   TABLESPOON DIJON MUSTARD

1   Preheat oven to 350°F.

2   In 12-inch nonstick skillet, heat oil over medium heat. Add celery and onion and cook until vegetables are tender, about 10 minutes, stirring occasionally. Add garlic and cook 1 minute. Transfer vegetables to large bowl; cool slightly.

3   To bowl with vegetables, add turkey, bread crumbs, milk, Worcestershire, egg whites, ¼ cup ketchup, salt, and pepper; mix with hands until well combined but not overmixed. In cup, mix Dijon and remaining ¼ cup ketchup.

4   In 13" by 9" metal baking pan, shape meat mixture into 9" by 5" loaf. Spread ketchup mixture over top of loaf. Bake meatloaf until instant-read thermometer inserted in center reaches 160°F, 55 to 60 minutes. (Temperature will rise to 165°F upon standing.)

5 Let meatloaf stand 10 minutes before removing from pan to set juices for easier slicing. Transfer meatloaf to platter and cut into slices to serve.

TIP For faster cooking, you can make smaller loaves. Shape the meat mixture into two loaves and you shave about 20 minutes off your cooking time; make 6 to 8 individual loaves and cut the time in half. (Place the loaves in a 13" by 9" pan or jelly-roll pan.)

EACH SERVING: ABOUT 230 CALORIES | 25G PROTEIN | 11G CARBOHYDRATE | 11G TOTAL FAT (3G SATURATED) | 1G FIBER | 80MG CHOLESTEROL | 500MG SODIUM

BULGUR MINI MEATLOAVES

What an effortless way to get your grains—in these individual-serving meatloaves. In addition to its nutritional goodness, the bulgur adds a delicious nutty, chewy quality to this dish of comfort.

ACTIVE TIME: 25 MIN · **TOTAL TIME:** 45 MIN

MAKES: 6 MAIN-DISH SERVINGS

2 TEASPOONS OLIVE OIL

1 MEDIUM ONION, CHOPPED

2 GARLIC CLOVES, CRUSHED WITH GARLIC PRESS

2 CUPS WATER

1 CUP BULGUR

1 POUND LEAN (90%) GROUND BEEF

½ CUP LOOSELY PACKED FRESH PARSLEY LEAVES, CHOPPED

1 LARGE EGG, LIGHTLY BEATEN

1 JAR (14 TO 16 OUNCES) MARINARA SAUCE

1 TEASPOON SALT

¼ TEASPOON GROUND BLACK PEPPER

1 In nonstick 1½-quart saucepan, heat oil over medium-high heat until hot. Add onion and cook until lightly browned, about 5 minutes, stirring occasionally. Stir in garlic; cook 30 seconds. Add water, and stir bulgur into saucepan with onion; cover and heat to boiling. Reduce heat to low and simmer, covered, until bulgur is tender and liquid is absorbed, about 15 minutes. Transfer bulgur to large plate and spread out to cool, about 5 minutes.

2 Meanwhile, preheat oven to 425°F. Line 15½" by 10½" jelly-roll pan with nonstick foil (or spray regular foil with nonstick spray).

3 In large bowl, combine beef, parsley, egg, ¾ cup marinara sauce, salt, and pepper. Add bulgur mixture and mix with fingertips just until blended. Shape meat mixture by scant cupfuls into six 4½" by 3½" mounds (about 1 inch high) in prepared pan.

4 Bake meatloaves until instant-read thermometer inserted into center of loaves reaches 160°F, 20 to 25 minutes.

5 In microwave-safe medium bowl or 4-cup liquid measuring cup, heat remaining marinara sauce, covered, in microwave oven on High 1 minute or until hot. Serve sauce with meatloaves.

EACH SERVING: ABOUT 300 CALORIES | 19G PROTEIN | 27G CARBOHYDRATE | 13G TOTAL FAT (4G SATURATED) | 7G FIBER | 82MG CHOLESTEROL | 725MG SODIUM

ACORN SQUASH WITH BROWN RICE AND TURKEY SAUSAGE

Here's a hearty fall dish that gives you your grains and reduces the fat without reducing the flavor.

ACTIVE TIME: 25 MIN · **TOTAL TIME:** 45 MIN

MAKES: 4 MAIN-DISH SERVINGS

---

2 ACORN SQUASH (1¼ POUNDS EACH), CUT CROSSWISE IN HALF AND SEEDED

1 TABLESPOON OLIVE OIL

½ POUND SWEET OR HOT ITALIAN TURKEY OR CHICKEN SAUSAGE, CASINGS REMOVED

1 SMALL ONION, CHOPPED

1 MEDIUM RED PEPPER, CHOPPED

½ TEASPOON SALT

¼ TEASPOON GROUND BLACK PEPPER

1 PACKAGE (8.8 OUNCES) PRECOOKED BROWN RICE (SCANT 2 CUPS)

2 TABLESPOONS CHOPPED FRESH PARSLEY

1 Lightly grease microwave-safe large plate; place squash halves, cut sides down, on plate (it's OK if halves overlap slightly). Cook squash in microwave on High 8 to 9 minutes or until fork-tender; set aside until cool enough to handle.

2 Meanwhile, preheat oven to 375°F. Line 15½" by 10½" jelly-roll pan with foil.

3 In nonstick 12-inch skillet, heat oil over medium-high heat until hot. Add sausage and cook until browned, breaking it up with side of spoon. With slotted spoon, transfer sausage to large bowl.

4 To same skillet, add onion, red pepper, salt, and black pepper, and cook over medium heat until lightly browned and tender, 6 to 8 minutes, stirring occasionally; add to sausage in bowl.

5 With spoon, scoop out squash, leaving ¼-inch-thick shell. Add scooped-out squash to bowl with sausage; stir in rice (it is not necessary to heat rice) and parsley until combined.

6 Spoon sausage mixture into squash shells; place in prepared pan. Bake until heated through, about 20 minutes.

EACH SERVING: ABOUT 365 CALORIES | 11G PROTEIN | 42G CARBOHYDRATE | 20G TOTAL FAT (6G SATURATED) | 5G FIBER | 30MG CHOLESTEROL | 610MG SODIUM

NEW FRIED CHICKEN

This is our answer to high-fat fried chicken: skinless drumsticks brushed with creamy mustard, coated with crushed whole-wheat cereal, and baked to a crispy golden brown.

ACTIVE TIME: 15 MIN · **TOTAL TIME:** 45 MIN
MAKES: 4 MAIN-DISH SERVINGS

8   LARGE CHICKEN DRUMSTICKS
     (1½ POUNDS)

1½ CUPS WHOLE-WHEAT-FLAKE CEREAL,
   COARSELY CRUSHED

2   TABLESPOONS DRIED PARSLEY FLAKES

⅓   CUP CREAMY MUSTARD BLEND

¾   TEASPOON SALT

1   Preheat oven to 400°F. Coat 15½" by 10½" jelly-roll pan with nonstick cooking spray.
2   Remove skin from chicken drumsticks. On waxed paper, mix cereal and parsley flakes. In small bowl, mix mustard blend and salt. Brush each drumstick with mustard mixture; coat with cereal mixture, then place in prepared jelly-roll pan. Bake drumsticks until coating is crisp and juices run clear when chicken is pierced with tip of knife, about 30 minutes.
3   Arrange drumsticks on platter.

EACH SERVING: ABOUT 241 CALORIES | 22G PROTEIN | 17G CARBOHYDRATE | 9G TOTAL FAT (2G SATURATED) | 2G FIBER | 65G CHOLESTEROL | 1,137MG SODIUM

HAM AND CHEESE GRITS CASSEROLE

This is perfect for an easy weeknight supper.

ACTIVE TIME: 25 MIN · TOTAL TIME: 1 HR 10 MIN

MAKES: 6 MAIN-DISH SERVINGS

3½ CUPS SKIM MILK

2¼ CUPS WATER

1 TEASPOON SALT

1¼ CUPS QUICK HOMINY GRITS

4 OUNCES COOKED HAM, DICED (¾ CUP)

3 OUNCES LOW-FAT MONTEREY JACK CHEESE, SHREDDED (¾ CUP)

2 TABLESPOONS FRESHLY GRATED PARMESAN CHEESE

1 PICKLED JALAPEÑO CHILE, MINCED

2 LARGE EGGS

3 LARGE EGG WHITES

1   Preheat oven to 325°F. Grease shallow 2-quart casserole.

2   In heavy 3-quart saucepan, heat 1½ cups milk, water, and salt to boiling over medium-high heat. Gradually stir in grits, beating constantly with wire whisk. Cover and simmer over low heat 5 minutes, stirring occasionally. Remove from heat; stir in ham, Monterey Jack, Parmesan, and jalapeño.

3   In large bowl, with whisk, beat whole eggs, egg whites, and remaining 2 cups milk. Gradually add grits to egg mixture (mixture will be lumpy).

4   Pour mixture into prepared casserole. Bake, uncovered, until top is set and edges are lightly golden, 45 to 50 minutes. Remove from oven; let stand 10 minutes.

EACH SERVING: ABOUT 300 CALORIES | 19G PROTEIN | 34G CARBOHYDRATE | 9G TOTAL FAT (5G SATURATED) | 1.5G FIBER | 98MG CHOLESTEROL | 870MG SODIUM

TURKEY AND POLENTA CASSEROLE

In this brand-new take on the tamale pie, ground turkey is layered with polenta and cheese.

ACTIVE TIME: 1 HR · **TOTAL TIME:** 1 HR 30 MIN

MAKES: 8 MAIN-DISH SERVINGS

---

2   MEDIUM (8 TO 10 OUNCES EACH) ZUCCHINI, DICED

2   TABLESPOONS VEGETABLE OIL

1½ POUNDS GROUND TURKEY

1   LARGE ONION, CHOPPED

1¾ TEASPOONS SALT

1   CAN (14½ OUNCES) ITALIAN-STYLE STEWED TOMATOES

1   CAN (8 OUNCES) TOMATO SAUCE

½   CUP LOOSELY PACKED UNSALTED DRIED TOMATOES (1 OUNCE), CHOPPED

4   CUPS WATER

2½ CUPS LOW-FAT MILK (1%)

2   CUPS CORNMEAL

1   PACKAGE (8 OUNCES) SHREDDED PART-SKIM MOZZARELLA CHEESE

1 In nonstick 12-inch skillet, heat 1 tablespoon oil over medium heat until hot. Cook zucchini until lightly browned and tender, 5 to 7 minutes, stirring often. Remove to bowl.

2 In same skillet, heat remaining 1 tablespoon oil until hot. Cook turkey, onion, and 1 teaspoon salt until turkey is browned and onion is tender, about 10 minutes, breaking up turkey with side of spoon. Stir stewed tomatoes, tomato sauce, dried tomatoes, and ½ cup water into turkey mixture; heat to boiling over high heat. Reduce heat to low; cover and simmer 5 minutes to blend flavors, stirring occasionally. Remove skillet from heat; stir in zucchini.

4 Preheat oven to 450°F. Grease 13" by 9" glass baking dish.

5 Meanwhile, in 3-quart saucepan over high heat, heat milk, remaining ¾ teaspoon salt, and remaining 3½ cups water to boiling. With wire whisk or fork, gradually stir in cornmeal, stirring constantly to prevent lumping. Reduce heat to low; simmer until polenta is very thick, about 10 minutes, stirring constantly.

6 Spread half of polenta in prepared baking dish; top with half of turkey mixture, then half of mozzarella. Repeat layering. Bake casserole until cheese on top is lightly browned, about 20 minutes.

EACH SERVING: ABOUT 465 CALORIES | 30G PROTEIN | 46G CARBOHYDRATE | 17G TOTAL FAT (6G SATURATED) | 4G FIBER | 86MG CHOLESTEROL | 1,105MG SODIUM

THREE-BEAN AND WILD-RICE CASSEROLE

Here's a wonderful vegetarian main course; a creamy, satisfying combination of mushrooms, wild rice, and protein-rich legumes.

ACTIVE TIME: 20 MIN · **TOTAL TIME:** 1 HR 45 MIN

MAKES: 6 MAIN-DISH SERVINGS

1 TABLESPOON VEGETABLE OIL	3¼ CUPS WATER
4 MEDIUM CARROTS, PEELED AND CUT INTO ¼-INCH-THICK SLICES	1½ CUPS WILD RICE (8 OUNCES)
1 LARGE ONION, THINLY SLICED	1 CAN (19 OUNCES) RED KIDNEY BEANS
1 PACKAGE (10 OUNCES) WHITE MUSHROOMS, TRIMMED AND CUT INTO ¼-INCH-THICK SLICES	1 CAN (19 OUNCES) GREAT NORTHERN OR WHITE KIDNEY BEANS (CANNELLINI)
¾ TEASPOON SALT	1 PACKAGE (10 OUNCES) FROZEN BABY LIMA BEANS, THAWED
1 CAN (10¾ OUNCES) CONDENSED CREAM OF MUSHROOM SOUP	½ TEASPOON COARSELY GROUND BLACK PEPPER

1 Preheat oven to 400°F.

2 In 12-inch skillet over medium-high heat, heat oil over medium-high heat until hot. Cook carrots, onion, mushrooms, and salt until vegetables are golden, 8 to 10 minutes.

3 Meanwhile, in 2-quart saucepan over medium-high heat, heat undiluted cream of mushroom soup and water to boiling over high heat.

4 In deep 2½-quart casserole, stir carrot mixture, hot soup mixture, and wild rice. Cover and bake 1 hour.

5 Rinse and drain kidney and Great Northern beans. Stir kidney, Great Northern, and lima beans and pepper into casserole; cover and bake until hot, about 20 minutes longer. Stir before serving.

EACH SERVING: ABOUT 498 CALORIES | 22G PROTEIN | 88G CARBOHYDRATE | 7G TOTAL FAT (1G SATURATED) | 19G FIBER | 0G CHOLESTEROL | 1,073MG SODIUM

BULGUR AND BEEF STUFFED PEPPERS

This dish is so delicious and it takes so little effort to double this recipe that it makes sense to make an extra casserole and have it at the ready in the freezer. To freeze it, wrap casserole completely in foil, crimping edges to seal well.

ACTIVE TIME: 40 MIN · **TOTAL TIME:** 1 HR 15 MIN

MAKES: 2 CASSEROLES, 4 MAIN-DISH SERVINGS EACH

8 LARGE RED, YELLOW, ORANGE, AND/OR GREEN PEPPERS, WITH STEMS, IF POSSIBLE	1 PACKAGE (10 OUNCES) FROZEN CHOPPED SPINACH, THAWED AND SQUEEZED DRY (SEE TIP)
2 CANS (14½ OUNCES EACH) CHICKEN BROTH	½ CUP LOOSELY PACKED FRESH DILL, CHOPPED
1½ CUPS BULGUR	2 CANS (28 OUNCES EACH) CRUSHED TOMATOES
1 TABLESPOON OLIVE OIL	4 OUNCES FETA CHEESE, CRUMBLED (1 CUP)
1 MEDIUM ONION, CHOPPED	¼ TEASPOON SALT
3 GARLIC CLOVES, CRUSHED WITH GARLIC PRESS	¼ TEASPOON COARSELY GROUND BLACK PEPPER
1 POUND LEAN (90%) GROUND BEEF	

1 Cut ¾-inch-thick slices from top of each pepper; reserve tops, including stems. Remove seeds and ribs, and cut a thin slice from bottom of each pepper so they will stand upright.

2 Arrange 4 peppers and their tops (separately) on same micro-wave-safe plate. Cook, uncovered, in microwave on High 4 minutes. With tongs, transfer tops to paper towel. Microwave peppers 4 to 5 minutes longer, until just tender. Invert peppers onto double thickness of paper towels to drain. Repeat with remaining peppers and tops.

3   In microwave-safe large bowl, combine broth and bulgur. Cook, uncovered, in microwave on High 12 to 15 minutes, until bulgur is tender but still
slightly chewy and most of broth is absorbed.

4   Meanwhile, in deep 12-inch skillet, heat oil over medium heat until hot.
Add onion and garlic, and cook until onion begins to turn golden, about
5 minutes, stirring frequently. Remove ¼ cup onion mixture and reserve.
Add beef to remaining onion in skillet and cook until beef is no longer
pink, 6 to 8 minutes, breaking up beef with side of spoon. Remove skillet
from heat.

5   Into beef in skillet, stir bulgur, spinach, dill, 1 cup crushed tomatoes,
and ¾ cup feta. Fill peppers with bulgur mixture, using a generous cup for
each; sprinkle with remaining ¼ cup feta. Replace pepper tops.

6   Preheat oven to 350°F. Wipe skillet clean.

7   In same skillet, combine remaining tomatoes, reserved onion mixture,
salt, and pepper; heat to boiling over medium-high heat, stirring occasionally. Divide tomato sauce evenly between two 2-quart shallow casseroles
or 8-inch square glass baking dishes. Place 4 peppers in each dish. Cover
one dish with foil and bake until peppers are hot, about 35 minutes. Wrap
second dish for freezing. To reheat, first defrost casserole in refrigerator for
24 hours. To reheat in oven, bake, loosely covered with foil, at 350°F 1 hour;
uncover and heat 45 minutes longer. To reheat in microwave, heat, covered
loosely with plastic wrap, on Low (30%) 50 minutes, then heat on High
15 minutes.

TIP To quickly and easily dry frozen spinach, thaw it in the microwave just until
the ice crystals melt, about 7 minutes on High, then place the defrosted spinach in a
sieve over a bowl or in the sink. Press the spinach with the back of a spoon to drain
off most of the excess water.

EACH SERVING: ABOUT 365 CALORIES | 24G PROTEIN | 45G CARBOHYDRATE | 12G TOTAL FAT
(5G SATURATED) | 12G FIBER | 49MG CHOLESTEROL | 1,220MG SODIUM

CABBAGE AND BULGUR CASSEROLE

We layered Napa cabbage with a filling that is healthy *and* tastes good.

ACTIVE TIME: 45 MIN · **TOTAL TIME:** 1 HR 25 MIN
MAKES: 6 MAIN-DISH SERVINGS

2   CUPS WATER

1½ CUPS BULGUR

1   TABLESPOON VEGETABLE OIL

2   MEDIUM CARROTS, PEELED AND DICED

2   MEDIUM STALKS CELERY, DICED

1   MEDIUM RED PEPPER, DICED

½   SMALL HEAD NAPA (CHINESE) CABBAGE, CORED AND CUT CROSSWISE INTO 2-INCH STRIPS

3   GARLIC CLOVES, CRUSHED WITH GARLIC PRESS

3   GREEN ONIONS, SLICED

2   TABLESPOONS MINCED, PEELED FRESH GINGER

2   TABLESPOONS PLUS 1 TEASPOON SOY SAUCE

2   TABLESPOONS SEASONED RICE VINEGAR

1   CAN (14½ OUNCES) DICED TOMATOES

2   TABLESPOONS BROWN SUGAR

2   TABLESPOONS CHOPPED FRESH PARSLEY FOR GARNISH

1 Preheat oven to 350°F.

2 In 2-quart saucepan, heat 1½ cups water to boiling over high heat; stir in bulgur. Remove saucepan from heat; cover and set aside.

3 In 5-quart Dutch oven, heat oil over medium-high heat. Add carrots, celery, and red pepper; cook 5 minutes. Add cabbage stems, and cook until vegetables are tender, 7 minutes longer. Reduce heat to low; add garlic, green onions, and ginger, and cook 1 minute longer, stirring.

4 Add remaining ½ cup water; heat to boiling over high heat. Reduce heat to low; simmer 1 minute, stirring. Remove Dutch oven from heat; stir in 2 tablespoons soy sauce, 1 tablespoon vinegar, and cooked bulgur.

5 In small bowl, combine tomatoes with their juice, brown sugar, and remaining 1 teaspoon soy sauce and 1 tablespoon vinegar.

6 In 3-quart casserole, place half of cabbage leaves; top with bulgur mixture, then remaining cabbage leaves. Spoon tomato mixture over top. Cover casserole and bake until hot in center and top layer of cabbage leaves is wilted, about 40 minutes. Sprinkle with parsley before serving.

EACH SERVING: ABOUT 220 CALORIES | 7G PROTEIN | 43G CARBOHYDRATE | 3G TOTAL FAT (0G SATURATED) | 12G FIBER | 0MG CHOLESTEROL | 800MG SODIUM

PASTA & NOODLES

A complete whole-grain makeover for your favorite pasta dishes simply means buying whole-grain or 100% whole-wheat pasta instead of the egg or semolina based pastas you may be used to eating. Changing over to a whole-grain pasta also contributes an added layer of flavor—whole-grain pastas have a distinct nuttiness.

When buying whole-grain pastas, it pays to read labels. A pasta may proclaim itself multigrain, but if you read the label, you might find that semolina, a refined flour, is the number one ingredient, with the whole-grain flours down at the bottom of the list. Most supermarkets offer a range of whole-wheat and whole-grain pastas (whole-grain pastas can contain a mix of whole-grain flours, including whole wheat, barley, and flour). If you don't find the shape you're looking for in a whole-grain version, try health food stores or online sources. Health food stores offer even more whole-grain opportunities, like pastas made from spelt flour.

Pasta isn't just about Italian noodles—think Asian, too. Udon noodles (which are now available in a lot of larger supermarkets) are made from a combination of buckwheat and wheat flour; check to make sure you buy a brand that uses whole-wheat flour, or you'll be getting refined flour mixed in with your buckwheat flour.

Orecchiette with Morels and Peas (page 89)

WHOLE-GRAIN ROTINI WITH ASPARAGUS AND SNAP PEAS

Fresh snap peas and asparagus lighten up a pasta dinner (and add plenty of vitamins). Choosing whole-grain pasta over regular helps triple the cholesterol-lowering fiber.

ACTIVE TIME: 10 MIN · **TOTAL TIME:** 30 MIN
MAKES: 4 MAIN-DISH SERVINGS

1 PACKAGE (13¼ OUNCES) WHOLE-GRAIN ROTINI OR FUSILLI PASTA

8 OUNCES ASPARAGUS, TRIMMED AND CUT INTO 1-INCH PIECES (SEE TIP)

1 BAG (8 OUNCES) STRINGLESS SNAP PEAS

1 TABLESPOON OLIVE OIL

1 SMALL ONION, CHOPPED

1 LEMON

½ CUP FRESHLY GRATED PECORINO-ROMANO CHEESE

¼ CUP LOOSELY PACKED FRESH BASIL LEAVES, THINLY SLICED

½ TEASPOON SALT

¼ TEASPOON COARSELY GROUND BLACK PEPPER

1 Heat large covered saucepot of **salted water** to boiling over high heat. Add pasta and cook as label directs, adding asparagus and snap peas when 3 minutes of cooking time remain.

2 Meanwhile, in 10-inch nonstick skillet, heat oil over medium heat until hot. Add onion and cook until tender and browned, 10 to 12 minutes. From lemon, grate 1 teaspoon peel and squeeze 2 tablespoons juice.

3 Reserve ½ **cup pasta cooking water**; drain pasta and vegetables. In large serving bowl, toss pasta and vegetables with reserved cooking water, onion, lemon peel and juice, Pecorino, basil, salt, and pepper.

TIP To trim asparagus, bend the stalk; it will break off at the spot where it becomes too tough to eat.

EACH SERVING: ABOUT 405 CALORIES | 18G PROTEIN | 72G CARBOHYDRATE | 8G TOTAL FAT (2G SATURATED) | 9G FIBER | 10MG CHOLESTEROL | 545MG SODIUM

ROASTED VEGETABLES WITH ARUGULA AND WHOLE-WHEAT FUSILLI

Roasted butternut squash, peppers, and onions are tossed with fresh arugula leaves, whole-wheat pasta, and a splash of vinegar. If you can't find precut butternut squash at your grocery store, buy one that weighs two pounds and peel, seed, and cut it up yourself.

ACTIVE TIME: 25 MIN · **TOTAL TIME:** 50 MIN
MAKES: 4 MAIN-DISH SERVINGS

1   PACKAGE (ABOUT 20 OUNCES) BUTTERNUT SQUASH CHUNKS, CUT INTO 1-INCH PIECES

4   GARLIC CLOVES, EACH CUT IN HALF

2   MEDIUM RED ONIONS, EACH CUT INTO 8 WEDGES

2   MEDIUM RED PEPPERS, CUT INTO ½-INCH-WIDE STRIPS

2   TABLESPOONS OLIVE OIL

½   TEASPOON COARSELY GROUND BLACK PEPPER

1   TEASPOON SALT

1   PACKAGE (16 OUNCES) WHOLE-WHEAT FUSILLI OR CORKSCREW PASTA

2   BUNCHES ARUGULA (4 OUNCES EACH), TRIMMED AND LEAVES COARSELY CHOPPED

2   TABLESPOONS WHITE OR DARK BALSAMIC VINEGAR

FRESHLY GRATED PARMESAN CHEESE (OPTIONAL)

1   Preheat oven to 450°F. Toss squash, garlic, onions, red peppers, oil, black pepper, and salt in 15½" by 10½" jelly-roll pan until evenly mixed. Roast until vegetables are tender and lightly golden, about 50 minutes, stirring occasionally.

2   Meanwhile, heat large pot of **salted water** to boiling over high heat; add fusilli and cook as label directs.

3   When pasta has cooked to desired doneness, remove ½ **cup pasta cooking water**; reserve. Drain pasta and return to pot. Add roasted vegetables, arugula, vinegar, and reserved pasta cooking water; toss until well mixed. Serve with Parmesan, if desired.

EACH SERVING: ABOUT 610 CALORIES | 19G PROTEIN | 115G CARBOHYDRATE | 9G TOTAL FAT (1G SATURATED) | 16G FIBER | 0MG CHOLESTEROL | 610MG SODIUM

ORECCHIETTE WITH MORELS AND PEAS

This veggie pasta is so fresh and delicious, you'll want to eat green every day. (See photo on page 84.)

ACTIVE TIME: 25 MIN · **TOTAL TIME:** 35 MIN

MAKES: 6 MAIN-DISH SERVINGS

3 TABLESPOONS UNSALTED BUTTER	1½ CUPS PEA SHOOTS
3 GARLIC CLOVES, CHOPPED	½ CUP MICROGREENS
3 OUNCES FRESH MOREL MUSHROOMS (OR ½ OUNCE DRIED AND RECONSTITUTED), QUARTERED LENGTHWISE AND RINSED WELL	¾ TEASPOON SALT
	SHAVED PARMESAN, FOR GARNISH (OPTIONAL)
1 POUND ORECCHIETTE PASTA	
8 OUNCES SUGAR SNAP PEAS, STRINGS REMOVED	
1 CUP FRESH OR FROZEN (THAWED) PEAS	
¼ CUP GRATED PARMESAN CHEESE	

1 Heat large covered pot of **salted water** to boiling over high heat.

2 In 8-inch skillet, heat butter over medium heat for 3 minutes or until light brown and foaming, swirling occasionally. Add garlic and morels; cook for 2 minutes, stirring occasionally. Remove from heat.

3 Cook pasta as label directs. Remove ½ **cup cooking water** 4 minutes before pasta is done; set aside. Add sugar snap peas and peas to boiling water. Continue cooking until pasta is al dente and vegetables are tender. Drain well; return to pot.

4 To pot with pasta, add mushroom mixture along with Parmesan, pea shoots, microgreens, ¼ cup cooking water, and salt; stir until well combined, adding more cooking water if necessary. Divide among serving bowls; garnish with shaved Parmesan, if desired.

EACH SERVING: ABOUT 381 CALORIES | 14G PROTEIN | 64G CARBOHYDRATE | 8G TOTAL FAT (4G SATURATED) | 6G FIBER | 28MG CHOLESTEROL | 396MG SODIUM

FUSILLI WITH SWISS CHARD, GARBANZO BEANS, AND BACON

Dark-green Swiss chard is loaded with vitamins K, A, and C, as well as minerals; toss it into an already good-for-you bean and whole-grain pasta dish, and you've got a nutrition powerhouse. The single slice of bacon lends rich flavor without adding much fat.

ACTIVE TIME: 20 MIN · TOTAL TIME: 30 MIN

MAKES: 4 MAIN-DISH SERVINGS

---

12 OUNCES WHOLE-WHEAT FUSILLI OR ROTINI PASTA

1 BUNCH SWISS CHARD (1 POUND), TOUGH ENDS TRIMMED

1 SLICE BACON, CUT INTO ½-INCH-WIDE STRIPS

1 GARLIC CLOVE, CRUSHED WITH GARLIC PRESS

¼ TEASPOON CRUSHED RED PEPPER

1 CAN (15 TO 19 OUNCES) GARBANZO BEANS, RINSED AND DRAINED

½ TEASPOON SALT

2 TABLESPOONS FRESH LEMON JUICE

1 Heat large covered saucepot of **salted water** to boiling over high heat. Add pasta and cook as label directs.

2 Meanwhile, cut ribs and stems from Swiss chard leaves. Cut ribs and stems into 1-inch pieces; cut leaves into 2-inch pieces. Rinse Swiss chard in large bowl of cold water; swish to remove any dirt. Transfer to colander. Do not spin dry.

3 In 12-inch nonstick skillet, cook bacon over medium-high heat until browned, tossing occasionally. With slotted spoon, transfer bacon to paper towels to drain. Reduce heat to medium. To bacon fat in skillet, add garlic and crushed red pepper; cook 30 seconds, stirring. Add chard, beans, and salt. Cover and cook until chard begins to wilt, about 2 minutes. Uncover and cook until stems are tender-crisp, about 5 minutes longer.

4 Drain pasta, reserving ¼ **cup pasta cooking water**. Return pasta to saucepot. Stir in Swiss chard mixture and lemon juice until combined. If mixture seems dry, add reserved pasta cooking water.

EACH SERVING: ABOUT 500 CALORIES | 21G PROTEIN | 93G CARBOHYDRATE | 8G TOTAL FAT (2G SATURATED) | 14G FIBER | 6MG CHOLESTEROL | 755MG SODIUM

SPAGHETTI WITH SZECHUAN CHICKEN AND PEANUTS

Pasta goes Asian with this tasty dish sparked with the delicious heat of fresh ginger.

ACTIVE TIME: 10 MIN · **TOTAL TIME:** 25 MIN

MAKES: 6 MAIN-DISH SERVINGS

---

1   PACKAGE (16 OUNCES) WHOLE-WHEAT SPAGHETTI

1   TEASPOON VEGETABLE OIL

2   BUNCHES GREEN ONIONS, CUT INTO ½-INCH PIECES

1   POUND GROUND CHICKEN OR TURKEY BREAST MEAT

2   TABLESPOONS GRATED, PEELED FRESH GINGER (SEE TIP PAGE 95)

3   GARLIC CLOVES, CRUSHED WITH GARLIC PRESS

1   BAG (12 TO 16 OUNCES) SHREDDED BROCCOLI, CAULIFLOWER, CARROT, CABBAGE BLEND

1   CAN (14½ OUNCES) CHICKEN BROTH

⅓   CUP STIR-FRY SAUCE

¼   CUP NATURAL PEANUT BUTTER

    HOT PEPPER SAUCE (OPTIONAL)

---

1   Heat large covered saucepot of **salted water** to boiling over high heat. Add spaghetti and cook as label directs.

2   Meanwhile, in 12-inch skillet, heat oil over high heat. Add green onions and cook until wilted, 1 to 2 minutes, stirring; transfer to bowl.

3   In same skillet over high heat, cook chicken, ginger, and garlic until chicken is no longer pink, about 3 minutes, breaking the chicken up with a spoon. Stir in vegetable blend, broth, stir-fry sauce, peanut butter, and green onions; heat to boiling. Reduce heat to medium and cook until vegetables are tender-crisp and sauce thickens slightly, 6 to 8 minutes, stirring.

4   Drain spaghetti; return to saucepot. Add chicken mixture and toss to combine. Serve with hot pepper sauce, if desired.

EACH SERVING: ABOUT 475 CALORIES │ 34G PROTEIN │ 70G CARBOHYDRATE │ 9G TOTAL FAT (1G SATURATED) │ 10G FIBER │ 44MG CHOLESTEROL │ 580MG SODIUM

DAN-DAN NOODLES

We made this specialty noodle dish of the Szechuan province with easy-to-find whole-wheat fettuccine, in place of sun mein, a Chinese wheat noodle.

ACTIVE TIME: 30 MIN · TOTAL TIME: 35 MIN

MAKES: 4 MAIN-DISH SERVINGS

½ CUP CHICKEN BROTH

¼ CUP SOY SAUCE

2 TABLESPOONS SUGAR

1 TABLESPOON CREAMY PEANUT BUTTER

2 TEASPOONS CORNSTARCH

2 TEASPOONS ASIAN SESAME OIL

¼ TEASPOON CRUSHED RED PEPPER

8 OUNCES GROUND PORK

1 TABLESPOON GRATED, PEELED FRESH GINGER (SEE TIP PAGE 95)

2 GARLIC CLOVES, CRUSHED WITH GARLIC PRESS

3 GREEN ONIONS, THINLY SLICED

12 OUNCES NAPA (CHINESE) CAPPAGE, SLICED (5 CUPS)

12 OUNCES WHOLE-WHEAT FETTUCCINE

---

1   In small bowl, with wire whisk or fork, mix broth, soy sauce, sugar, peanut butter, cornstarch, sesame oil, and crushed red pepper; set aside.

2   Heat nonstick 12-inch skillet over medium-high heat until very hot. Add pork, ginger, garlic, and green onions, and cook until pork is browned, 6 to 8 minutes, breaking it up with side of spoon and stirring occasionally. Transfer pork mixture to small bowl.

3   In same skillet, cook cabbage until lightly browned, about 5 minutes, stirring frequently.

4   Meanwhile, heat large saucepot of **salted water** to boiling over high heat; add fettuccine and cook as label directs.

5   Return pork mixture to skillet. Stir in broth mixture; heat to boiling. Reduce heat to medium and simmer 2 minutes to blend flavors and thicken sauce slightly.

6   To serve, drain fettuccine; toss with pork mixture in skillet.

EACH SERVING: ABOUT 555 CALORIES | 26G PROTEIN | 77G CARBOHYDRATE | 18G TOTAL FAT (5G SATURATED) | 13G FIBER | 41MG CHOLESTEROL | 1,204MG SODIUM

SOBA NOODLES WITH SHRIMP, SNOW PEAS, AND CARROTS

Soba (thin Japanese noodles made from buckwheat flour) cook quickly and the shrimp, peas, and carrots cook in the same water as the noodles. Then just toss with a delicious peanut sauce that takes a couple of minutes to put together and dinner is served.

ACTIVE TIME: 15 MIN · **TOTAL TIME:** 35 MIN

MAKES: 4 MAIN-DISH SERVINGS

¼ CUP CREAMY PEANUT BUTTER

2 TEASPOONS GRATED, PEELED FRESH GINGER (SEE TIP)

2 TABLESPOONS REDUCED-SODIUM SOY SAUCE

1 TABLESPOON DISTILLED WHITE VINEGAR

1 TEASPOON ASIAN SESAME OIL

½ TEASPOON HOT PEPPER SAUCE

1 TEASPOON SALT

1 PACKAGE (8 OUNCES) WHOLE-WHEAT SOBA NOODLES

½ BAG (10 OUNCES) SHREDDED OR MATCHSTICK CARROTS (1½ CUPS)

1 POUND LARGE SHRIMP, SHELLED AND DEVEINED, WITH TAIL PART LEFT ON IF YOU LIKE

4 OUNCES SNOW PEAS, STRINGS REMOVED

½ CUP LOOSELY PACKED FRESH CILANTRO LEAVES, CHOPPED, PLUS ADDITIONAL SPRIGS FOR GARNISH

1 In small bowl, place peanut butter, ginger, soy sauce, vinegar, sesame oil, and hot pepper sauce; set aside.

2 Heat covered 5- to 6-quart saucepot of **water** and salt to boiling over high heat. Add noodles and cook 4 minutes. Add carrots and cook 1 minute. Add shrimp and snow peas and cook 2 minutes more. Reserve ½ **cup noodle cooking water.** Drain noodles, shrimp, and vegetables into large colander. Transfer noodle mixture to large bowl.

3 With wire whisk, beat peanut-butter mixture until well blended. Add peanut sauce and chopped cilantro to noodle mixture in bowl and toss until evenly coated.

4 To serve, spoon into four large bowls; garnish each serving with a cilantro sprig.

EACH SERVING: ABOUT 430 CALORIES | 33G PROTEIN | 53G CARBOHYDRATE | 12G TOTAL FAT (2G SATURATED) | 6G FIBER | 140MG CHOLESTEROL | 960MG SODIUM

TIP Use a vegetable peeler to peel ginger; be careful to remove only the very top layer of skin because the flesh directly beneath is the youngest and most delicate. Then, chop, slice, or shred the ginger as directed with a sharp knife or box grater. A ginger grater works best for fine grating because it yields plenty of juice with minimal fibers.

CHICKEN-NOODLE STIR-FRY

We love the nutty flavor of dark, slender soba noodles, combined with a simple stir-fry of chicken breasts, bok choy, and red pepper.

ACTIVE TIME: 15 MIN · **TOTAL TIME:** 30 MIN

MAKES: 4 MAIN-DISH SERVINGS

1   PACKAGE (8 OUNCES) WHOLE-WHEAT SOBA NOODLES

2   TABLESPOONS VEGETABLE OIL

1   POUND BONELESS, SKINLESS CHICKEN BREASTS, CUT LENGTHWISE INTO ½-INCH-WIDE STRIPS

2   TABLESPOONS SOY SAUCE, PLUS ADDITIONAL FOR SERVING

3   GREEN ONIONS, THINLY SLICED

1   LARGE RED PEPPER, CUT LENGTHWISE INTO ¼-INCH-WIDE STRIPS

1   MEDIUM HEAD BOK CHOY (1½ POUNDS), CUT CROSSWISE INTO ½-INCH-WIDE RIBBONS

1   CUP CHICKEN BROTH

2   GARLIC CLOVES, CRUSHED WITH GARLIC PRESS

1   TABLESPOON GRATED, PEELED FRESH GINGER (SEE TIP PAGE 95)

1   TABLESPOON SEASONED RICE VINEGAR

2   TEASPOONS CORNSTARCH

1   TEASPOON SUGAR

1   Heat large saucepot of **water** to boiling over high heat; add soba noodles and cook as label directs. Drain noodles; rinse under cold running water and drain again. Set aside.

2   Meanwhile, in nonstick 12-inch skillet, heat 1 tablespoon oil over medium-high heat until hot. Add chicken and 1 tablespoon soy sauce, and cook until chicken loses its pink color throughout, about 5 minutes, stirring often. Transfer chicken to plate.

3   Add remaining 1 tablespoon oil to skillet; add green onions and red pepper, and cook 3 minutes, stirring often. Add bok choy and cook until vegetables are tender-crisp, about 3 minutes longer.

4   Meanwhile, in 2-cup glass measuring cup, whisk together broth, garlic, ginger, vinegar, cornstarch, sugar, and remaining 1 tablespoon soy sauce.

5   Add noodles and sauce mixture to bok-choy mixture and heat to boiling; cook 1 minute, stirring to coat noodles. Add chicken and toss just until heated through. Serve with extra soy sauce, if desired.

EACH SERVING: ABOUT 440 CALORIES | 38G PROTEIN | 55G CARBOHYDRATE | 10G TOTAL FAT (1G SATURATED) | 5G FIBER | 66MG CHOLESTEROL | 1,505MG SODIUM

COUSCOUS PAELLA

A box of couscous makes paella quick enough for a weeknight.

TOTAL TIME: 20 MIN

MAKES: 4 MAIN-DISH SERVINGS

¼ CUP WATER

1 CAN (14½ OUNCES) CHICKEN BROTH

1 PACKAGE (10 OUNCES) WHOLE-WHEAT COUSCOUS (MOROCCAN PASTA)

1 PACKAGE (10 OUNCES) FROZEN PEAS

2 TEASPOONS OLIVE OIL

1 RED OR GREEN PEPPER, DICED

2 OUNCES LOW-FAT KIELBASA (SMOKED POLISH SAUSAGE), SLICED

12 OUNCES SKINLESS, BONELESS CHICKEN BREAST, CUT INTO 1-INCH PIECES

1 GARLIC CLOVE, CRUSHED WITH GARLIC PRESS

½ TEASPOON SALT

½ TEASPOON DRIED THYME

¼ TEASPOON COARSELY GROUND BLACK PEPPER

1½ CUPS CHERRY TOMATOES, EACH CUT IN HALF

1 In 3-quart saucepan, heat broth and water to boiling over high heat. Remove saucepan from heat; stir in couscous and frozen peas. Cover saucepan and let stand 5 minutes or until ready to use.

2 Meanwhile, in nonstick 12-inch skillet, heat oil over medium-high heat until hot. Add red or green pepper and kielbasa and cook 5 minutes, stirring occasionally. Add chicken, garlic, salt, thyme, and black pepper, and cook until chicken loses its pink color throughout, about 5 minutes, stirring occasionally. Remove skillet from heat, and stir in cherry-tomato halves.

3 Fluff couscous with fork; add to chicken mixture in skillet, and toss gently until combined.

EACH SERVING: ABOUT 520 CALORIES | 38G PROTEIN | 73G CARBOHYDRATE | 8G TOTAL FAT (1G SATURATED) | 14G FIBER | 50MG CHOLESTEROL | 725MG SODIUM

JEWELED CINNAMON COUSCOUS

Although it looks like a whole grain, couscous is actually tiny pasta made from semolina (ground wheat flour). If you crave something green, toss in a half cup of frozen peas.

ACTIVE TIME: 20 MIN · **TOTAL TIME:** 25 MIN PLUS STANDING
MAKES: 4 MAIN-DISH SERVINGS

1 TABLESPOON BUTTER OR MARGARINE	½ CUP DRIED CRANBERRIES
½ MEDIUM RED ONION, CHOPPED	½ CUP GOLDEN RAISINS
1 PACKAGE (8 OUNCES) SLICED MUSHROOMS	¼ CUP DRY SHERRY
	1 TEASPOON SALT
1 CAN (14½ OUNCES) LOW-SODIUM VEGETABLE BROTH	½ TEASPOON GROUND CINNAMON
¼ CUP WATER	¼ TEASPOON GROUND BLACK PEPPER
1 CAN (15 TO 19 OUNCES) LOW-SODIUM GARBANZO BEANS, RINSED AND DRAINED	1 PACKAGE (10 OUNCES) WHOLE-WHEAT COUSCOUS (MOROCCAN PASTA)

1 In deep 12-inch skillet, melt butter over medium-high heat. Add onion and mushrooms; cook 3 minutes.

2 While mushrooms are cooking, in 1-quart saucepan, heat broth and water to boiling over high heat.

3 Stir beans, cranberries, raisins, sherry, salt, cinnamon, and pepper into mushroom mixture. Remove skillet from heat.

4 Add couscous to skillet; stir in hot broth. Cover and let mixture stand until liquid is absorbed, about 5 minutes. Fluff with fork before serving.

EACH SERVING: ABOUT 570 CALORIES | 19G PROTEIN | 110G CARBOHYDRATE | 6G TOTAL FAT (1G SATURATED) | 17G FIBER | 0MG CHOLESTEROL | 710MG SODIUM

KASHA VARNISHKES

Groats are the whole, hulled seeds of buckwheat. What is sold as kasha are groats that have been roasted. This traditional comfort-food dish is a delicious way to enjoy the heart-healthy benefits of buckwheat.

ACTIVE TIME: 30 MIN · **TOTAL TIME:** 40 MIN
MAKES 7 CUPS OR 6 SIDE-DISH SERVINGS

2 CUPS MINI BOW-TIE PASTA	2 MEDIUM ONIONS, CHOPPED
1 LARGE EGG WHITE	1 CAN (14½ OUNCES) LOW-SODIUM CHICKEN BROTH
1 CUP KASHA (ROASTED BUCKWHEAT GROATS)	½ TEASPOON SALT
2 TEASPOONS CANOLA OR VEGETABLE OIL	1 TABLESPOON BUTTER
	¼ TEASPOON GROUND BLACK PEPPER

1 Cook pasta according to package directions until al dente; drain.

2 Meanwhile, in medium bowl, beat egg white lightly with fork. Add kasha and stir to evenly coat with egg white.

3 Heat a large nonstick skillet over medium-high heat until hot. Add kasha and reduce heat to medium-low. Cook, stirring constantly, until kasha is toasted and grains separate, about 5 minutes. Transfer to a bowl and set aside.

4 Measure broth and add water to equal 2 cups. In medium saucepan, bring broth, kasha, and ¼ teaspoon salt to boiling. Reduce heat to low; cover and simmer until broth is absorbed, about 10 minutes.

5 Meanwhile, in large nonstick skillet over medium heat, heat oil until hot. Add onions and cook, stirring frequently, until golden brown, about 12 minutes. Add pasta, kasha, butter, remaining ¼ teaspoon salt, and pepper to onions; stir to combine. Heat through and serve.

EACH SERVING: ABOUT 290 CALORIES | 10G PROTEIN | 52G CARBOHYDRATE | 5G TOTAL FAT (2G SATURATED) | 5G FIBER | 5MG CHOLESTEROL | 245MG SODIUM

STOVETOP DINNERS

Like casseroles from the oven, it's easy to introduce whole grains to skillet meals. We offer up a delicious selection of always easy and often fast dishes for you to choose from. With a stir-fry, you can simply serve it up over brown rice, or try adding cooked udon or whole-wheat spaghetti as one of the ingredients. Serve satisfying sautés over brown rice, whole-wheat couscous, or a golden mound of grits or polenta.

Pilafs aren't just about rice and they can have main-course star power. We've got some mouthwatering choices, both with and without meat, prepared with barley, bulgur, and wheat berries.

Fried rice is the ultimate last-minute, what-have-I-got-in-the-refrigerator stovetop savior dish. Try our quick version to get the technique down, then make sure you have cold cooked brown rice in the fridge and dinner will always be just minutes away.

Chicken and Mushrooms with Brown Rice and Baby Squash (page 109)

STIR-FRIED STEAK AND VEGETABLES

A stir-fry is always a great choice for a busy weekday meal, especially if you buy already-sliced mushrooms and skillet-ready veggies.

ACTIVE TIME: 10 MIN · **TOTAL TIME:** 10 MIN

MAKES: 4 MAIN-DISH SERVINGS

---

1   BEEF TOP ROUND STEAK (1 POUND)

⅓   CUP REDUCED-SODIUM SOY SAUCE

2   LARGE GARLIC CLOVES, CRUSHED WITH GARLIC PRESS

1   MEDIUM ONION, PEELED

1   RED PEPPER

2   TEASPOONS VEGETABLE OIL

1   PACKAGE (8 OUNCES) SLICED CREMINI MUSHROOMS

1   BAG (16 OUNCES) FRESH VEGETABLES FOR STIR-FRYING (SUCH AS BROCCOLI, CARROTS, SNOW PEAS)

2   TABLESPOONS GRATED, PEELED FRESH GINGER (SEE TIP PAGE 95)

¾   CUP WATER

1   PACKAGE (8.8 OUNCES) PRECOOKED BROWN RICE, HEATED AS LABEL DIRECTS

1   With knife held in slanting position, almost parallel to cutting surface, cut round steak crosswise into ⅛-inch-thick slices. In medium bowl, toss steak slices with 1 tablespoon soy sauce and 1 crushed garlic clove. Let stand 5 minutes.

2   Meanwhile cut onion in half, then thinly slice crosswise. Cut red pepper into ¼-inch-thick slices. Set vegetables aside.

3   In deep nonstick 12-inch skillet, heat 1 teaspoon oil over medium-high heat until very hot but not smoking. Add half of beef and stir-fry just until beef is no longer pink, 30 to 45 seconds. Transfer to a plate and set aside. Repeat with remaining beef, without adding additional oil.

4   In same skillet, heat remaining 1 teaspoon oil until hot. Add mushrooms and onion; cover and cook until mushrooms are browned, 3 to 4 minutes, stirring occasionally.

5   Add vegetables for stir-frying, red pepper, ginger, water, and remaining soy sauce to skillet. Cook until vegetables are tender-crisp, 5 to 6 minutes, stirring frequently. Remove skillet from heat; stir in beef with its juices. Serve over rice.

EACH SERVING: ABOUT 380 CALORIES | 34G PROTEIN | 34G CARBOHYDRATE | 12G TOTAL FAT (4G SATURATED) | 7G FIBER | 68MG CHOLESTEROL | 790MG SODIUM

TIP It's hard to buy just the amount of ginger you need for a single dish. You can store what you don't use unpeeled, wrapped first in a paper towel, then tightly in plastic wrap. It will keep in the refrigerator up to 2 weeks. Or peel and slice or cut the ginger into chunks, and preserve in a tightly covered jar of dry sherry or mirin (Japanese rice wine) in the fridge for several months.

FAST FRIED RICE

The secrets to this dish are quick-cooking brown rice, precut frozen vegetables, and ready-to-use stir-fry sauce.

ACTIVE TIME: 20 MIN · **TOTAL TIME:** 20 MIN

MAKES: 4 MAIN-DISH SERVINGS

1½ CUPS INSTANT (10-MINUTE) BROWN RICE

1 POUND FIRM TOFU, DRAINED AND CUT INTO 1-INCH CUBES

6 TEASPOONS OLIVE OIL

1 PACKAGE (16 OUNCES) FROZEN VEGETABLES FOR STIR-FRY

2 LARGE EGGS, LIGHTLY BEATEN

½ CUP STIR-FRY SAUCE

¼ CUP WATER

1 Prepare rice as label directs.

2 Meanwhile, in medium bowl, place 3 layers of paper towels. Place tofu on towels and top with 3 more layers paper towels. Gently press tofu with hands to extract excess moisture.

3 In nonstick 12-inch skillet, heat 2 teaspoons oil over medium-high heat until hot. Add frozen vegetables; cover and cook 5 minutes, stirring occasionally. Transfer vegetables to bowl; keep warm.

4 In same skillet, heat remaining 4 teaspoons oil until hot. Add tofu and cook 5 minutes, gently stirring. Stir in rice and cook 4 minutes longer.

5 With spatula, push rice mixture around edge of skillet, leaving space in center. Add eggs to center of skillet; cook 1 minute, stirring eggs until scrambled. Add stir-fry sauce, vegetables, and water; cook 1 minute, stirring. Serve immediately.

EACH SERVING: ABOUT 360 CALORIES | 17G PROTEIN | 41G CARBOHYDRATE | 15G TOTAL FAT (2G SATURATED) | 5G FIBER | 106MG CHOLESTEROL | 760MG SODIUM

CITRUS SHRIMP

The couscous absorbs all the delicious orange pan juices from the shrimp.

ACTIVE TIME: 15 MIN · **TOTAL TIME:** 20 MIN
MAKES: 4 MAIN-DISH SERVINGS

---

3   NAVEL ORANGES

1½ CUPS WATER

1   CUP WHOLE-WHEAT COUSCOUS
     (MOROCCAN PASTA)

½   TEASPOON SALT

¼   TEASPOON GROUND BLACK PEPPER

1   TABLESPOON OLIVE OIL

1   POUND LARGE SHRIMP, SHELLED AND
     DEVEINED, WITH TAIL PART LEFT ON IF
     YOU LIKE

1   CUP FROZEN PEAS, THAWED

2   TABLESPOONS FINELY CHOPPED RED
     ONION

1 From 1 orange, grate 1 teaspoon peel and squeeze ¼ cup juice. Peel and slice remaining 2 oranges; cut each slice in half and set aside.

2 In 1-quart saucepan, heat water to boiling over high heat. Stir in couscous, salt, and ⅛ teaspoon pepper. Cover saucepan and remove from heat; let stand 5 minutes.

3 Meanwhile, in nonstick 12-inch skillet, heat oil over medium-high heat until very hot but not smoking. Stir in shrimp, orange peel and juice, and remaining ⅛ teaspoon pepper. Cook shrimp until they just turn opaque throughout, 3 to 4 minutes, stirring occasionally.

4 With fork, fluff couscous; transfer to large bowl. Stir in peas, onion, and reserved orange slices. Serve couscous with shrimp.

EACH SERVING: ABOUT 405 CALORIES | 30G PROTEIN | 61G CARBOHYDRATE | 6G TOTAL FAT (1G SATURATED) | 11G FIBER | 140MG CHOLESTEROL | 470MG SODIUM

SPICY CHICKEN AND SAUSAGE JAMBALAYA

This hearty Creole classic gets slimmed down with chicken tenders and turkey sausage (in place of high-fat pork). Brown rice boosts the fiber and key phytonutrients, while peppers and tomatoes deliver half the daily recommendation of vitamin C—and it's all cooked in one skillet.

ACTIVE TIME: 15 MIN · **TOTAL TIME:** 30 MIN

MAKES: 4 MAIN-DISH SERVINGS

- 8 OUNCES TURKEY ANDOUILLE SAUSAGE, SLICED ¼ INCH THICK
- 1 GREEN OR YELLOW PEPPER, CHOPPED
- 1 CAN (15½ OUNCES) STEWED TOMATOES
- 1 CUP INSTANT (10-MINUTES) BROWN RICE
- 8 OUNCES CHICKEN TENDERS, EACH CUT CROSSWISE IN HALF
- ½ CUP WATER
- ¼ TEASPOON SALT
- 1 BUNCH GREEN ONIONS, SLICED

1 Heat 12-inch skillet over medium heat until hot. Add sausage and pepper, and cook 5 minutes, stirring occasionally.

2 Stir in tomatoes, brown rice, chicken, water, and salt; heat to boiling over high heat. Reduce heat to low; cover and simmer until rice is just tender, about 10 minutes. Remove skillet from heat; stir in green onions.

EACH SERVING: ABOUT 265 CALORIES | 26G PROTEIN | 30G CARBOHYDRATE | 6G TOTAL FAT (2G SATURATED) | 4G FIBER | 73MG CHOLESTEROL | 830MG SODIUM

MEATBALLS IN SPICY TOMATO SAUCE

Meatballs are perfect for injecting whole-grain healthiness into your diet.

ACTIVE TIME: 35 MIN · **TOTAL TIME:** 55 MIN
MAKES: 6 MAIN-DISH SERVINGS

½ CUP CRACKED WHEAT (COARSE)

¾ CUP WATER

1 MEDIUM ONION

1 POUND LEAN GROUND BEEF (SIRLOIN)

¼ CUP LIGHTLY PACKED FRESH MINT LEAVES, CHOPPED

1 LARGE EGG, LIGHTLY BEATEN

1 TEASPOON GROUND CUMIN

1 TEASPOON SALT

½ TEASPOON GROUND BLACK PEPPER

1 TABLESPOON OLIVE OIL

2 LARGE GARLIC CLOVES, MINCED

¼ TEASPOON GROUND CINNAMON

⅛ TO ¼ TEASPOON GROUND RED PEPPER (CAYENNE)

1 CAN (28 OUNCES) PLUM TOMATOES

⅓ CUP GOLDEN RAISINS

3 TABLESPOONS CRUMBLED FETA CHEESE

¼ CUP FRESH MINT LEAVES, TORN

1 Place cracked wheat in medium bowl and pour 2 cups boiling water over. Cover bowl with plastic wrap and let stand 30 minutes. Drain.

2 Meanwhile, preheat oven to 400°F. Line 15½" by 10½" jelly roll pan with foil and spray with nonstick cooking spray. On large holes of box grater, grate onion to measure ¼ cup. Chop remaining onion.

3 In large bowl, combine cracked wheat, grated onion, ground beef, chopped mint, egg, ½ teaspoon cumin, ½ teaspoon salt, ¼ teaspoon black pepper, and ¼ cup cold water until well blended, but not overmixed.

4 Shape mixture by heaping tablespoonfuls into 24 meatballs. Place 1 inch apart on prepared pan. Bake until cooked through, about 20 minutes.

5 Meanwhile, in large nonstick skillet over medium heat, heat oil until hot. Add chopped onion and cook until tender and starting to brown, about 8 minutes, stirring often. Stir in garlic, cinnamon, ground red pepper, remaining ½ teaspoon cumin, ½ teaspoon salt, and ¼ teaspoon black pepper; cook until fragrant, about 30 seconds. Add tomatoes with their juice, raisins, and remaining ½ cup water; bring to boiling over high heat, breaking up tomatoes with side of spoon. Reduce heat, cover, and simmer, stirring occasionally, until sauce thickens, about 20 minutes.

6 Add meatballs and simmer until meatballs are hot, about 5 minutes. Sprinkle with feta and torn mint leaves, or serve over brown rice.

EACH SERVING: ABOUT 250 CALORIES | 20G PROTEIN | 24G CARBOHYDRATE | 8G TOTAL FAT (3G SATURATED) | 4G FIBER | 80MG CHOLESTEROL | 776MG SODIUM

CHICKEN AND MUSHROOMS WITH BROWN RICE AND BABY SQUASH

Here's another great recipe for weeknight cooking. (See photo on page 101.)

ACTIVE TIME: 10 MIN · **TOTAL TIME:** 45 MIN
MAKES: 4 MAIN-DISH SERVINGS

2 TABLESPOONS OLIVE OIL

1¼ POUNDS SKINLESS, BONELESS CHICKEN THIGHS

1 PACKAGE (10 OUNCES) SLICED CREMINI MUSHROOMS

2 MEDIUM STALKS CELERY, THINLY SLICED

1 TEASPOON CHOPPED FRESH THYME

1 CAN (14½ OUNCES) CHICKEN BROTH

1 CUP INSTANT (10-MINUTE) BROWN RICE

½ CUP DRY WHITE WINE

¼ TEASPOON SALT

¼ TEASPOON COARSELY GROUND BLACK PEPPER

8 BABY SUMMER SQUASH, HALVED, STEAMED, AND KEPT WARM

1 In 12-inch skillet, heat oil over medium-high heat until hot. Add chicken and cook, covered, 5 minutes. Reduce heat to medium; turn chicken and cook, covered, 5 more minutes. Transfer to plate.

2 To skillet, add mushrooms, celery, and thyme; cook until vegetables are softened, about 5 minutes, stirring occasionally. Add broth, brown rice, wine, salt, and pepper; heat to boiling.

3 Return chicken to skillet. Reduce heat to low; cover and simmer until juices run clear when thickest part of chicken is pierced with knife and rice is cooked, about 12 minutes. Serve with squash.

EACH SERVING: ABOUT 350 CALORIES │ 33G PROTEIN │ 21G CARBOHYDRATE, │ 13G TOTAL FAT (2G SATURATED) │ 2G FIBER │ 118MG CHOLESTEROL │ 702MG SODIUM

BEEF AND BARLEY WITH CARROTS AND MUSHROOMS

This is a hearty dinner of sautéed beef tossed with a rich barley-and-mushroom pilaf. Because top round steak is a very lean cut, it must be thinly sliced across the grain—otherwise it may be tough.

ACTIVE TIME: 30 MIN · **TOTAL TIME:** 1 HR 10 MIN
MAKES: 6 MAIN-DISH SERVINGS

- 3 CUPS BOILING WATER
- 1 PACKAGE (½ OUNCE) DRIED PORCINI MUSHROOMS
- 1 POUND BEEF TOP ROUND STEAK, ¾ INCH THICK
- 1 TEASPOON OLIVE OIL
- 1 TABLESPOON SOY SAUCE
- 1 PACKAGE (8 OUNCES) SLICED WHITE MUSHROOMS
- 2 MEDIUM CARROTS, PEELED, CUT LENGTHWISE IN HALF, THEN CROSSWISE INTO ¼-INCH-THICK SLICES

- 1 MEDIUM ONION, FINELY CHOPPED
- ½ TEASPOON SALT
- ¼ TEASPOON GROUND BLACK PEPPER
- ¼ TEASPOON DRIED THYME
- 1½ CUPS PEARL BARLEY
- 1 CAN (14½ OUNCES) CHICKEN BROTH
- ½ CUP LOOSELY PACKED FRESH PARSLEY LEAVES

1 Into medium bowl, pour boiling water over porcini; let stand 10 minutes.

2 Meanwhile, cut steak lengthwise in half. With knife held in slanted position, almost parallel to cutting surface, slice each half of steak crosswise into ⅛-inch-thick slices.

3 In deep nonstick 12-inch skillet, heat oil over medium-high heat until very hot. Add half of steak slices and cook until they just lose their pink color, about 2 minutes, stirring constantly. Transfer steak to medium bowl; repeat with remaining steak. Toss steak with soy sauce; set aside.

4 To same skillet, add white mushrooms, carrots, onion, salt, pepper, and thyme and cook over medium-high heat until vegetables are tender-crisp, about 10 minutes, stirring occasionally.

5 While vegetables are cooking, with slotted spoon, remove porcini from soaking water, reserving liquid. Rinse porcini to remove any sand; coarsely chop. Strain soaking water through sieve lined with paper towel into medium bowl and set aside.

6 Add barley, broth, porcini, and mushroom-soaking water to vegetables in skillet; heat mixture to boiling over medium-high heat. Reduce heat to medium-low; cover and simmer until barley and vegetables are tender and most of the liquid has evaporated, 35 to 40 minutes, stirring occasionally. Stir in steak mixture and parsley; heat through.

EACH SERVING: ABOUT 320 CALORIES | 47G CARBOHYDRATE | 20G PROTEIN | 7G TOTAL FAT (2G SATURATED) | 10G FIBER | 34MG CHOLESTEROL | 695MG SODIUM

TOASTED CHICKEN AND BARLEY PILAF

Cut up the chicken, carrots, celery, and onion the night before and this dish will come together in minutes.

ACTIVE TIME: 10 MIN · **TOTAL TIME:** 1 HR
MAKES: 4 MAIN-DISH SERVINGS

1½ CUPS PEARL BARLEY

3 TEASPOONS OLIVE OIL

4 SKINLESS, BONELESS CHICKEN THIGHS (1 POUND), CUT INTO 1-INCH CHUNKS

2 MEDIUM CARROTS, PEELED AND CHOPPED

2 STALKS CELERY, CHOPPED

1 SMALL ONION, CHOPPED

1 PACKAGE (8 OUNCES) SLICED MUSHROOMS

1 CAN (14½ OUNCES) CHICKEN BROTH

2 CUPS WATER

½ TEASPOON DRIED THYME

¼ TEASPOON GROUND NUTMEG

½ TEASPOON SALT

¼ TEASPOON GROUND BLACK PEPPER

PARSLEY LEAVES FOR GARNISH

1 Heat deep nonstick 12-inch skillet over medium-high heat until hot. Add barley and cook until toasted and fragrant, 4 to 6 minutes, stirring occasionally. Transfer barley to large bowl.

2 In same skillet, heat 2 teaspoons oil over medium-high heat until hot. Add chicken and cook just until it loses its pink color on the outside, about 5 minutes, stirring occasionally. Transfer chicken to bowl with barley.

3 In same skillet, in remaining 1 teaspoon oil, cook carrots, celery, and onion over medium heat until tender-crisp, 7 to 8 minutes. Stir in mushrooms and cook until most of liquid evaporates and vegetables are tender and lightly browned, about 10 minutes longer.

4 Return chicken and barley to skillet; stir in broth, water, thyme, nutmeg, salt, and pepper. Heat to boiling over medium-high heat. Reduce heat to low; cover and simmer until barley is tender and chicken is no longer pink in center, 30 to 35 minutes. Serve pilaf garnished with parsley leaves.

EACH SERVING: ABOUT 485 CALORIES | 33G PROTEIN | 67G CARBOHYDRATE | 10G TOTAL FAT (2G SATURATED) | 14G FIBER | 94MG CHOLESTEROL | 865MG SODIUM

FARRO RISOTTO WITH BUTTERNUT SQUASH

This is a wonderful way to try farro, the granddaddy of all grains. It contains starches very similar to those in the short-grain risotto rices, making it the perfect whole-grain substitute. Farro has a firm, chewy texture that pairs beautifully with the sweet creaminess of butternut squash.

ACTIVE TIME: 20 MIN · **TOTAL TIME:** 55 MIN

MAKES: 4 MAIN-DISH SERVINGS

---

1   TABLESPOON OLIVE OIL

1   SMALL ONION, FINELY CHOPPED

½   TEASPOON SALT

¼   TEASPOON GROUND BLACK PEPPER

1½ CUPS FARRO (EMMER WHEAT)

½   CUP DRY WHITE WINE

1¼ CUPS WATER

1   CAN (14½ OUNCES) CHICKEN BROTH

⅛   TEASPOON DRIED THYME

⅛   TEASPOON CRUSHED DRIED ROSEMARY

1   BUTTERNUT SQUASH (2 POUNDS), PEELED, SEEDED, AND CUT INTO ½-INCH PIECES

½   CUP FRESHLY GRATED PARMESAN CHEESE, PLUS ADDITIONAL FOR SERVING

¼   CUP LOOSELY PACKED FRESH PARSLEY LEAVES, CHOPPED

1   In deep nonstick 12-inch skillet, heat oil over medium heat until hot. Add onion, salt, and pepper, and cook until onion is tender and lightly browned, 5 to 7 minutes. Add farro and cook until lightly browned, 2 to 3 minutes, stirring constantly. Add wine and cook until absorbed, about 1 minute.

2   Add water, then broth, thyme, and rosemary; cover skillet and heat to boiling over high heat. Stir in squash; reduce heat to medium-low. Cover and simmer until farro is just tender (mixture will still be soupy), about 20 minutes longer.

3   Uncover and cook 1 to 2 minutes longer over high heat, stirring constantly, until most of liquid is absorbed. Remove skillet from heat and stir in Parmesan and parsley. Serve risotto with additional Parmesan, if you like.

EACH SERVING: ABOUT 415 CALORIES | 16G PROTEIN | 74G CARBOHYDRATE | 9G TOTAL FAT (3G SATURATED) | 5G FIBER | 8MG CHOLESTEROL | 925MG SODIUM

ORANGE-ROSEMARY TURKEY CUTLETS WITH COUSCOUS AND ARUGULA

Turkey can stand up to strong flavors and this striking combination of orange, rosemary, and arugula is particularly tasty.

ACTIVE TIME: 15 MIN · TOTAL TIME: 20 MIN

MAKES: 4 MAIN-DISH SERVINGS

3   NAVEL ORANGES

1½ CUPS WATER

3   TABLESPOONS OLIVE OIL

½   TEASPOON SALT

1   PACKAGE (10 OUNCES) WHOLE-WHEAT COUSCOUS (MOROCCAN PASTA)

1   TABLESPOON CHOPPED FRESH ROSEMARY LEAVES

¼   TEASPOON GROUND BLACK PEPPER

1   POUND TURKEY CUTLETS

2   TABLESPOONS SEASONED RICE VINEGAR

1   BAG (5 OUNCES) BABY ARUGULA

1   From oranges, grate 2 tablespoons peel and squeeze ¾ cup juice. In 4-quart saucepan, heat water, ½ cup orange juice, 1 tablespoon orange peel, 2 tablespoons oil, and ¼ teaspoon salt to boiling over high heat. Stir in couscous; cover saucepan and remove from heat. Let couscous stand 5 minutes.

2   Meanwhile, heat ridged grill pan over medium-high heat. In cup, combine remaining 1 tablespoon orange peel with rosemary, 1 teaspoon oil, remaining ¼ teaspoon salt, and pepper. Pat turkey cutlets dry with paper towels, then rub both sides of each cutlet with rosemary mixture. Add cutlets to hot grill pan and cook until they just lose their pink color throughout, 4 to 5 minutes, turning cutlets once.

3   In small bowl, prepare orange vinaigrette. Whisk together vinegar and remaining ¼ cup orange juice; slowly whisk in remaining 2 tablespoons oil until blended.

4   To serve, fluff couscous with fork. Toss arugula with ¼ cup vinaigrette. Arrange arugula on 4 dinner plates; sop with couscous and turkey; drizzle with remaining vinaigrette.

EACH SERVING: ABOUT 410 CALORIES | 33G PROTEIN | 44G CARBOHYDRATE | 12G TOTAL FAT (2G SATURATED) | 6G FIBER | 71MG CHOLESTEROL | 610MG SODIUM

BULGUR PILAF WITH GARBANZO BEANS AND APRICOTS

This meatless dish turns grain and beans into a hearty entrée.

ACTIVE TIME: 10 MIN · TOTAL TIME: 30 MIN
MAKES: 4 MAIN-DISH SERVINGS

¾ CUP WATER

1 CAN (14½ OUNCES) VEGETABLE OR CHICKEN BROTH

1 CUP BULGUR

1 TABLESPOON OLIVE OIL

1 SMALL ONION, CHOPPED

2 TEASPOONS CURRY POWDER

1 GARLIC CLOVE, CRUSHED WITH GARLIC PRESS

1 CAN (15 TO 19 OUNCES) GARBANZO BEANS, RINSED AND DRAINED

½ CUP DRIED APRICOTS

½ TEASPOON SALT

¼ CUP LOOSELY PACKED FRESH PARSLEY LEAVES, CHOPPED

1 In 2-quart covered saucepan, heat water and 1¼ cups broth to boiling over high heat. Stir in bulgur; heat to boiling. Reduce heat to medium-low; cover and simmer until liquid is absorbed, 12 to 15 minutes. Remove saucepan from heat. Uncover and fluff bulgur with fork to separate grains.

2 Meanwhile, in 12-inch nonstick skillet, heat oil over medium heat 1 minute. Add onion and cook 10 minutes, stirring occasionally. Stir in curry powder and garlic; cook 1 minute.

3 Stir in garbanzo beans, apricots, ½ teaspoon salt, and remaining broth; heat to boiling. Remove saucepan from heat; stir in bulgur and parsley.

EACH SERVING: ABOUT 370 CALORIES | 13G PROTEIN | 71G CARBOHYDRATE | 6G TOTAL FAT (1G SATURATED) | 15G FIBER | 0MG CHOLESTEROL | 815MG SODIUM

ON THE **SIDE**

Side dishes are the perfect way to experiment with whole grains. They allow you get to know a grain before making a main-course commitment to it.

This chapter gives you tasty starter recipes for bulgur, wheat berries, barley, brown rice, couscous, wild rice, quinoa, and polenta, not to mention cracked wheat, faro, and millet, as well as all sorts of flavor variations. You can enjoy your grains kicked up with a variety of tasty additions: cranberries, toasted nuts, chopped fresh herbs, and piquant citrus juices. You can learn how to make stovetop polenta, then chill it, cut it into wedges, and enjoy it crispy hot from a trip under the broiler.

And no one said you have to eat your grains one at a time. We have tasty recipes for sides that combine grains—brown rice, wild rice, bulgur, barley, and wheat berries—in multiple delicious pairings.

At the end of the chapter you'll find a diverse selection of stuffings that get their whole-grain goodness from whole-grain bread, wild rice, cornbread, brown rice, bulgur, and wheat berries. Serve one up with your next roast chicken or turkey and your family will be asking for seconds.

Also remember that you can transform many of these recipes from sides to main courses with the addition of your favorite protein.

Wild Rice and Mushroom Stuffing (page 136)

AROMATIC BROWN RICE

Think of rice as a blank canvas to which you can add any number of flavorings for your own taste creation. Below is a basic recipe for cooking brown rice, followed by two very different variations.

ACTIVE TIME: 5 MIN · **TOTAL TIME:** 45 MIN
MAKES: 4 SIDE-DISH SERVINGS

---

1 CUP LONG-GRAIN BROWN RICE	¾ CUP WATER
1 CUP CHICKEN BROTH	¼ TEASPOON SALT

In a medium saucepan, combine rice, broth, water, and salt and bring to boiling, uncovered, over high heat. Cover and simmer over low heat until rice is tender and liquid is absorbed, 40 to 45 minutes.

EACH SERVING: ABOUT 175 CALORIES | 4G PROTEIN | 36G CARBOHYDRATE | 2G TOTAL FAT (0G SATURATED) | 3G FIBER | 0MG CHOLESTEROL | 385MG SODIUM

LEMON-PARSLEY BROWN RICE

After rice has cooked, stir in **2 tablespoons chopped fresh parsley** and **1 teaspoon freshly grated lemon peel.**

EACH SERVING: ABOUT 175 CALORIES | 4G PROTEIN | 37G CARBOHYDRATE | 1G TOTAL FAT (0G SATURATED) | 3G FIBER | 3MG CHOLESTEROL | 385MG SODIUM

ASIAN BROWN RICE

Omit salt when cooking rice. After rice has cooked, stir in **2 green onions,** chopped, **2 teaspoons soy sauce,** and **¼ teaspoon Asian sesame oil.**

EACH SERVING: ABOUT 180 CALORIES | 4G PROTEIN | 38G CARBOHYDRATE | 1G TOTAL FAT (0G SATURATED) | 3G FIBER | 3MG CHOLESTEROL | 390MG SODIUM

BROWN RICE AND VEGETABLE PILAF

Fragrant herbs and a variety of fresh vegetables complement the nutty flavor of brown rice in this tasty vegetarian dish.

ACTIVE TIME: 15 MIN · **TOTAL TIME:** 1 HR 25 MIN

MAKES: 6 SIDE-DISH SERVINGS

---

1   TABLESPOON OLIVE OR VEGETABLE OIL

1   MEDIUM ONION, FINELY CHOPPED

1   STALK CELERY, FINELY CHOPPED

1   PACKAGE (8 OUNCES) MUSHROOMS, TRIMMED AND SLICED

1   GARLIC CLOVE, FINELY CHOPPED

1   CUP LONG-GRAIN BROWN RICE

2¼ CUPS WATER

2   CARROTS, PEELED AND CHOPPED

1¼ TEASPOONS SALT

¼   TEASPOON DRIED THYME

⅛   TEASPOON GROUND BLACK PEPPER

PINCH DRIED SAGE

1 In 10-inch skillet, heat oil over medium heat. Add onion and celery; cook until onion is tender, about 5 minutes, stirring frequently. Stir in mushrooms; increase heat to medium-high and cook until mushrooms begin to brown and liquid has evaporated. Stir in garlic. Add rice; cook, stirring, 30 seconds. Stir in water, carrots, salt, thyme, pepper, and sage; heat to boiling. **2** Reduce heat; cover and simmer until rice is tender and all liquid has been absorbed, about 45 minutes. Fluff with fork.

EACH SERVING: ABOUT 165 CALORIES | 4G PROTEIN | 31G CARBOHYDRATE | 3G TOTAL FAT (0G SATURATED) | 3G FIBER | 0MG CHOLESTEROL | 503MG SODIUM

TOASTED BARLEY PILAF WITH TART CHERRIES AND PECANS

Nutty whole-grain flavor is heightened by tangy dried cherries and rich toasted pecans for a wonderful wintertime accompaniment that holds up nicely on a buffet table.

ACTIVE TIME: 25 MIN · **TOTAL TIME:** 55 MIN

MAKES: 24 SIDE-DISH SERVINGS

2 BAGS (1 POUND EACH) PEARL BARLEY	LEAVES FROM 2 BUNCHES FRESH PARSLEY, CHOPPED (2 CUPS)
8 CUPS WATER	1 CUP SEASONED RICE VINEGAR
2 TEASPOONS SALT	½ CUP OLIVE OIL
2 CUPS PECANS, TOASTED (SEE TIP, PAGE 29) AND CHOPPED	½ TEASPOON GROUND BLACK PEPPER
2 CUPS DRIED TART CHERRIES	PARSLEY SPRIGS FOR GARNISH

1 Preheat oven to 400°F.

2 In two 15½" by 10½" jelly-roll pans, toast barley until fragrant and lightly browned, about 20 minutes, shaking pans occasionally.

3 In 5- to 6-quart Dutch oven, heat barley, water, and salt to boiling over high heat. Reduce heat to low; cover and simmer until barley is tender and all liquid is absorbed, about 30 minutes.

4 Spoon barley into large serving bowl; stir in pecans, cherries, chopped parsley, vinegar, oil, and pepper. Serve warm or at room temperature, garnished with parsley sprigs.

EACH SERVING: ABOUT 275 CALORIES | 5G PROTEIN | 43G CARBOHYDRATE | 10G TOTAL FAT (1G SATURATED) | 10G FIBER | 0MG CHOLESTEROL | 510MG SODIUM

FRUITED MULTIGRAIN PILAF WITH ALMONDS

Get a double dose of grain goodness (brown rice and bulgur) in this delicious pilaf studded with dried fruit and toasted almonds.

ACTIVE TIME: 5 MIN · **TOTAL TIME:** 40 MIN PLUS STANDING
MAKES: 6 SIDE-DISH SERVINGS

1   TEASPOON OLIVE OIL

1   MEDIUM ONION, CHOPPED

½   CUP INSTANT (10-MINUTE) BROWN RICE

1   CAN (14½ OUNCES) CHICKEN BROTH

½   CUP WATER

½   CUP BULGUR

½   CUP DRIED FRUIT BITS

½   CUP SLICED ALMONDS, TOASTED (SEE TIP PAGE 29)

1   In 3-quart saucepan, heat oil over medium heat. Add onion and cook until lightly browned, about 4 minutes, stirring. Stir in rice; cook 1 minute. Add broth and water; heat to boiling. Reduce heat to low; cover and simmer 15 minutes.

2   Stir in bulgur; heat to boiling over high heat. Reduce heat to low; cover and simmer until rice and bulgur are tender and liquid is absorbed, 10 to 12 minutes.

3   Remove from heat. Stir in fruit; cover and let stand 5 minutes, then stir in almonds.

EACH SERVING: ABOUT 180 CALORIES | 5G PROTEIN | 28G CARBOHYDRATE | 7G TOTAL FAT (1G SATURATED) | 4G FIBER | 0MG CHOLESTEROL | 295MG SODIUM

DOUBLE RICE PILAF WITH FENNEL AND CRANBERRIES

Sautéed vegetables and tart fruit add flavor and color to this savory and nutritious wild and brown rice mix.

ACTIVE TIME: 45 MIN · TOTAL TIME: 1 HR 25 MIN

MAKES: 12 SIDE-DISH SERVINGS

---

1   CUP WILD RICE (6 OUNCES), RINSED

4   CUPS WATER

¾   CUP DRIED CRANBERRIES

4   TABLESPOONS BUTTER OR MARGARINE

3   MEDIUM CARROTS, PEELED AND DICED

1   MEDIUM STALK CELERY, DICED

1   SMALL FENNEL BULB (8 OUNCES), TRIMMED AND DICED

1   MEDIUM ONION, DICED

1½ TEASPOONS CHOPPED FRESH THYME

2   CUPS LONG-GRAIN BROWN RICE

1   CAN (14½ OUNCES) CHICKEN BROTH

¾   TEASPOON SALT

¼   TEASPOON COARSELY GROUND BLACK PEPPER

FRESH THYME LEAVES FOR GARNISH

---

1 In 3-quart saucepan, heat wild rice and 2 cups water to boiling over high heat. Reduce heat to low; cover and simmer until wild rice is tender, 35 to 40 minutes. Stir in cranberries; heat 1 minute. Drain wild-rice mixture, if necessary.

2 Meanwhile, in 5-quart Dutch oven, melt butter over medium-high heat. Add carrots, celery, fennel, and onion and cook until all vegetables are tender and lightly browned, about 20 minutes, stirring occasionally. Stir in chopped thyme; cook 1 minute. Remove vegetables to medium bowl.

3 In same 5-quart Dutch oven, heat brown rice, broth, and remaining 2 cups water to boiling over high heat. Reduce heat to low; cover and simmer until rice is tender, 18 to 20 minutes. Stir in salt, pepper, wild-rice mixture, and vegetable mixture; heat through. Spoon into serving bowl; sprinkle with thyme leaves.

EACH SERVING: ABOUT 245 CALORIES │ 6G PROTEIN │ 46G CARBOHYDRATE │ 4G TOTAL FAT (1G SATURATED) │ 3G FIBER │ 0MG CHOLESTEROL │ 315MG SODIUM

BASIC COUSCOUS AND VARIATIONS

Couscous is the perfect side for a busy weekday meal, taking all of ten minutes to put together from start to finish. It's satisfying as is, but it only takes another couple of minutes to put your own personal spin on it. Below is the basic method for couscous, plus three flavor variation.

ACTIVE TIME: 5 MIN · **TOTAL TIME:** 10 MIN PLUS STANDING

MAKES: 4 SIDE-DISH SERVINGS

---

1   CUP WHOLE-WHEAT COUSCOUS
     (MOROCCAN PASTA)

1¼ CUPS WATER

½   TEASPOON SALT

Prepare couscous as the label directs, adding seasoning to the water before boiling. Do not add margarine or butter.

EACH SERVING: ABOUT 105 CALORIES │ 4G PROTEIN │ 23G CARBOHYDRATE │ 0.5G TOTAL FAT
4G FIBER │ 0MG CHOLESTEROL │ 405MG SODIUM

LIME COUSCOUS

Add **1 tablespoon fresh lime juice** and **1 teaspoon freshly grated lime peel** to water when preparing couscous.

EACH SERVING: ABOUT 175 CALORIES │ 6G PROTEIN │ 36G CARBOHYDRATE │ 0G TOTAL FAT
4G FIBER │ 0MG CHOLESTEROL │ 405MG SODIUM

MOROCCAN COUSCOUS

Add **¼ cup golden raisins, ¼ teaspoon ground cinnamon, ¼ teaspoon ground turmeric,** and **¼ teaspoon ground cumin** to water when preparing couscous.

EACH SERVING: ABOUT 200 CALORIES │ 6G PROTEIN │ 43G CARBOHYDRATE │ 0G TOTAL FAT
4G FIBER │ 0MG CHOLESTEROL │ 405MG SODIUM

APRICOT COUSCOUS

This quick-to-the-table side dish cooks in five minutes. Stir in parsley or cilantro, depending on the flavorings in the main meal.

MAKES: 4 SIDE-DISH SERVINGS · **ACTIVE TIME:** 5 MIN
TOTAL TIME: 10 MIN PLUS STANDING

1   CUP CHICKEN BROTH

¼   CUP WATER

3   STRIPS (3" BY 1" EACH) ORANGE PEEL

½   CUP DRIED APRICOT HALVES, CUT
     INTO THIN STRIPS

1   CUP WHOLE-WHEAT COUSCOUS
     (MOROCCAN PASTA)

⅓   CUP CHOPPED FRESH PARSLEY OR
     CILANTRO

1   In 2-quart saucepan, heat broth, water, orange peel, and apricots to boiling over high heat. Remove saucepan from heat; stir in couscous. Cover saucepan, and let stand 5 minutes or until ready to serve.
2   Remove orange-peel strips. Fluff couscous with fork, and stir in parsley.

EACH SERVING: ABOUT 225 CALORIES │ 8G PROTEIN │ 46G CARBOHYDRATE │ 1G TOTAL FAT (0G SATURATED) │ 5G FIBER │ 0MG CHOLESTEROL │ 205MG SODIUM

SPICED COUSCOUS WITH VEGETABLES

A blend of cumin, curry powder, and paprika complements this tasty Moroccan-style side dish.

ACTIVE TIME: 15 MIN · **TOTAL TIME:** 30 MIN PLUS STANDING
MAKES: 8 SIDE-DISH SERVINGS

1   PACKAGE (10 OUNCES) WHOLE-WHEAT COUSCOUS (MOROCCAN PASTA)

¼   TEASPOON COARSELY GROUND BLACK PEPPER

2   TABLESPOONS OLIVE OIL

1   TEASPOON SALT

2   MEDIUM CARROTS, PEELED AND CUT INTO ¼-INCH DICE

1   MEDIUM RED ONION, CUT INTO ¼-INCH DICE

1   MEDIUM (8 TO 10 OUNCES) ZUCCHINI, CUT INTO ¼-INCH DICE

3   RIPE MEDIUM TOMATOES, CUT INTO ¼-INCH DICE

1   TABLESPOON GROUND CUMIN

2   TEASPOONS CURRY POWDER

2   TEASPOONS PAPRIKA

¼   CUP PINE NUTS (PIGNOLI), TOASTED

¼   CUP LOOSELY PACKED FRESH PARSLEY LEAVES, CHOPPED

¼   CUP PITTED PRUNES, CUT INTO SLIVERS

1   Prepare couscous as label directs, but instead of the salt or butter called for, stir in pepper, 1 tablespoon oil, and ½ teaspoon salt; cover and keep warm.

2   Meanwhile, in nonstick 12-inch skillet, heat remaining 1 tablespoon oil over medium heat until hot. Add carrots and onion, and cook 5 minutes, stirring occasionally. Add zucchini, and cook until vegetables are tender, about 5 minutes longer. Stir in tomatoes, cumin, curry, paprika, and remaining ½ teaspoon salt, and cook 2 minutes longer.

3   Stir vegetable mixture into couscous; sprinkle with pine nuts, parsley, and prunes.

EACH SERVING: ABOUT 230 CALORIES | 7G PROTEIN | 38G CARBOHYDRATE | 6G TOTAL FAT (1G SATURATED) | 7G FIBER | 0MG CHOLESTEROL | 285MG SODIUM

CREAMY POLENTA

Long a popular staple of northern Italy, polenta has acquired a devoted American following.

ACTIVE TIME: 5 MIN · **TOTAL TIME:** 35 MIN
MAKES: 8 SIDE-DISH SERVINGS

---

2   CUPS COLD WATER

1   TEASPOON SALT

1½ CUPS YELLOW CORNMEAL

4½ CUPS BOILING WATER

½   CUP FRESHLY GRATED PARMESAN CHEESE

4   TABLESPOON BUTTER OR MARGARINE, CUT INTO PIECES

1 In 5-quart Dutch oven, combine cold water and salt. With wire whisk, gradually beat in cornmeal until smooth. Whisk in boiling water. Heat to boiling over high heat. Reduce heat to medium-low and cook until mixture is very thick, 20 to 25 minutes, stirring frequently with wooden spoon.
2 Stir Parmesan and butter into polenta until butter has melted. Serve immediately.

EACH SERVING: ABOUT 175 CALORIES | 5G PROTEIN | 20G CARBOHYDRATE | 8G TOTAL FAT (5G SATURATED) | 1G FIBER | 20MG CHOLESTEROL | 464MG SODIUM

BROILED POLENTA WEDGES

Line 13" by 9" baking pan with foil, extending foil over rim. Prepare Creamy Polenta as directed but only use **3½ cups boiling water** and cook until mixture is very thick and indentation remains when a spoon is dragged through it, 30 to 35 minutes. Stir in Parmesan and butter as directed. Spoon mixture into prepared pan, smoothing top. Refrigerate until very firm, at least 1 hour. Preheat broiler. Lift foil with polenta from baking pan; place on cookie sheet. Cut polenta into 16 triangles; separate them. Brush **1 table-spoon butter or margarine,** melted, on wedges. Broil 5 to 7 inches away from heat source until lightly browned and heated through, about 10 minutes.

ROSEMARY POLENTA WEDGES

Prepare Broiled Polenta Wedges as directed but add **½ teaspoon chopped fresh rosemary or ¼ teaspoon dried rosemary,** crumbled, to melted butter before brushing.

POLENTA AND SPINACH GRATIN

A creamy spinach topping is layered over slices of ready-made polenta for a satisfying side dish. You can assemble this casserole completely up to one day ahead, but do not bake. Cover and refrigerate. Increase baking time to 40 minutes because you are starting with a chilled caserole.

ACTIVE TIME: 20 MIN · **TOTAL TIME:** 55 MIN

MAKES: 16 SIDE-DISH SERVINGS

2   LOGS (24 OUNCES EACH) PRECOOKED PLAIN POLENTA

2   TABLESPOONS OLIVE OIL

1   LARGE ONION, CHOPPED

2   GARLIC CLOVES, MINCED

¼   TEASPOON CRUSHED RED PEPPER

3   PACKAGES (10 OUNCES EACH) FROZEN CHOPPED SPINACH, THAWED AND SQUEEZED DRY

3½ CUPS WHOLE MILK

2   TABLESPOONS CORNSTARCH

1   TEASPOON SALT

1   CUP FRESHLY GRATED PARMESAN CHEESE

1 Cut each polenta log crosswise in half, then cut each half lengthwise into 6 slices. In 13" by 9" ceramic or glass baking dish, place half of polenta slices, overlapping slightly.

2 Preheat oven to 425°F.

3 In 4-quart saucepan, heat oil over medium heat until hot. Add onion and cook until tender and golden, 10 to 12 minutes, stirring occasionally. Add garlic and crushed red pepper and cook 1 minute, stirring. Add spinach and cook 3 minutes to heat through, stirring frequently and separating spinach with fork.

4 In medium bowl, with wire whisk, mix milk and cornstarch. Stir in salt and all but 2 tablespoons Parmesan. Add milk mixture to spinach mixture in saucepan; heat to boiling over medium-high heat. Reduce heat to low; cook 2 minutes, stirring occasionally. Remove saucepan from heat.

5 Spoon half of spinach mixture over polenta slices in baking dish. Repeat layering with remaining polenta slices and spinach mixture. Sprinkle with reserved Parmesan. Bake until hot and bubbly, about 20 minutes.

EACH SERVING: ABOUT 155 CALORIES | 8G PROTEIN | 19G CARBOHYDRATE | 5G TOTAL FAT (3G SATURATED) | 2G FIBER | 12MG CHOLESTEROL | 625MG SODIUM

QUINOA AND FRESH CORN SAUTÉ

Although unfamiliar to many, quinoa has been a staple grain since the time of the Incas, who called it the "mother grain." If you've never prepared quinoa before, this basic recipe is a great place to start.

ACTIVE TIME: 15 MIN · **TOTAL TIME:** 30 MIN
MAKES: 6 SIDE-DISH SERVINGS

1 CUP QUINOA	1 TABLESPOON BUTTER OR MARGARINE
1½ CUPS WATER	4 GREEN ONIONS, SLICED
¾ TEASPOON SALT	¼ TEASPOON GROUND BLACK PEPPER
3 MEDIUM EARS CORN, HUSKS AND SILK REMOVED	½ TEASPOON FRESHLY GRATED LEMON PEEL

1 In sieve, rinse quinoa with cold running water. In 2-quart saucepan, combine water, quinoa, and ½ teaspoon salt; heat to boiling over high heat. Reduce heat, cover, and simmer until water has been absorbed, about 15 minutes.

2 Meanwhile, cut kernels from cobs. In 10-inch skillet, melt butter over medium-high heat. Add corn, green onions, remaining ¼ teaspoon salt, and pepper. Cook until corn is tender-crisp, about 3 minutes, stirring frequently. Stir in lemon peel. Add quinoa and cook until evenly combined, stirring.

EACH SERVING: ABOUT 190 CALORIES | 6G PROTEIN | 34G CARBOHYDRATE | 4G TOTAL FAT (1G SATURATED) | 3G FIBER | 5MG CHOLESTEROL | 340MG SODIUM

WHOLE-GRAIN BREAD AND MUSHROOM STUFFING

Artisanal, or hand-shaped, breads vary greatly, so depending on the density of the bread, you may need more or less broth when preparing this stuffing. Add the broth slowly to be sure it is completely absorbed. If there is extra broth in the bottom of the bowl, you have added enough.

ACTIVE TIME: 40 MIN · **TOTAL TIME:** 1 HR 45 MIN
MAKES: 8 CUPS OR 16 SERVINGS

---

1   POUND ARTISANAL WHOLE-GRAIN BREAD

4   SLICES BACON

1   MEDIUM ONION, CHOPPED

2   STALKS CELERY, CHOPPED

1   TEASPOON POULTRY SEASONING

2   PACKAGES (8 OUNCES EACH) SLICED MUSHROOMS

½   CUP LOOSELY PACKED FRESH PARSLEY LEAVES, CHOPPED

¼   TEASPOON SALT

¼   TEASPOON GROUND BLACK PEPPER

1¾ TO 2½ CUPS CHICKEN BROTH

1   Preheat oven to 325°F. Cut bread into ¾-inch cubes (you should have about 8 cups) and place in 15½" by 10½" jelly-roll pan or large cookie sheet. Toast bread in oven until golden and dry, 25 to 30 minutes, stirring bread halfway through toasting. Cool bread in pan on wire rack.

2   Meanwhile, cut bacon into ½-inch pieces. In 12-inch skillet, cook bacon over medium heat until browned, 8 to 10 minutes, stirring occasionally. With slotted spoon, transfer bacon to very large bowl.

3   To bacon drippings in skillet, add onion, celery, and poultry seasoning, and cook over medium-high heat 10 minutes, stirring occasionally. Add mushrooms and cook until vegetables are tender and lightly browned, another 10 minutes, stirring occasionally.

4   To bowl with bacon, add bread, vegetable mixture, parsley, salt, and pepper. Gradually drizzle in broth until cubes are moistened.

5   Use stuffing to fill cavity of 12- to 16-pound turkey, or spoon into greased 2½- to 3-quart glass or ceramic baking dish. Cover dish with foil and bake stuffing in preheated 325°F oven 20 minutes. Remove foil and bake until heated through and lightly browned on top, 20 to 25 minutes longer.

EACH SERVING: ABOUT 120 CALORIES | 4G PROTEIN | 13G CARBOHYDRATE 6G | TOTAL FAT (2G SATURATED) | 2G FIBER | 6MG CHOLESTEROL | 215MG SODIUM

TIP If you want to make enough to serve 24, double all ingredients in recipe except chicken broth. Toast bread in two jelly-roll pans and cook vegetables in two skillets. When adding the broth, drizzle in only 2½ to 3 cups. Bake the stuffing in two 2½- to 3-quart glass or ceramic baking dishes.

CORNBREAD AND SAUSAGE STUFFING

We jazzed up a packaged cornbread stuffing mix with sausage and peppers—easy and delicious!

ACTIVE TIME: 45 MIN · **TOTAL TIME:** 1 HR 25 MIN

MAKES: 13 CUPS OR 26 SERVINGS

---

1   PACKAGE (12 OUNCES) FROZEN PORK SAUSAGE, THAWED

3   LARGE STALKS CELERY, CHOPPED

1   LARGE ONION, CHOPPED

1   RED PEPPER, CUT INTO ½-INCH PIECES

1   GREEN PEPPER, CUT INTO ½-INCH PIECES

1   CAN (14½ OUNCES) CHICKEN BROTH

1   CUP WATER

1   BAG (16 OUNCES) CORNBREAD-STUFFING MIX

1   CUP LOOSELY PACKED FRESH PARSLEY LEAVES, CHOPPED

1   Heat nonstick 12-inch skillet over medium-high heat until hot. Add sausage and cook until browned, 5 to 8 minutes, stirring frequently. With slotted spoon, transfer sausage to very large bowl. Spoon off and discard all but 1 tablespoon sausage drippings.

2   Add celery, onion, and red and green peppers and cook over medium heat until golden, about 20 minutes. Stir in broth and water; heat to boiling.

3   Add vegetable mixture, stuffing mix, and parsley to sausage in bowl; toss to mix well. Spoon stuffing into greased 13" by 9" baking dish or shallow 3½-quart casserole. Cover with foil.

4   Preheat oven to 325°F; bake until heated through, about 40 minutes (see Tip).

TIP If not serving right away, complete the recipe but do not bake. Cover and refrigerate up to 2 days. Bake as directed but increase the cooking time to 1 hour.

EACH SERVING: ABOUT 90 CALORIES | 3G PROTEIN | 15G CARBOHYDRATE | 2G TOTAL FAT (1G SATURATED) | 1G FIBER | 3MG CHOLESTEROL | 420MG SODIUM

WILD RICE AND MUSHROOM STUFFING

This recipe makes an elegant alternative to ordinary bread stuffing. It's richly flavored with two kinds of mushrooms and other vegetables. (See photo on page 118.)

ACTIVE TIME: 45 MIN · **TOTAL TIME:** 1 HR 5 MIN
MAKES: 13 CUPS OR 26 SERVINGS

1 CUP WILD RICE (6 OUNCES), RINSED

3¾ CUPS WATER

1 CUP DRIED CRANBERRIES OR RAISINS

4 TABLESPOONS BUTTER OR MARGARINE

3 MEDIUM CARROTS, PEELED AND CUT INTO ¼-INCH DICE

2 STALKS CELERY, CUT INTO ¼-INCH DICE

1 MEDIUM ONION, CUT INTO ¼-INCH DICE

1 TEASPOON SALT

½ TEASPOON DRIED THYME

¼ TEASPOON COARSELY GROUND BLACK PEPPER

8 OUNCES SHIITAKE MUSHROOMS, STEMS DISCARDED, CAPS SLICED

10 OUNCES WHITE MUSHROOMS, TRIMMED AND SLICED

2 CUPS LONG-GRAIN BROWN RICE

1 CAN (14½ OUNCES) CHICKEN BROTH

1 In 2-quart saucepan, heat wild rice and 2 cups water to boiling over high heat. Reduce heat to low; cover and simmer until wild rice is tender, 35 to 40 minutes. Stir in cranberries; heat 1 minute. Drain wild rice mixture if necessary.

2 Meanwhile, in nonstick 5- to 6-quart Dutch oven, melt 2 tablespoons butter over medium heat. Add carrots, celery, and onion, and cook until tender and golden, 12 to 15 minutes. Stir in salt, thyme, and pepper, and cook 1 minute; transfer to medium bowl.

3 In same Dutch oven, melt remaining 2 tablespoons butter over medium heat. Add both mushrooms, and cook until tender and golden and liquid evaporates, about 12 minutes; transfer to bowl with vegetables.

4 Preheat oven to 325°F.

5 In same Dutch oven, heat brown rice, broth, and remaining 1¾ cups water to boiling over high heat. Reduce heat to low; cover and simmer until tender, 18 to 20 minutes. Stir wild-rice and vegetable mixtures into rice.

6 Spoon stuffing into 13" by 9" glass baking dish or shallow ½-quart casserole. Cover with foil and bake until heated through, about 20 minutes.

EACH SERVING: ABOUT 120 CALORIES | 3G PROTEIN | 23G CARBOHYDRATE | 2G TOTAL FAT (0G SATURATED) | 2G FIBER | 0MG CHOLESTEROL | 190MG SODIUM

WHEAT BERRIES WITH BROWN BUTTER AND PECANS

Wheat berries have an appealing chewy texture. Combining them with pecans and brown butter brings out the grain's nutty flavor.

ACTIVE TIME: 10 MIN · TOTAL TIME: 1 HR 30 MIN PLUS OVERNIGHT SOAKING
MAKES: 6 SIDE-DISH SERVINGS

---

1 CUP WHEAT BERRIES (WHOLE-WHEAT KERNELS)

2 TABLESPOONS BUTTER OR MARGARINE

1 MEDIUM ONION, CHOPPED

½ CUP PECANS, COARSELY CHOPPED

½ TEASPOON SALT

⅛ TEASPOON GROUND BLACK PEPPER

1 TABLESPOON WATER

2 TABLESPOONS CHOPPED FRESH PARSLEY

1 In medium bowl, soak wheat berries overnight in enough **water** to cover by 2 inches. Drain.

2 In 3-quart saucepan, combine wheat berries and **3 cups water**; heat to boiling over high heat. Reduce heat; cover and simmer until wheat berries are tender but still firm to the bite, about 1 hour. Drain.

3 In same clean saucepan, melt butter over medium heat. Add onion and cook until tender, about 5 minutes, stirring frequently. Stir in pecans, salt, and pepper. Cook until pecans are lightly toasted and butter begins to brown, about 3 minutes, stirring. Stir in wheat berries and 1 tablespoon water; heat through. Stir in parsley.

EACH SERVING: ABOUT 210 CALORIES | 5G PROTEIN | 27G CARBOHYDRATE | 11G TOTAL FAT (3G SATURATED) | 5G FIBER | 10MG CHOLESTEROL | 233MG SODIUM

BREADS, BISCUITS & ROLLS

It's certainly easier to buy your sandwich or toasting bread and there are plenty of whole-grains choices available (like pasta, beware—read the label and make sure the whole-grain ingredients are at the top of the ingredient list). But nothing can top the satisfaction of baking your own bread and slicing into it when it's still warm. We've included here a few of our favorite whole-grain recipes, filled with the goodness of oats, whole-wheat flour, rye flour, wheat germ, barley, and wheat bran.

Corn bread is in a class of its own; you'll find in these pages a cheesy skillet recipe, a flavor twist with dried cranberries, and a crunchy delicious recipe for corn sticks made with sweet potatoes. Just make sure you buy stone- or water-ground cornmeal—it leaves more of the bran and germ intact, making for a more nutritious baked product.

When it comes to rolls and biscuits, the supermarket refrigerator case and bread aisle can be a disappointment when you're looking for whole grains. Try making your own from scratch. We think there's a good chance you might never go back to supermarket-bought.

Cranberry-Cornmeal Biscuits (page 149)

WHOLE WHEAT–OATMEAL BREAD

This recipe makes two slightly flat breads with a sweet flavor and dense texture. (See photo of walnut variation, opposite.)

ACTIVE TIME: 45 MIN · **TOTAL TIME:** 1 HR 20 MIN PLUS RISING

MAKES: 2 OVAL LOAVES, 12 SLICES EACH

---

2   CUPS WARM WATER (105° TO 115°F)

2   PACKAGES ACTIVE DRY YEAST

½   TEASPOON SUGAR

½   CUP HONEY

4   TABLESPOONS BUTTER OR MARGARINE

1   CUP QUICK-COOKING OR OLD-FASHIONED OATS

1   TABLESPOON SALT

4   CUPS WHOLE-WHEAT FLOUR

1   LARGE EGG

ABOUT 2½ CUPS ALL-PURPOSE FLOUR OR 2 CUPS BREAD FLOUR

1 In large bowl, combine ½ cup warm water, yeast, and sugar; stir to dissolve. Let stand until foamy, about 5 minutes. Stir in remaining 1½ cups warm water, honey, butter, oats, salt, and 2 cups whole-wheat flour until smooth. Stir in egg. Gradually stir in remaining 2 cups whole-wheat flour, then 2 cups all-purpose flour or 1½ cups bread flour.

2 Turn dough onto lightly floured surface and knead until smooth but slightly sticky, about 7 minutes, working in enough of remaining ½ cup flour just to keep dough from sticking.

3 Shape dough into ball; place in greased large bowl, turning dough to grease top. Cover bowl loosely with plastic wrap and let rise in warm place (80° to 85°F) until doubled in volume, about 1 hour.

4 Punch down dough. Turn dough onto lightly floured surface and cut in half; cover and let rest 15 minutes. Grease large cookie sheet.

5 Shape each dough half into 7" by 4" oval; place on prepared cookie sheet. Cover and let rise in warm place until doubled in volume, about 1 hour.

6 Meanwhile, preheat oven to 350°F. With serrated knife or single-edge razor blade, cut three to five ¼-inch-deep crisscross slashes across top of each loaf. Lightly dust tops of loaves with all-purpose flour. Bake until loaves sound hollow when lightly tapped on bottom, 35 to 40 minutes. Transfer to wire racks to cool.

EACH SLICE: ABOUT 175 CALORIES | 5G PROTEIN | 34G CARBOHYDRATE | 3G TOTAL FAT (1G SATURATED) | 3G FIBER | 14MG CHOLESTEROL | 315MG SODIUM

WHOLE WHEAT–WALNUT BREAD

Prepare Whole Wheat Oatmeal Bread as directed, using **½ cup milk** heated to warm (105° to 115°F) instead of water and only **1 package active dry yeast**. Stir in **1 cup warm water**, **3 tablespoons butter or margarine**, softened, **2 tablespoons molasses**, **1½ teaspoons salt**, **2 cups whole-wheat flour**, and only **½ cup all-purpose or bread flour**. Proceed as directed, but after punching down dough in Step 4, knead in **2 cups walnuts**, toasted (see Tip page 29) and coarsely chopped. In Step 5, reduce rising time to about 45 minutes. Preheat oven to 375°F. Just before baking, with sharp knife or single-edge razor blade, cut three 3-inch-long and ¼-inch deep diagonal slashes across tops of loaves. Bake loaves about 30 minutes.

EACH SLICE: ABOUT 155 CALORIES | 4G PROTEIN | 17G CARBOHYDRATE | 9G TOTAL FAT (2G SATURATED) | 2G FIBER | 5MG CHOLESTEROL | 165MG SODIUM

MULTIGRAIN BREAD

The trick to maintaining the light texture of these loaves is to keep the dough slightly sticky while kneading. Adding more flour than what's called for will make your bread too dense.

ACTIVE TIME: 40 MIN · **TOTAL TIME:** 1 HR 15 MIN
MAKES: 2 LOAVES, 12 SLICES EACH

1	CUP OLD-FASHIONED OATS	⅓ CUP FLAX SEEDS, GROUND (SEE BOX)
2	PACKAGES ACTIVE DRY YEAST	¼ CUP LIGHT (MILD) MOLASSES
1	TABLESPOON SUGAR	3 TABLESPOONS OLIVE OIL
2	CUPS WARM WATER (105° TO 115°F)	2½ TEASPOONS SALT
1	CUP WHOLE-WHEAT FLOUR	ABOUT 2½ CUPS ALL-PURPOSE FLOUR
1	CUP STONE-GROUND RYE FLOUR	1 CUP PITTED PRUNES, COARSELY CHOPPED

1 Preheat oven to 350°F. Place oats in small baking pan; bake in oven until lightly toasted, about 10 minutes, stirring occasionally.

2 Meanwhile, in cup, mix yeast, sugar, and ½ cup warm water; stir to dissolve. Let stand until foamy, about 5 minutes.

3 In large bowl, with wooden spoon, stir toasted oats, yeast mixture, whole-wheat and rye flours, flax seeds, molasses, olive oil, salt, and remaining 1½ cups warm water until smooth. Gradually stir in 2½ cups all-purpose flour. With hands, knead in bowl until dough comes together.

4 Turn dough onto lightly floured surface and knead until elastic and almost smooth, about 8 minutes, working in more all-purpose flour (¼ cup) while kneading (dough will be sticky). Knead in prunes.

5 Shape dough into a ball; place in greased large bowl, turning dough over to grease top. Cover bowl loosely with plastic wrap and let rise in warm place (80° to 85°F) until doubled in volume, about 1 hour.

6 Punch down dough. Turn dough onto floured surface; cut in half. Lightly sprinkle large cookie sheet (17" by 14") with flour. With hands, flatten half of dough on one end of cookie sheet into 10" by 8" rectangle. Fold dough over lengthwise to make a 10" by 4" rectangle. Turn dough seam side down and pinch edges to seal; shape into 11" by 4" loaf. Repeat with remaining dough on other end of same cookie sheet.

FLAX FACTS

You can buy flax seeds already ground. The problem with that is, it may have been sitting at the health-food store for months, and be past its prime. The beneficial omega-3 fatty acids in flax can rapidly become rancid after the seeds are milled; you'll notice a strong paintlike smell if this happens. (In its other life, flax seeds are used to make linseed oil, a key ingredient in paint, varnish, and linoleum.)

The best way to keep a fresh supply of flax seeds on hand is to buy the seeds whole, store in an airtight container in a cool area, and pulverize as needed in a coffee grinder. Stored this way, the seeds should keep well up to a year. If you have leftover ground flax seeds, refrigerate them for up to 1 month or freeze for up to 6 months.

7 Cover loaves loosely with greased plastic wrap and let rise in warm place until doubled in volume, about 45 minutes.

8 Preheat oven to 350°F. With sharp knife, cut 6 diagonal slashes about ¼ inch deep across top of each loaf. Sprinkle loaves with all-purpose flour if you like. Bake until loaves are lightly browned and sound hollow when lightly tapped with fingers, about 35 minutes. Transfer loaves to wire rack to cool.

EACH SLICE: ABOUT 160 CALORIES | 4G PROTEIN | 30G CARBOHYDRATE | 3G TOTAL FAT (0G SATURATED) | 2G FIBER | 0MG CHOLESTEROL | 225MG SODIUM

GREAT PLAINS OATMEAL-MOLASSES ROLLS

These tender moist rolls are topped with oats and a butter molasses glaze.

ACTIVE TIME: 1 HR · **TOTAL TIME:** 1 HR 25 MIN PLUS RISING
MAKES: 18 ROLLS

---

1   CUP BOILING WATER

1   CUP PLUS 2 TABLESPOONS OLD-FASHIONED OATS, UNCOOKED

1   PACKAGE ACTIVE DRY YEAST

1   TEASPOON SUGAR

¾   CUP WARM WATER (105° TO 115°F)

5   TABLESPOONS BUTTER OR MARGARINE, SLIGHTLY SOFTENED

⅓   CUP PLUS 2 TEASPOONS LIGHT (MILD) MOLASSES

1½ TEASPOONS SALT

ABOUT 4½ CUPS ALL-PURPOSE FLOUR

1 In medium bowl, pour boiling water over 1 cup oats, stirring to combine. Let stand until oats absorb water, about 10 minutes. In small bowl, combine yeast, sugar, and warm water; stir to dissolve. Let stand until foamy.

2 In large bowl, with mixer at low speed, beat 4 tablespoons butter until smooth; add ⅓ cup molasses, beating until combined. Beat in oat mixture, yeast mixture, and salt just until blended. Gradually beat in 2 cups of the flour, 1 cup at a time, just until blended. With wooden spoon, stir in 2 more cups flour. Turn dough onto lightly floured surface and knead until smooth and elastic, about 5 minutes, working in more flour (about ¼ cup) while kneading. Place dough in greased bowl, turning dough to grease top. Cover loosely with plastic wrap and let rise in warm place (80° to 85°F) until doubled in volume, about 1 hour.

3 Punch down dough. On lightly floured surface, divide dough into 18 equal pieces. Shape each piece into a ball and place in a greased 13" by 9" metal baking pan in 3 rows of 6 balls each. Cover and let rise in warm place until doubled in volume, about 1 hour.

4 Preheat oven to 350°F. Bake rolls until very lightly browned, about 30 minutes. Meanwhile, melt remaining 1 tablespoon butter; stir in remaining 2 teaspoons molasses. After rolls have baked 30 minutes, remove from oven and brush with molasses butter; sprinkle with remaining 2 tablespoons oats. Bake rolls until golden, another 15 minutes. Remove rolls from pan to wire rack; cool slightly to serve warm.

EACH ROLL: ABOUT 195 CALORIES | 5G PROTEIN | 35G CARBOHYDRATE | 4G TOTAL FAT (1G SATURATED) | 1G FIBER | 0MG CHOLESTEROL | 220MG SODIUM

PORTUGUESE PEASANT BREAD

This dense bread is called *broa* in Portugal. Our "secret" ingredient for its unusual flavor and texture: barley cereal for babies, found in the baby-food section of your supermarket! The loaves are also sprayed with water during baking to help give them the characteristic crisp and chewy crust.

ACTIVE TIME: 30 MIN · **TOTAL TIME:** ABOUT 30 MIN

MAKES: 2 LOAVES, 12 SLICES EACH

---

2 TABLESPOONS SUGAR	2½ CUPS STONE-GROUND CORNMEAL, PREFERABLY WHITE
2 PACKAGES ACTIVE DRY YEAST	
3 CUPS WARM WATER (105° TO 115°F)	4 TEASPOONS SALT
1 PACKAGE (8 OUNCES, 4½ CUPS) BARLEY CEREAL	4¾ CUPS (MORE OR LESS, AS NECESSARY) ALL-PURPOSE FLOUR

1 In small bowl, stir sugar and yeast into ½ cup warm water; stir to dissolve. Let stand until foamy, about 5 minutes.

2 In large bowl, combine barley cereal, cornmeal, salt, and 4 cups flour. With wooden spoon, stir in yeast mixture and remaining 2½ cups warm water until combined. With floured hands, shape dough into a ball in bowl. Cover bowl loosely with plastic wrap and let rise in warm place (80° to 85°F) until doubled in volume, about 1 hour.

3 Punch down dough and turn onto well-floured surface. Knead dough until smooth, about 5 minutes, working in more flour (about ¾ cup) as necessary while kneading.

4 Grease large cookie sheet. Cut dough in half and shape each half into 6-inch round. Coat each round with flour; place on cookie sheet. Cover loaves and let rise in warm place until doubled in volume, about 1 hour.

5 Preheat oven to 400°F. Bake loaves until golden brown, about 35 minutes, using spray bottle to spritz loaves with water after first 5 minutes of baking, and again 10 minutes later. Cool on wire racks before slicing.

EACH SLICE: ABOUT 175 CALORIES | 5G PROTEIN | 36G CARBOHYDRATE | 1G TOTAL FAT (1G SATURATED) | 4G FIBER | 0MG CHOLESTEROL | 390MG SODIUM

SKILLET CORN BREAD

This delicious homemade corn bread is baked in an oven-safe skillet—preferably one that's heavyweight, such as cast iron.

ACTIVE TIME: 10 MIN · **TOTAL TIME:** 25 MIN
MAKES: 8 SERVINGS

1 CUP ALL-PURPOSE FLOUR

1 CUP YELLOW CORNMEAL

2 TABLESPOONS SUGAR

2 TEASPOONS BAKING POWDER

¼ TEASPOON SALT

¼ TEASPOON COARSELY GROUND BLACK PEPPER

4 TABLESPOONS COLD BUTTER OR MARGARINE

1 CAN (8½ OUNCES) CREAM-STYLE CORN

1 LARGE EGG, BEATEN

2 OUNCES MONTEREY JACK CHEESE WITH JALAPEÑO CHILES, SHREDDED (½ CUP)

1 Preheat oven to 400°F. Grease 10-inch skillet with oven-safe handle.

2 In large bowl, mix flour, cornmeal, sugar, baking powder, salt, and pepper. With pastry blender or two knives used scissor-fashion, cut in butter until mixture resembles coarse crumbs. With fork, stir corn, egg, and Monterey Jack into flour mixture just until blended (batter will be very stiff).

3 Place greased skillet in oven; preheat pan 5 minutes (to help brown bottom of corn bread). Remove pan from oven; spoon batter into skillet and spread evenly with small metal spatula.

4 Bake corn bread until toothpick inserted in center comes out clean and corn bread is just firm to the touch, 15 to 20 minutes. Cut into 8 wedges and serve warm.

EACH SERVING: ABOUT 290 CALORIES | 7G PROTEIN | 44G CARBOHYDRATE | 9G TOTAL FAT (3G SATURATED) | 1G FIBER | 34MG CHOLESTEROL | 375MG SODIUM

SWEET-POTATO CORN STICKS

Your family is going to love these—and what a fun way to introduce them to the goodness of grains. Plus sweet potatoes are rich in antioxidants in the form of beta-carotene and vitamin C, as well as vitamin B6, potassium, magnesium, and also provide a healthy dose of fiber.

ACTIVE TIME: 20 MIN · **TOTAL TIME:** 45 MIN

MAKES: 14 CORN STICKS

2 MEDIUM SWEET POTATOES (12 OUNCES EACH)	1 TEASPOON SALT
1¼ CUPS ALL-PURPOSE FLOUR	4 TABLESPOONS BUTTER
1 CUP YELLOW CORNMEAL	1¼ CUPS MILK
2½ TEASPOONS BAKING POWDER	⅓ CUP PACKED BROWN SUGAR
	1 LARGE EGG

1 Peel sweet potatoes; cut each into quarters. In 3-quart saucepan, heat sweet potatoes and enough **water** to cover to boiling over high heat. Reduce heat to low; cover and simmer until sweet potatoes are fork-tender, 15 to 20 minutes; drain.

2 Meanwhile, grease well 14 corn-stick molds (2 pans, 7 molds each).

3 In large bowl, combine flour, cornmeal, baking powder, and salt. With pastry blender or two knives used scissor-fashion, cut in butter until mixture resembles coarse crumbs.

4 Preheat oven to 400°F. In small bowl, with potato masher, mash sweet potatoes with milk, brown sugar, and egg until smooth. Stir into dry ingredients until batter is just blended. Spoon batter into prepared corn-stick molds.

5 Bake until toothpick inserted in center comes out clean, 10 to 15 minutes. Cool corn sticks in molds on wire rack 5 minutes. Remove from molds; cool on wire rack. Just before serving, reheat, if desired.

EACH CORN STICK: ABOUT 170 CALORIES | 4G PROTEIN | 29G CARBOHYDRATE | 5G TOTAL FAT (3G SATURATED) | 2G FIBER | 26MG CHOLESTEROL | 316MG SODIUM

CRANBERRY-CORNMEAL BISCUITS

If you'd like to make these biscuits ahead, wrap the cooled biscuits in foil in single layer. You can leave them at room temperature overnight or freeze up to one month. To warm, place in 325°F oven for five minutes.

ACTIVE TIME: 15 MIN · **TOTAL TIME:** 30 MIN
MAKES: 12 BISCUITS

1¼ CUPS CORNMEAL

¾ CUP ALL-PURPOSE FLOUR

½ CUP DRIED CRANBERRIES

2 TABLESPOONS SUGAR

2 TEASPOONS BAKING POWDER

½ TEASPOON SALT

4 TABLESPOONS BUTTER OR MARGARINE, MELTED

¾ CUP MILK

1 Preheat oven to 400°F. Grease large cookie sheet.

2 In medium bowl, stir cornmeal, flour, cranberries, sugar, baking powder, and salt until combined. Stir in melted butter, then mix just until it forms a soft dough.

3 Drop dough by scant ¼ cups, 2 inches apart, on prepared cookie sheet. Bake biscuits until golden, about 15 minutes. Cool biscuits slightly on wire rack to serve warm, or cool completely to serve later. Reheat biscuits if you like.

EACH BISCUIT: ABOUT 150 CALORIES | 3G PROTEIN | 24G CARBOHYDRATE | 5G TOTAL FAT (3G SATURATED) | 2G FIBER | 13MG CHOLESTEROL | 210MG SODIUM

DELICIOUS DESSERTS

Desserts are the sweetest way of all to add grains to your diet. You can try adding oats for extra crunch and good-for-you-fiber to chocolate chip cookies, or experiment with whole grains in other cookie recipes. You'll find oats providing delicious good flavor in our Granola Jumbo cookies, as well as in the crispy, chewy toppings for two fruit crisps, one made with blueberries and the other with nectarines and dark sweet fresh cherries.

Using whole-wheat flour when baking is another effortless way to up your grains. You'll find four cookie-tin perfect recipes that have gotten a whole-wheat flour makeover—gingersnaps, brownies, sugar cookies, and fig bars.

Finally, a taste of the past can be a great choice for good health right now. Try Nantucket Indian Pudding, a comforting dessert made from cornmeal, milk, sugar, and molasses, spiced up with ginger, cinnamon, and nutmeg. Served topped with a dollop of ice cream, it's a scrumptious way to get your daily dose of grains.

Blueberry Crisp (page 160)

WHOLE-GRAIN GINGERSNAPS

Get a dose of whole-wheat goodness in these spicy gingersnaps.

ACTIVE TIME: 25 MIN · **TOTAL TIME:** 35 MIN PLUS CHILLING
MAKES: 3½ DOZEN COOKIES

1 CUP ALL-PURPOSE FLOUR	½ CUP SUGAR
1 CUP WHOLE-WHEAT FLOUR	6 TABLESPOONS TRANS-FAT-FREE VEGETABLE OIL SPREAD (60% TO 70% OIL)
1 TEASPOON GROUND GINGER	
1 TEASPOON BAKING SODA	1 LARGE EGG
½ TEASPOON GROUND CINNAMON	½ CUP DARK MOLASSES
½ TEASPOON SALT	NONPAREILS OR ROUND WHITE SPRINKLES (OPTIONAL)

1 On sheet of waxed paper, combine all-purpose and whole-wheat flours, ginger, baking soda, cinnamon, and salt.

2 In large bowl, with mixer on low speed, beat sugar and vegetable oil spread until blended. Increase speed to high; beat until light and creamy, occasionally scraping down bowl with rubber spatula. Beat in egg and molasses. Reduce speed to low; beat in flour mixture just until blended. Cover dough in bowl with plastic wrap and refrigerate until easier to handle (dough will be slightly sticky), about 1 hour.

3 Preheat oven to 350°F.

4 With lightly greased hands, shape dough by heaping measuring teaspoons into 1-inch balls. If desired, dip top of each ball in nonpareils. Place balls, 2½ inches apart, on ungreased cookie sheet.

5 Bake cookies until tops are slightly cracked, 9 to 11 minutes. (Cookies will be very soft.) Place cookie sheet on wire rack 1 minute to cool. With thin metal spatula, transfer cookies to rack to cool completely. Repeat with remaining dough. Store cookies in tightly covered container at room temperature up to 3 days or in freezer up to 1 month.

EACH COOKIE: ABOUT 55 CALORIES | 1G PROTEIN | 9G CARBOHYDRATE | 2G TOTAL FAT (0G SATURATED) | 1G FIBER | 5MG CHOLESTEROL | 75MG SODIUM

BROWNIE BITES

Espresso powder gives these brownies a nice flavor edge. The cocoa frosting takes them over the top.

ACTIVE TIME: 30 MIN · **TOTAL TIME:** 38 MIN
MAKES: 28 COOKIES

BROWNIE BITES

- 1 TEASPOON INSTANT ESPRESSO COFFEE POWDER
- 1 TEASPOON HOT WATER
- ½ CUP UNSWEETENED COCOA
- ⅓ CUP ALL-PURPOSE FLOUR
- ⅓ CUP WHOLE-WHEAT FLOUR
- ½ TEASPOON BAKING POWDER
- ¼ TEASPOON SALT
- ⅛ TEASPOON GROUND CINNAMON
- ¾ CUP GRANULATED SUGAR
- 3 TABLESPOONS CANOLA OIL
- 2 TABLESPOONS HONEY
- 1 TEASPOON VANILLA EXTRACT
- 1 LARGE EGG WHITE

FROSTING

- 1 OUNCE UNSWEETENED CHOCOLATE, COARSELY CHOPPED
- 3 TABLESPOONS WATER
- 1 TEASPOON TRANS FAT–FREE VEGETABLE OIL SPREAD (60% TO 70% OIL)
- ⅔ CUP CONFECTIONERS' SUGAR
- ½ TEASPOON VANILLA EXTRACT

1 Prepare Brownie Bites: Preheat oven to 350°F. Grease large cookie sheet. In cup, stir espresso powder into hot water until dissolved. Set aside.
2 In large bowl, combine cocoa, both flours, baking powder, salt, and cinnamon. In medium bowl, whisk granulated sugar, oil, honey, vanilla, egg white, and espresso mixture. With spoon, stir oil mixture into flour mixture; with hands, press into a dough.
3 With lightly greased hands, shape dough by rolling heaping teaspoons into 1-inch balls and place on prepared cookie sheet, 2 inches apart; press to flatten slightly. Bake until brownies have cracked slightly, 7 to 8 minutes. Transfer to wire rack to cool. Repeat with remaining dough.
4 Prepare Frosting: In microwave-safe small bowl, heat chocolate and water in microwave oven on High 45 seconds; stir until smooth. Stir in vegetable oil spread, then confectioners' sugar and vanilla. Cool frosting slightly. Dip top of each cookie in frosting. Set aside to allow frosting to dry.

EACH COOKIE: ABOUT 99 CALORIES | 1G PROTEIN | 19G CARBOHYDRATE | 3G TOTAL FAT (0.5G SATURATED) | 0.5G FIBER | 0MG CHOLESTEROL | 74MG SODIUM

WHOLE-WHEAT SUGAR COOKIES

What an effortless way to get your daily grains!

ACTIVE TIME: 1 HR · TOTAL TIME: 2 HR PLUS CHILLING

MAKES: 6 DOZEN COOKIES

1   CUP ALL-PURPOSE FLOUR

1   CUP WHITE WHOLE-WHEAT FLOUR

½   TEASPOON BAKING POWDER

¼   TEASPOON SALT

1   CUP SUGAR

½   CUP TRANS-FAT-FREE VEGETABLE OIL SPREAD (60% TO 70% OIL)

1   LARGE EGG

2   TEASPOONS VANILLA EXTRACT

1   On sheet of waxed paper, combine all-purpose and whole-wheat flours, baking powder, and salt.

2   In large bowl, with mixer on low speed, beat sugar and vegetable oil spread until blended. Increase speed to high; beat until light and creamy, about 3 minutes, occasionally scraping down bowl with rubber spatula. Reduce speed to low; beat in egg and vanilla, then beat in flour mixture just until blended.

3   Divide dough in half; flatten each half into a disk. Wrap each disk with plastic wrap and refrigerate until dough is firm enough to roll, about 2 hours.

4   Preheat oven to 375°F.

5   On lightly floured surface, with floured rolling pin, roll one piece of dough ⅛ inch thick. With 2-inch cookie cutters, cut out as many cookies as possible; wrap and refrigerate trimmings. With lightly floured spatula, place cookies, 1 inch apart, on ungreased cookie sheet.

6   Bake cookies until lightly browned, 10 to 12 minutes. With thin metal spatula, transfer cookies to wire rack to cool. Repeat with remaining dough and trimmings. Store cookies in tightly covered containers up to 1 week or freeze up to 3 months.

EACH COOKIE: ABOUT 35 CALORIES | 1G PROTEIN | 5G CARBOHYDRATE | 1G TOTAL FAT (0G SATURATED) | 0G FIBER | 3MG CHOLESTEROL | 20MG SODIUM

BERRY-ORANGE LINZER JEWELS

Prepare Whole-Wheat Sugar Cookies as directed, but in steps 1 and 2, add **1 teaspoon grated orange peel** with egg and vanilla. Chill, roll, and cut as above in steps 3 and 4, but use scalloped 2-inch square or round cookie cutter. Use small star-shaped or other decorative cutter to cut out centers of half the cookies. Bake and cool as above in step 5. When cookies are cool, if you like, sprinkle **confectioners' sugar** through sieve over cookies with cutout centers. From **¼ cup seedless red raspberry jam**, spread scant ½ teaspoon jam on each whole cookie; top with cookie with cutout center. Makes about 3 dozen.

EACH COOKIE: ABOUT 70 CALORIES │ 2G PROTEIN │ 10G CARBOHYDRATE │ 2G TOTAL FAT (0G SATURATED) │ 0G FIBER │ 6MG CHOLESTEROL │ 5MG SODIUM

WHOLE-WHEAT FLOUR THAT'S WHITE

Struggling to eat the recommended three servings of whole grains a day because you don't like the flavor and texture of whole wheat? Try baking with white whole-wheat flour instead like we do in Whole-Wheat Sugar Cookies. King Arthur Flour makes it, among other brands. Milled from an albino variety of wheat, it's as healthy as traditional whole wheat—with the same levels of fiber, nutrients, and minerals—but it lacks the heartier taste and grainy heft. It's ideal for all whole-grain recipes and can be substituted for up to half of the all-purpose flour in many other recipes without substantially changing the taste.

CHOCOLATE-CHIP OATMEAL DROPS

Though the chocolate-chip cookie, America's most popular cookie, was invented in 1930, it wasn't until 1939 that Nestlé introduced packaged chocolate chips. In the early 1940s, many variations on this cookie evolved, including this GH classic featuring oats.

ACTIVE TIME: 30 MIN · **TOTAL TIME:** 1 HR 35 MIN

MAKES: 5½ DOZEN COOKIES

---

1   CUP QUICK-COOKING OR OLD-FASHIONED OATS

¾   CUP ALL-PURPOSE FLOUR

½   TEASPOON BAKING SODA

¼   TEASPOON GROUND CINNAMON

⅔   CUP SUGAR

½   CUP BUTTER OR MARGARINE (1 STICK), SOFTENED

1   LARGE EGG

1   TEASPOON VANILLA EXTRACT

1   PACKAGE (6 OUNCES) SEMISWEET-CHOCOLATE CHIPS (1 CUP)

⅓   CUP WALNUTS, FINELY CHOPPED (OPTIONAL)

1   Preheat oven to 350°F. Grease large cookie sheet.

2   Place oats in blender or food processor with knife blade attached and pulse until finely ground. Transfer oats to medium bowl; stir in flour, baking soda, and cinnamon.

3   In small bowl, with mixer at medium speed, beat sugar with butter until creamy. At low speed, beat in egg and vanilla (mixture may look curdled). Add flour mixture and beat until just blended, occasionally scraping down bowl with rubber spatula. With spoon, stir in chocolate chips and nuts, if using.

4   Drop dough by rounded teaspoons, 1 inch apart, on prepared cookie sheet. Bake cookies until lightly browned around the edges, 12 to 14 minutes. Transfer cookies to wire rack to cool completely. Repeat with remaining dough. Repeat with remaining dough. Store cookies in tightly covered container up to 1 week.

EACH COOKIE: ABOUT 120 CALORIES | 2G PROTEIN | 16G CARBOHYDRATE | 6G TOTAL FAT (2G SATURATED) | 1G FIBER | 9MG CHOLESTEROL | 60MG SODIUM

PEANUTTY YUMMY BARS

This rich peanut-butter bar with an oatmeal crust is sure to be a winner with kids twelve months of the year.

ACTIVE TIME: 30 MIN · **TOTAL TIME:** 1 HR 25 MIN

MAKES: 4 DOZEN BARS

⅓ CUP QUICK-COOKING OATS

1⅔ CUPS ALL-PURPOSE FLOUR

⅓ CUP PLUS 1½ CUPS PACKED LIGHT BROWN SUGAR

½ CUP BUTTER OR MARGARINE (1 STICK), SOFTENED

3 TABLESPOONS PLUS ⅓ CUP CHUNKY PEANUT BUTTER

3 LARGE EGGS

4½ TEASPOONS LIGHT (MILD) MOLASSES

2½ TEASPOONS BAKING POWDER

½ TEASPOON SALT

1 CUP SALTED COCKTAIL PEANUTS, CHOPPED

1 PACKAGE (6 OUNCES) SEMISWEET-CHOCOLATE PIECES (1 CUP)

CONFECTIONERS' SUGAR FOR GARNISH

1 Preheat oven to 350°F. Grease 13" by 9" metal baking pan.

2 Prepare crust: In large bowl, with mixer at low speed, beat oats, 1 cup flour, ⅓ cup brown sugar, 4 tablespoons butter, and 3 tablespoons peanut butter until blended. Pat dough evenly into pan and bake 15 minutes.

3 Meanwhile, in large bowl, with mixer at medium speed, beat eggs, molasses, remaining 1½ cups brown sugar, remaining ⅓ cup peanut butter, and remaining 4 tablespoons butter until well combined, constantly scraping down bowl with rubber spatula. Reduce speed to low; add baking powder, salt, and remaining ⅔ cup flour and beat until blended, occasionally scraping down bowl. With spoon, stir in peanuts and chocolate pieces.

4 Spread mixture evenly over hot crust. Bake until golden, about 40 minutes longer. Cool completely in pan on wire rack. Sprinkle with confectioners' sugar if you like. When cool, cut lengthwise into 4 strips, then cut each strip crosswise into 12 pieces.

EACH BAR: ABOUT 125 CALORIES | 3G PROTEIN | 16G CARBOHYDRATE | 6G TOTAL FAT (1G SATURATED) | 4G FIBER | 13MG CHOLESTEROL | 100MG SODIUM

FLAPJACKS

Flapjacks, nothing like an American pancake, are a British treat made from oats and baked in a flat tin. Traditionally, they're thick and biscuit-like, but this version is more like a crisp, crumbly cookie.

ACTIVE TIME: 15 MIN · **TOTAL TIME:** 31 MIN PLUS COOLING
MAKES: 16 COOKIES

---

5 TABLESPOONS BUTTER OR MARGARINE	1⅓ CUPS OLD-FASHIONED OATS
⅓ CUP PACKED BROWN SUGAR	PINCH SALT

1 Preheat oven to 350°F. Grease 8-inch round cake pan. Line pan with foil; grease foil.

2 In 2-quart saucepan, melt butter over low heat. Add brown sugar and cook until well blended, about 1 minute, stirring. Remove saucepan from heat; stir in oats and salt until evenly mixed.

3 Sprinkle oat mixture into cake pan; with spatula, firmly pat down mixture. Bake until golden, 16 to 18 minutes. Let cool in pan on wire rack 10 minutes. Lift cookie out of pan with foil and place on cutting board. While still warm, cut into 16 wedges. Transfer flapjacks with foil to wire rack to cool completely. Store cookies in single layer in tightly covered container up to 1 week or freeze up to 3 months.

EACH COOKIE: ABOUT 100 CALORIES | 2G PROTEIN | 13G CARBOHYDRATE | 5G TOTAL FAT (3G SATURATED) | 1G FIBER | 10MG CHOLESTEROL | 50MG SODIUM

NANTUCKET INDIAN PUDDING

This is a baked cornmeal and molasses pudding adapted by the early English settlers in New England and later known as "hasty pudding" by the colonists.

ACTIVE TIME: 30 MIN · **TOTAL TIME:** 2 HR 30 MIN PLUS COOLING
MAKES: 8 SERVINGS

⅔ CUP YELLOW CORNMEAL

4 CUPS MILK

½ CUP LIGHT (MILD) MOLASSES

4 TABLESPOONS BUTTER OR MARGARINE, CUT UP

¼ CUP SUGAR

1 TEASPOON GROUND GINGER

1 TEASPOON GROUND CINNAMON

½ TEASPOON SALT

¼ TEASPOON GROUND NUTMEG

VANILLA ICE CREAM OR WHIPPED CREAM (OPTIONAL)

1 Preheat oven to 350°F. Grease shallow 1½-quart glass or baking dish.

2 In small bowl, combine cornmeal and 1 cup milk. In 4-quart saucepan, heat remaining 3 cups milk to boiling over high heat. Stir in cornmeal mixture; heat to boiling. Reduce heat to low and cook, stirring often to avoid lumps, 20 minutes. (Mixture will be very thick.) Remove saucepan from heat; stir in molasses, butter, sugar, ginger, cinnamon, salt, and nutmeg until blended.

4 Pour batter evenly into prepared baking dish. Place dish in roasting pan; place on oven rack. Carefully pour **boiling water** into roasting pan to come halfway up side of baking dish. Cover with foil and bake pudding 1 hour. Remove foil and bake pudding until lightly browned and just set, about 1 hour longer.

5 Carefully remove baking dish from water. Cool pudding in dish on wire rack 30 minutes. Serve pudding warm with vanilla ice cream, if desired.

TIP You can mix the batter and pour it into the baking dish up to 2 hours before baking. Then pop it into the oven and let it cook, maintenance-free.

EACH SERVING: ABOUT 245 CALORIES | 5G PROTEIN | 34G CARBOHYDRATE | 10G TOTAL FAT (4G SATURATED) | 1G FIBER | 17MG CHOLESTEROL | 275MG SODIUM

BLUEBERRY CRISP

What a great combination—the crunchy brown sugar goodness of oat-meal and the plump blueberry taste of summer.

ACTIVE TIME: 15 MIN · TOTAL TIME: 50 MIN

MAKES: 8 SERVINGS

⅓ CUP GRANULATED SUGAR

2 TABLESPOONS CORNSTARCH

3 PINTS BLUEBERRIES (7½ CUPS)

1 TABLESPOON FRESH LEMON JUICE

¾ CUP OLD-FASHIONED OR QUICK-COOKING OATS

½ CUP PACKED BROWN SUGAR

⅓ CUP ALL-PURPOSE FLOUR

½ TEASPOON GROUND CINNAMON

4 TABLESPOONS COLD BUTTER OR MARGARINE, CUT UP

1 In large bowl, stir granulated sugar and cornstarch until blended. Add blueberries and lemon juice; toss to coat. Pour blueberry mixture into shallow 2½-quart glass or ceramic baking dish; spread evenly.

2 In same bowl, combine oats, brown sugar, flour, and cinnamon. With fingertips, work in butter until coarse crumbs form. Press crumb mixture together and sprinkle on top of blueberry mixture.

3 Bake crisp until top is browned and fruit is bubbling at edge, 35 to 40 minutes. Cool on wire rack 1 hour to serve warm, or cool completely to serve later.

EACH SERVING: ABOUT 270 CALORIES | 3G PROTEIN | 52G CARBOHYDRATE | 7G TOTAL FAT (4G SATURATED) | 5G FIBER | 16MG CHOLESTEROL | 75MG SODIUM

VEGETARIAN

Penne with Green Beans and Basil (page 239)

INTRODUCTION

For generations, the mealtime mantra of mothers across America has been "Eat your vegetables!" Well, as usual, mother is right. So too are the health professionals who, for decades, have advocated a healthy diet of less meat and more fruits, vegetables, whole grains, lowfat or fat-free dairy products to help us live longer and better.

Americans have finally gotten the message. Tens of millions of people in the U.S. today have changed their eating habits to include more produce and grains and fewer animal products.

While you may not consider yourself a vegetarian, you probably do, in fact, eat a few meatless meals each week. Pancakes for brunch, yogurt and fruit for breakfast, an after-movie pizza with mushrooms and peppers, a quick lunch of vegetable-and-bean burritos, comforting mac-and-cheese casserole or take-out vegetable lo mein for dinner are all satisfying and nutritious fare, yet free of meat, fish, or poultry.

TYPES OF VEGETARIANS

Vegetarians choose to eliminate animal products from their diets for any number of reasons—ethical, environmental, economic, or religious. But according to a recent Gallup Poll, the majority of people who choose to go meatless do so for health reasons. Vegetarians usually fall into one of these groups:

- The vegan, or total vegetarian, diet includes only foods from plant sources: fruits, vegetables, legumes (dried beans and peas), whole grains, seeds, and nuts.

- The lactovegetarian diet includes plant foods plus cheese and other dairy products.

- The ovo-lactovegetarian diet is the same as the lactovegetarian, but also includes eggs.

- The semivegetarian diet, which is frequently favored by those who are just easing into a vegetarian lifestyle or who want to add more meatless meals to their diet, does not include red meat but does include chicken and fish along with plant foods, dairy products, and eggs.

EATING VEGETARIAN

Good Housekeeping does not advocate a vegetarian diet in this book. Rather, we assembled a collection of our favorite healthful, flavor-packed recipes because, like many of our readers, you want to add more nutritious meatless dishes to your family's meals. Perhaps you have a member of your family who is a vegetarian, or your child has just announced that he or she wants to give up all animal foods. Or you simply want to introduce more vegetables, fruits, whole grains, legumes, and lowfat products into your meals. In these pages, you'll find a veritable garden of tasty, appealing, meat-free dishes to please everyone at your table.

Like life, variety is the key to delicious vegetarian meals. Experiment with the many available grains, legumes, fruits, and vegetables and combine them with several of the vast array of herbs and spices to marry flavors and add punch. You'll discover that the possibilities are endless.

NUTRITIONAL GUIDELINES

The most important consideration for a nutritionally sound vegetarian diet is to consume a variety of foods and in sufficient amounts to meet the caloric and nutritional needs of each individual. If you are incorporating more meatless meals into your family's menus and fewer animal products, there are several nutrients that you need to focus on to be sure everyone is getting an adequate amount, particularly youngsters:

PROTEIN. You don't need to consume meat, fish, or poultry to have enough protein in your diet. Protein needs can easily be met by eating a variety of plant foods. It is not necessary to include specific combinations of foods (such as rice and beans) in the same meal. A mixture of proteins from grains, legumes, seeds, and vegetables eaten throughout the day will provide enough of all the amino acids, the building blocks of protein, your body needs.
Some sources of protein for vegetarians: legumes (dried peas and beans), seeds, nuts and nut butters, soy protein, cheese, milk and yogurt, eggs, grains, and some vegetables.

IRON. An integral part of hemoglobin which carries oxygen in the blood. Vegetarians who eliminate all meat, poultry and seafood (the primary sources of iron) may be prone to an iron deficiency.

Some sources of iron for vegetarians: legumes, dark green leafy vegetables (except spinach), enriched and whole-grain breads and cereals, nuts, and seeds. Cooking foods in cast-iron cookware can also boost their iron content.

CALCIUM: The major building material for building bones and teeth.
Some sources of calcium for vegetarians: milk and milk products, dark green leafy vegetables (except spinach), calcium-fortified soy products, fortified juices and cereals.

ZINC. Essential for growth and development and proper functioning of the immune system.
Some sources of zinc for vegetarians: legumes, wheat germ, whole grains, nuts, pumpkin and sunflower seeds, milk and milk products.

VITAMIN B-12. Essential for formation of red blood cells and proper functioning of the nervous system. Animal products are the only natural food source of this vitamin.
Some sources of B-12 for vegetarians: milk and milk products, eggs, fortified foods and supplements.

THE VEGETARIAN FOOD GROUPS

Adopting a healthful vegetarian or semivegetarian diet is as simple as choosing a variety of different foods daily from among each of the following seven categories. Try any of the suggested recipes.

- **BREADS AND GRAINS.** Choose whole or unrefined grain products whenever possible or use fortified or enriched cereals.

- **VEGETABLES AND FRUITS.** Always try to use the freshest produce you can get. When fresh is not available, opt first for frozen, then canned. Go for the deepest colors for the highest nutritional content: Most dark green leafy vegetables contain calcium and iron. Deep yellow and orange fruits and vegetables are good sources of beta carotene. Veggies and fruits are also rich in potassium, fiber, folic acid, and vitamin C.

- **BEANS, PEAS, SOY, AND OTHER LEGUMES.** Use beans, peas, and other legumes as a main dish or part of a meal often. They are excellent sources of protein, and also contribute zinc, calcium, and iron.

- **DAIRY PRODUCTS OR CALCIUM-RICH SUBSTITUTES.** If using dairy products, select reduced-fat, lowfat, or fat-free varieties whenever possible.

- **NUTS AND SEEDS.** Eat a variety of nuts and seeds as a snack, on fruit or vegetable salads, or in main dishes. They are a source of protein, zinc, and iron. Don't overdo—they are high in calories.

- **FATS:** Essential in any diet, but ideally, most fats should come from whole plant foods such as nuts, seeds, and avocado. Moderate amounts of plant oils such as olive, canola, and sesame are good choices for cooking or for salad dressings.

- **EGGS.** Because of their high cholesterol content, you may want to limit eggs to three or four a week or consider using commercial egg substitutes, which contain no cholesterol and can be used freely as a protein source.

PLANNING MEALS

The key to serving delicious vegetarian meals everyone will enjoy is to create dishes that include some of each food group and have a variety of tastes, colors, and textures.

If you're just beginning on the path to more meatless meals, you may find some resistance from the carnivores in your family. Understand that it will take some time for those who are used to thinking of vegetables as side dishes to see them as the main event. Ask everyone to contribute a list of his or her favorite foods. Many dishes that contain meat can be easily modified to make them vegetarian. Chili, stir-fries, and pasta dishes naturally lend themselves to meatless recipes.

In general, plan your meals around one main dish that is vegetable-, bean-, or grain-based. Then add the appropriate go-withs. For example, if your main course is a vegetable tart, accompany it with potato, grain, or corn for a nutritionally complete meal. With a main course of pasta, add a salad and whole-grain bread. A bean-and-vegetable casserole calls for a side of rice pilaf or other grain.

TIPS FOR BUSY PEOPLE

Most of us spend our days on the go: at work, shuttling kids back and forth, shopping, doing chores. Preparing good, wholesome vegetarian meals for your family shouldn't be a burden. Here are a few shortcuts for healthier cooking.

• Plan menus, make lists, then shop.

• Make sure there are plenty of good-quality ingredients on hand for quick and/or last-minute meals such as pastas, canned beans and tomatoes, frozen vegetables, and cheeses.

• Make two big casseroles or a double-batch of a one-pot dish that will feed your family for two nights. Serve with a salad and whole-grain bread.

• On the weekend, do some basic prep work of foods that can be incorporated into meals during the week: Cook up some rice or other grain, make pasta sauce, or cook a pot of beans.

• Get everyone involved in planning, shopping, and preparing meals. That way, they'll be more likely to eat and enjoy the meal. This approach is also a great way to get children started on healthy eating habits.

SOUPS
& STEWS

What is it about a steaming pot of soup or a hearty stew, slowly simmering on the stove and filling the house with enticing aromas, that instinctively reminds us of childhood? Possibly it's because carefully prepared soups and stews have come to symbolize the comforts of home. They warm us when the weather turns cold and console us after a trying day.

For busy cooks with families on the go, soups and stews are a godsend. They need minimal prep work, usually just chopping vegetables and measuring the required amounts of liquid, grains, herbs, and spices that go into the pot. Then, depending on the recipe, the whole lot can simmer slowly or quickly on the stove, in the oven, or in a slow cooker. What's more, many taste even better the next day, which means leftovers are sure to be satisfying.

On days when schedules dictate that everyone has to eat dinner at a different time, it's great to know there's a warm pot of something nutritious and flavorful ready for each person to tuck into. And when you find yourself with a few more hungry mouths to feed than you'd counted on, just add some more veggies or beans to the pot or to the accompanying salad, heat up a hearty loaf of bread, and call the gang in for dinner.

Curried Sweet-Potato and Lentil Soup (page 192)

BLACK BEAN SOUP

For extra south-of-the-border flavor, serve this shortcut soup with thinly sliced pickled jalapeño peppers and crumbled *queso fresco*.

ACTIVE TIME: 10 MIN · **TOTAL TIME:** 30 MIN
MAKES: 6½ CUPS OR 4 MAIN-DISH SERVINGS

1	TABLESPOON VEGETABLE OIL	2	CANS (16 TO 19 OUNCES EACH) BLACK BEANS, RINSED AND DRAINED
1	MEDIUM ONION, FINELY CHOPPED		
2	GARLIC CLOVES, CRUSHED WITH GARLIC PRESS	1	CAN (14½ OUNCES) VEGETABLE BROTH (1¾ CUPS)
2	TEASPOONS CHILI POWDER	2	CUPS WATER
1	TEASPOON GROUND CUMIN	½	CUP LOOSELY PACKED FRESH CILANTRO LEAVES, CHOPPED
¼	TEASPOON CRUSHED RED PEPPER		
			LIME WEDGES

1 In 3-quart saucepan, heat oil over medium heat until hot. Add onion and cook until tender, about 5 minutes. Stir in garlic, chili powder, cumin, and crushed red pepper; cook 30 seconds. Stir in beans, broth, and water; heat to boiling over high heat. Reduce heat to low; simmer, uncovered, 15 minutes.

2 Spoon half of mixture into blender; cover, with center part of cover removed to let steam escape, and puree until almost smooth. Pour into medium bowl. Repeat with remaining mixture.

3 Return soup to saucepan; heat through. Sprinkle with cilantro and serve with lime wedges.

EACH SERVING: ABOUT 265 CALORIES | 22G PROTEIN | 46G CARBOHYDRATE | 6G TOTAL FAT (1G SATURATED) | 0MG CHOLESTEROL | 965MG SODIUM

STOVETOP CHILI

A quick weeknight chili that's packed with buttery black soybeans, tender-crisp green beans, and melt-in-your-mouth sweet potatoes. Serve with a chunk of warm corn bread.

ACTIVE TIME: 20 MIN · **TOTAL TIME:** 55 MIN

MAKES: 11 CUPS OR 6 MAIN-DISH SERVINGS

1 TABLESPOON OLIVE OIL

1 MEDIUM ONION, CHOPPED

2 TABLESPOONS CHILI POWDER

1 TEASPOON GROUND CUMIN

1 TEASPOON GROUND CORIANDER

2 GARLIC CLOVES, CRUSHED WITH GARLIC PRESS

1 JALAPEÑO CHILE, SEEDED AND MINCED

1 CAN (28 OUNCES) WHOLE TOMATOES

½ POUND GREEN BEANS, TRIMMED AND EACH CUT CROSSWISE IN HALF

3 MEDIUM SWEET POTATOES (ABOUT 1½ POUNDS), PEELED AND CUT INTO 1½-INCH PIECES

1 TEASPOON SUGAR

1 TEASPOON SALT

2 CUPS WATER

2 CANS (15 OUNCES) BLACK SOYBEANS OR BLACK BEANS, RINSED AND DRAINED

SOUR CREAM (OPTIONAL)

1 In nonstick 5- to 6-quart Dutch oven, heat oil over medium heat until hot. Add onion and cook, stirring occasionally, until tender, about 10 minutes. Add chili powder, cumin, coriander, garlic, and jalapeño; cook, stirring, 1 minute.

2 Add tomatoes with their juice, green beans, sweet potatoes, sugar, salt, and water; heat to boiling over medium-high heat, breaking up tomatoes with side of spoon. Reduce heat to low; cover and simmer, stirring occasionally, until sweet potatoes are tender, about 25 minutes.

3 Add soybeans and heat through, about 2 minutes longer. Serve with sour cream, if you like.

EACH SERVING: ABOUT 275 CALORIES | 14G PROTEIN | 45G CARBOHYDRATE | 5G TOTAL FAT (1G SATURATED) | 0MG CHOLESTEROL | 635MG SODIUM

MEATLESS CHILI

So thick and hearty, you'll never miss the meat. Serve by the bowlful, with warm tortillas.

ACTIVE TIME: 30 MIN · **TOTAL TIME**: 2 HR PLUS SOAKING BEANS
MAKES: 12½ CUPS OR 6 MAIN-DISH SERVINGS

1½ POUNDS MIXED DRY BEANS, SUCH AS RED KIDNEY, WHITE KIDNEY (CANNELLINI), AND BLACK (3 CUPS TOTAL)

1 TABLESPOON VEGETABLE OIL

3 MEDIUM CARROTS, PEELED AND CUT CROSSWISE INTO ¼-INCH-THICK SLICES

2 MEDIUM ONIONS, FINELY CHOPPED

1 STALK CELERY, FINELY CHOPPED

1 MEDIUM RED PEPPER, FINELY CHOPPED

3 GARLIC CLOVES, MINCED

1 JALAPEÑO CHILE, MINCED

2 TEASPOONS GROUND CUMIN

½ TEASPOON GROUND CORIANDER

1 CAN (28 OUNCES) TOMATOES IN PUREE

1 CHIPOTLE CHILE IN ADOBO, MINCED

2 TEASPOONS SALT

¼ TEASPOON DRIED OREGANO

1 PACKAGE (10 OUNCES) FROZEN WHOLE-KERNEL CORN

1¼ CUPS LOOSELY PACKED FRESH CILANTRO LEAVES AND STEMS, CHOPPED

1 Place beans in colander and pick through, discarding any stones or debris. Rinse beans with cold running water and drain. Transfer beans to large bowl. Add enough **water** to cover by 2 inches. Cover and let stand at room temperature overnight. (Or, in 5-quart Dutch oven or saucepot, combine beans and enough water to cover by 2 inches; heat to boiling over high heat. Boil 2 minutes. Remove from heat; cover and let stand 1 hour.) Drain and rinse beans.

2 Preheat oven to 375°F. In 5-quart Dutch oven, combine beans and 8 cups water; heat to boiling over high heat. Cover and bake, stirring occasionally, until beans are tender, about 1 hour. Drain beans and return to Dutch oven.

3 Meanwhile, in 10-inch skillet, heat vegetable oil over medium heat until hot. Add carrots, onions, celery, and red pepper; cook, stirring frequently, until vegetables are tender, about 10 minutes. Stir in garlic, jalapeño, cumin, and coriander; cook, stirring, 30 seconds. Stir in tomatoes with their puree, chipotle chile, salt, and oregano, breaking up tomatoes with side of spoon; heat to boiling over high heat. Reduce heat to low; simmer, uncovered, 10 minutes.

4 Stir tomato mixture, corn, and **2 cups water** into beans; cover and bake 30 minutes longer. Remove Dutch oven from oven; stir in cilantro.

EACH SERVING: ABOUT 360 CALORIES | 20G PROTEIN | 66G CARBOHYDRATE | 4G TOTAL FAT (0G SATURATED) | 0MG CHOLESTEROL | 1,195MG SODIUM

VEGETARIAN CHILI

Black soybeans, sold in convenient cans, have a better texture and flavor than the usual beige variety and add extra oomph to winter chili.

ACTIVE TIME: 30 MIN · **TOTAL TIME:** 1 HR 20 MIN

MAKES: 10 CUPS OR 6 MAIN-DISH SERVINGS

---

4   TEASPOONS OLIVE OIL

1   MEDIUM BUTTERNUT SQUASH (ABOUT 2 POUNDS), PEELED AND CUT INTO ¾-INCH PIECES

3   MEDIUM CARROTS, PEELED AND CUT INTO ¼-INCH PIECES

1   LARGE ONION (12 OUNCES), CHOPPED

2   TABLESPOONS CHILI POWDER

2   GARLIC CLOVES, CRUSHED WITH GARLIC PRESS

1   CAN (28 OUNCES) PLUM TOMATOES

3   JALAPEÑO CHILES, SEEDED AND MINCED

1   CUP VEGETABLE BROTH

1   TABLESPOON SUGAR

½   TEASPOON SALT

2   CANS (15 OUNCES EACH) BLACK SOYBEANS, RINSED AND DRAINED

1   CUP LIGHTLY PACKED FRESH CILANTRO LEAVES, CHOPPED

PLAIN NONFAT YOGURT (OPTIONAL)

---

1 In nonstick 5-quart Dutch oven or saucepot, heat 2 teaspoons oil over medium-high heat until hot. Add squash and cook, stirring occasionally, until golden, 8 to 10 minutes. Transfer squash to bowl; set aside.

2 In same Dutch oven, heat remaining 2 teaspoons oil. Add carrots and onion and cook, stirring occasionally, until golden, about 10 minutes. Stir in chili powder and garlic; cook, stirring, 1 minute longer.

3 Add tomatoes with their juice, jalapeños, broth, sugar, and salt; heat to boiling over medium-high heat, stirring to break up tomatoes with side of spoon. Stir in soybeans and squash; heat to boiling over medium-high heat. Reduce heat to low; cover and simmer until squash is tender, about 30 minutes.

4 Remove Dutch oven from heat; stir in cilantro. Serve chili with yogurt, if you like.

EACH SERVING: ABOUT 265 CALORIES | 15G PROTEIN | 40G CARBOHYDRATE | 6G TOTAL FAT (1G SATURATED) | 0MG CHOLESTEROL | 480MG SODIUM

WHITE BEAN AND TOMATILLO CHILI

A spicy vegetarian chili with fresh tomatillos—tart, green, tomatolike fruits (with papery husks) that are staples in Southwestern cuisine. For this recipe, we used canned, not dry, white kidney beans. Serve with warm tortillas and a dollop of plain yogurt.

ACTIVE TIME: 5 MIN · **TOTAL TIME:** 30 MIN
MAKES: 9 CUPS OR 4 MAIN-DISH SERVINGS

2   TABLESPOONS OLIVE OIL

3   GARLIC CLOVES, CRUSHED WITH GARLIC PRESS

1   SMALL ONION, CUT IN HALF AND THINLY SLICED

1   JALAPEÑO CHILE, SEEDED AND MINCED

1   TEASPOON GROUND CUMIN

1   POUND TOMATILLOS, HUSKED, RINSED, AND COARSELY CHOPPED

1¼ TEASPOONS SALT

½   TEASPOON SUGAR

1   CAN (14½ OUNCES) VEGETABLE BROTH (1¾ CUPS)

1   CAN (4 OUNCES) CHOPPED MILD GREEN CHILES, DRAINED

1   CUP WATER

2   CANS (15 TO 19 OUNCES EACH) WHITE KIDNEY BEANS (CANNELLINI), RINSED, DRAINED, AND COARSELY MASHED

1   CUP LOOSELY PACKED FRESH CILANTRO LEAVES, CHOPPED

1 In nonstick 10-inch skillet, heat oil over medium heat until hot. Add garlic, onion, jalapeño, and cumin, and cook, stirring often, until light golden, 7 to 10 minutes.

2 Meanwhile, in 5- to 6-quart saucepot, combine tomatillos, salt, sugar, broth, green chiles, and water; heat to boiling over high heat. Reduce heat to low. Stir in onion mixture; cover and simmer 15 minutes.

3 Stir in beans and cilantro; heat through.

EACH SERVING: ABOUT 335 CALORIES | 13G PROTEIN | 50G CARBOHYDRATE | 10G TOTAL FAT (1G SATURATED) | 0MG CHOLESTEROL | 1,610MG SODIUM

CRANBERRY BEAN SOUP

A Chilean-style soup made with butternut squash, tomatoes, fresh basil, and jalapeño. Cranberry beans have large, knobby beige pods speckled with red; the beans inside are cream-colored with red streaks and have a nutlike taste.

ACTIVE TIME: 40 MIN · **TOTAL TIME:** 1 HR 25 MIN
MAKES: 9 CUPS OR 4 MAIN-DISH SERVINGS

4 TEASPOONS OLIVE OIL	2 MEDIUM TOMATOES, CHOPPED
1 MEDIUM BUTTERNUT SQUASH (2 POUNDS), PEELED AND CUT INTO ¾-INCH PIECES	1½ POUNDS FRESH CRANBERRY BEANS, SHELLED (ABOUT 2 CUPS BEANS)
1 MEDIUM ONION, CHOPPED	1 TEASPOON SALT
2 GARLIC CLOVES, MINCED	1 TEASPOON SUGAR
1 JALAPEÑO CHILE, SEEDED AND MINCED	1¼ CUPS LOOSELY PACKED FRESH BASIL LEAVES, CHOPPED
1 TEASPOON GROUND CUMIN	2¼ CUPS WATER
1 CAN (14½ OUNCES) VEGETABLE BROTH (1¾ CUPS)	2 CUPS CORN KERNELS CUT FROM COBS (ABOUT 4 MEDIUM EARS)

1 In 5-quart Dutch oven, heat 2 teaspoons oil over medium heat until hot. Add squash and onion and cook, stirring occasionally, until golden, about 10 minutes. Transfer squash mixture to bowl.

2 In same Dutch oven, heat remaining 2 teaspoons olive oil over medium heat; add garlic, jalapeño, and cumin and cook, stirring, 1 minute. Stir in broth, tomatoes, beans, salt, sugar, squash mixture, ¼ cup basil, and water; heat to boiling over high heat. Reduce heat to low; cover and simmer, stirring occasionally, until beans are tender, about 30 minutes.

3 Stir in corn; heat to boiling over high heat. Reduce heat to low; cover and simmer 5 minutes longer. Stir in remaining 1 cup chopped basil.

EACH SERVING: ABOUT 353 CALORIES | 15G PROTEIN | 68G CARBOHYDRATE | 7G TOTAL FAT (1G SATURATED) | 0MG CHOLESTEROL | 854MG SODIUM

CARIBBEAN BLACK BEAN SOUP

Our new take on black bean soup is made with allspice, thyme, and brown sugar for authentic island flair.

ACTIVE TIME: 45 MIN · **TOTAL TIME:** 3 HR 15 MIN PLUS SOAKING BEANS

MAKES: 13 CUPS OR 6 MAIN-DISH SERVINGS

1 POUND DRY BLACK BEANS	8 CUPS WATER
2 TABLESPOONS VEGETABLE OIL	2 MEDIUM SWEET POTATOES (ABOUT 12 OUNCES EACH), PEELED AND CUT INTO ¾-INCH PIECES
2 MEDIUM RED ONIONS, CHOPPED	
4 JALAPEÑO CHILES, SEEDED AND MINCED	1 TABLESPOON DARK BROWN SUGAR
2 TABLESPOONS MINCED, PEELED FRESH GINGER	2 TEASPOONS SALT
	1 BUNCH GREEN ONIONS, TRIMMED AND THINLY SLICED
4 GARLIC CLOVES, MINCED	1 CUP LIGHTLY PACKED FRESH CILANTRO LEAVES, CHOPPED
½ TEASPOON GROUND ALLSPICE	
½ TEASPOON DRIED THYME	2 LIMES, CUT INTO WEDGES (OPTIONAL)

1 Place beans in colander and pick through, discarding any stones or debris. Rinse beans with cold running water and drain. Transfer beans to large bowl. Add enough **water** to cover by 2 inches. Cover and let stand at room temperature overnight. (Or, in 5-quart Dutch oven or saucepot, combine beans and enough water to cover by 2 inches; heat to boiling over high heat. Boil 2 minutes. Remove from heat; cover and let stand 1 hour.) Drain and rinse beans.

2 In 6-quart saucepot, heat vegetable oil over medium heat until hot. Add onions and cook, stirring occasionally, until tender, about 10 minutes. Add jalapeños, ginger, garlic, allspice, and thyme and cook, stirring, 3 minutes.

3 Add beans and water; heat to boiling over high heat. Reduce heat to low; cover and simmer 1 hour 30 minutes.

4 Add sweet potatoes, brown sugar, and salt; heat to boiling over high heat. Reduce heat to low; cover and simmer until beans and sweet potatoes are tender, about 30 minutes longer.

5 Transfer 1 cup bean mixture to blender; cover, with center part of cover removed to let steam escape, and puree until smooth. Return to saucepot. Stir in green onions and cilantro. Serve with lime wedges, if you like.

EACH SERVING: ABOUT 390 CALORIES | 17G PROTEIN | 70G CARBOHYDRATE | 6G TOTAL FAT (1G SATURATED) | 0MG CHOLESTEROL | 705MG SODIUM

LENTIL AND MACARONI SOUP

This flavorful and filling soup, chock-full of vegetables, lentils, and pasta, needs only some crusty bread to become a meal. And there's enough to enjoy another day.

ACTIVE TIME: 20 MIN · **TOTAL TIME:** 1 HR 10 MIN

MAKES: 12 CUPS OR 6 MAIN-DISH SERVINGS

1   TABLESPOON OLIVE OIL

2   MEDIUM CARROTS, PEELED AND CUT INTO ¼-INCH PIECES

1   MEDIUM ONION, CHOPPED

2   GARLIC CLOVES, CRUSHED WITH GARLIC PRESS

1   CAN (14½ OUNCES) WHOLE TOMATOES IN PUREE

1   CAN (14½ OUNCES) VEGETABLE BROTH (1¾ CUPS)

¾   CUP DRY LENTILS, RINSED AND PICKED THROUGH

½   TEASPOON SALT

½   TEASPOON COARSELY GROUND BLACK PEPPER

¼   TEASPOON DRIED THYME

6   CUPS WATER

1   BUNCH SWISS CHARD (ABOUT 1 POUND), TRIMMED AND COARSELY CHOPPED

¾   CUP ELBOW MACARONI (ABOUT 3½ OUNCES)

1   CUP FRESH BASIL LEAVES, CHOPPED

FRESHLY GRATED PARMESAN CHEESE (OPTIONAL)

1 In nonstick 5- to 6-quart Dutch oven, heat oil over medium heat until hot. Add carrots, onion, and garlic and cook, stirring occasionally, until vegetables are tender and golden, about 10 minutes.

2 Add tomatoes with their puree, broth, lentils, salt, pepper, thyme, and water; heat to boiling, stirring to break up tomatoes with side of spoon. Reduce heat to low; cover and simmer until lentils are almost tender, about 20 minutes.

3 Stir in Swiss chard and macaroni; heat to boiling over medium-high heat. Reduce heat to medium; cook, uncovered, until macaroni is tender, about 10 minutes. Stir in basil. Serve with Parmesan, if you like.

EACH SERVING WITHOUT PARMESAN: ABOUT 200 CALORIES | 12G PROTEIN | 34G CARBOHYDRATE | 3G TOTAL FAT (0G SATURATED) | 0MG CHOLESTEROL | 810MG SODIUM

RED BEAN AND COLLARD GUMBO

Gumbo is traditionally made with a variety of meats and shellfish, but you're not likely to be disappointed with this all-vegetable version.

ACTIVE TIME: 20 MIN · **TOTAL TIME:** 50 MIN

MAKES: 8 CUPS OR 4 MAIN-DISH SERVINGS

¼ CUP ALL-PURPOSE FLOUR

1 TABLESPOON OLIVE OIL

1 MEDIUM ONION, THINLY SLICED

1 MEDIUM RED PEPPER, CUT INTO ½-INCH PIECES

1 LARGE STALK CELERY, THINLY SLICED

2 GARLIC CLOVES, CRUSHED WITH GARLIC PRESS

½ TEASPOON SALT

¼ TEASPOON GROUND RED PEPPER (CAYENNE)

¼ TEASPOON DRIED THYME

¼ TEASPOON GROUND ALLSPICE

1 CAN (14½ OUNCES) VEGETABLE BROTH (1¾ CUPS)

3 CUPS WATER

1 BUNCH COLLARD GREENS (ABOUT 1¼ POUNDS), TOUGH STEMS TRIMMED AND LEAVES COARSELY CHOPPED

2 CANS (15 TO 19 OUNCES EACH) SMALL RED BEANS, RINSED AND DRAINED

1 In dry nonstick 5- to 6-quart saucepot, toast flour over medium heat, stirring frequently, until pale golden, about 5 minutes. Transfer flour to medium bowl; set aside.

2 In same saucepot, heat oil over medium-high heat until hot. Add onion, red pepper, and celery and cook, stirring occasionally, until vegetables are tender-crisp, about 10 minutes. Add garlic, salt, ground red pepper, thyme, and allspice and cook, stirring, 2 minutes.

3 Whisk broth into toasted flour until blended. Stir broth mixture and water into vegetables in saucepot; heat to boiling over medium-high heat. Add collard greens, stirring until wilted; stir in beans. Heat gumbo to boiling. Reduce heat to medium-low; cover and simmer until greens are tender, about 10 minutes.

EACH SERVING: ABOUT 330 CALORIES | 17G PROTEIN | 58G CARBOHYDRATE | 6G TOTAL FAT (1G SATURATED) | 0MG CHOLESTEROL | 1,190MG SODIUM

TOMATO AND RICE SOUP

Serve this old-fashioned comfort food with crusty bread and a tossed salad for a satisfying winter meal. If you can't find either Wehani (an aromatic, reddish-brown rice that splits slightly when cooked and has a chewy texture) or black Japonica (a dark rice that tastes like a cross between basmati and wild rice), you can use long-grain brown rice.

ACTIVE TIME: 20 MIN · **TOTAL TIME:** 1 HR 10 MIN
MAKES: 7½ CUPS OR 4 MAIN-DISH SERVINGS

½ CUP WEHANI, BLACK JAPONICA, OR LONG-GRAIN BROWN RICE

1 TABLESPOON BUTTER OR MARGARINE

1 MEDIUM ONION, FINELY CHOPPED

1 MEDIUM STALK CELERY, FINELY CHOPPED

1 MEDIUM CARROT, PEELED AND CHOPPED

1 GARLIC CLOVES, CRUSHED WITH GARLIC PRESS

¼ TEASPOON DRIED THYME

1 CAN (28 OUNCES) PLUM TOMATOES IN JUICE

1 CAN (14½ OUNCES) VEGETABLE BROTH (1¾ CUPS)

½ TEASPOON SALT

¼ TEASPOON COARSELY GROUND BLACK PEPPER

1 BAY LEAF

1 CUP WATER

½ CUP LOOSELY PACKED FRESH PARSLEY LEAVES, CHOPPED

1 Prepare rice as label directs but do not add salt or butter; set rice aside.

2 Meanwhile, in 4-quart saucepan, melt butter over medium heat. Add onion, celery, and carrot and cook, stirring occasionally, until tender, about 10 minutes. Stir in garlic and thyme; cook 1 minute.

3 Add tomatoes with their juice, broth, salt, pepper, bay leaf, and water; heat to boiling over high heat, breaking up tomatoes with side of spoon. Reduce heat to medium-low and cook, covered, 30 minutes. Discard bay leaf.

4 Spoon one-third of mixture into blender; cover, with center part of cover removed to let steam escape, and puree until almost smooth. Pour into large bowl. Repeat with remaining mixture.

5 Return soup to saucepan; heat over high heat until hot. Remove saucepan from heat; add cooked rice and chopped parsley.

EACH SERVING: ABOUT 190 CALORIES | 6G PROTEIN | 32G CARBOHYDRATE | 6G TOTAL FAT (4G SATURATED) | 8MG CHOLESTEROL | 960MG SODIUM

MACARONI, CABBAGE, AND BEAN SOUP

Small pasta, such as macaroni or mini penne is perfect for this dish— you can spoon up every last morsel.

ACTIVE TIME: 5 MIN · **TOTAL TIME:** 20 MIN

MAKES: 12 CUPS OR 6 MAIN-DISH SERVINGS

1½ CUPS ELBOW MACARONI OR MINI PENNE PASTA

1 TABLESPOON OLIVE OIL

1 MEDIUM ONION, CUT IN HALF AND THINLY SLICED

½ SMALL HEAD SAVOY CABBAGE (ABOUT 1 POUND), THINLY SLICED

2 GARLIC CLOVES, CRUSHED WITH GARLIC PRESS

¼ TEASPOON GROUND BLACK PEPPER

3 CANS (14½ OUNCES EACH) VEGETABLE BROTH (5¼ CUPS)

2 CANS (15 TO 19 OUNCES EACH) WHITE KIDNEY BEANS (CANNELLINI), RINSED AND DRAINED

1½ CUPS WATER

FRESHLY GRATED PARMESAN CHEESE (OPTIONAL)

---

1 In 4-quart saucepan, cook pasta as label directs.

2 Meanwhile, in 5- to 6-quart saucepot, heat oil over medium-high heat until hot. Add onion, cabbage, garlic, and pepper; cook, stirring often, until cabbage begins to wilt, 6 to 8 minutes. Stir in broth, beans, and water; heat to boiling.

3 Drain macaroni; stir into cabbage mixture and heat through. Serve with Parmesan, if you like.

EACH SERVING: ABOUT 310 CALORIES | 14G PROTEIN | 52G CARBOHYDRATE | 5G TOTAL FAT (1G SATURATED) | 0MG CHOLESTEROL | 1,170MG SODIUM

PASTA E FAGIOLI

A fast-lane version of our favorite Italian bean soup.

ACTIVE TIME: 5 MIN · **TOTAL TIME:** 30 MIN

MAKES: 8 CUPS OR 4 MAIN-DISH SERVINGS

---

1   TABLESPOON OLIVE OIL

1   SMALL ONION, SLICED

1   LARGE STALK CELERY, SLICED

1   CAN (14½ OUNCES) VEGETABLE BROTH
    (1¾ CUPS)

2   CUPS WATER

1   CAN (15 TO 19 OUNCES) WHITE
    KIDNEY BEANS (CANNELLINI), RINSED
    AND DRAINED

1   CAN (14½ OUNCES) DICED TOMATOES

2   GARLIC CLOVES, CRUSHED
    WITH GARLIC PRESS

1   TEASPOON SUGAR

¼   TEASPOON SALT

¼   TEASPOON GROUND BLACK PEPPER

¼   CUP TUBETTINI OR DITALINI PASTA

1   PACKAGE (10 OUNCES) FROZEN
    CHOPPED SPINACH

1 In 5- to 6-quart Dutch oven, heat oil over medium heat until hot. Add onion and celery and cook, stirring occasionally, until vegetables are tender, about 10 minutes.

2 Meanwhile, in 2-quart saucepan, heat broth and water to boiling over high heat.

3 Add beans, tomatoes, garlic, sugar, salt, and pepper to onion mixture; heat to boiling over high heat. Add broth mixture and pasta; heat to boiling. Reduce heat to medium and cook 5 minutes. Add frozen spinach; cook, stirring frequently to separate spinach, 3 to 4 minutes longer.

EACH SERVING: ABOUT 220 CALORIES | 10G PROTEIN | 33G CARBOHYDRATE | 5G TOTAL FAT (1G SATURATED) | 0MG CHOLESTEROL | 1,265MG SODIUM

FRENCH ONION SOUP

Slowly cooked onions add great, caramelized flavor to this classic. If you double the recipe, be sure to cook the onions in two skillets.

ACTIVE TIME: 15 MIN · **COOK/BAKE:** 2 HR 5 MIN
MAKES: 6½ CUPS OR 4 MAIN-DISH SERVINGS

3   TABLESPOONS BUTTER OR MARGARINE

7   MEDIUM ONIONS (ABOUT 2½ POUNDS), EACH CUT LENGTHWISE IN HALF AND THINLY SLICED

¼   TEASPOON SALT

4   CUPS WATER

1   CAN (14½ OUNCES) VEGETABLE BROTH (1¾ CUPS)

¼   TEASPOON DRIED THYME

4   SLICES (½ INCH THICK) FRENCH BREAD

4   OUNCES GRUYÈRE OR SWISS CHEESE, SHREDDED (1 CUP)

1 In 12-inch skillet, melt butter over medium heat. Add onions and salt and cook, stirring occasionally, until onions are very tender and begin to caramelize, about 45 minutes. Reduce heat to low; cook, stirring often, until onions are deep golden brown, about 15 minutes longer.

2 Transfer onions to 3-quart saucepan. Add ½ cup water to skillet; heat to boiling over high heat, stirring until browned bits are loosened from bottom of pan. Pour into saucepan with onions. Add broth, thyme, and remaining water; heat to boiling over high heat. Reduce heat to low; cover and simmer until onions are very tender, about 30 minutes.

3 Meanwhile, preheat oven to 450°F. Place bread slices on small cookie sheet; bake until lightly toasted, about 5 minutes.

4 Place four 2½-cup oven-safe bowls in 15½" by 10½" jelly-roll pan. Spoon onion soup into bowls; top with toasted bread, pressing toast lightly into soup. Sprinkle toast with cheese. Bake until cheese melts and begins to brown, 12 to 15 minutes.

EACH SERVING: ABOUT 375 CALORIES | 15G PROTEIN | 38G CARBOHYDRATE | 23G TOTAL FAT (11G SATURATED) | 54MG CHOLESTEROL | 808MG SODIUM

VIETNAMESE NOODLE SOUP

This Asian-style broth is brimming with delicate rice noodles, fresh snow peas, shiitake mushrooms, and pungent herbs.

ACTIVE TIME: 20 MIN · **TOTAL TIME:** 45 MIN

MAKES: 8 CUPS OR 4 MAIN-DISH SERVINGS

- 1 LARGE LIME
- 4 OUNCES DRIED FLAT RICE NOODLES (ABOUT ¼ INCH WIDE)
- 2 CANS (14½ OUNCES EACH) VEGETABLE BROTH
- 1 SMALL BUNCH FRESH BASIL
- 2 GARLIC CLOVES, CRUSHED WITH SIDE OF CHEF'S KNIFE
- 1 PIECE (2 INCHES) PEELED FRESH GINGER, THINLY SLICED

- 2 CUPS WATER
- ¼ POUND SHIITAKE MUSHROOMS, STEMS DISCARDED AND CAPS THINLY SLICED
- 4 OUNCES SNOW PEAS, STRINGS REMOVED AND EACH POD CUT DIAGONALLY IN HALF
- 1 TABLESPOON SOY SAUCE
- 1 CUP LOOSELY PACKED FRESH CILANTRO LEAVES, CHOPPED

1 From lime, with vegetable peeler, remove peel and reserve; squeeze 1 tablespoon juice.

2 In large bowl, pour enough boiling water over rice noodles to cover; let soak until softened, 7 to 10 minutes.

3 Meanwhile, in 3-quart saucepan, combine broth, basil, garlic, ginger, lime peel, and water; heat to boiling over high heat. Reduce heat to low; cover and simmer 10 minutes. Strain broth through sieve; discard solids and return broth to saucepan.

4 Drain noodles; rinse with cold running water and drain again. Stir mushrooms, snow peas, soy sauce, and noodles into broth mixture; heat to boiling over high heat. Reduce heat to low; cover and simmer 3 minutes. Stir in cilantro and lime juice just before serving.

EACH SERVING: ABOUT 155 CALORIES | 5G PROTEIN | 30G CARBOHYDRATE | 2G TOTAL FAT (1G SATURATED) | 0MG CHOLESTEROL | 1,120MG SODIUM

CALDO VERDE

This thick green soup is a Portuguese classic made with potatoes and very thinly sliced kale.

ACTIVE TIME: 15 MIN · **TOTAL TIME:** 1 HR
MAKES: 10 CUPS OR 5 MAIN-DISH SERVINGS

---

2 TABLESPOONS OLIVE OIL

1 LARGE ONION, DICED

3 GARLIC CLOVES, MINCED

2½ POUNDS ALL-PURPOSE POTATOES (ABOUT 8 MEDIUM), PEELED AND CUT INTO 2-INCH CHUNKS

2 CANS (14½ OUNCES EACH) VEGETABLE BROTH (3½ CUPS)

3 CUPS WATER

1 TEASPOON SALT

¼ TEASPOON COARSELY GROUND BLACK PEPPER

1 POUND KALE, COARSE STEMS AND VEINS REMOVED, VERY THINLY SLICED

1 In 5-quart Dutch oven, heat olive oil over medium heat. Add onion and garlic; cook until lightly browned, about 10 minutes.

2 Add potatoes, broth, water, salt, and pepper; heat to boiling over high heat. Reduce heat to low; cover and simmer until potatoes are fork-tender, about 20 minutes.

3 With potato masher, mash potatoes in broth until potatoes are lumpy. Stir in kale; simmer, uncovered, until tender, 5 to 8 minutes.

EACH SERVING: ABOUT 250 CALORIES | 8G PROTEIN | 42G CARBOHYDRATE | 7G TOTAL FAT (1G SATURATED) | 8 MG CHOLESTEROL | 925 MG SODIUM

SWEET-POTATO AND PEANUT STEW

A tasty vegetarian dish with tomatoes, warm spices, and a touch of creamy peanut butter. Microwaving the sweet potatoes helps you finish in a flash.

ACTIVE TIME: 15 MIN · **TOTAL TIME:** 30 MIN

MAKES: 8 CUPS OR 4 MAIN-DISH SERVINGS

---

3 MEDIUM SWEET POTATOES (ABOUT 12 OUNCES EACH), WELL SCRUBBED AND CUT INTO 1½-INCH PIECES

1 TABLESPOON OLIVE OIL

2 GARLIC CLOVES, CRUSHED WITH GARLIC PRESS

1½ TEASPOONS GROUND CUMIN

½ TEASPOON SALT

¼ TEASPOON GROUND CINNAMON

⅛ TEASPOON CRUSHED RED PEPPER

2 CANS (15 TO 19 OUNCES EACH) GARBANZO BEANS, RINSED AND DRAINED

1 CAN (14½ OUNCES) VEGETABLE BROTH (1¾ CUPS)

1 CAN (14½ OUNCES) DICED TOMATOES

¼ CUP CREAMY PEANUT BUTTER

½ CUP LOOSELY PACKED FRESH CILANTRO LEAVES, CHOPPED

1 Place potatoes in 2½-quart microwave-safe dish. Cover dish and microwave on High until fork-tender, about 8 minutes.

2 Meanwhile, in 5- to 6-quart saucepot, heat oil over medium-high heat until hot. Add garlic, cumin, salt, cinnamon, and crushed red pepper and cook, stirring, 30 seconds. Stir in beans, broth, tomatoes, and peanut butter until blended; heat to boiling and cook, stirring occasionally, 1 minute.

3 Reduce heat to medium-low; add sweet potatoes and simmer, stirring occasionally, 2 minutes. Stir in cilantro.

EACH SERVING: ABOUT 585 CALORIES | 22G PROTEIN | 92G CARBOHYDRATE | 16G TOTAL FAT (2G SATURATED) | 0MG CHOLESTEROL | 1,725MG SODIUM

CURRIED SWEET-POTATO AND LENTIL SOUP

This thick and hearty soup is packed with spicy flavor. Get it going, then call a friend or spend some time with the kids while it simmers.

ACTIVE TIME: 15 MIN · **TOTAL TIME:** 1 HR 30 MIN
MAKES: 14 CUPS OR 8 MAIN-DISH SERVINGS

2   TABLESPOONS BUTTER OR MARGARINE

2   MEDIUM SWEET POTATOES (ABOUT 12 OUNCES EACH), PEELED AND CUT INTO ½-INCH CHUNKS

2   LARGE STALKS CELERY, CUT INTO ¼-INCH PIECES

1   LARGE ONION (12 OUNCES), CUT INTO ¼-INCH PIECES

1   GARLIC CLOVE, MINCED

1   TABLESPOON CURRY POWDER

1   TABLESPOON GRATED, PEELED FRESH GINGER

1   TEASPOON GROUND CUMIN

1   TEASPOON GROUND CORIANDER

1   TEASPOON SALT

⅛   TEASPOON GROUND RED PEPPER (CAYENNE)

2   CANS (14½ OUNCES EACH) VEGETABLE BROTH (3½ CUPS)

1   PACKAGE (16 OUNCES) DRY LENTILS, RINSED AND PICKED THROUGH

6   CUPS WATER

YOGURT, TOASTED COCONUT, AND LIME WEDGES (OPTIONAL)

1 In 6-quart Dutch oven, melt butter over medium heat. Add the sweet potatoes, celery, and onion and cook, stirring occasionally, until onion is tender, about 10 minutes. Add garlic, curry powder, ginger, cumin, coriander, salt, and ground red pepper; cook, stirring, 1 minute.
2 To vegetables in Dutch oven, add broth, lentils, and water; heat to boiling over high heat. Reduce heat to low; cover and simmer, stirring occasionally, until lentils are tender, 40 to 45 minutes. Serve with yogurt, toasted coconut, and lime wedges, if you like.

EACH SERVING WITHOUT YOGURT, COCONUT, AND LIME: ABOUT 295 CALORIES | 15G PROTEIN | 15G CARBOHYDRATE | 5G TOTAL FAT (2G SATURATED) | 8MG CHOLESTEROL | 646MG SODIUM

CORN AND BEAN CHOWDER

This rich and creamy-looking soup—without a drop of cream—is easy to make, taking advantage of the convenience of canned beans and frozen corn.

ACTIVE TIME: 20 MIN · **TOTAL TIME:** 55 MIN

MAKES: 12 CUPS OR 6 MAIN-DISH SERVINGS

---

2   TABLESPOONS OLIVE OIL

3   MEDIUM CARROTS, PEELED AND CUT LENGTHWISE IN HALF, THEN CROSS-WISE INTO ¼-INCH-THICK SLICES

1   LARGE STALK CELERY, CUT LENGTH-WISE IN HALF, THEN CROSSWISE INTO ¼-INCH-THICK SLICES

1   LARGE ONION (12 OUNCES), CHOPPED

1   MEDIUM RED PEPPER, CUT INTO ½-INCH PIECES

2   PACKAGES (10 OUNCES EACH) FROZEN WHOLE-KERNEL CORN

2   CUPS WATER

2   CANS (15 TO 16 OUNCES EACH) PINK BEANS, RINSED AND DRAINED

2   CANS (14½ OUNCES EACH) VEGETABLE BROTH (3½ CUPS)

2   TEASPOONS SUGAR

½   TEASPOON SALT

¼   TEASPOON DRIED THYME

⅛   TEASPOON GROUND RED PEPPER (CAYENNE)

1 In 5- to 6-quart Dutch oven or saucepot, heat oil over medium heat until hot. Add carrots, celery, onion, and red pepper, and cook, stirring frequent-ly, until vegetables are tender-crisp, about 10 minutes.

2 Meanwhile, in blender, combine 1 package frozen corn and water and puree until almost smooth.

3 To Dutch oven, add pureed corn mixture, remaining package frozen corn, beans, broth, sugar, salt, thyme, and ground red pepper; heat to boil-ing over high heat. Reduce heat to low; cover and simmer, stirring occa-sionally, 20 minutes.

TIP Cool soup slightly, and spoon into containers with tight-fitting lids. Refrigerate up to two days or freeze up to one month ahead. Reheat, without thawing, in Dutch oven, adding about two tablespoons **water** to pan to prevent scorching, or use the microwave.

EACH SERVING: ABOUT 280 CALORIES | 12G PROTEIN | 50G CARBOHYDRATE | 8G TOTAL FAT (2G SATURATED) | 0MG CHOLESTEROL | 1270MG SODIUM

INDIAN VEGETABLE STEW

A fast, fragrant skillet dish flavored with rich Indian spices, raisins, and tomatoes. Serve over rice or with pita bread and plain yogurt.

ACTIVE TIME: 30 MIN · **TOTAL TIME:** 1 HR 10 MIN

MAKES: 10 CUPS OR 5 MAIN-DISH SERVINGS

---

1   TABLESPOON OLIVE OIL

1   MEDIUM ONION, COARSELY CHOPPED

5   CUPS SMALL CAULIFLOWER FLOWERETS (ABOUT 1 SMALL HEAD CAULIFLOWER)

4   MEDIUM CARROTS, PEELED AND EACH CUT LENGTHWISE IN HALF, THEN CROSSWISE INTO ¼-INCH-THICK SLICES

1   TABLESPOON MINCED, PEELED FRESH GINGER

3   GARLIC CLOVES, CRUSHED WITH GARLIC PRESS

1   TABLESPOON CURRY POWDER

1   TEASPOON GROUND CUMIN

¾   TEASPOON SALT

⅛   TO ¼ TEASPOON GROUND RED PEPPER (CAYENNE)

2   CANS (15 TO 19 OUNCES EACH) GARBANZO BEANS, RINSED AND DRAINED

1   CAN (14½ OUNCES) DICED TOMATOES

¼   CUP GOLDEN RAISINS

½   CUP WATER

½   CUP LOOSELY PACKED FRESH CILANTRO LEAVES, CHOPPED

---

1 In nonstick 12-inch skillet, heat oil over medium heat until hot. Add onion and cook, stirring occasionally, 5 minutes. Increase heat to medium-high; add cauliflower and carrots and cook, stirring occasionally, until vegetables are lightly browned, about 10 minutes. Add the ginger, garlic, curry powder, cumin, salt, and ground red pepper; cook, stirring, 1 minute.

2 Add garbanzo beans, tomatoes with their juice, raisins, and water; heat to boiling over high heat. Reduce heat to low; cover and simmer until vegetables are tender and sauce thickens slightly, 15 to 20 minutes. Stir in cilantro and serve.

EACH SERVING: ABOUT 430 CALORIES | 18G PROTEIN | 74G CARBOHYDRATE | 10G TOTAL FAT (1G SATURATED) | 0MG CHOLESTEROL | 1,430MG SODIUM

CHILLED BUTTERMILK-VEGETABLE SOUP

The refreshing, cool flavors of summer vegetables make this chunky soup a delightful first course.

ACTIVE TIME: 20 MIN PLUS CHILLING

MAKES: 10 CUPS OR 6 MAIN-DISH SERVINGS

---

2   LIMES

1½ QUARTS BUTTERMILK (6 CUPS)

3   MEDIUM TOMATOES (ABOUT 1 POUND), SEEDED AND CUT INTO ¼-INCH PIECES

1   ENGLISH (SEEDLESS) CUCUMBER, UNPEELED AND CUT INTO ¼-INCH PIECES

1   RIPE AVOCADO, CUT INTO ¼-INCH PIECES

1   CUP LOOSELY PACKED FRESH CILANTRO LEAVES, CHOPPED

1   TEASPOON SALT

¼   TEASPOON COARSELY GROUND BLACK PEPPER

CILANTRO SPRIGS FOR GARNISH

1 From limes, grate 1 teaspoon peel and squeeze 3 tablespoons juice.

2 In large bowl, combine lime peel and juice, buttermilk, tomatoes, cucumber, avocado, cilantro, salt, and pepper; stir until blended. Cover and refrigerate at least 2 hours or up to one day. Garnish each serving with a cilantro sprig.

EACH SERVING: ABOUT 175 CALORIES | 10G PROTEIN | 18G CARBOHYDRATE | 6G TOTAL FAT (2G SATURATED) | 8MG CHOLESTEROL | 632MG SODIUM

GREEN PEA AND LETTUCE SOUP

Fresh chives add color as well as flavor to this simplified lowfat version of the delicate French classic.

ACTIVE TIME: 5 MIN · **TOTAL TIME:** 20 MIN
MAKES: 6 CUPS OR 4 MAIN-DISH SERVINGS

2 TEASPOONS BUTTER OR MARGARINE

1 MEDIUM ONION, FINELY CHOPPED

1 CAN (14½ OUNCES) VEGETABLE BROTH (1¾ CUPS)

1 PACKAGE (10 OUNCES) FROZEN PEAS

1 HEAD BOSTON LETTUCE (ABOUT 10 OUNCES), COARSELY CHOPPED

¾ TEASPOON SALT

⅛ TEASPOON GROUND BLACK PEPPER

⅛ TEASPOON DRIED THYME

1 CUP WATER

½ CUP FAT-FREE (SKIM) MILK

1 TABLESPOON FRESH LEMON JUICE

FRESH CHIVES FOR GARNISH

1 In 4-quart saucepan, melt butter over medium heat. Add onion and cook, stirring occasionally, until tender, about 5 minutes. Stir in broth, frozen peas, lettuce, salt, pepper, thyme, and water; heat to boiling over high heat. Reduce heat to low; simmer 5 minutes. Stir in milk.

2 Spoon half of pea mixture into blender; cover, with center part of cover removed to let steam escape, and puree until smooth. Pour soup into large bowl. Repeat with remaining mixture.

3 Return soup to same saucepan; heat through. Stir in lemon juice and remove from heat. Transfer soup to serving bowl; garnish with chives.

EACH SERVING: ABOUT 120 CALORIES | 8G PROTEIN | 17G CARBOHYDRATE | 4G TOTAL FAT (2G SATURATED) | 6MG CHOLESTEROL | 829MG SODIUM

MUSHROOM-BARLEY MISO SOUP

Never boil miso; high heat destroys its delicate flavor and nutrients.

ACTIVE TIME: 20 MIN · **TOTAL TIME:** 1 HR 20 MIN
MAKES: 10 CUPS OR 6 MAIN-DISH SERVINGS

1	PACKAGE (1 OUNCE) DRIED SHIITAKE MUSHROOMS	½	CUP PEARL BARLEY
1	TABLESPOON OLIVE OIL	½	TEASPOON SALT
3	MEDIUM CARROTS, PEELED AND CUT INTO ¼-INCH PIECES	¼	TEASPOON COARSELY GROUND BLACK PEPPER
1	MEDIUM ONION, CHOPPED	1½	POUNDS BOK CHOY, TRIMMED AND CHOPPED
2	GARLIC CLOVES, MINCED	6	TABLESPOONS DARK RED MISO
1	TABLESPOON GRATED, PEELED FRESH GINGER	1	TABLESPOON BROWN SUGAR

1 In 2-quart saucepan, heat 4 cups water to boiling over high heat. Remove saucepan from heat; add dried shiitake mushrooms and let stand until softened, about 15 minutes. With slotted spoon, remove mushrooms. Rinse to remove any grit; drain on paper towels. Cut stems from mushrooms and discard; thinly slice caps. Strain soaking liquid through sieve lined with paper towels into 4-cup glass measuring cup. Add enough water to liquid in cup to equal 4 cups and set aside.

2 In nonstick 5-quart Dutch oven, heat oil over medium heat until hot. Add carrots, onion, and mushrooms and cook until vegetables are tender, about 15 minutes. Add garlic and ginger and cook 1 minute longer.

3 Add barley, salt, pepper, reserved mushroom liquid, and an additional **4 cups water;** heat to boiling over medium-high heat. Reduce heat to low; cover and simmer until barley is tender, about 40 minutes.

4 Add bok choy; heat to boiling over medium-high heat. Reduce heat to low and simmer, uncovered, until bok choy is tender-crisp and wilted, 5 to 7 minutes, stirring occasionally.

5 With ladle, transfer ½ cup broth from soup to small bowl. Add miso and brown sugar to broth and stir until smooth paste forms.

6 Remove Dutch oven from heat; stir in miso mixture.

EACH SERVING: ABOUT 170 CALORIES | 7G PROTEIN | 29G CARBOHYDRATE | 4G TOTAL FAT (0G SATURATED) | 0MG CHOLESTEROL | 985MG SODIUM

THAI COCONUT SOUP

For a more authentic—fiery—flavor, increase the ground red pepper to taste or, if available, add a small red Szechuan pepper or two (be sure to remove the peppers before serving).

ACTIVE TIME: 14 MIN · **TOTAL TIME:** 20 MIN

MAKES: 9 CUPS OR 4 MAIN-DISH SERVINGS

2   SMALL CARROTS, PEELED AND EACH CUT CROSSWISE IN HALF

½   MEDIUM RED PEPPER

1   CAN (14 OUNCES) LIGHT UNSWEETENED COCONUT MILK (NOT CREAM OF COCONUT), WELL STIRRED

2   GARLIC CLOVES, CRUSHED WITH GARLIC PRESS

1   PIECE (2 INCHES) PEELED FRESH GINGER, CUT INTO 4 PIECES

½   TEASPOON GROUND CORIANDER

½   TEASPOON GROUND CUMIN

¼   TEASPOON GROUND RED PEPPER (CAYENNE)

12 OUNCES FIRM TOFU, CUT INTO 1-INCH CUBES

2   CANS (14½ OUNCES EACH) VEGETABLE BROTH (3½ CUPS)

1   TABLESPOON ASIAN FISH SAUCE (SEE TIP)

1   TABLESPOON FRESH LIME JUICE

1   CUP WATER

2   GREEN ONIONS, TRIMMED AND SLICED

½   CUP CHOPPED FRESH CILANTRO LEAVES

1 With vegetable peeler, remove lengthwise strips from carrots and edge of red pepper; set aside.

2 In 5-quart Dutch oven, heat ½ cup coconut milk to boiling over medium heat. Add garlic, ginger, coriander, cumin, and ground red pepper and cook, stirring, 1 minute.

3 Increase heat to medium-high. Stir in tofu, broth, carrot strips, pepper strips, fish sauce, lime juice, water, and remaining coconut milk; heat just to simmering. Discard ginger. Just before serving, stir in green onions and cilantro.

TIP Asian fish sauce (nuoc nam or nam pla) is available in the specialty sections of some supermarkets and in Asian groceries.

EACH SERVING: ABOUT 210 CALORIES | 11G PROTEIN | 14G CARBOHYDRATE | 17G TOTAL FAT (6G SATURATED) | 0MG CHOLESTEROL | 1,060MG SODIUM

HOT AND SOUR SOUP

We streamlined seasonings to help get this popular Asian soup on the table in record time—without sacrificing the great taste.

ACTIVE TIME: 10 MIN · **TOTAL TIME:** 30 MIN

MAKES: 8 CUPS OR 4 MAIN-DISH SERVINGS

---

1   TABLESPOON VEGETABLE OIL

4   OUNCES SHIITAKE MUSHROOMS, STEMS REMOVED AND CAPS THINLY SLICED

3   TABLESPOONS REDUCED-SODIUM SOY SAUCE

1   PACKAGE (15 TO 16 OUNCES) EXTRA-FIRM TOFU, DRAINED, PATTED DRY, AND CUT INTO 1-INCH CUBES

2   TABLESPOONS CORNSTARCH

1   CONTAINER (32 OUNCES) VEGETABLE BROTH (4 CUPS)

3   TABLESPOONS SEASONED RICE VINEGAR

2   TABLESPOONS GRATED, PEELED FRESH GINGER

1   TABLESPOON WORCESTERSHIRE SAUCE

½   TEASPOON ASIAN SESAME OIL

¼   TEASPOON GROUND RED PEPPER (CAYENNE)

2   LARGE EGGS, BEATEN

2   GREEN ONIONS, TRIMMED AND SLICED

1 In nonstick 5-quart saucepot, heat vegetable oil over medium-high heat until hot. Add mushrooms, soy sauce, and tofu and cook, gently stirring often, until liquid has evaporated, about 5 minutes.

2 In cup, with fork, blend cornstarch and ¼ cup water until smooth; set aside. Add broth and ¾ cup water to tofu mixture; heat to boiling. Stir in cornstarch mixture and boil, stirring, 30 seconds. Reduce heat to medium-low; add vinegar, ginger, Worcestershire, sesame oil, and pepper and simmer 5 minutes.

3 Remove saucepot from heat. In a thin, steady stream, slowly pour beaten eggs into soup around side of saucepot. Carefully stir soup once in circular motion to separate egg into strands. Sprinkle with green onions.

TIP To brown, tofu should be dry. Wrap in paper towels and set it on a plate. Cover with a second plate; place a heavy can on top and let drain fifteen minutes. Discard towels.

EACH SERVING: ABOUT 280 CALORIES | 18G PROTEIN | 17G CARBOHYDRATE | 15G TOTAL FAT (3G SATURATED) | 106MG CHOLESTEROL | 1,790MG SODIUM

HARVEST MEXICAN SOUP

This soup is full of savory ingredients, including corn, avocado, and lime; a jalapeño chile adds a burst of heat.

ACTIVE TIME: 25 MIN · **TOTAL TIME:** 55 MIN

MAKES: 9½ CUPS OR 4 MAIN-DISH SERVINGS

---

4   TEASPOONS OLIVE OIL

1   JUMBO ONION (1 POUND), CUT INTO
    ¼-INCH PIECES

2   MEDIUM CARROTS, PEELED AND CUT
    INTO ¼-INCH PIECES

2   GARLIC CLOVES, CRUSHED
    WITH GARLIC PRESS

1   JALAPEÑO CHILE, SEEDED AND MINCED

3   LIMES

12 OUNCES RED POTATOES, UNPEELED
    AND CUT INTO ¼-INCH PIECES

1   CAN (14½ OUNCES) VEGETABLE BROTH
    (1¾ CUPS)

½   TEASPOON SALT

4   CUPS WATER

2   CUPS CORN KERNELS CUT FROM COBS
    (3 TO 4 EARS)

1   CUP LOOSELY PACKED FRESH
    CILANTRO LEAVES, CHOPPED

1   AVOCADO, CUT INTO ¼-INCH PIECES

PLAIN TORTILLA CHIPS, COARSELY
BROKEN (OPTIONAL)

---

1 In nonstick 5- to 6-quart saucepot or Dutch oven, heat oil over medium-high heat until hot. Add onion, carrots, garlic, and jalapeño, and cook, stirring occasionally, until vegetables are golden, 15 minutes.

2 Meanwhile, from limes, grate ½ teaspoon peel and squeeze $1/3$ cup juice; set aside.

3 Add potatoes, broth, salt, and water to saucepot; heat to boiling over medium-high heat. Reduce heat to low; cover and simmer 5 minutes. Add corn; cover and simmer until potatoes are tender, about 5 minutes.

4 Stir in cilantro, lime peel, and lime juice. Ladle soup into 4 bowls; top with avocado and sprinkle with tortilla chips, if you like.

EACH SERVING: ABOUT 350 CALORIES | 8G PROTEIN | 58G CARBOHYDRATE | 14G TOTAL FAT (2G SATURATED) | 0MG CHOLESTEROL | 945MG SODIUM

LUNCH
& BRUNCH

Whether you spend your days at work, at school, or at home, weekday lunch has become a meal to be consumed quickly, between getting to the next meeting, class, or activity. Finding time to have a relaxing, well-balanced, wholesome lunch can be difficult.

But weekends are another story. Life slows to a more manageable pace and, while there may be chores to do or places to go, we can sleep late and get out of the weekday routine. Many of us use the extra time to start the day off with a leisurely brunch—that weekend meal that combines the best of both breakfast and lunch, and that carries us right through to dinner.

Of course, when you think brunch, the first thing that comes to mind are eggs, one of nature's most nutrient-rich and versatile foods. Not only are eggs an inexpensive protein source, they provide a tasty base for using up leftover veggies, cheese, and herbs. And for added convenience, most egg recipes can be doubled to accommodate a crowd.

In addition to being healthful and palate-pleasing, the recipes in this chapter yield leftovers that are ideal for packing in a brown bag or lunch box. Now there's no excuse for not eating healthy all week long.

French Potato Pancake (page 228)

FRITTATA SANDWICHES WITH PEPPERS AND ONIONS

This hot sandwich can be wrapped in foil and carried along to serve later at a backyard picnic or concert in the park.

ACTIVE TIME: 30 MIN · **TOTAL TIME:** 40 MIN

MAKES: 4 SANDWICHES

---

2 TABLESPOONS OLIVE OIL	¾ CUP FRESHLY GRATED PARMESAN CHEESE
2 MEDIUM ONIONS, EACH CUT IN HALF AND THINLY SLICED	¼ CUP CHOPPED FRESH PARSLEY
4 ITALIAN FRYING PEPPERS (ABOUT 2 OUNCES EACH), THINLY SLICED	¼ TEASPOON GROUND BLACK PEPPER
½ TEASPOON SALT	1 ROUND OR SQUARE (8-INCH) FOCACCIA BREAD, CUT HORIZONTALLY IN HALF
6 LARGE EGGS	

1 In 12-inch skillet, heat 1 tablespoon oil over medium heat. Add onions and cook, stirring frequently, until tender, about 8 minutes. Add peppers; sprinkle with ¼ teaspoon salt and cook until peppers are tender, about 12 minutes longer. Keep warm.

2 Meanwhile, preheat oven to 375°F. In large bowl, with wire whisk beat eggs, Parmesan, parsley, black pepper, and remaining ¼ teaspoon salt until blended.

3 In oven-safe nonstick 10-inch skillet (if skillet is not oven-safe, wrap handle with double layer of foil), heat remaining 1 tablespoon olive oil over medium heat. Pour in egg mixture and cook, without stirring, until egg mixture begins to set around the edge, 3 to 4 minutes.

4 Place skillet in oven; bake until frittata is just set and knife inserted in center comes out clean, about 10 minutes longer. Slide frittata onto plate.

5 Place frittata on bottom of focaccia; top with onion mixture. Replace top of focaccia. To serve, cut into 4 wedges.

EACH SANDWICH: ABOUT 535 CALORIES | 29G PROTEIN | 49G CARBOHYDRATE | 26G TOTAL FAT (7G SATURATED) | 341MG CHOLESTEROL | 1,225MG SODIUM

PORTOBELLO BURGERS

Marinate the "burgers" in a broth mixture accented with thyme before grilling, and serve on buns with a lemon and green-onion mayonnaise.

ACTIVE TIME: 15 MIN · TOTAL TIME: 20 MIN PLUS MARINATING
MAKES: 4 SANDWICHES

¼ CUP VEGETABLE BROTH

2 TABLESPOONS OLIVE OIL

2 TEASPOONS BALSAMIC VINEGAR

1 TEASPOON CHOPPED FRESH THYME LEAVES

¼ TEASPOON SALT

¼ TEASPOON COARSELY GROUND BLACK PEPPER

4 MEDIUM (ABOUT 4 OUNCES EACH) PORTOBELLO MUSHROOMS, STEMS REMOVED

1 LEMON

⅓ CUP MAYONNAISE

1 SMALL GREEN ONION, TRIMMED AND MINCED

4 LARGE (ABOUT 4-INCH) BUNS

1 BUNCH ARUGULA, TRIMMED

1 In glass baking dish just large enough to hold mushrooms in a single layer, mix broth, oil, vinegar, thyme, ⅛ teaspoon salt, and ⅛ teaspoon pepper. Add mushrooms, turning to coat. Let stand, turning occasionally, 30 minutes.

2 Prepare grill.

3 Meanwhile, from lemon, grate ½ teaspoon peel and squeeze ½ teaspoon juice. In small bowl, stir lemon peel and juice, mayonnaise, green onion, and remaining ⅛ teaspoon salt and ⅛ teaspoon pepper.

4 Place mushrooms on hot grill rack over medium heat and grill, turning occasionally and brushing with remaining marinade, until mushrooms are browned and cooked through, 8 to 10 minutes per side.

5 Cut each bun horizontally in half. Spread cut sides of buns with mayonnaise mixture; top with arugula leaves. Place warm mushrooms on bottom halves of buns; replace top half of buns to serve.

EACH SANDWICH: ABOUT 355 CALORIES | 6G PROTEIN | 30G CARBOHYDRATE | 25G TOTAL FAT (4G SATURATED) | 7MG CHOLESTEROL | 585MG SODIUM

GREEK SALAD PITAS

Hummus—the Middle Eastern spread made with mashed garbanzo beans—is fast work in a food processor or blender.

TOTAL TIME: 20 MIN

MAKES: 4 SANDWICHES

---

1   CAN (15 TO 19 OUNCES) GARBANZO
    BEANS, RINSED AND DRAINED

¼   CUP PLAIN LOWFAT YOGURT

2   TABLESPOONS OLIVE OIL

2   TABLESPOONS FRESH LEMON JUICE

½   TEASPOON SALT

¼   TEASPOON COARSELY GROUND
    BLACK PEPPER

¼   TEASPOON GROUND CUMIN

1   GARLIC CLOVE, PEELED

4   (6- TO 7-INCH) WHOLE-WHEAT PITAS

3   CUPS SLICED ROMAINE LETTUCE

2   MEDIUM TOMATOES, CUT INTO
    ¼-INCH PIECES

1   MEDIUM CUCUMBER, PEELED AND
    THINLY SLICED

2   OUNCES FETA CHEESE, CRUMBLED
    (ABOUT ½ CUP)

2   TABLESPOONS CHOPPED FRESH
    MINT LEAVES

FRESH MINT LEAVES FOR GARNISH

1 In food processor, with knife blade attached, or in blender, combine beans, yogurt, oil, lemon juice, salt, pepper, cumin, and garlic and puree until smooth.

2 Cut off top third of each pita to form pocket. Use half of the bean mixture to spread inside pockets.

3 Combine lettuce, tomatoes, cucumber, feta, and chopped mint; use to fill pockets. Top with remaining bean mixture and mint leaves.

EACH SANDWICH: ABOUT 440 CALORIES | 17G PROTEIN | 66G CARBOHYDRATE | 15G TOTAL FAT (4G SATURATED) | 13MG CHOLESTEROL | 1,105MG SODIUM

HUEVOS RANCHEROS

This traditional Mexican dish is a quick and easy way to liven up breakfast or brunch.

ACTIVE TIME: 5 MIN · TOTAL TIME: 12 MIN
MAKES: 4 MAIN-DISH SERVINGS

1   CAN (15 TO 19 OUNCES) BLACK BEANS, RINSED AND DRAINED

1¼ CUPS MILD OR MEDIUM-HOT SALSA (ABOUT 11 OUNCES)

¼   CUP WATER

4   LARGE EGGS

3   OUNCES SHREDDED MEXICAN CHEESE BLEND (¾ CUP)

CHOPPED FRESH CILANTRO OR PARSLEY LEAVES FOR GARNISH

WARM FLOUR TORTILLAS (OPTIONAL)

1   In 10-inch skillet, mix black beans, salsa, and water; heat to boiling over high heat, stirring frequently.

2   Break eggs, one at a time, into custard cup and slip into skillet on top of bean mixture. Reduce heat to medium-low; cover and simmer until whites are completely set and yolks begin to thicken, about 5 minutes, or until eggs are cooked to desired firmness.

3   To serve, sprinkle bean mixture and eggs with shredded cheese and garnish with chopped cilantro. Serve with warm tortillas, if you like.

EACH SERVING WITHOUT TORTILLAS: ABOUT 250 CALORIES | 17G PROTEIN | 23G CARBOHYDRATE | 12G TOTAL FAT (6G SATURATED) | 231MG CHOLESTEROL | 1,110MG SODIUM

EGGS IN SPICY TOMATO SAUCE

This classic Italian dish pairs an easy homemade tomato sauce with eggs poached right in the sauce. A delicious one-skillet dish to add to your quick-cook repertoire.

ACTIVE TIME: 15 MIN · **TOTAL TIME:** 45 MIN
MAKES: 4 MAIN-DISH SERVINGS

1   LOAF (8 OUNCES) ITALIAN BREAD
1   TABLESPOON OLIVE OIL
1   JUMBO ONION (1 POUND), CUT INTO ¼-INCH PIECES
2   MEDIUM CARROTS, PEELED AND CUT INTO ¼-INCH PIECES
1   STALK CELERY, CUT INTO ¼-INCH PIECES

2   GARLIC CLOVES, CRUSHED WITH GARLIC PRESS
1   CAN (28 OUNCES) WHOLE TOMATOES
½   TEASPOON SALT
¼   TEASPOON CRUSHED RED PEPPER
1   TABLESPOON BUTTER OR MARGARINE
8   LARGE EGGS
¼   CUP LOOSELY PACKED FRESH BASIL LEAVES, CHOPPED

1 Preheat oven to 350°F. Cut bread diagonally into 1-inch-thick slices. Place bread slices on cookie sheet and bake until lightly toasted, about 5 minutes. Set aside.

2 In nonstick 12-inch skillet, heat oil over medium-high heat until hot. Add onion, carrots, celery, and garlic and cook, stirring occasionally, until vegetables are lightly browned, 12 to 15 minutes.

3 Stir in tomatoes with their juice, salt, and crushed red pepper, breaking up tomatoes with side of spoon; heat to boiling over medium-high heat. Reduce heat to low; simmer, stirring occasionally, 5 minutes. Stir in butter.

4 Break 1 egg into custard cup. With back of spoon, make small well in sauce and slip egg into well. Repeat with remaining eggs. Heat sauce to boiling over medium-high heat. Reduce heat to medium-low; cover and simmer until egg whites are set and yolks begin to thicken, 7 to 10 minutes, or until eggs are cooked to desired firmness.

5 To serve, place 1 bread slice in each of 4 large soup bowls. Spoon 2 eggs and some tomato mixture over each slice; sprinkle with basil. Serve with remaining bread.

EACH SERVING: ABOUT 455 CALORIES | 21G PROTEIN | 52G CARBOHYDRATE | 20G TOTAL FAT (6G SATURATED) | 433MG CHOLESTEROL | 1,091MG SODIUM

CREAM CHEESE AND CHIVE SCRAMBLED EGGS

Serve this versatile dish for a formal brunch or for a late-night family supper. A salad on the side rounds out the meal.

ACTIVE TIME: 5 MIN · **TOTAL TIME:** 10 MIN

MAKES: 4 MAIN-DISH SERVINGS

---

1 BAG (5 OUNCES) BABY MIXED SALAD GREENS

1 TABLESPOON OLIVE OIL

2 TEASPOONS RED WINE VINEGAR

   PINCH PLUS ½ TEASPOON SALT

8 LARGE EGGS

2 TABLESPOONS CHOPPED FRESH CHIVES

¼ TEASPOON COARSELY GROUND BLACK PEPPER

¼ CUP WATER

2 TEASPOONS BUTTER OR MARGARINE

4 OUNCES (HALF 8-OUNCE PACKAGE) NEUFCHÂTEL OR LIGHT CREAM CHEESE, CUT INTO ½-INCH PIECES

4 SLICES MULTIGRAIN BREAD, TOASTED AND EACH CUT DIAGONALLY IN HALF

1 In medium bowl, toss greens with oil, vinegar, and pinch salt; set aside.

2 In large bowl, with wire whisk, beat eggs, chives, pepper, remaining ½ teaspoon salt, and water until blended.

3 In nonstick 10-inch skillet, melt butter over medium-high heat; add egg mixture. With heat-safe rubber spatula, gently push egg mixture as it begins to set to form soft curds. When eggs are partially cooked, top with Neufchâtel and continue cooking, stirring occasionally, until eggs have thickened and no visible liquid egg remains.

4 To serve, divide greens among 4 dinner plates. Place 2 toast halves on each plate; spoon eggs over toast.

EACH SERVING: ABOUT 340 CALORIES | 18G PROTEIN | 15G CARBOHYDRATE | 24G TOTAL FAT (9G SATURATED) | 451MG CHOLESTEROL | 716MG SODIUM

LEEK AND GOAT CHEESE QUICHE

Meltingly tender sweet leeks and tangy goat cheese are delicious partners in this rich tart.

ACTIVE TIME: 30 MIN · **TOTAL TIME:** 1 HR 30 MIN PLUS CHILLING AND COOLING
MAKES: 8 MAIN-DISH SERVINGS

PASTRY FOR 11-INCH TART (RECIPE FOLLOWS)

FILLING

1 POUND LEEKS (ABOUT 3 MEDIUM)

2 TABLESPOONS BUTTER OR MARGARINE

½ TEASPOON SALT

½ CUP WATER

3 LARGE EGGS

1 LOG (3½ TO 4 OUNCES) MILD GOAT CHEESE SUCH AS MONTRACHET

⅛ TEASPOON GROUND BLACK PEPPER

1½ CUPS HALF-AND-HALF OR LIGHT CREAM

1 Prepare Pastry for 11-inch Tart as recipe directs.

2 On lightly floured surface, with floured rolling pin, roll dough into 14-inch round. Ease dough into 11" by 1" round tart pan with removable bottom. Fold overhang in and press dough against side of pan so it extends ⅛ inch above rim. With fork, prick dough at 1-inch intervals. Refrigerate 30 minutes or freeze 10 minutes. Preheat oven to 425°F.

3 Line tart shell with foil; fill with pie weights or dry beans. Bake 10 minutes. Remove foil with weights; bake until lightly golden, about 10 minutes longer. (If pastry puffs up during baking, gently press down with back of spoon.) Cool in pan on wire rack 20 minutes. Turn oven control to 350°F.

4 While tart shell bakes and cools, prepare filling: Cut off roots and trim dark green tops from leeks. Cut each leek lengthwise in half, then crosswise into ½-inch-thick slices. Rinse leeks in large bowl of cold water, swishing to remove sand; transfer to colander to drain, leaving sand in bottom of bowl.

5 In 12-inch skillet, melt butter over medium heat. Add leeks, ¼ teaspoon salt, and water; cook, uncovered, until leeks are tender and all liquid has evaporated, about 10 minutes, stirring occasionally. Remove skillet from heat.

6 In medium bowl, with wire whisk, beat eggs, goat cheese, pepper, and remaining ¼ teaspoon salt until well blended. Stir in half-and-half.

7 Place tart pan on foil-lined cookie sheet to catch any overflow. Sprinkle leeks over bottom of tart shell; pour egg mixture over leeks. Bake until knife inserted in center comes out clean, 35 to 40 minutes. Cool on wire rack 10 minutes. Just before serving, remove side of pan. Serve hot or at room temperature.

EACH SERVING: ABOUT 410 CALORIES | 10G PROTEIN | 26G CARBOHYDRATE | 31G TOTAL FAT (17G SATURATED) | 149MG CHOLESTEROL | 551MG SODIUM

PASTRY FOR 11-INCH TART

ACTIVE TIME: 10 MIN PLUS CHILLING
MAKES: ONE 11-INCH TART SHELL

1½ CUPS ALL-PURPOSE FLOUR

½ TEASPOON SALT

½ CUP COLD BUTTER OR MARGARINE (1 STICK), CUT INTO PIECES

2 TABLESPOONS VEGETABLE SHORTENING

3 TO 4 TABLESPOONS ICE WATER

1 In large bowl, mix flour and salt. With pastry blender or two knives used scissor-fashion, cut in butter and shortening until mixture resembles coarse crumbs.
2 Sprinkle in ice water, 1 tablespoon at a time, mixing lightly with fork after each addition, until dough is just moist enough to hold together. Shape dough into disk; wrap disk in plastic wrap. Refrigerate 30 minutes or up to overnight. (If chilled overnight, let stand 30 minutes at room temperature before rolling.)

EACH ⅛ PASTRY: ABOUT 222 CALORIES | 3G PROTEIN | 20G CARBOHYDRATE | 15G TOTAL FAT (8G SATURATED) | 32MG CHOLESTEROL | 263MG SODIUM

ASPARAGUS QUICHE

We made the delicate custard filling with half-and-half instead of heavy cream to save fat and calories—but it still tastes rich.

ACTIVE TIME: 45 MIN · **TOTAL TIME:** 1 HR 30 MIN PLUS CHILLING AND COOLING
MAKES: 8 MAIN-DISH SERVINGS

1¼ CUPS ALL-PURPOSE FLOUR

¾ TEASPOON SALT

4 TABLESPOONS BUTTER OR MARGARINE

2 TABLESPOONS SHORTENING

4 TABLESPOONS ICE WATER

1 POUND ASPARAGUS, TRIMMED AND CUT INTO ¾-INCH PIECES

4 LARGE EGGS

2 CUPS HALF-AND-HALF OR LIGHT CREAM

⅛ TEASPOON GROUND BLACK PEPPER

PINCH GROUND NUTMEG

4 OUNCES GRUYÈRE OR SWISS CHEESE, COARSELY SHREDDED (1 CUP)

1 In medium bowl, mix flour and ¼ teaspoon salt. With pastry blender or two knives used scissor-fashion, cut in butter and shortening until mixture resembles coarse crumbs. Sprinkle in ice water, 1 tablespoon at a time, mixing lightly with fork after each addition, until dough is just moist enough to hold together. Shape dough into disk; wrap in plastic wrap. Refrigerate 30 minutes or up to overnight. (If chilled overnight, let stand 30 minutes at room temperature before rolling.)

2 Meanwhile, in 2-quart saucepan, heat 4 cups water to boiling over high heat. Add asparagus and cook until tender, 6 to 8 minutes. Drain asparagus and rinse under cold water. Drain and set aside.

3 Preheat oven to 425°F. On lightly floured surface, with floured rolling pin, roll dough into 11-inch round. Gently ease dough into 9-inch pie plate. Fold overhang in and press dough against side of pan so it extends ⅛ inch above rim. Make decorative edge. With fork, prick dough at 1-inch intervals.

4 Line pie shell with foil; fill with pie weights or dry beans. Bake 15 minutes. Remove foil with weights; bake until golden, about 10 minutes longer. (If crust puffs up during baking, gently press it down with back of spoon.) Turn oven control to 350°F.

5 Meanwhile, in medium bowl, with wire whisk, beat eggs, half-and-half, pepper, nutmeg, and remaining ½ teaspoon salt until well blended.

6 Place pie plate on foil-lined cookie sheet to catch any overflow. Sprinkle asparagus and cheese over bottom of crust; pour egg mixture over asparagus and cheese. Bake until knife inserted in center comes out clean, 40 to 45 minutes. Serve hot or at room temperature.

EACH SERVING: ABOUT 325 CALORIES | 12G PROTEIN | 19G CARBOHYDRATE | 25G TOTAL FAT (12G SATURATED) | 157MG CHOLESTEROL | 362MG SODIUM

ASPARAGUS OMELET

If you don't have pale yellow, nutty-flavored Gruyère cheese, substitute the same amount of shredded Swiss or Jarlsberg, or a few shavings of fresh Parmesan.

ACTIVE TIME: 10 MIN · **TOTAL TIME:** 15 MIN
MAKES: 4 MAIN-DISH SERVINGS

FILLING

1   POUND ASPARAGUS, TRIMMED

⅛ TEASPOON COARSELY GROUND BLACK PEPPER

4   OUNCES GRUYÈRE CHEESE, SHREDDED (1 CUP)

OMELETS

8   LARGE EGGS (SEE TIP)

½ TEASPOON SALT

½ CUP COLD WATER

4   TEASPOONS BUTTER OR MARGARINE

1 Prepare filling: In deep 12-inch skillet, heat 1 inch water to boiling over high heat. Add asparagus; heat to boiling. Reduce heat and simmer, uncovered, just until tender, about 5 minutes. Drain and rinse with cold running water. Drain. Sprinkle pepper over cheese.

2 To make omelets: In medium bowl, with wire whisk, beat eggs, salt, and cold water. For each omelet, in nonstick 8-inch skillet, melt 1 teaspoon butter over medium-high heat. Pour in ½ cup egg mixture; cook, gently lifting edge of eggs with heat-safe rubber spatula and tilting pan to allow uncooked eggs to run underneath, until eggs are set, about 1 minute. Sprinkle one-fourth of cheese mixture over half of omelet; top with one-fourth of asparagus spears. Fold unfilled half over filling and slide onto warm plate. Repeat with remaining butter, egg mixture, and filling. If desired, keep omelets warm in 200°F oven until all are cooked.

TIP For lighter omelets, substitute 4 large eggs and 8 large egg whites for the whole eggs.

EACH OMELET: ABOUT 310 CALORIES | 23G PROTEIN | 3G CARBOHYDRATE | 25G TOTAL FAT (11G SATURATED) | 467MG CHOLESTEROL | 528MG SODIUM

SPRING ONION, SPINACH, AND PECORINO FRITTATA

For a less assertive flavor, substitute Parmigiano-Reggiano for the Pecorino Romano or use a combination of the two for a more complex flavor.

ACTIVE TIME: 30 MIN · **TOTAL TIME:** 40 MIN

MAKES: 4 MAIN-DISH SERVINGS

---

2 SPRING ONIONS WITH TOPS (ABOUT 12 OUNCES), OR 1 LARGE (12 OUNCES) SWEET ONION

2 TEASPOONS OLIVE OIL

1 BAG (5 TO 6 OUNCES) BABY SPINACH

8 LARGE EGGS

¼ CUP FRESHLY GRATED PECORINO ROMANO CHEESE

¼ CUP WATER

½ TEASPOON SALT

¼ TEASPOON COARSELY GROUND BLACK PEPPER

1 Preheat oven to 425°F. Trim tough green leaves from top of spring onions. Cut stems crosswise into ¼-inch-thick slices. Cut each onion bulb in half and thinly slice.

2 In oven-safe nonstick 12-inch skillet (if skillet is not oven-safe, wrap handle with double layer of foil), heat oil over medium heat until hot. Add sliced onions and stems and cook, stirring occasionally, until soft and golden brown, about 10 minutes. Stir in spinach and cook, stirring constantly, just until wilted, about 1 minute. Spread onion mixture evenly in skillet; remove skillet from heat.

3 In medium bowl with wire whisk, beat eggs, Pecorino Romano, water, salt, and pepper until blended. Carefully pour egg mixture over onion mixture; do not stir. Return skillet to medium-high heat and cook until egg mixture begins to set around the edge, 2 to 3 minutes.

4 Place skillet in oven; bake until frittata is set, 8 to 10 minutes. Slide frittata onto cutting board. Cut into wedges to serve.

EACH SERVING: ABOUT 215 CALORIES | 16G PROTEIN | 7G CARBOHYDRATE | 14G TOTAL FAT (4G SATURATED) | 430MG CHOLESTEROL | 530MG SODIUM

ASPARAGUS AND GREEN ONION FRITTATA

Everyone loves a skillet omelet, especially when it's filled with bits of cream cheese and sautéed vegetables.

ACTIVE TIME: 25 MIN · **TOTAL TIME:** 35 MIN
MAKES: 4 MAIN-DISH SERVINGS

8 LARGE EGGS	12 OUNCES ASPARAGUS, TRIMMED
½ CUP WHOLE MILK	1 TABLESPOON BUTTER OR MARGARINE
⅛ TEASPOON GROUND BLACK PEPPER	1 BUNCH GREEN ONIONS, CHOPPED
¾ TEASPOON SALT	2 OUNCES LIGHT CREAM CHEESE (NEUFCHÂTEL)

1 Preheat oven to 375°F. In medium bowl, with wire whisk, beat eggs, milk, pepper, and ½ teaspoon salt until blended; set aside. If using thin asparagus, cut each stalk crosswise in half; if using medium asparagus, cut stalks into 1-inch pieces.

2 In oven-safe nonstick 10-inch skillet (if skillet is not oven-safe, wrap handle with double layer of foil), melt butter over medium heat. Add the asparagus and the remaining ¼ teaspoon salt and cook, stirring often, 4 minutes for thin stalks or 6 minutes for medium-size stalks. Stir in green onions and cook, stirring occasionally, until vegetables are tender, 2 to 3 minutes longer.

3 Reduce heat to medium-low. Pour egg mixture over vegetables; drop scant teaspoonfuls of cream cheese over egg mixture. Cook, without stirring, until egg mixture begins to set around edge, 3 to 4 minutes. Place skillet in oven and bake until frittata is set and knife inserted in center comes out clean, 10 to 12 minutes. Cut into wedges to serve.

EACH SERVING: ABOUT 250 CALORIES | 17G PROTEIN | 6G CARBOHYDRATE | 19G TOTAL FAT (7G SATURATED) | 448MG CHOLESTEROL | 671MG SODIUM

SPINACH AND JACK CHEESE BREAD PUDDING

A delicious departure from quiche, this savory bread pudding is easier to prepare and very satisfying.

ACTIVE TIME: 5 MIN · **TOTAL TIME:** 30 MIN

MAKES: 6 MAIN-DISH SERVINGS

---

6   LARGE EGGS

2   CUPS LOW-FAT MILK (1%)

¼   TEASPOON DRIED THYME

¼   TEASPOON SALT

¼   TEASPOON COARSELY GROUND BLACK PEPPER

PINCH GROUND NUTMEG

1   PACKAGE (10 OUNCES) FROZEN CHOPPED SPINACH, THAWED AND SQUEEZED DRY

1   CUP SHREDDED MONTEREY JACK CHEESE (4 OUNCES)

8   SLICES FIRM WHITE BREAD, CUT INTO ¾-INCH PIECES

1 Preheat oven to 375°F. In large bowl, with wire whisk, beat eggs, milk, thyme, salt, pepper, and nutmeg until blended. With rubber spatula, stir in spinach, Monterey Jack, and bread.

2 Pour mixture into lightly greased 13" by 9" ceramic or glass baking dish. Bake bread pudding until browned and puffed, and knife inserted in center comes out clean, 20 to 25 minutes.

3 Remove bread pudding from oven; let stand 5 minutes before serving.

EACH SERVING: ABOUT 280 CALORIES | 17G PROTEIN | 22G CARBOHYDRATE | 13G TOTAL FAT (6G SATURATED) | 233MG CHOLESTEROL | 545MG SODIUM

SPINACH STRATA

You can assemble this a day ahead, then pop it in the oven—right from the refrigerator—just one hour before serving.

ACTIVE TIME: 15 MIN · **TOTAL TIME:** 1 HR 15 MIN PLUS CHILLING
MAKES: 6 MAIN-DISH SERVINGS

8   SLICES FIRM WHITE BREAD

4   OUNCES MOZZARELLA CHEESE, SHREDDED (1 CUP)

1   PACKAGE (10 OUNCES) FROZEN CHOPPED SPINACH, THAWED AND SQUEEZED DRY

1   TABLESPOON BUTTER OR MARGARINE, SOFTENED

2   CUPS MILK

6   LARGE EGGS

½   CUP LOOSELY PACKED FRESH BASIL LEAVES, CHOPPED

½   TEASPOON SALT

¼   TEASPOON GROUND BLACK PEPPER

1 Grease 8" by 8" glass baking dish. Place 4 bread slices in dish; top with ½ cup cheese, all spinach, then remaining cheese. Spread butter on 1 side of each remaining bread slice; place in dish, buttered side up.

2 In medium bowl, with wire whisk, beat milk, eggs, basil, salt, and pepper until blended. Slowly pour egg mixture over bread slices. Prick bread with fork and press slices down to absorb egg mixture. Cover baking dish with plastic wrap and refrigerate at least 30 minutes or overnight.

3 Preheat oven to 350°F. Remove cover from baking dish; bake strata until knife inserted in center comes out clean, about 1 hour. Remove from oven and let stand 5 minutes before serving.

EACH SERVING: ABOUT 290 CALORIES | 17G PROTEIN | 22G CARBOHYDRATE | 16G TOTAL FAT (7G SATURATED) | 245MG CHOLESTEROL | 569MG SODIUM

SAVORY RICE AND RICOTTA TART

An irresistible combination of rice and creamy ricotta cheese baked with spinach in a golden crust.

ACTIVE TIME: 30 MIN · **TOTAL TIME:** 1 HR 30 MIN
MAKES: 8 MAIN-DISH SERVINGS

PASTRY FOR 11-INCH TART (PAGE 213)

RICE FILLING

½ CUP LONG-GRAIN WHITE RICE

¾ TEASPOON SALT

1 CUP WATER

1 TABLESPOON BUTTER OR MARGARINE

1 MEDIUM ONION, FINELY CHOPPED

1 PACKAGE (10 OUNCES) FROZEN CHOPPED SPINACH, THAWED AND SQUEEZED DRY

¼ TEASPOON COARSELY GROUND BLACK PEPPER

⅛ TEASPOON GROUND NUTMEG

1 CONTAINER (15 OUNCES) PART-SKIM RICOTTA CHEESE

½ CUP LOW-FAT MILK (1%)

3 LARGE EGGS

¾ CUP FRESHLY GRATED PARMESAN CHEESE

1 Prepare Pastry for 11-inch Tart as recipe directs.

2 Preheat oven to 425°F. On lightly floured surface, with floured rolling pin, roll dough into 14-inch round. Ease dough into 11" by 1" round tart pan with removable bottom. Fold overhang in and press dough against side of pan so it extends ⅛ inch above rim. With fork, prick dough at 1-inch intervals.

3 Line tart shell with foil and fill with pie weights or dry beans. Bake tart shell 20 minutes; remove foil with weights, and bake until golden, about 10 minutes longer. (If pastry puffs up during baking, gently press down with back of spoon.) Turn oven control to 350°F.

4 While tart shell is baking, prepare filling: In 1-quart saucepan, heat rice, ¼ teaspoon salt, and water to boiling over high heat. Reduce heat to low; cover and simmer until rice is tender and liquid has been absorbed, 15 to 18 minutes.

5 While rice is cooking, in 2-quart saucepan, melt butter over medium heat. Add onion and cook until tender, about 8 minutes. Stir in spinach, pepper, nutmeg, and remaining ½ teaspoon salt; remove from heat.
6 In large bowl, with wire whisk, mix ricotta, milk, eggs, and ½ cup Parmesan until well blended. Stir in cooked rice and spinach mixture.
7 Spoon rice mixture into warm tart shell; spread evenly. Sprinkle remaining ¼ cup Parmesan over filling. Bake until set, about 30 minutes. (To brown top after baking, turn oven control to broil. Place tart on rack in broiling pan. Place pan in broiler at closest position to heat source; broil 3 to 5 minutes.) Remove side of pan and serve tart warm.

EACH SERVING: ABOUT 415 CALORIES | 17G PROTEIN | 34G CARBOHYDRATE | 29G TOTAL FAT (14G SATURATED) | 139MG CHOLESTEROL | 690MG SODIUM

PORTOBELLO "CHEESE STEAKS"

A hearty hand-held meal wrapped in pita and served gyro style.

ACTIVE TIME: 15 MIN · TOTAL TIME: 35 MIN
MAKES: 4 SANDWICHES

2 MEDIUM PORTOBELLO MUSHROOMS (ABOUT 4 OUNCES EACH), STEMS REMOVED

2 TABLESPOONS OLIVE OIL

2 MEDIUM YELLOW PEPPERS, THINLY SLICED

1 JUMBO SWEET ONION (1 POUND) SUCH AS VIDALIA OR WALLA WALLA, THINLY SLICED

½ TEASPOON SALT

¼ TEASPOON COARSELY GROUND BLACK PEPPER

2 TABLESPOONS WATER

1 TABLESPOON BALSAMIC VINEGAR

4 (7-INCH) POCKETLESS PITAS

8 OUNCES PART-SKIM MOZZARELLA CHEESE, SHREDDED (2 CUPS)

1 Preheat oven to 400°F. Heat nonstick 12-inch skillet over medium-high heat until hot. Brush both sides of mushrooms using 1 tablespoon oil. Add mushrooms to skillet and cook until tender and lightly browned, about 5 minutes on each side. Transfer mushrooms to cutting board and cut into ¼-inch-thick slices; set aside.

2 In same skillet, heat remaining 1 tablespoon oil over medium heat until hot. Add yellow peppers, onion, salt, black pepper, and water; cook, stirring frequently, until the vegetables are tender and golden, about 15 minutes. Stir in vinegar; remove skillet from heat. Gently stir in sliced portobellos.

3 Meanwhile, place pitas on large cookie sheet; sprinkle with mozzarella cheese. Heat pitas until cheese has melted, about 5 minutes.

4 Roll each pita into a cone; tightly wrap bottom half of each with kitchen parchment or foil to help hold its shape and prevent leakage. Fill pita cones with warm mushroom mixture.

EACH SANDWICH: ABOUT 460 CALORIES | 24G PROTEIN | 52G CARBOHYDRATE | 18G TOTAL FAT (7G SATURATED) | 41MG CHOLESTEROL | 1,060MG SODIUM

FRENCH POTATO PANCAKE

We've taken the classic Swiss shredded-potato pancake and come up with a choice of fillings designed to please everyone. This versatile recipe can serve as a main dish or an accompaniment.

ACTIVE TIME: 25 MIN · TOTAL TIME: 50 MIN
MAKES: 4 MAIN-DISH SERVINGS

PEPPER FILLING

2   TEASPOONS OLIVE OIL

1   MEDIUM RED PEPPER, CUT INTO
    ¼-INCH PIECES

3½ TO 4 OUNCES PLAIN GOAT CHEESE,
    CRUMBLED

POTATO PANCAKE

2¼ POUNDS BAKING POTATOES
    (ABOUT 4 MEDIUM)

½   TEASPOON SALT

½   TEASPOON COARSELY GROUND
    BLACK PEPPER

2   TABLESPOONS OLIVE OIL

1 Prepare filling: In oven-safe nonstick 10-inch skillet (if skillet is not oven-safe, wrap handle with double layer of foil), heat oil over medium heat until hot. Add red pepper and cook, stirring occasionally, until tender and lightly browned, 10 to 12 minutes. Transfer pepper to small bowl; set aside. Wipe skillet with paper towel.

2 Meanwhile, prepare potato pancake: Preheat oven to 400°F. Peel and coarsely shred potatoes; pat dry with paper towels. In large bowl, toss potatoes with salt and black pepper.

3 In same skillet, heat 1 tablespoon oil over medium heat. Working quickly, add half of potatoes, gently patting with rubber spatula to cover bottom of skillet. Leaving 1-inch border, top potatoes with red pepper and goat cheese. Cover filling with remaining potatoes, gently patting to edge of skillet. Cook, gently shaking skillet occasionally to keep pancake from sticking, until browned, 10 minutes.

4 Carefully invert pancake onto large, flat plate. Add remaining 1 tablespoon oil to skillet, then slide pancake back into skillet. Cook, gently shaking skillet occasionally, 10 minutes longer.

5 Place skillet, uncovered, in oven and bake until potatoes are tender throughout, 20 to 25 minutes.

EACH SERVING: ABOUT 340 CALORIES | 10G PROTEIN | 36G CARBOHYDRATE | 18G TOTAL FAT (8G SATURATED) | 22MG CHOLESTEROL | 550MG SODIUM

SWISS POTATO PANCAKE

Prepare French Potato Pancake as above, but in step 1, instead of preparing pepper filling, heat **1 tablespoon oil** in skillet over medium heat until hot. Add **1 large onion** (12 ounces), cut into ¼-inch pieces, and cook, stirring occasionally, until tender and golden brown, about 15 minutes. Transfer onion to small bowl. Complete recipe as in steps 2 through 5, substituting **caramelized onion** and **1 cup shredded Gruyère cheese** (4 ounces) for red pepper and goat cheese.

EACH SERVING: ABOUT 370 CALORIES | 12G PROTEIN | 38G CARBOHYDRATE |
20G TOTAL FAT (6G SATURATED) | 30MG CHOLESTEROL | 380MG SODIUM

MEXICAN POTATO PANCAKE

Prepare French Potato Pancake as above, but in step 1, instead of preparing pepper filling, in small bowl, stir **1 cup canned black beans**, rinsed, drained, and mashed; **1 tablespoon water, 1 teaspoon fresh lime juice**, and **½ teaspoon ground cumin** until well mixed. (If bean mixture is too stiff to spread, stir in 1 or 2 teaspoons water.) Complete recipe as in steps 2 through 5, substituting black-bean mixture and **1 cup shredded Monterey Jack cheese** (4 ounces) for red pepper and goat cheese.

EACH SERVING: ABOUT 360 CALORIES | 12G PROTEIN | 42G CARBOHYDRATE |
16G TOTAL FAT (6G SATURATED) | 30MG CHOLESTEROL | 530MG SODIUM

FRESH MOZZARELLA AND TOMATO SANDWICHES

The essence of summer, with garden tomatoes and our versatile Italian herb sauce, which makes a terrific sandwich spread.

TOTAL TIME: 15 MIN

MAKES: 4 SANDWICHES

½ CUP SALSA VERDE (BELOW)

8 SLICES (½ INCH THICK) TUSCAN BREAD

2 RIPE MEDIUM TOMATOES, EACH CUT INTO 4 SLICES

8 OUNCES FRESH MOZZARELLA CHEESE, CUT INTO 8 SLICES

Spread about 1 tablespoon Salsa Verde on 1 side of each bread slice. On each of 4 bread slices, sauce side up, place 2 tomato slices and 2 mozzarella slices. Top with remaining bread slices, sauce side down. Cut each sandwich in half to serve.

EACH SANDWICH: ABOUT 455 CALORIES | 17G PROTEIN | 38G CARBOHYDRATE | 26G TOTAL FAT (9G SATURATED) | 44MG CHOLESTEROL | 690MG SODIUM

SALSA VERDE

1 GARLIC CLOVE, CUT IN HALF

¼ TEASPOON SALT

2 CUPS PACKED FRESH FLAT-LEAF PARSLEY LEAVES (ABOUT 3 BUNCHES)

⅓ CUP OLIVE OIL

3 TABLESPOONS CAPERS, DRAINED

3 TABLESPOONS FRESH LEMON JUICE

1 TEASPOON DIJON MUSTARD

⅛ TEASPOON GROUND BLACK PEPPER

In food processor with knife blade attached, or in blender, combine garlic, salt, parsley, oil, capers, lemon juice, mustard, and pepper and puree until almost smooth. If not using right away, cover and refrigerate up to 3 days. Makes about ¾ cup.

EACH TABLESPOON: ABOUT 60 CALORIES | 0G PROTEIN | 1G CARBOHYDRATE | 6G TOTAL FAT (1G SATURATED) | 0MG CHOLESTEROL | 140MG SODIUM

VEGETARIAN SOUVLAKI

No one will miss the meat in these yummy sandwiches. Make the filling by cutting up your favorite veggie burgers.

ACTIVE TIME: 15 MIN · TOTAL TIME: 35 MIN

MAKES: 4 MAIN-DISH SERVINGS

1 TABLESPOON OLIVE OIL	8 OUNCES ENGLISH (SEEDLESS) CUCUMBER, CUT INTO ¼-INCH PIECES
1 LARGE ONION (12 OUNCES), CUT IN HALF AND THINLY SLICED	1 TEASPOON DRIED MINT
4 FROZEN VEGETARIAN SOY BURGERS (10- TO 12-OUNCE PACKAGE), CUT INTO 1-INCH PIECES	1 SMALL GARLIC CLOVE, CRUSHED WITH GARLIC PRESS
½ TEASPOON SALT	4 (6- TO 7-INCH) PITAS, WARMED
¼ TEASPOON GROUND BLACK PEPPER	1 MEDIUM TOMATO, CUT INTO ½-INCH PIECES
8 OUNCES PLAIN NONFAT YOGURT	1 OUNCE FETA CHEESE, CRUMBLED

1 In nonstick 12-inch skillet, heat oil over medium heat until hot. Add onion and cook, stirring occasionally, until tender and golden, 12 to 15 minutes. Add burgers, ¼ teaspoon salt, and pepper and cook until heated through, about 5 minutes.

2 Meanwhile, in medium bowl, stir yogurt, cucumber, mint, garlic, and remaining ¼ teaspoon salt until blended. Add burger mixture and toss gently to combine.

3 Cut 1-inch slice from each pita to form pocket. Spoon one-fourth burger mixture into each pita. Sprinkle with tomato and feta.

EACH SANDWICH: ABOUT 390 CALORIES | 24G PROTEIN | 45G CARBOHYDRATE | 13G TOTAL FAT (3G SATURATED) | 9MG CHOLESTEROL | 945MG SODIUM

MAIN-DISH
SALADS

Salads can be an extremely versatile part of vegetarian menus year round. They can be served chilled in the summer and warm during the colder months. Although we usually think of salads as a combination of vegetables tossed with greens, they can take many forms. Pasta, grains, beans and legumes, eggs, potatoes, even bread can serve as the foundation of a salad. Then just add fresh seasonal fruits or vegetables and other vegetarian staples, and maybe some whole-grain bread as an accompaniment, and you have a hearty, nutritious meal.

The art of salad making lies in the composition and combination of ingredients. Essential to any salad is the freshest, finest-quality produce available. The best salads contrast and balance textures, colors, and flavors. Crunchy and soft ingredients, tangy flavors with slightly sweet or mild ones, and bright colors combined with muted ones create salads that are pleasing to both the eyes and the taste buds.

Include a basket of whole-grain breads or crackers and perhaps another vegetarian dish on the table as accompaniments for an especially hearty meal. If you want to add extra protein in the form of nuts or seeds, toast them briefly for best flavor. For protein, you can also add full-flavored cheeses like feta, Parmesan, or gorgonzola; crumbled hard-cooked eggs; or other tasty add-ins that complement the ingredients.

Flatbread with Salad (page 244)

RICE NOODLES WITH MANY HERBS

Whip up this light summer main dish with fast-cooking noodles, carrots, cucumber, herbs, and our delicious Asian dressing. Serve warm or at room temperature.

ACTIVE TIME: 20 MIN · **TOTAL TIME:** 30 MIN

MAKES: 4 MAIN-DISH SERVINGS

3 SMALL CARROTS, PEELED AND CUT INTO 2" BY ¼" MATCHSTICK STRIPS (1⅓ CUPS)

⅓ CUP SEASONED RICE VINEGAR

1 PACKAGE (1 POUND) ½-INCH-WIDE FLAT RICE NOODLES

⅓ ENGLISH (SEEDLESS) CUCUMBER, UNPEELED AND CUT INTO 2" BY ¼" MATCHSTICK STRIPS (1 CUP)

1 CUP LOOSELY PACKED FRESH CILANTRO LEAVES

½ CUP LOOSELY PACKED FRESH MINT LEAVES

⅓ CUP LOOSELY PACKED SMALL FRESH BASIL LEAVES

⅓ CUP SNIPPED FRESH CHIVES

2 TEASPOONS ASIAN SESAME OIL

1 In small bowl, stir carrots with rice vinegar. Let stand at room temperature while preparing noodles.

2 In 8-quart saucepot, heat **5 quarts water** to boiling over high heat. Add noodles and cook just until cooked through, about 3 minutes. Drain noodles; rinse under cold running water and drain again.

3 Transfer noodles to large shallow serving bowl. Add carrots with their liquid, cucumber, cilantro, mint, basil, chives, and sesame oil; toss well.

EACH SERVING: ABOUT 470 CALORIES | 7G PROTEIN | 105G CARBOHYDRATE | 3G TOTAL FAT (0G SATURATED) | 0MG CHOLESTEROL | 550MG SODIUM

BLACK BEAN AND AVOCADO SALAD WITH CILANTRO DRESSING

A satisfying combination of summer veggies, romaine lettuce, and black beans tossed with a creamy cilantro-lime dressing.

TOTAL TIME: 30 MIN

MAKES: 16 CUPS OR 4 MAIN-DISH SERVINGS

CILANTRO DRESSING

- 2 LIMES
- ¼ CUP LIGHT MAYONNAISE
- ½ CUP PACKED FRESH CILANTRO LEAVES
- 2 TABLESPOONS REDUCED-FAT SOUR CREAM
- ½ TEASPOON GROUND CUMIN
- ¼ TEASPOON SUGAR
- ⅛ TEASPOON SALT
- ⅛ TEASPOON COARSELY GROUND BLACK PEPPER

SALAD

- 1 SMALL HEAD ROMAINE LETTUCE (ABOUT 1 POUND), CUT INTO ¾-INCH PIECES (ABOUT 8 CUPS)
- 2 MEDIUM TOMATOES, CUT INTO ½-INCH PIECES
- 2 KIRBY CUCUMBERS (ABOUT 4 OUNCES EACH), UNPEELED, EACH CUT LENGTH-WISE INTO QUARTERS, THEN CROSS-WISE INTO ¼-INCH-THICK PIECES
- 1 RIPE AVOCADO, CUT INTO ½-INCH PIECES
- 1 CAN (15 TO 19 OUNCES) BLACK BEANS, RINSED AND DRAINED

1 Prepare dressing: From limes, grate ½ teaspoon peel and squeeze 3 tablespoons juice. In blender, combine lime peel and juice, mayonnaise, cilantro, sour cream, cumin, sugar, salt, and pepper and puree, occasionally scraping down sides of blender, until smooth. Cover and refrigerate if not using right away. Makes about ½ cup.

2 Prepare salad: In large serving bowl, combine romaine, tomatoes, cucumbers, avocado, and beans. Add dressing and toss until evenly coated.

EACH SERVING: ABOUT 230 CALORIES | 9G PROTEIN | 34G CARBOHYDRATE | 10G TOTAL FAT (2G SATURATED) | 3MG CHOLESTEROL | 520MG SODIUM

RICE SALAD WITH BLACK BEANS

A satisfying meal in one, packed with the zesty flavors of citrus, salsa, and cilantro.

ACTIVE TIME: 10 MIN · **TOTAL TIME:** 30 MIN

MAKES: 7 CUPS OR 4 MAIN-DISH SERVINGS

¾ CUP REGULAR LONG-GRAIN RICE

2 LARGE LIMES

2 CANS (15 TO 19 OUNCES) BLACK BEANS, RINSED AND DRAINED

1 BUNCH WATERCRESS, TOUGH STEMS REMOVED

½ CUP BOTTLED SALSA

1 CUP CORN KERNELS CUT FROM COBS (2 MEDIUM EARS)

¼ CUP PACKED FRESH CILANTRO LEAVES, CHOPPED

1 TABLESPOON OLIVE OIL

½ TEASPOON SALT

¼ TEASPOON COARSELY GROUND BLACK PEPPER

---

1 Prepare rice as label directs. Meanwhile, from limes, grate ½ teaspoon peel and squeeze 3 tablespoons juice.

2 In large bowl, mix cooked rice, lime peel and juice, black beans, watercress, salsa, corn, cilantro, oil, salt, and pepper; toss well. Cover and refrigerate if not serving right away.

EACH SERVING: ABOUT 405 CALORIES | 24G PROTEIN | 81G CARBOHYDRATE | 6G TOTAL FAT (1G SATURATED) | 0MG CHOLESTEROL | 1,125MG SODIUM

GREEK PASTA TOSS

A great Greek salad (minus the lettuce) with hot pasta and beans folded in makes a complete meal.

ACTIVE TIME: 25 MIN · **TOTAL TIME:** 40 MIN

MAKES: 6 MAIN-DISH SERVINGS

1   POUND ROTINI OR FUSILLI PASTA

¼   CUP OLIVE OIL

2   TABLESPOONS BALSAMIC VINEGAR

1   GARLIC CLOVE, CRUSHED WITH GARLIC PRESS

½   TEASPOON SALT

¼   TEASPOON COARSELY GROUND BLACK PEPPER

9   RIPE MEDIUM TOMATOES (ABOUT 3 POUNDS), CUT INTO THIN WEDGES

2   CANS (15 TO 19 OUNCES EACH) GARBANZO BEANS, RINSED AND DRAINED

8   OUNCES FETA CHEESE, COARSELY CRUMBLED

2   KIRBY CUCUMBERS (ABOUT 4 OUNCES EACH), UNPEELED AND CUT INTO ¼-INCH PIECES

½   CUP KALAMATA OLIVES, PITTED AND CHOPPED

½   CUP PACKED FRESH PARSLEY LEAVES, CHOPPED

½   CUP PACKED FRESH DILL, CHOPPED

1 In large saucepot, cook pasta as label directs.

2 Meanwhile, in large serving bowl, with wire whisk, mix oil, vinegar, garlic, salt, and pepper until blended. Add tomatoes, beans, feta, cucumbers, olives, parsley, and dill. Toss until evenly mixed and coated with dressing.

3 Drain pasta. Add pasta to tomato mixture in bowl; toss well.

EACH SERVING: ABOUT 685 CALORIES | 26G PROTEIN | 97G CARBOHYDRATE | 22G TOTAL FAT (8G SATURATED) | 34MG CHOLESTEROL | 1,154MG SODIUM

PENNE WITH GREEN BEANS AND BASIL

This cool pasta salad is perfect for a hot night.

ACTIVE TIME: 15 MIN · TOTAL TIME: 35 MIN
MAKES: 8 CUPS OR 4 MAIN-DISH SERVINGS

---

8   OUNCES PENNE OR BOW-TIE PASTA

1   POUND GREEN BEANS,
    TRIMMED AND EACH CUT IN HALF

1½ TEASPOONS SALT

1   TABLESPOON WATER

1   CUP LOOSELY PACKED FRESH
    BASIL LEAVES

¼   CUP EXTRA-VIRGIN OLIVE OIL

½   TEASPOON COARSELY GROUND
    BLACK PEPPER

1   MEDIUM TOMATO, CHOPPED

SMALL BASIL LEAVES FOR GARNISH

1 In large saucepot, cook penne as label directs.

2 Meanwhile, in 12-inch skillet, heat **1 inch water** to boiling over high heat. Add green beans and ½ teaspoon salt; heat to boiling. Cook beans until tender-crisp, 8 to 10 minutes. Drain beans. Rinse beans under cold running water to cool slightly; drain again.

3 In blender at high speed, combine basil, oil, and water and puree until almost smooth, stopping blender occasionally and scraping down sides with rubber spatula. Transfer basil puree to large bowl; stir in remaining 1 teaspoon salt and pepper.

4 Drain pasta; rinse under cold running water and drain again. In warm serving bowl, toss pasta, beans, tomato, and basil puree. Garnish with basil leaves.

EACH SERVING: ABOUT 370 CALORIES | 10G PROTEIN | 52G CARBOHYDRATE | 15G TOTAL FAT (2G SATURATED) | 0MG CHOLESTEROL | 680MG SODIUM

TOMATO AND ORZO SALAD

This perfect pasta toss requires little cooking but yields big flavor.

ACTIVE TIME: 20 MIN · TOTAL TIME: 28 MIN
MAKES: 7½ CUPS OR 4 MAIN-DISH SERVINGS

SALT

1¼ CUPS ORZO PASTA

½ POUND GREEN BEANS, TRIMMED AND EACH CUT INTO THIRDS

2 LARGE LEMONS

2 TABLESPOONS EXTRA-VIRGIN OLIVE OIL

2 TEASPOONS FRESH OREGANO LEAVES, CHOPPED

¼ TEASPOON COARSELY GROUND BLACK PEPPER

1 POUND RIPE TOMATOES (ABOUT 3 MEDIUM), CUT INTO ½-INCH PIECES

4 OUNCES RICOTTA SALATA CHEESE, CRUMBLED, OR PARMESAN CHEESE, SHAVED

1 In 4-quart saucepan, heat 3 quarts of salted water to boiling over high heat. Add orzo; heat to boiling and cook 4 minutes. Add green beans and cook until orzo and beans are tender, about 4 minutes longer. Drain well.

2 Meanwhile, from lemons, grate 1 teaspoon peel and squeeze ¼ cup juice. In large bowl, with wire whisk or fork, mix oil, oregano, ¾ teaspoon salt, pepper, and lemon peel and juice until blended.

3 Add warm orzo and beans to dressing in bowl and toss well. Gently stir in tomatoes and ricotta salata.

EACH SERVING: ABOUT 340 CALORIES | 12G PROTEIN | 44G CARBOHYDRATE | 14G TOTAL FAT (6G SATURATED) | 26MG CHOLESTEROL | 1,010MG SODIUM

FATTOUSH

This Lebanese salad is packed with juicy summer-ripe tomatoes and fresh herbs. Pieces of toasted pita absorb the tasty dressing.

TOTAL TIME: 25 MIN PLUS STANDING

MAKES: 16 CUPS OR 4 MAIN-DISH SERVINGS

3 TABLESPOONS FRESH LEMON JUICE

3 TABLESPOONS OLIVE OIL

1 TEASPOON SALT

½ TEASPOON COARSELY GROUND BLACK PEPPER

4 MEDIUM TOMATOES (ABOUT 1¼ POUNDS), CUT INTO ½-INCH PIECES

3 GREEN ONIONS, TRIMMED AND CHOPPED

1 MEDIUM CUCUMBER (8 OUNCES), PEELED, SEEDED, AND CUT INTO ½-INCH PIECES

1 CUP LOOSELY PACKED FRESH PARSLEY LEAVES

½ CUP LOOSELY PACKED FRESH MINT LEAVES, CHOPPED

4 (6-INCH) PITAS, EACH SPLIT HORIZONTALLY IN HALF

1 SMALL HEAD ROMAINE LETTUCE (ABOUT 1 POUND), COARSELY CHOPPED

1 In large salad bowl, with wire whisk or fork, mix lemon juice, oil, salt, and pepper. Add tomatoes, green onions, cucumber, parsley, and mint; toss to coat. Let tomato mixture stand 15 minutes to allow flavors to blend.

2 Meanwhile, toast pitas; cool. Break pitas into 1-inch pieces.

3 Just before serving, toss lettuce and pitas with tomato mixture.

EACH SERVING: ABOUT 315 CALORIES | 9G PROTEIN | 47G CARBOHYDRATE | 12G TOTAL FAT (2G SATURATED) | 0MG CHOLESTEROL | 935MG SODIUM

GREEK PEASANT SALAD

Serve this cool Mediterranean-style salad on a summer night.

TOTAL TIME: 25 MIN

MAKES: 6½ CUPS OR 4 MAIN-DISH SERVINGS

---

4   KIRBY CUCUMBERS (ABOUT 1 POUND)

2   TABLESPOONS FRESH LEMON JUICE

1   TABLESPOON OLIVE OIL

¼   TEASPOON SALT

⅛   TEASPOON GROUND BLACK PEPPER

2   POUNDS RIPE RED AND/OR YELLOW TOMATOES (ABOUT 6 MEDIUM), CUT INTO 1-INCH PIECES

½   CUP LOOSELY PACKED FRESH MINT LEAVES, CHOPPED

⅓   CUP KALAMATA OLIVES, PITTED AND COARSELY CHOPPED

¼   CUP LOOSELY PACKED FRESH DILL, CHOPPED

2   OUNCES FETA CHEESE, CRUMBLED (½ CUP)

1 With vegetable peeler, remove 3 or 4 evenly spaced lengthwise strips of peel from each cucumber. Cut each cucumber lengthwise into quarters, then crosswise into ½-inch pieces.

2 In large bowl, with wire whisk or fork, mix lemon juice, oil, salt, and pepper until blended. Add cucumbers, tomatoes, mint, olives, and dill, and toss until evenly mixed and coated with dressing. Top with feta.

EACH SERVING: ABOUT 150 CALORIES | 5G PROTEIN | 17G CARBOHYDRATE | 9G TOTAL FAT (3G SATURATED) | 12MG CHOLESTEROL | 42G SODIUM

FLATBREAD WITH SALAD

Try this salad "pizza" as an alternative to the usual tomato-and-cheese kind. It's especially good because it starts with our excellent crusty Grilled Flatbread.

TOTAL TIME: 20 MIN PLUS PREPARATION OF FLATBREADS
MAKES: 4 MAIN-DISH SERVINGS

GRILLED FLATBREAD

1 PACKAGE ACTIVE DRY YEAST

1 TEASPOON SUGAR

1¼ CUPS WARM WATER (105° TO 115°F)

ABOUT 4 CUPS ALL-PURPOSE FLOUR

ABOUT 3 TABLESPOONS OLIVE OIL

2 TEASPOONS SALT

SALAD

2 TABLESPOONS EXTRA-VIRGIN OLIVE OIL

2 TABLESPOONS RED WINE VINEGAR

1 TEASPOON SUGAR

1 TEASPOON DIJON MUSTARD

¼ TEASPOON SALT

⅛ TEASPOON GROUND BLACK PEPPER

6 CUPS SALAD GREENS, SUCH AS RADICCHIO, ENDIVE, AND ARUGULA, TORN INTO ½-INCH PIECES

2 RIPE MEDIUM TOMATOES, CUT INTO ½-INCH PIECES

1 SMALL CUCUMBER, PEELED AND CUT INTO ½-INCH PIECES

1 Prepare flatbread: In large bowl, combine yeast, sugar, and ¼ cup warm water; stir to dissolve. Let stand until foamy, about 5 minutes. With a wooden spoon, stir in 1½ cups flour, 2 tablespoons olive oil, salt, and remaining 1 cup warm water until blended. With spoon, gradually stir in 2 cups flour. With floured hand, knead mixture in bowl to combine.

2 Turn dough onto lightly floured surface and knead, working in more flour (about ½ cup), until smooth and elastic, about 10 minutes.

3 Shape dough into ball and place in greased large bowl, turning to grease top. Cover bowl with plastic wrap and let rise in warm place (80° to 85°F) until doubled in volume, about 1 hour. (After dough has risen, if not using dough right away, punch down and leave in bowl, cover loosely with greased plastic wrap, and refrigerate until ready to use, up to 24 hours. When ready to use, follow directions below.)

4 Punch down dough. Turn dough onto lightly floured surface. Cover and let rest 15 minutes.

5 Meanwhile, prepare grill. Grease two large cookie sheets.

6 Shape dough into 4 balls. On lightly floured surface, with floured rolling pin, roll 1 dough ball at a time into 12-inch round about ⅛ inch thick. (The diameter or shape of round is not as important as even thickness.) Place rounds on prepared cookie sheets; brush tops with some remaining oil.

7 About 10 minutes before grilling flatbread, prepare salad topping: In large bowl, with wire whisk, mix oil, vinegar, sugar, mustard, salt, and pepper until blended. Add salad greens, tomatoes, and cucumber; toss to coat well. Set aside.

8 With hands, place 1 round at a time, greased side down, on hot grill rack over medium heat. Grill until grill marks appear on underside and dough stiffens (dough may puff slightly), 2 to 3 minutes. Brush top with some oil. With tongs, turn bread and grill until grill marks appear on underside and bread is cooked through, 2 to 3 minutes longer. Transfer flatbread to tray; keep warm. Repeat with remaining dough rounds.

9 To serve, top each flatbread with about 2 cups salad. Cut each round into quarters. Serve 4 wedges per person.

EACH SERVING OF FLATBREAD: ABOUT 370 CALORIES | 10G PROTEIN | 64G CARBOHYDRATE | 8G TOTAL FAT (2G SATURATED) | 0MG CHOLESTEROL | 610MG SODIUM

EACH SERVING OF FLATBREAD WITH SALAD: ABOUT 620 CALORIES | 16G PROTEIN | 106G CARBOHYDRATE | 14G TOTAL FAT (2G SATURATED) | 0MG CHOLESTEROL | 1,250MG SODIUM

SZECHUAN PEANUT-NOODLE SALAD

A tasty pasta salad packed with great Asian flavors. To serve cold, chill the pasta and toss with the vegetables just before serving.

ACTIVE TIME: 25 MIN · **TOTAL TIME:** 50 MIN

MAKES: 8 MAIN-DISH SERVINGS

---

1   PACKAGE (16 OUNCES) LINGUINE OR SPAGHETTI

2½ TEASPOONS SALT

4   OUNCES SNOW PEAS, STRINGS REMOVED

½   CUP CREAMY PEANUT BUTTER

1   TABLESPOON GRATED, PEELED FRESH GINGER

¼   CUP SOY SAUCE

2   TABLESPOONS DISTILLED WHITE VINEGAR

2   TEASPOONS ASIAN SESAME OIL

¼   TEASPOON HOT PEPPER SAUCE

1   SMALL CUCUMBER (6 OUNCES), PEELED, SEEDED, AND CUT INTO 2" BY ¼" MATCHSTICK STRIPS

¼   CUP DRY-ROASTED PEANUTS

1   GREEN ONION, TRIMMED AND CHOPPED

1   In large saucepot, cook linguine as label directs, using 2 teaspoons salt.

2   Meanwhile, in 3-quart saucepan, heat **1 inch water** to boiling; add snow peas. Reduce heat and simmer 2 min; drain. Rinse with cold running water; drain. Cut snow peas lengthwise into ¼-inch-wide matchstick strips; set aside.

3   Drain linguine, reserving 1 cup pasta water.

4   Prepare dressing: In large bowl, with wire whisk, mix peanut butter, ginger, reserved pasta water, soy sauce, vinegar, sesame oil, hot pepper sauce, and remaining ½ teaspoon salt until smooth.

5   Add linguine to dressing in bowl and toss to coat. Add snow peas and cucumber; toss to combine. Sprinkle with peanuts and green onion.

EACH SERVING: ABOUT 358 CALORIES | 14G PROTEIN | 49G CARBOHYDRATE | 13G TOTAL FAT (2G SATURATED) | 0MG CHOLESTEROL | 1,121MG SODIUM

TOFU "EGG" SALAD

A real surprise! Looks and tastes just like egg salad but has no cholesterol. Enjoy it on its own or make into sandwiches on whole-grain bread with sliced tomato and crisp lettuce.

TOTAL TIME: 15 MIN

MAKES: 4 MAIN-DISH SERVINGS

- 1 PACKAGE (16 OUNCES) FIRM OR EXTRA-FIRM TOFU, DRAINED
- 1 MEDIUM STALK CELERY, CHOPPED
- ½ SMALL RED PEPPER, CHOPPED
- 1 GREEN ONION, TRIMMED AND CHOPPED

- ¼ CUP LIGHT MAYONNAISE
- ½ TEASPOON DIJON MUSTARD
- ½ TEASPOON SALT
- ⅛ TEASPOON TURMERIC

In medium bowl, with fork, mash tofu until it resembles scrambled eggs. Stir in celery, red pepper, green onion, mayonnaise, mustard, salt, and tumeric. Cover and refrigerate if not serving right away.

EACH SERVING: ABOUT 195 CALORIES | 18G PROTEIN | 10G CARBOHYDRATE | 11G TOTAL FAT (1G SATURATED) | 0MG CHOLESTEROL | 445MG SODIUM

EGG SALAD DELUXE

Hard-cooked eggs are chopped and mixed with sautéed onions, mushrooms, and celery for a new take on the classic egg salad. If you like, serve with toasted whole-grain bread.

ACTIVE TIME: 20 MIN · **TOTAL TIME:** 40 MIN
MAKES: 4½ CUPS OR 6 MAIN-DISH SERVINGS

8 LARGE EGGS

3 TABLESPOONS OLIVE OIL

1 MEDIUM ONION, CUT IN HALF AND THINLY SLICED

10 OUNCES MUSHROOMS, SLICED

2 MEDIUM STALKS CELERY, FINELY CHOPPED

¼ CUP LOOSELY PACKED FRESH PARSLEY LEAVES, CHOPPED

½ TEASPOON SALT

¼ TEASPOON COARSELY GROUND BLACK PEPPER

1 HEAD BOSTON LETTUCE, LEAVES SEPARATED

1 In 3-quart saucepan, place eggs and enough cold water to cover by at least 1 inch; heat to boiling over high heat. Immediately remove saucepan from heat and cover tightly; let stand 15 minutes. Pour off hot water and run cold water over eggs until easy to handle.

2 Meanwhile, in nonstick 12-inch skillet, heat 1 tablespoon oil over medium heat until hot. Add onion and cook, stirring occasionally, until tender and golden, 10 to 12 minutes. Increase heat to medium-high; add mushrooms and cook until mushrooms are golden and all liquid has evaporated, about 8 minutes.

3 Peel hard-cooked eggs and finely chop. In large bowl, combine eggs with mushroom mixture, celery, parsley, salt, pepper, and remaining 2 tablespoons oil; toss well.

4 To serve, line platter with lettuce leaves and top with egg salad.

EACH SERVING: ABOUT 190 CALORIES | 11G PROTEIN | 5G CARBOHYDRATE | 14G TOTAL FAT (3G SATURATED) | 283MG CHOLESTEROL | 290MG SODIUM

PROVENÇAL PASTA SALAD

The robust flavors of this colorful salad—complete with eggplant, tomatoes, garlic, basil, and olives—will transport you and your guests to sunny southern France.

ACTIVE TIME: 30 MIN · **TOTAL TIME:** 1 HR

MAKES: 12 CUPS OR 6 MAIN-DISH SERVINGS

12 OUNCES BOW-TIE PASTA

2 MEDIUM RED PEPPERS OR 1 JAR (7 OUNCES) ROASTED RED PEPPERS, DRAINED AND CUT INTO ½-INCH PIECES

2 TABLESPOONS OLIVE OIL

1 MEDIUM ONION, CHOPPED

1 SMALL EGGPLANT (ABOUT ¾ POUND), CUT INTO ½-INCH PIECES

2 GARLIC CLOVES, MINCED

¾ TEASPOON SALT

¼ TEASPOON COARSELY GROUND BLACK PEPPER

1 PINT CHERRY TOMATOES, EACH CUT IN HALF

1 CUP LOOSELY PACKED FRESH BASIL LEAVES, COARSELY CHOPPED

⅓ CUP KALAMATA OLIVES, PITTED AND COARSELY CHOPPED

1 In large saucepot, cook pasta as label directs. Reserve ¼ cup pasta water. Drain and rinse pasta under cold running water; drain again.

2 Meanwhile, roast peppers if using fresh ones: Preheat broiler. Line broiling pan with foil. Cut each pepper lengthwise in half; remove and discard stems and seeds. Arrange peppers, cut side down, in prepared pan. With hand, flatten each pepper half. Place pan in broiler 5 to 6 inches from heat source. Broil until skin is charred and blistered, 8 to 10 minutes. Wrap peppers in foil and allow to steam at room temperature until cool enough to handle, about 15 minutes. Remove peppers from foil. Peel off skin and discard. Cut peppers into ½-inch pieces.

3 In nonstick 12-inch skillet, heat oil over medium heat until hot. Add onion and cook, stirring often, until tender and golden, about 10 minutes. Increase heat to medium-high. Add eggplant, garlic, salt, and black pepper and cook, stirring often, until eggplant is tender and golden, about 8 minutes longer.

4 To pasta, add roasted peppers, onion mixture, tomatoes, basil, olives, and reserved pasta water; toss gently. Transfer pasta mixture to serving bowl. Cover and refrigerate if not serving right away.

EACH SERVING: ABOUT 300 CALORIES | 9G PROTEIN | 52G CARBOHYDRATE | 7G TOTAL FAT (1G SATURATED) | 0MG CHOLESTEROL | 495MG SODIUM

QUICK
DINNERS

We all live hectic lives today. Few of us have time to spend hours preparing from-scratch meals seven days a week. Even if we did have the time, there are thousands of other things competing for each extra minute. So in this chapter, we've put together a collection of scrumptious meatless recipes that require the bare minimum of muss, fuss, labor—perfect for busy households.

What's the secret? Making smart use of convenience foods and staples from the pantry and refrigerator, then adding your own vegetables, herbs, and spices. In no more than forty minutes you can have any of the dishes in this chapter on the table and ready to eat. These are not mere thrown-together, ho-hum meals either. They are wholesome, satisfying vegetarian dishes that everyone will find delicious.

Ample use is made of canned beans and tomato products, quick-cooking grains and pasta, jars of olives and salsa, packaged shredded cheeses, and bags of precut vegetables. Cuisines from around the world offer many palate-pleasing vegetarian recipes. Most supermarkets, specialty food shops, and markets stock a wide array of ethnic products that can easily be stored in your pantry for quick and hassle-free dinners.

Another great feature of the time-saving nature of these dishes is that few pots and pans are used in preparation. That means cleanup is a breeze, allowing you to spend more time with your family, which is, after all, the most valuable use of your time.

Spinach Soufflé (page 260)

BOW TIES WITH TOMATOES, HERBS, AND LEMON

The easy late-summer sauce "cooks" from the heat of the drained pasta. While the pasta boils, slice and warm a loaf of semolina bread for a simple go-along.

ACTIVE TIME: 15 MIN · TOTAL TIME: 30 MIN

MAKES: 11 CUPS OR 4 MAIN-DISH SERVINGS

6 MEDIUM TOMATOES (ABOUT 2 POUNDS), CHOPPED	1 TEASPOON GRATED LEMON PEEL
¼ CUP LOOSELY PACKED FRESH MINT LEAVES, CHOPPED	1 GARLIC CLOVES, CRUSHED WITH GARLIC PRESS
¼ CUP LOOSELY PACKED FRESH BASIL LEAVES, CHOPPED	1 TEASPOON SALT
2 TABLESPOONS OLIVE OIL	¼ TEASPOON GROUND BLACK PEPPER
	1 PACKAGE (16 OUNCES) BOW-TIE OR ZITI PASTA

1 In large serving bowl, stir tomatoes, mint, basil, olive oil, lemon peel, garlic, salt and pepper; set mixture aside to allow flavors to develop.

2 Meanwhile, in large saucepot, cook pasta as label directs. Drain well.

3 Add hot pasta to tomato mixture in bowl; toss well.

EACH SERVING: ABOUT 530 CALORIES | 17G PROTEIN | 96G CARBOHYDRATE | 9G TOTAL FAT (1G SATURATED) | 0MG CHOLESTEROL | 695MG SODIUM

COUSCOUS WITH GARBANZO BEANS

A vegetarian entrée fragrant with the flavors of Morocco—warm spices, green olives, and garlic—gets a quick start from preseasoned couscous mix.

ACTIVE TIME: 5 MIN · TOTAL TIME: 15 MIN
MAKES: 4 MAIN-DISH SERVINGS

1   BOX (5.6 OUNCES) COUSCOUS (MOROCCAN PASTA) WITH TOASTED PINE NUTS
⅓   CUP DARK SEEDLESS RAISINS
1   TABLESPOON OLIVE OIL
1   MEDIUM ZUCCHINI (ABOUT 10 OUNCES), CUT LENGTHWISE IN HALF, THEN CROSSWISE INTO ½-INCH-THICK SLICES
1   GARLIC CLOVE, CRUSHED WITH GARLIC PRESS

¾   TEASPOON GROUND CUMIN
¾   TEASPOON GROUND CORIANDER
⅛   TEASPOON GROUND RED PEPPER (CAYENNE)
2   CANS (15 TO 19 OUNCES EACH) GARBANZO BEANS, RINSED AND DRAINED
½   CUP SALAD OLIVES, DRAINED, OR CHOPPED PIMIENTO-STUFFED OLIVES
¼   CUP WATER

1   Prepare couscous as label directs, except add raisins to cooking water.
2   Meanwhile, in nonstick 12-inch skillet, heat oil over medium-high heat until hot. Add zucchini and cook, stirring occasionally, 5 minutes. Add garlic, cumin, coriander, and red pepper and cook, stirring, 30 seconds. Add beans, olives, and water and cook, stirring often, until heated through, about 5 minutes.
3   Add cooked couscous to bean mixture and toss gently. Spoon into serving bowl.

EACH SERVING: ABOUT 555 CALORIES | 20G PROTEIN | 101G CARBOHYDRATE | 10G TOTAL FAT (1G SATURATED) | 0MG CHOLESTEROL | 1,110MG SODIUM

FUSILLI WITH GARBANZO BEANS AND SPINACH

A staple of Italian cuisine, beans show up almost everywhere, including pasta dishes. For this dish, we use canned garbanzo beans to reduce preparation and cooking time.

ACTIVE TIME: 8 MIN · TOTAL TIME: 20 MIN
MAKES: 6 MAIN-DISH SERVINGS

1   POUND FUSILLI PASTA

2   TABLESPOONS OLIVE OIL

1   MEDIUM ONION, CHOPPED

2   GARLIC CLOVES, CRUSHED
    WITH GARLIC PRESS

½   TEASPOON DRIED OREGANO

1   CAN (29 OUNCES) GARBANZO BEANS,
    RINSED AND DRAINED

3   TABLESPOONS BALSAMIC VINEGAR

1¼ TEASPOONS SALT

¼   TEASPOON COARSELY GROUND
    BLACK PEPPER

2   BAGS (6 OUNCES EACH)
    BABY SPINACH

1   In large saucepot, cook pasta as label directs.

2   Meanwhile, in 12-inch skillet, heat oil over medium-high heat until hot. Add onion; cook, covered, 5 minutes, stirring often. Stir in garlic and oregano and cook 30 seconds. Stir in beans, vinegar, salt, and pepper; cook, stirring often, 5 minutes.

3   Drain pasta, reserving 1 cup pasta water. Return pasta to saucepot. Add spinach, bean mixture, and reserved pasta water; toss gently to combine.

EACH SERVING: ABOUT 500 CALORIES | 20G PROTEIN | 85G CARBOHYDRATE | 8G TOTAL FAT (1G SATURATED) | 0MG CHOLESTEROL | 980MG SODIUM

PASTA WITH EGGPLANT SAUCE

Leftovers from our Eggplant Parmesan make a quick weeknight pasta supper. Serve this easy pasta toss with mixed greens and crusty bread.

ACTIVE TIME: 5 MIN · TOTAL TIME: 25 MIN

MAKES: 4 MAIN-DISH SERVINGS

1   PACKAGE (16 OUNCES) RIGATONI OR FUSILLI PASTA

2   CUPS TOMATO SAUCE RESERVED FROM EGGPLANT PARMESAN (PAGE 304)

1   QUARTER (ABOUT 6" BY 4" PIECE) RESERVED EGGPLANT PARMESAN (PAGE 304) CUT INTO ¾-INCH PIECES (ABOUT 2½ CUPS)

1   In large saucepot, cook pasta as label directs.

2   Meanwhile, in 2-quart saucepan, heat Tomato Sauce and cut-up Eggplant Parmesan over medium heat, stirring occasionally, until hot, about 15 minutes.

3   Drain pasta, reserving **¼ cup pasta water**. Return pasta to saucepot; add eggplant mixture and reserved pasta water and toss well.

EACH SERVING: ABOUT 615 CALORIES | 24G PROTEIN | 107G CARBOHYDRATE | 10G TOTAL FAT (3G SATURATED) | 15MG CHOLESTEROL | 1,280MG SODIUM

CAVATELLI WITH RICOTTA AND FRESH TOMATO SAUCE

We used frozen cavatelli, a short, curled, rippled pasta. If you can't find it, substitute frozen gnocchi. Serve with mixed Italian salad greens and sesame breadsticks. Just before serving, toss the greens with olive oil and a squeeze of lemon juice.

ACTIVE TIME: 5 MIN · TOTAL TIME: 30 MIN
MAKES: 4 MAIN-DISH SERVINGS

1 BAG (16 OUNCES) FROZEN CAVATELLI	½ TEASPOON SALT
1 TABLESPOON OLIVE OIL	¼ TEASPOON COARSELY GROUND BLACK PEPPER
1 GARLIC CLOVES, CRUSHED WITH GARLIC PRESS	¾ CUP PART-SKIM RICOTTA CHEESE
4 MEDIUM TOMATOES (ABOUT 1½ POUNDS), CHOPPED	¼ CUP FRESHLY GRATED PECORINO ROMANO OR PARMESAN CHEESE

1 In large saucepot, cook pasta as label directs.

2 Meanwhile, in nonstick 10-inch skillet, heat oil over medium heat until hot. Add garlic and cook, stirring, 1 minute. Stir in tomatoes, salt, and pepper and cook, stirring occasionally, until tomatoes break up slightly, about 5 minutes.

3 Drain cavatelli; transfer to warm serving bowl. Stir in ricotta and Romano. Pour tomato mixture on top; toss before serving.

EACH SERVING: ABOUT 455 CALORIES | 20G PROTEIN | 71G CARBOHYDRATE | 11G TOTAL FAT (5G SATURATED) | 40MG CHOLESTEROL | 560MG SODIUM

PASTA RIBBONS WITH CHUNKY VEGETABLES

Just as satisfying as lasagna, but with half the work and half the time.

ACTIVE TIME: 10 MIN · **TOTAL TIME:** 25 MIN

MAKES: 4 MAIN-DISH SERVINGS

SALT

1   PACKAGE (8 TO 9 OUNCES) OVEN-READY LASAGNA NOODLES (6½" BY 3½" EACH)

1   TABLESPOON OLIVE OIL

2   MEDIUM YELLOW SUMMER SQUASH AND/OR ZUCCHINI (10 OUNCES EACH), CUT INTO ¾-INCH-THICK SLICES

1   PACKAGE (10 OUNCES) MUSHROOMS, TRIMMED AND CUT INTO HALVES OR QUARTERS, IF LARGE

2   CUPS TOMATO-BASIL PASTA SAUCE

¼   CUP HEAVY OR WHIPPING CREAM

1   SMALL CHUNK (2 OUNCES) PARMESAN CHEESE

1 In 4-quart saucepan, heat **3 quarts of salted water** to boiling over high heat. Add lasagna noodles, 1 noodle at a time to avoid sticking; cook until tender, 7 to 8 minutes.

2 Meanwhile, in nonstick 12-inch skillet, heat oil over medium-high heat until very hot. Add squash and mushrooms; cover and cook, stirring occasionally, until vegetables are tender-crisp, 4 to 5 minutes. Add pasta sauce and cream; heat to boiling, stirring frequently.

3 Drain noodles. In serving bowl, toss noodles with squash mixture. With vegetable peeler, shave thin strips from Parmesan. Top pasta with Parmesan shavings to serve.

EACH SERVING: ABOUT 515 CALORIES | 19G PROTEIN | 70G CARBOHYDRATE | 18G TOTAL FAT (7G SATURATED) | 32MG CHOLESTEROL | 770MG SODIUM

SPINACH SOUFFLÉ

Serve this delicious soufflé with crusty rolls and a simple salad of mixed baby greens.

ACTIVE TIME: 20 MIN · TOTAL TIME: 40 MIN
MAKES: 4 MAIN-DISH SERVINGS

---

3 TABLESPOONS PLAIN DRIED BREAD CRUMBS

1½ CUPS LOW-FAT MILK (1%)

⅓ CUP CORNSTARCH

2 LARGE EGGS, SEPARATED

1 PACKAGE (10 OUNCES) FROZEN CHOPPED SPINACH, THAWED AND SQUEEZED DRY

3 TABLESPOONS FRESHLY GRATED PARMESAN CHEESE

½ TEASPOON SALT

¼ TEASPOON COARSELY GROUND BLACK PEPPER

½ TEASPOON CREAM OF TARTAR

4 LARGE EGG WHITES (SEE TIP)

1 Preheat oven to 425°F. Spray 10-inch quiche dish or shallow 2-quart casserole with nonstick cooking spray; sprinkle with bread crumbs to coat. Set aside.

2 In 2-quart saucepan, with wire whisk, beat milk with cornstarch until blended. Heat milk mixture over medium-high heat, stirring constantly, until mixture thickens and boils; boil 1 minute. Remove pan from heat.

3 In large bowl, with rubber spatula, mix egg yolks, spinach, Parmesan, salt, and pepper until blended; stir in warm milk mixture. Cool slightly (if spinach mixture is too warm, it will deflate beaten egg whites).

4 In another large bowl, with mixer at high speed, beat cream of tartar and 6 egg whites until stiff peaks form. Gently fold egg-white mixture, one-third at a time, into spinach mixture.

5 Spoon soufflé mixture into quiche dish. Bake soufflé until top is golden and puffed, about 20 minutes. Serve immediately.

TIP If you prefer, you can use liquid egg substitute or pasteurized liquid egg whites, which are sold in 1-pint containers in the dairy case of most supermarkets.

EACH SERVING: ABOUT 195 CALORIES | 15G PROTEIN | 23G CARBOHYDRATE | 5G TOTAL FAT (2G SATURATED) | 114MG CHOLESTEROL | 590MG SODIUM

CAPELLINI FRITTATA

A satisfying meal made with sautéed onion and red pepper baked in an egg-and-pasta custard. If you have leftover spaghetti in the fridge, use one cup of it instead of the cooked capellini. Serve with a green salad, tossed with our Spicy Tomato Dressing (recipe follows) and a chunk of hearty peasant bread.

ACTIVE TIME: 14 MIN · TOTAL TIME: 20 MIN

MAKES: 4 MAIN-DISH SERVINGS

---

2   OUNCES CAPELLINI OR ANGEL HAIR PASTA, BROKEN INTO PIECES (ABOUT ½ CUP)

2   TEASPOONS OLIVE OIL

1   SMALL ONION, THINLY SLICED

1   SMALL RED PEPPER, CHOPPED

6   LARGE EGG WHITES (SEE TIP PAGE 260)

2   LARGE EGGS

⅓   CUP FRESHLY GRATED PARMESAN CHEESE

¼   CUP FAT-FREE (SKIM) MILK

½   TEASPOON SALT

¼   TEASPOON HOT PEPPER SAUCE

1   In 2-quart saucepan, heat 3 cups water to boiling over high heat. Add pasta, and cook just until tender, about 2 minutes. Drain and set aside.

2   Meanwhile, preheat oven to 425°F. In oven-safe nonstick 10-inch skillet (if skillet is not oven-safe, wrap handle with double layer of foil), heat oil over medium heat. Add onion and red pepper and cook, stirring frequently, until tender, about 7 minutes.

3   In large bowl, with wire whisk or fork, beat egg whites, whole eggs, Parmesan, milk, salt, and hot pepper sauce; stir in pasta. Pour egg mixture over onion mixture; cover and cook until egg mixture is set around edge, about 3 minutes. Remove cover and place skillet in oven. Bake until frittata is set in center, about 6 minutes longer.

4   To serve, invert frittata onto warm serving plate, and cut into wedges.

EACH SERVING: ABOUT 190 CALORIES | 15G PROTEIN | 15G CARBOHYDRATE | 8G TOTAL FAT (3G SATURATED) | 113MG CHOLESTEROL | 545MG SODIUM

SPICY TOMATO DRESSING

Made with vegetable juice and just a bit of olive oil, it's destined to be a new favorite.

TOTAL TIME: 3 MIN

MAKES: 1 CUP

---

1   CAN (5½ OUNCES) SPICY-HOT
     VEGETABLE JUICE

3   TABLESPOONS RED WINE VINEGAR

1   TABLESPOON OLIVE OIL

1   GARLIC CLOVE, CRUSHED
     WITH GARLIC PRESS

½   TEASPOON SUGAR

½   TEASPOON DRY MUSTARD

In small bowl or jar, combine juice, vinegar, oil, garlic, sugar, and mustard. With wire whisk or fork, mix (or cover jar and shake) until blended. Cover and refrigerate. Stir or shake before using.

EACH TABLESPOON: ABOUT 15 CALORIES | 0G PROTEIN | 1G CARBOHYDRATE | 1G TOTAL FAT (0G SATURATED) | 0MG CHOLESTEROL | 35MG SODIUM

NACHO CASSEROLE

Warning: This soup-based casserole may become a family favorite! For less "heat," omit the jalapeños.

ACTIVE TIME: 10 MIN · TOTAL TIME: 30 MIN

MAKES: 6 MAIN-DISH SERVINGS

---

1   CAN (10¾ OUNCES) CONDENSED CHEDDAR CHEESE SOUP

½   CUP LOW-FAT MILK (1%)

1   JAR (16 OUNCES) MILD OR MEDIUM-HOT SALSA

1   BAG (7 OUNCES) BAKED, UNSALTED TORTILLA CHIPS

1   CAN (16 OUNCES) FAT-FREE REFRIED BEANS

1   OR 2 JALAPEÑO CHILES, THINLY SLICED

1   CUP SHREDDED CHEDDAR CHEESE

Preheat oven to 400°F. In 13" by 9" ceramic or glass baking dish, stir undiluted soup with milk until well blended; spread evenly. Top with half of salsa and half of chips. Carefully spread beans over chips. Top with remaining chips and salsa. Sprinkle evenly with chiles and Cheddar. Bake until hot, about 20 minutes.

EACH SERVING: ABOUT 385 CALORIES | 17G PROTEIN | 60G CARBOHYDRATE | 12G TOTAL FAT (5G SATURATED) | 27MG CHOLESTEROL | 1,370MG SODIUM

MEXICAN POTATO FRITTATA

This flat, baked omelet combines a jar of salsa with a bit of sharp Cheddar cheese. Toss a package of prewashed baby spinach with sliced red onions, sliced fresh pears, and bottled salad dressing while the frittata bakes.

ACTIVE TIME: 20 MIN · TOTAL TIME: 25 MIN
MAKES: 4 MAIN-DISH SERVINGS

1   TEASPOON OLIVE OIL

12 OUNCES RED-SKINNED POTATOES, CUT INTO ½-INCH PIECES

6   LARGE EGGS

1   JAR (11 TO 12 OUNCES) MEDIUM-HOT SALSA

½   TEASPOON SALT

¼   TEASPOON COARSELY GROUND BLACK PEPPER

¼   CUP SHREDDED SHARP CHEDDAR CHEESE (1 OUNCE)

1   MEDIUM TOMATO

1 Preheat oven to 425°F. In oven-safe nonstick 10-inch skillet (if skillet is not oven-safe, wrap handle with double layer of foil), heat oil over medium-high heat until hot; add potatoes and cook, covered, until potatoes are tender and golden brown, about 10 minutes, stirring occasionally.
2 Meanwhile, in medium bowl, with wire whisk or fork, beat eggs with ¼ cup salsa (chopped, if necessary), salt, and pepper. Stir in cheese; set aside. Chop tomato and stir into remaining salsa.
3 Stir egg mixture into potatoes in skillet and cook over medium heat, covered, until egg mixture begins to set around edge, about 3 minutes. Remove cover and place skillet in oven; bake until frittata is set, 4 to 6 minutes.
4 To serve, transfer frittata to cutting board. Cut into wedges and top with salsa mixture.

EACH SERVING: ABOUT 235 CALORIES | 14G PROTEIN | 20G CARBOHYDRATE | 11G TOTAL FAT (4G SATURATED) | 327MG CHOLESTEROL | 795MG SODIUM

TOFU STIR-FRY

We call for a bag of broccoli flowerets to save cutting and trimming time. Choose extra-firm tofu; other types will fall apart during stir-frying. To serve, spoon the saucy mixture over quick-cooking brown rice, another time-saver.

ACTIVE TIME: 25 MIN · TOTAL TIME: 40 MIN
MAKES: 4 MAIN-DISH SERVINGS

3   TABLESPOONS SOY SAUCE

1   TABLESPOON BROWN SUGAR

1   TABLESPOON CORNSTARCH

1   CUP WATER

2   TEASPOONS VEGETABLE OIL

3   GARLIC CLOVES, CRUSHED
    WITH GARLIC PRESS

1   TABLESPOON PEELED, GRATED FRESH
    GINGER

⅛   TO ¼ TEASPOON CRUSHED
    RED PEPPER

1   BAG (12 OUNCES) BROCCOLI
    FLOWERETS, CUT INTO UNIFORM
    PIECES IF NECESSARY

8   OUNCES SHIITAKE MUSHROOMS,
    STEMS REMOVED AND CAPS
    THINLY SLICED

1   MEDIUM RED PEPPER,
    CUT INTO 1-INCH PIECES

1   PACKAGE (15 OUNCES) EXTRA-FIRM
    TOFU, PATTED DRY AND CUT INTO
    1-INCH CUBES

3   GREEN ONIONS, TRIMMED AND
    THINLY SLICED

1 In small bowl, with wire whisk, mix soy sauce, brown sugar, cornstarch, and water until blended; set aside.

2 In deep nonstick 12-inch skillet, heat oil over medium-high heat until hot. Add garlic, ginger, and crushed red pepper and cook, stirring frequently (stir-frying), 30 seconds. Add broccoli, mushrooms, and red pepper and cook, covered, 8 minutes, stirring occasionally.

3 Add tofu and green onions and cook, uncovered, 2 minutes, stirring occasionally. Stir soy-sauce mixture to blend and add to skillet; heat to boiling. Boil, stirring, 1 minute.

EACH SERVING: ABOUT 225 CALORIES | 16G PROTEIN | 23G CARBOHYDRATE | 9G TOTAL FAT (1G SATURATED) | 0MG CHOLESTEROL | 775MG SODIUM

RICOTTA-SPINACH CALZONE

Using refrigerated pizza-crust dough simplifies and shortens the preparation of these rich cheese and spinach–filled "pies."

ACTIVE TIME: 10 MIN · TOTAL TIME: 35 MIN

MAKES: 4 MAIN-DISH SERVINGS

---

1   CUP PART-SKIM RICOTTA CHEESE

1   CUP SHREDDED MOZZARELLA CHEESE (4 OUNCES)

1   TABLESPOON CORNSTARCH

½   TEASPOON DRIED OREGANO

1   TUBE (10 OUNCES) REFRIGERATED PIZZA-CRUST DOUGH

½   CUP MARINARA SAUCE

1   PACKAGE (10 OUNCES) FROZEN CHOPPED SPINACH, THAWED AND SQUEEZED DRY

1 Preheat oven to 400°F. In small bowl, combine ricotta, mozzarella, cornstarch, and oregano; stir until blended. Set aside.

2 Spray large cookie sheet with nonstick cooking spray. Unroll pizza dough in center of cookie sheet. With fingertips, press dough into 14" by 10" rectangle.

3 Spread cheese mixture lengthwise on half of dough, leaving 1-inch border. Spoon marinara sauce over cheese mixture; top with spinach. Fold other half of dough over filling. Pinch edges together to seal.

4 Bake calzone until well browned on top, 20 to 25 minutes. Cut calzone into 4 equal pieces to serve.

EACH SERVING: ABOUT 400 CALORIES | 21G PROTEIN | 43G CARBOHYDRATE | 15G TOTAL FAT (5G SATURATED) | 19MG CHOLESTEROL | 1,055MG SODIUM

PIEROGI AND SAUERKRAUT-SLAW CASSEROLE

This recipe couldn't be easier: just toss coleslaw mix with sauerkraut and seasonings, top with mini pierogi, then let the microwave do all the work!

ACTIVE TIME: 5 MIN · TOTAL TIME: 17 MIN
MAKES: 4 MAIN-DISH SERVINGS

1   BAG (16 OUNCES) SHREDDED CABBAGE
    MIX FOR COLESLAW
1   BAG (16 OUNCES) SAUERKRAUT,
    DRAINED
¼   CUP APPLE CIDER OR APPLE JUICE
½   TEASPOON CARAWAY SEEDS

⅛   TEASPOON GROUND BLACK PEPPER
1   BOX (12 OUNCES) FROZEN MINI
    PIEROGI
2   TABLESPOONS CHOPPED FRESH DILL
2   TABLESPOONS BUTTER OR
    MARGARINE, CUT INTO PIECES

1 In shallow 3-quart microwave-safe casserole, stir cabbage mix, sauer-kraut, cider, caraway seeds, and pepper. In microwave oven, cook coleslaw mixture, covered, on High 5 minutes, stirring once halfway through cook-ing.
2 Arrange frozen pierogi over coleslaw mixture (it's OK if they overlap slightly). Sprinkle pierogi with dill and top with butter. Return casserole to microwave oven and cook, covered, on High until pierogi are hot, 5 to 7 minutes longer. Toss before serving.

EACH SERVING: ABOUT 260 CALORIES | 7G PROTEIN | 37G CARBOHYDRATE | 13G TOTAL FAT (6G SATURATED) | 65MG CHOLESTEROL | 837MG SODIUM

SKILLET VEGETABLE CURRY

A package of precut cauliflower shortens prep time. As vegetables simmer, toast pita bread.

ACTIVE TIME: 15 MIN · TOTAL TIME: 40 MIN

MAKES: 8 CUPS OR 4 MAIN-DISH SERVINGS

¾ POUND CAULIFLOWER FLOWERETS

1 LARGE ALL-PURPOSE POTATO (ABOUT 8 OUNCES), PEELED AND CUT INTO 1-INCH PIECES

1 LARGE SWEET POTATO (ABOUT 12 OUNCES), PEELED AND CUT INTO 1-INCH PIECES

2 TABLESPOONS LIGHTLY PACKED SWEETENED FLAKED COCONUT

2 TEASPOONS OLIVE OIL

1 MEDIUM ONION, FINELY CHOPPED

1 TEASPOON MUSTARD SEEDS

1½ TEASPOONS GROUND CUMIN

1½ TEASPOONS GROUND CORIANDER

⅛ TEASPOON GROUND RED PEPPER (CAYENNE)

2 MEDIUM TOMATOES, CHOPPED

1 CUP FROZEN PEAS, THAWED

1¼ TEASPOONS SALT

½ CUP LOOSELY PACKED FRESH CILANTRO LEAVES, CHOPPED

1 In 4-quart saucepan, combine cauliflower, potato, sweet potato, and enough **water** to cover; heat to boiling over high heat. Reduce heat to low; cover and simmer until vegetables are tender, 8 to 10 minutes. Drain well, reserving ¾ cup cooking water.

2 Meanwhile, in dry nonstick 12-inch skillet, cook coconut over medium heat, stirring constantly, until lightly browned, about 3 minutes; transfer to small bowl.

3 In same skillet, heat oil over medium heat until hot; add onion and cook 5 minutes. Add mustard seeds, cumin, coriander, and ground red pepper; cover and cook, shaking skillet frequently, until onion is tender and lightly browned and seeds start to pop, 5 minutes longer.

4 Spoon cauliflower mixture into skillet. Add tomatoes, peas, salt, and reserved cooking water; heat through. Sprinkle with cilantro to serve.

EACH SERVING: ABOUT 230 CALORIES | 8G PROTEIN | 43G CARBOHYDRATE | 4G TOTAL FAT (1G SATURATED) | 0MG CHOLESTEROL | 735MG SODIUM

BARLEY-VEGETABLE STEW

A simple Italian gremolata of parsley, garlic, and lemon peel tops the stew to add a distinctive tangy element.

ACTIVE TIME: 10 MIN · TOTAL TIME: 25 MIN

MAKES: 9 CUPS OR 4 MAIN-DISH SERVINGS

1   CUP QUICK-COOKING BARLEY

1   TABLESPOON OLIVE OIL

1   PACKAGE (20 OUNCES) PEELED BUTTERNUT SQUASH, CUT INTO ½-INCH PIECES (4 CUPS)

2   MEDIUM STALKS CELERY, CUT INTO ½-INCH PIECES

1   MEDIUM ONION, CHOPPED

1   JAR (14 TO 16 OUNCES) MARINARA SAUCE

1   PACKAGE (9 OUNCES) FROZEN CUT GREEN BEANS

1   CUP VEGETABLE BROTH

½   TEASPOON SALT

¼   TEASPOON GROUND BLACK PEPPER

½   CUP LOOSELY PACKED FRESH PARSLEY LEAVES, CHOPPED

½   TEASPOON GRATED FRESH LEMON PEEL

1   SMALL GARLIC CLOVE, MINCED

1   Cook barley as label directs.

2   Meanwhile, in nonstick 12-inch skillet, heat oil over medium-high heat until hot. Add squash, celery, and onion; cover and cook, stirring occasionally, until lightly browned, about 10 minutes. Stir in marinara sauce, frozen beans, broth, salt, and pepper. Simmer, uncovered, 4 minutes, or until slightly thickened.

3   Meanwhile, in small bowl, with fork, mix parsley, lemon peel, and garlic; set aside.

4   Drain liquid, if any, from barley. Stir barley into vegetables. Sprinkle with parsley mixture to serve.

EACH SERVING: ABOUT 320 CALORIES | 9G PROTEIN | 60G CARBOHYDRATE | 7G TOTAL FAT (1G SATURATED) | 0MG CHOLESTEROL | 985MG SODIUM

VEGETARIAN PHYLLO PIZZA

Delicate layers of phyllo form the crust of this rich, savory pizza.

ACTIVE TIME: 10 MIN · TOTAL TIME: 25 MIN

MAKES: 4 MAIN-DISH SERVINGS

6 SHEETS (17" BY 12" EACH) FRESH OR FROZEN (THAWED) PHYLLO

2 TABLESPOONS BUTTER OR MARGARINE, MELTED

4 OUNCES SOFT, MILD GOAT CHEESE SUCH AS MONTRÂCHET

1 JAR (6 OUNCES) MARINATED ARTICHOKE HEARTS, DRAINED AND CUT INTO ¼-INCH PIECES

1½ CUPS GRAPE OR CHERRY TOMATOES, EACH CUT IN HALF

1 Preheat oven to 450°F. Place 1 sheet of phyllo on ungreased large cookie sheet; brush with some melted butter. Repeat layering with remaining phyllo and butter. Do not brush top layer.

2 Crumble goat cheese over phyllo; top with artichokes and tomatoes. Bake pizza until golden brown around the edges, 12 to 15 minutes.

3 Transfer pizza to large cutting board. With pizza cutter or knife, cut pizza lengthwise in half, then cut each half crosswise into 4 pieces.

EACH SERVING: ABOUT 245 CALORIES | 8G PROTEIN | 20G CARBOHYDRATE | 19G TOTAL FAT (9G SATURATED) | 29MG CHOLESTEROL | 387MG SODIUM

FALAFEL CONES

Falafel is a staple of Middle Eastern cuisine. It is typically served as a snack or part of an appetizer plate.

ACTIVE TIME: 15 MIN · TOTAL TIME: 25 MIN
MAKES: 4 MAIN-DISH SERVINGS

2   CANS (15 TO 19 OUNCES EACH) LOW-SODIUM GARBANZO BEANS, RINSED AND WELL DRAINED

2   GARLIC CLOVES, PEELED

1   LARGE EGG

1   CUP LOOSELY PACKED FRESH PARSLEY LEAVES

¼   CUP TAHINI (SESAME SEED PASTE)

1   TABLESPOON DRIED MINT LEAVES

2   TEASPOONS GROUND CUMIN

¼   TEASPOON GROUND RED PEPPER (CAYENNE)

¼   CUP VEGETABLE OIL

2   PLUM TOMATOES, CHOPPED

1   GREEN ONION, TRIMMED AND CHOPPED

1   CONTAINER (8 OUNCES) PLAIN LOW-FAT YOGURT

¼   TEASPOON SALT

4   POCKETLESS PITAS, WARMED

1   In food processor, with knife blade attached, combine beans, garlic, egg, parsley, tahini, mint, cumin, and ground red pepper and puree until smooth. Shape mixture into sixteen 2-inch balls.

2   In nonstick 12-inch skillet, heat oil over medium-high heat until very hot but not smoking. Add falafel balls and cook, turning frequently, until evenly golden, 10 minutes.

3   Meanwhile, in small bowl, combine tomatoes, green onion, yogurt, and salt and stir until mixed.

4   To serve, shape each pita into a cone; tightly wrap bottom of each with kitchen parchment or foil to help hold its shape and prevent leakage. Fill each cone with 4 falafel balls and top with some yogurt mixture.

EACH SERVING: ABOUT 670 CALORIES | 28G PROTEIN | 94G CARBOHYDRATE | 22G TOTAL FAT (4G SATURATED) | 57MG CHOLESTEROL | 740MG SODIUM

VEGETARIAN TORTILLA PIE

This dish can be assembled in a jiffy, thanks to its no-cook filling of canned black beans and corn, prepared salsa, and preshredded Jack cheese. A wedge of iceberg lettuce on the side with our Spicy Tomato Dressing (page 263) adds the missing crunch.

ACTIVE TIME: 8 MIN · TOTAL TIME: 20 MIN
MAKES: 4 MAIN-DISH SERVINGS

1   JAR (11 TO 12 OUNCES) MEDIUM SALSA

1   CAN (8 OUNCES) NO-SALT-ADDED TOMATO SAUCE

1   CAN (15 TO 16 OUNCES) NO-SALT-ADDED BLACK BEANS, RINSED AND DRAINED

1   CAN (15¼ OUNCES) NO-SALT-ADDED WHOLE-KERNEL CORN, DRAINED

½   CUP PACKED FRESH CILANTRO LEAVES

4   (10-INCH) LOW-FAT FLOUR TORTILLAS

6   OUNCES SHREDDED REDUCED-FAT MONTEREY JACK CHEESE (1½ CUPS)

REDUCED-FAT SOUR CREAM (OPTIONAL)

1   Preheat oven to 500°F. Spray 15½" by 10½" jelly-roll pan with nonstick cooking spray.

2   In small bowl, mix salsa and tomato sauce. In medium bowl, mix black beans, corn, and cilantro.

3   Place 1 tortilla in jelly-roll pan. Spread one-third of salsa mixture over tortilla. Top with one-third of bean mixture and one-third of cheese. Repeat layering 2 more times, ending with last tortilla.

4   Bake pie until cheese has melted and filling is hot, 10 to 12 minutes. Serve with reduced-fat sour cream, if you like.

EACH SERVING WITHOUT SOUR CREAM: ABUT 440 CALORIES | 25G PROTEIN | 65G CARBO-HYDRATE, 11G TOTAL FAT (5G SATURATED) | 30MG CHOLESTEROL | 820MG SODIUM

QUESO-BLANCO SOFT TACOS

These tacos are filled with *queso blanco,* a white cheese that's a bit firmer than mozzarella, so it holds its shape when melted. Don't confuse it with *queso fresco,* a crumbly fresh cow's milk cheese that's found in almost every Latin American country.

ACTIVE TIME: 20 MIN · TOTAL TIME: 25 MIN

MAKES: 4 MAIN-DISH SERVINGS

3 GREEN ONIONS, TRIMMED AND THINLY SLICED

3 PLUM TOMATOES, CUT INTO ½-INCH PIECES

1 RIPE AVOCADO, PEELED, PITTED, AND CUT INTO ½-INCH PIECES

¼ SMALL HEAD ROMAINE LETTUCE, THINLY SLICED (2 CUPS)

¼ CUP LOOSELY PACKED FRESH CILANTRO LEAVES

1 CUP MILD OR MEDIUM-HOT SALSA

1 PACKAGE (12 OUNCES) QUESO BLANCO (MEXICAN FRYING CHEESE), CUT INTO 12 SLICES

12 (6-INCH) CORN TORTILLAS, WARMED

1 LIME, CUT INTO 4 WEDGES

1 On platter, arrange green onions, tomatoes, avocado, lettuce, and cilantro. Pour salsa into serving bowl.

2 Heat nonstick 12-inch skillet over medium-high heat until hot. Add cheese and heat, turning once, until dark brown in spots, 2 to 3 minutes.

3 Place 1 cheese slice in each tortilla and fold in half. Serve tortillas immediately, adding green onions, tomatoes, avocado, lettuce, cilantro, salsa, and a squeeze of lime juice.

EACH SERVING: ABOUT 545 CALORIES | 26G PROTEIN | 49G CARBOHYDRATE | 29G TOTAL FAT (13G SATURATED) | 60MG CHOLESTEROL | 1,300MG SODIUM

ONE-DISH
MEALS

Is there a cook anywhere without a favorite one-dish meal in her or his repertoire? Maybe it's a comforting casserole you turn to when you're entertaining or an easy stir-fry on PTA night.

Whatever our favorites, most of us share a deep affection for one-dish meals—for good reason:

- Many can be prepared ahead of time.
- They free the cook from preparing time-consuming side dishes.
- Most require a minimum of prep time.
- They can be served from the vessel in which they were cooked, making cleanup a snap.

Those planning to add more meatless meals to their weekly menus will be delighted to know that in vegetarian cooking, one-dish meals are much more the norm than in traditional meat-based cooking.

This collection of one-dish meals includes almost fifty versatile, simple-to-fix recipes. There are creamy risottos, quick stir-fries, individual pizzas, pasta dishes aplenty, ethnic meals with authentic flair, pies and tarts that appeal to the eyes as well as to the palate. You'll find dishes to please everyone at your table.

As you work your way through these delectable recipes, don't be surprised to find that your repertoire of favorite one-dish meals has grown to include many of those on these pages.

Gazpacho-Style Pasta (page 295)

LENTIL SHEPHERD'S PIE

A steaming skillet of Indian-spiced lentils are topped with piping-hot curried mashed sweet potatoes for this nonmeat takeoff on an old comfort-food favorite.

ACTIVE TIME: 20 MIN · TOTAL TIME: 55 MIN
MAKES: 4 MAIN-DISH SERVINGS

1 CUP DRY LENTILS, RINSED

1 TABLESPOON GRATED, PEELED
FRESH GINGER

1 TEASPOON GROUND CUMIN

1 CAN (14½ OUNCES) VEGETABLE BROTH
(1¾ CUPS)

1 BAY LEAF

2 CUPS WATER

1 TABLESPOON OLIVE OIL

1 TEASPOON CURRY POWDER

⅛ TEASPOON CRUSHED
RED PEPPER

3 LARGE SWEET POTATOES (ABOUT
2 POUNDS), PEELED AND CUT INTO
1-INCH PIECES

1 TEASPOON SALT

2 GREEN ONIONS, TRIMMED AND
THINLY SLICED

PLAIN YOGURT (OPTIONAL)

1 In 12-inch skillet, combine lentils, ginger, cumin, broth, bay leaf, and 1¼ cups **water**; heat to boiling over high heat. Reduce heat to medium; cover and cook until lentils are tender, about 20 minutes. Discard bay leaf.

2 Meanwhile, in 3-quart saucepan, heat oil over medium-high heat until hot. Add curry powder and red pepper and cook, stirring, 15 seconds; add sweet potatoes, salt, and remaining ¾ cup water; heat to boiling. Reduce heat to medium-low; cover and cook, stirring occasionally, until potatoes are tender, about 15 minutes.

3 With potato masher or fork, mash potato mixture until almost smooth. Spoon mashed potatoes over lentil mixture in skillet; sprinkle with green onions. Serve with yogurt, if you like.

EACH SERVING: ABOUT 410 CALORIES | 18G PROTEIN | 77G CARBOHYDRATE | 5G TOTAL FAT (1G SATURATED) 0MG CHOLESTEROL | 1,040MG SODIUM

COUSCOUS TABBOULEH

Instead of the traditional bulgur wheat, this quick tabbouleh is made with couscous. Garbanzo beans add extra protein.

TOTAL TIME: 20 MIN

MAKES: 4 MAIN-DISH SERVINGS

- ¾ CUP WATER
- ¾ CUP COUSCOUS
- ¾ TEASPOON SALT
- 1 CAN (15 TO 19 OUNCES) GARBANZO BEANS, DRAINED AND RINSED
- 4 MEDIUM TOMATOES (ABOUT 1¼ POUNDS), CUT INTO ½-INCH PIECES
- 2 KIRBY (PICKLING) CUCUMBERS (ABOUT 4 OUNCES EACH), UNPEELED AND CUT INTO ½-INCH PIECES
- ¾ CUP LOOSELY PACKED FRESH FLAT-LEAF PARSLEY LEAVES, CHOPPED
- ½ CUP LOOSELY PACKED FRESH MINT LEAVES, CHOPPED
- ¼ CUP FRESH LEMON JUICE (FROM ABOUT 2 LEMONS)
- 2 TABLESPOONS OLIVE OIL
- ¼ TEASPOON COARSELY GROUND BLACK PEPPER

1 In microwave-safe 3-quart bowl, heat water to boiling in microwave oven on High, 1½ to 2 minutes. Remove bowl from microwave. Stir in couscous and ¼ teaspoon salt; cover and let stand until liquid has been absorbed, about 5 minutes.

2 Fluff couscous with fork. Stir in beans, tomatoes, cucumbers, parsley, mint, lemon juice, oil, pepper, and remaining ½ teaspoon salt. Serve couscous at room temperature or cover and refrigerate up to 6 hours.

EACH SERVING: ABOUT 350 CALORIES | 13G PROTEIN | 56G CARBOHYDRATE | 9G TOTAL FAT (1G SATURATED) | 0MG CHOLESTEROL | 700MG SODIUM

CARROT RISOTTO

This quick microwave risotto gets its lovely color and great flavor from shredded carrots and carrot juice.

ACTIVE TIME: 10 MIN · TOTAL TIME: 35 MIN
MAKES: 6 CUPS OR 4 MAIN-DISH SERVINGS

---

1 CAN OR BOTTLE (12 TO 15 OUNCES) CARROT JUICE PLUS ENOUGH WATER TO EQUAL 2 CUPS

1 CAN (14½ OUNCES) VEGETABLE BROTH (1¾ CUPS)

½ CUP DRY WHITE WINE

1¼ CUPS WATER

1 TABLESPOON OLIVE OIL

2 CUPS SHREDDED CARROTS

½ SMALL ONION, FINELY CHOPPED

2 CUPS ARBORIO RICE (ITALIAN SHORT-GRAIN RICE) OR MEDIUM-GRAIN RICE

⅓ CUP FRESHLY GRATED PARMESAN CHEESE

¾ TEASPOON SALT

¼ TEASPOON GROUND BLACK PEPPER

2 TABLESPOONS COARSELY CHOPPED FRESH MINT OR PARSLEY (OPTIONAL)

1 In 2-quart saucepan, heat carrot juice, broth, wine, and water to boiling over high heat. Reduce heat to low to maintain simmer; cover.

2 In 3- to 3½-quart microwave-safe casserole, combine oil, carrots, and onion. Cook, uncovered, in microwave oven on High until onion has softened, about 2 minutes. Add rice and stir until rice grains are opaque. Cook on High 1 minute.

3 Stir hot liquid into rice mixture. Cover casserole with lid or vented plastic wrap and cook on Medium (50% power) until most of liquid has been absorbed and rice is tender but still firm, 15 to 20 minutes. Stir in Parmesan, salt, and pepper. Sprinkle with mint, if you like.

EACH SERVING: ABOUT 570 CALORIES | 15G PROTEIN | 105G CARBOHYDRATE | 7G TOTAL FAT (2G SATURATED) | 7MG CHOLESTEROL | 1,110MG SODIUM

SPAGHETTI PRIMAVERA

A vegetable medley of asparagus, broccoli, and carrots tossed with spaghetti, fresh basil, and Parmesan.

ACTIVE TIME: 20 MIN · TOTAL TIME: 50 MIN

MAKES: 4 MAIN-DISH SERVINGS

---

4 TABLESPOONS BUTTER OR MARGARINE	1 POUND ASPARAGUS, TRIMMED AND CUT DIAGONALLY INTO 1-INCH PIECES
3 MEDIUM CARROTS, CUT LENGTHWISE INTO MATCHSTICK-THIN STRIPS	¾ TEASPOON SALT
1 MEDIUM ONION, CHOPPED	⅛ TO ¼ TEASPOON CRUSHED RED PEPPER
2 GARLIC CLOVES, CRUSHED WITH GARLIC PRESS	½ CUP WATER
SALT	1 CUP LOOSELY PACKED FRESH BASIL LEAVES, CHOPPED
1 PACKAGE (16 OUNCES) SPAGHETTI	½ CUP FRESHLY GRATED PARMESAN CHEESE
1 BAG (16 OUNCES) BROCCOLI FLOWERETS	

1 In nonstick 12-inch skillet, melt 2 tablespoons butter over medium heat. Add carrots and onion and cook, stirring occasionally, until tender and golden, about 10 minutes. Add garlic; cook, stirring, 1 minute.

2 Meanwhile, in large saucepot cook pasta as label directs.

3 To carrot mixture in skillet, add broccoli, asparagus, salt, crushed red pepper, and water; heat to boiling over medium-high heat. Reduce heat to medium; cover and cook, stirring occasionally, until vegetables are tender, 6 to 10 minutes longer.

4 Drain pasta, reserving ¾ cup pasta water; return pasta to saucepot. Add basil, Parmesan, remaining 2 tablespoons butter, and reserved pasta water; toss well. Add vegetable mixture and gently toss to combine.

EACH SERVING: ABOUT 655 CALORIES | 25G PROTEIN | 101G CARBOHYDRATE | 22G TOTAL FAT (9G SATURATED) | 39MG CHOLESTEROL | 946MG SODIUM

TRIPLE-MUSHROOM FETTUCCINE

The rich, earthy flavors of shiitake, cremini, and oyster mushrooms are combined with hearty fettuccine noodles to make a satisfying and easy family dish that's special enough for company.

ACTIVE TIME: 20 MIN · TOTAL TIME: 45 MIN

MAKES: 4 MAIN-DISH SERVINGS

1 PACKAGE (16 OUNCES) FETTUCCINE OR LINGUINE

2 TABLESPOONS BUTTER OR MARGARINE

1 MEDIUM ONION, FINELY CHOPPED

3 PACKAGES (4 OUNCES EACH) SLICED WILD MUSHROOM BLEND OR 1 POUND MIXED WILD MUSHROOMS, STEMS DISCARDED AND CAPS THINLY SLICED

2 GARLIC CLOVES, CRUSHED WITH GARLIC PRESS

¼ TEASPOON DRIED THYME

½ TEASPOON SALT

¼ TEASPOON COARSELY GROUND BLACK PEPPER

1 CAN (14½ OUNCES) REDUCED-SODIUM VEGETABLE BROTH (1¾ CUPS)

1 CUP LOOSELY PACKED FRESH PARSLEY LEAVES, CHOPPED

1 In large saucepot, cook pasta as label directs.

2 Meanwhile, in nonstick 12-inch skillet, melt butter over medium heat. Add onion and cook, stirring occasionally, until tender, 8 to 10 minutes. Increase heat to medium-high. Add mushrooms, garlic, thyme, salt, and pepper and cook, stirring often, until mushrooms are golden and liquid has evaporated, 10 minutes.

3 Add broth to mushroom mixture and heat to boiling, stirring occasionally.

4 Drain pasta; return to saucepot. Add mushroom mixture and parsley; toss well.

EACH SERVING: ABOUT 530 CALORIES | 19G PROTEIN | 95G CARBOHYDRATE | 11G TOTAL FAT (4G SATURATED) | 16MG CHOLESTEROL | 762MG SODIUM

QUICK-COMFORT EGG NOODLES AND CABBAGE

Old-fashioned curly egg noodles are combined with caramelized onion, cabbage, and peas for a cozy family dinner.

ACTIVE TIME: 15 MIN · TOTAL TIME: 45 MIN
MAKES: 4 MAIN-DISH SERVINGS

1 PACKAGE (12 OUNCES) CURLY WIDE EGG NOODLES

1 TABLESPOON BUTTER OR MARGARINE

1 TABLESPOON OLIVE OIL

1 JUMBO ONION (1 POUND), THINLY SLICED

1 SMALL HEAD (ABOUT 1¼ POUNDS) SAVOY CABBAGE, THINLY SLICED, WITH TOUGH RIBS DISCARDED

1 TEASPOON FRESH THYME LEAVES OR ¼ TEASPOON DRIED THYME

¾ TEASPOON SALT

¼ TEASPOON COARSELY GROUND BLACK PEPPER

1 PACKAGE (10 OUNCES) FROZEN PEAS

1 CUP VEGETABLE BROTH

¼ CUP FRESHLY GRATED PARMESAN CHEESE

THYME SPRIGS FOR GARNISH

1 In large saucepot, cook pasta as label directs.

2 Meanwhile, in nonstick 12-inch skillet, heat butter and oil over medium heat until melted and hot. Add onion and cook, stirring occasionally, until onion is tender and golden, about 20 minutes. Increase heat to medium-high; add cabbage, thyme, salt, and pepper and cook, stirring occasionally, until cabbage is tender-crisp and golden, 5 minutes. Stir in frozen peas and broth; cook, stirring, 2 minutes.

3 Drain noodles; return to saucepot. Add cabbage mixture and Parmesan; toss well. Garnish with thyme sprigs.

EACH SERVING: ABOUT 540 CALORIES | 22G PROTEIN | 88G CARBOHYDRATE | 13G TOTAL FAT (4G SATURATED) | 93MG CHOLESTEROL | 1,041MG SODIUM

LASAGNA TOSS WITH SPINACH AND RICOTTA

This recipe has all the flavor of a layered and baked lasagna, without the wait! Lasagna noodles are tossed with a speedy tomato-spinach skillet sauce, then dolloped with ricotta cheese to serve.

ACTIVE TIME: 20 MIN · **TOTAL TIME:** 55 MIN

MAKES: 4 MAIN-DISH SERVINGS

- 1 PACKAGE (16 OUNCES) LASAGNA NOODLES
- 1 TABLESPOON OLIVE OIL
- 1 MEDIUM ONION, FINELY CHOPPED
- 2 GARLIC CLOVES, CRUSHED WITH GARLIC PRESS
- 1 CAN (28 OUNCES) PLUM TOMATOES
- ¾ TEASPOON SALT
- ¼ TEASPOON COARSELY GROUND BLACK PEPPER
- 1 PACKAGE (10 OUNCES) FROZEN CHOPPED SPINACH
- ½ CUP LOOSELY PACKED FRESH BASIL LEAVES, CHOPPED
- ¼ CUP FRESHLY GRATED PARMESAN CHEESE, PLUS ADDITIONAL FOR SERVING (OPTIONAL)
- 1 CUP PART-SKIM RICOTTA CHEESE

1 In large saucepot, cook lasagna noodles as label directs, increasing cooking time to 12 to 14 minutes.

2 Meanwhile, in nonstick 12-inch skillet, heat oil over medium heat until hot. Add onion and cook, stirring occasionally, until tender, about 10 minutes. Add garlic and cook, stirring, 30 seconds.

3 Stir in tomatoes with their juice, salt, and pepper, breaking up tomatoes with side of spoon; heat to boiling over high heat. Reduce heat to medium and cook, uncovered, 8 minutes. Add frozen spinach and cook, covered, until spinach is tender, about 10 minutes, stirring occasionally. Stir in basil.

4 Drain noodles; return to saucepot. Add tomato mixture and Parmesan; toss well. Spoon into 4 pasta bowls; top with dollops of ricotta cheese. Serve with additional Parmesan, if you like.

EACH SERVING: ABOUT 620 CALORIES | 28G PROTEIN | 100G CARBOHYDRATE | 12G TOTAL FAT (5G SATURATED) | 23MG CHOLESTEROL | 1,640MG SODIUM

FETTUCCINE WITH FRESH HERBS AND TOMATOES

Toss fettuccine with basil, mint, sage, rosemary, and tomatoes, and sprinkle with ricotta salata cheese.

ACTIVE TIME: 15 MIN · TOTAL TIME: 30 MIN

MAKES: 4 MAIN-DISH SERVINGS

---

1 PACKAGE (16 OUNCES) FETTUCCINE OR LINGUINE

1 CUP LOOSELY PACKED FRESH BASIL LEAVES, CHOPPED

¾ CUP LOOSELY PACKED FRESH MINT LEAVES, CHOPPED

2 TABLESPOONS FRESH ROSEMARY LEAVES, CHOPPED

1 TABLESPOON FRESH SAGE LEAVES, CHOPPED

2 LARGE TOMATOES (ABOUT 8 OUNCES EACH), CHOPPED

2 TABLESPOONS EXTRA-VIRGIN OLIVE OIL

¾ TEASPOON SALT

¼ TEASPOON GROUND BLACK PEPPER

½ CUP CRUMBLED RICOTTA SALATA OR ¼ CUP FRESHLY GRATED PARMESAN CHEESE

1 In large saucepot, cook pasta as label directs.

2 Meanwhile, in large serving bowl, toss basil, mint, rosemary, sage, tomatoes, oil, salt, and pepper; set aside.

3 Drain pasta, reserving ½ cup pasta water. Add pasta and reserved pasta water to herb mixture; toss well. Sprinkle with cheese to serve.

EACH SERVING: ABOUT 565 CALORIES | 19G PROTEIN | 93G CARBOHYDRATE | 13G TOTAL FAT (4G SATURATED) | 17MG CHOLESTEROL | 920MG SODIUM

ROTELLE WITH RATATOUILLE

Roasting the eggplant, pepper, and onion for this dish may take a little longer than top-of-the-range cooking, but it's low maintenance and the resulting rich flavor is worth it.

ACTIVE TIME: 20 MIN · TOTAL TIME: 1 HR
MAKES: 4 MAIN-DISH SERVINGS

1   MEDIUM EGGPLANT (ABOUT 1½ POUNDS), CUT INTO 1-INCH PIECES

1   MEDIUM RED PEPPER, CUT INTO 1-INCH PIECES

1   LARGE RED ONION, CUT INTO 1-INCH PIECES

2   GARLIC CLOVES, CRUSHED WITH GARLIC PRESS

3   TABLESPOONS OLIVE OIL

1½ TEASPOONS SALT

½   TEASPOON GROUND BLACK PEPPER

1   PINT RED AND/OR YELLOW CHERRY TOMATOES, EACH CUT IN HALF

1   CUP LOOSELY PACKED FRESH BASIL LEAVES, COARSELY CHOPPED

1   TABLESPOON RED WINE VINEGAR

1   PACKAGE (16 OUNCES) ROTELLE OR FUSILLI PASTA

FRESH BASIL LEAVES FOR GARNISH

1 Preheat oven to 450°F. In large roasting pan (17" by 11½") or 15½" by 10½" jelly-roll pan, toss eggplant, red pepper, onion, garlic, oil, salt, and pepper until vegetables are well coated. Roast, stirring occasionally, until vegetables are tender and lightly browned, 35 to 40 minutes.

2 In large bowl, toss tomatoes, chopped basil, and vinegar; set aside to allow flavors to develop.

3 Meanwhile, in large saucepot, cook pasta as label directs. Drain pasta, reserving ¼ cup pasta water.

4 Add pasta, roasted vegetables, and reserved pasta water to tomatoes in bowl; toss well. Garnish each serving with basil leaves.

EACH SERVING: ABOUT 595 CALORIES | 18G PROTEIN | 104G CARBOHYDRATE | 13G TOTAL FAT (2G SATURATED) | 0MG CHOLESTEROL | 1,040MG SODIUM

BOW TIES WITH BUTTERNUT SQUASH AND PEAS

This vegetarian main dish of pasta tossed with butternut squash, peas, and a creamy Parmesan sauce makes a great family dinner. For a low-fat version, use fat-free half-and-half.

ACTIVE TIME: 20 MIN · TOTAL TIME: 35 MIN

MAKES: 6 MAIN-DISH SERVINGS

1 PACKAGE (16 OUNCES) BOW-TIE OR CORKSCREW PASTA

1 MEDIUM BUTTERNUT SQUASH (2¼ POUNDS), PEELED, SEEDED, AND CUT INTO 1-INCH PIECES

1 PACKAGE (10 OUNCES) FROZEN PEAS

¾ CUP HALF-AND-HALF OR LIGHT CREAM

1 TEASPOON MINCED FRESH SAGE LEAVES

⅓ CUP FRESHLY GRATED PARMESAN CHEESE

1 TEASPOON SALT

¼ TEASPOON COARSELY GROUND BLACK PEPPER

1 In large saucepot, cook pasta as label directs. Drain.

2 Meanwhile, place squash chunks in 2½-quart microwave-safe baking dish; cover and cook in microwave oven on High, stirring once, 12 minutes. Stir in peas, half-and-half, and sage and cook, uncovered, 2 minutes.

3 In large warm serving bowl, toss pasta with squash mixture, Parmesan, salt, and pepper.

EACH SERVING: ABOUT 430 CALORIES | 16G PROTEIN | 78G CARBOHYDRATE | 7G TOTAL FAT (3G SATURATED) | 15MG CHOLESTEROL | 650MG SODIUM

GAZPACHO-STYLE PASTA

Classic gazpacho soup ingredients get pulsed in the food processor while the small seashell pasta cooks. Serve with soup spoons!

ACTIVE TIME: 15 MIN · TOTAL TIME: 30 MIN
MAKES: 4 MAIN-DISH SERVINGS

1   PACKAGE (16 OUNCES) SMALL SHELL OR ORECCHIETTE PASTA

1   ENGLISH (SEEDLESS) CUCUMBER (ABOUT 1 POUND), UNPEELED AND CUT INTO 2-INCH PIECES

½   MEDIUM YELLOW PEPPER, CUT INTO 1-INCH PIECES

½   MEDIUM RED PEPPER, CUT INTO 1-INCH PIECES

½   MEDIUM RED ONION, CUT INTO 1-INCH PIECES

1   JALAPEÑO CHILE, SEEDED AND CUT INTO ½-INCH PIECES

1   GARLIC CLOVE, CUT INTO THIRDS

1½ POUNDS TOMATOES (ABOUT 5 MEDIUM), CUT INTO ½-INCH PIECES

2   TABLESPOONS OLIVE OIL

2   TABLESPOONS SHERRY OR RED WINE VINEGAR

1½ TEASPOONS SALT

1   SMALL BUNCH FRESH PARSLEY, STEMS DISCARDED

CUCUMBER SLICES AND CHERRY TOMATOES FOR GARNISH

1   In large saucepot, cook pasta as label directs. Drain.

2   Meanwhile, in food processor, with knife blade attached, finely chop cucumber, peppers, onion, chile, and garlic. Do not puree.

3   In large serving bowl, toss vegetable mixture with tomatoes, oil, vinegar, and salt until well mixed. Set aside 4 parsley leaves for garnish; chop remaining parsley.

4   Add pasta and chopped parsley to vegetable mixture; toss well to combine. Garnish each serving with cucumber slices, cherry tomatoes, and reserved parsley leaves.

EACH SERVING: ABOUT 555 CALORIES | 18G PROTEIN | 100G CARBOHYDRATE | 9G TOTAL FAT (1G SATURATED) | 0MG CHOLESTEROL | 1,045MG SODIUM

PASTA WITH NO-COOK TOMATO AND BOCCONCINI SAUCE

Bocconcini (Italian for "little mouthfuls") are small balls of mozzarella that can be found packed in whey or water in gourmet shops and in the dairy case of some supermarkets. Sometimes they have been tossed with herbs such as basil and black and crushed red pepper. If so, adjust the seasonings that are called for accordingly.

ACTIVE TIME: 20 MIN · TOTAL TIME: 35 MIN PLUS STANDING

MAKES: 6 MAIN-DISH SERVINGS

---

2 PINTS CHERRY TOMATOES, EACH CUT IN HALF	¼ TEASPOON COARSELY GROUND BLACK PEPPER
½ CUP LOOSELY PACKED FRESH FLAT-LEAF PARSLEY LEAVES, CHOPPED	1 GARLIC CLOVES, CRUSHED WITH GARLIC PRESS
½ CUP LOOSELY PACKED FRESH BASIL LEAVES, THINLY SLICED	1 PACKAGE (16 OUNCES) PENNE OR CORKSCREW PASTA
¼ CUP OLIVE OIL	12 OUNCES SMALL MOZZARELLA BALLS (BOCCONCINI), EACH CUT IN HALF
1 TEASPOON SALT	

1 In large serving bowl, stir cherry tomatoes, parsley, basil, oil, salt, pepper, and garlic. Let stand at room temperature at least 1 hour or up to 4 hours to blend flavors.

2 In large saucepot, cook pasta as label directs. Drain well.

3 Add pasta to tomato mixture; toss with bocconcini.

EACH SERVING: ABOUT 545 CALORIES | 21G PROTEIN | 64G CARBOHYDRATE | 23G TOTAL FAT (9G SATURATED) | 44MG CHOLESTEROL | 540MG SODIUM

PASTA PUTTANESCA WITH ARUGULA

For a refreshing summer meal, mix pasta with a perky caper and shallot dressing and lots of cut-up fresh tomatoes, chopped arugula, and basil.

ACTIVE TIME: 15 MIN · TOTAL TIME: 30 MIN

MAKES: 4 MAIN-DISH SERVINGS

---

1 PACKAGE (16 OUNCES) GEMELLI OR CORKSCREW PASTA

1½ POUNDS TOMATOES (ABOUT 5 MEDIUM), CUT INTO ½-INCH PIECES

1 MEDIUM SHALLOT, MINCED (ABOUT ¼ CUP)

1 GARLIC CLOVE, CRUSHED WITH GARLIC PRESS

2 TABLESPOONS OLIVE OIL

2 TABLESPOONS CAPERS, DRAINED AND CHOPPED

1 TABLESPOON RED WINE VINEGAR

½ TEASPOON GRATED FRESH LEMON PEEL

¼ TEASPOON CRUSHED RED PEPPER

2 BUNCHES ARUGULA (ABOUT 4 OUNCES EACH), TOUGH STEMS REMOVED, LEAVES COARSELY CHOPPED

1 CUP PACKED FRESH BASIL LEAVES, CHOPPED

1 In large saucepot, cook pasta as label directs. Drain.

2 Meanwhile, in large serving bowl, toss tomatoes with shallot, garlic, oil, capers, vinegar, lemon peel, and crushed red pepper until well mixed.

3 Add pasta to tomato mixture and toss to combine. Just before serving, gently toss warm pasta mixture with arugula and basil until greens are slightly wilted.

EACH SERVING: ABOUT 540 CALORIES | 18G PROTEIN | 97G CARBOHYDRATE | 10G TOTAL FAT (1G SATURATED) | 0MG CHOLESTEROL | 310MG SODIUM

MACARONI AND CHEESE ON THE LIGHT SIDE

Our pasta recipe is amazingly creamy, and it sneaks vegetables into the kids' dinner without a lot of fuss.

ACTIVE TIME: 20 MIN · TOTAL TIME: 40 MIN

MAKES: 8 MAIN-DISH SERVINGS

1 PACKAGE (16 OUNCES) CAVATELLI PASTA

2 TABLESPOONS BUTTER OR MARGARINE

3 TABLESPOONS ALL-PURPOSE FLOUR

½ TEASPOON SALT

¼ TEASPOON GROUND BLACK PEPPER

PINCH GROUND NUTMEG

3½ CUPS LOW-FAT MILK (1%)

6 OUNCES (1 ½ CUPS) REDUCED-FAT SHARP CHEDDAR CHEESE, SHREDDED

⅓ CUP GRATED PARMESAN CHEESE

1 PACKAGE (10 OUNCES) FROZEN MIXED VEGETABLES

1 In large saucepot, cook pasta as label directs.

2 Meanwhile, in 3-quart nonreactive saucepan, melt butter over medium heat. With wire whisk, stir in flour, salt, pepper, and nutmeg; cook, stirring constantly, 1 minute. Gradually whisk in milk and cook over medium-high heat, stirring constantly, until sauce boils and thickens slightly. Boil, stirring, 1 minute.

3 Remove saucepan from heat; stir in Cheddar and Parmesan just until melted. Following manufacturer's instructions, use immersion blender to blend mixture in saucepan until smooth. (Or, in blender at low speed, with center part of cover removed to let steam escape, puree sauce mixture in small batches until smooth. Pour the sauce into bowl after each batch.)

4 Place frozen vegetables in colander; drain pasta over vegetables. Return pasta and vegetables to saucepot; stir in cheese sauce.

EACH SERVING: ABOUT 340 CALORIES | 18G PROTEIN | 43G CARBOHYDRATE | 12G TOTAL FAT (5G SATURATED) | 40MG CHOLESTEROL | 576MG SODIUM

SOBA NOODLES PRIMAVERA WITH MISO

A quick and easy Asian-inspired pasta primavera made with packaged broccoli flowerets and shredded carrots. For a nutritional boost, we used soba noodles (Japanese buckwheat noodles) and miso (concentrated soybean paste).

ACTIVE TIME: 20 MIN · TOTAL TIME: 40 MIN
MAKES: 4 MAIN-DISH SERVINGS

1   PACKAGE (15 OUNCES) EXTRA-FIRM TOFU, RINSED, DRAINED, AND PATTED DRY

1   PACKAGE (8 OUNCES) SOBA NOODLES

1   TABLESPOON OLIVE OIL

1   MEDIUM RED PEPPER, THINLY SLICED

1   LARGE ONION (12 OUNCES), SLICED

2   GARLIC CLOVES, CRUSHED WITH GARLIC PRESS

1   TABLESPOON GRATED, PEELED FRESH GINGER

¼   TEASPOON CRUSHED RED PEPPER

1   BAG (16 OUNCES) BROCCOLI FLOWERETS, CUT INTO 1½-INCH PIECES

1   BAG (10 OUNCES) SHREDDED CARROTS

¼   CUP WATER

¼   CUP RED (DARK) MISO PASTE

2   GREEN ONIONS, TRIMMED AND THINLY SLICED

1   Cut tofu horizontally in half. Cut each half into 1-inch pieces; set aside.

2   In large saucepot, cook noodles as label directs.

3   Meanwhile, in nonstick 5- to 6-quart Dutch oven, heat oil over medium-high heat until hot. Add red pepper and onion and cook, stirring occasionally, until golden, about 10 minutes. Add garlic, ginger, crushed red pepper, and tofu; cook, stirring, 1 minute. Add broccoli, carrots, and water; heat to boiling over medium-high heat. Reduce heat to medium; cook, covered, until vegetables are tender, about 7 minutes.

4   Drain noodles, reserving ¾ cup noodle water. Return noodles to saucepot.

5   With wire whisk, mix miso paste and reserved noodle water until blended. To serve, toss noodles with tofu mixture, green onions, and miso-paste mixture.

EACH SERVING: ABOUT 455 CALORIES | 26G PROTEIN | 68G CARBOHYDRATE | 11G TOTAL FAT (2G SATURATED) | 0MG CHOLESTEROL | 1,290MG SODIUM

BROCCOLI STIR-FRY WITH RICE NOODLES

Inspired by our favorite Thai noodle dishes, this dish incorporates colorful fresh vegetables and herbs into a lime-spiked coconut sauce.

ACTIVE TIME: 30 MIN · TOTAL TIME: 50 MIN   MAKES: 4 MAIN-DISH SERVINGS

---

3   LIMES

8   OUNCES DRIED FLAT RICE NOODLES (ABOUT ¼ INCH WIDE)

2   TABLESPOONS VEGETABLE OIL

1   BAG (16 OUNCES) BROCCOLI FLOWERETS

3   MEDIUM CARROTS, PEELED AND EACH CUT LENGTHWISE IN HALF, THEN CROSSWISE INTO ¼-INCH-THICK SLICES

2   HEADS BABY BOK CHOY (ABOUT 6 OUNCES EACH), CUT CROSSWISE INTO 1-INCH-THICK SLICES

1   CUP LIGHT UNSWEETENED COCONUT MILK (NOT CREAM OF COCONUT)

2   TABLESPOONS BROWN SUGAR

3   TABLESPOONS REDUCED-SODIUM SOY SAUCE

2   TABLESPOONS ASIAN FISH SAUCE (SEE TIP PAGE 199)

¼   TEASPOON CRUSHED RED PEPPER

3   GARLIC CLOVES, CRUSHED WITH GARLIC PRESS

1   TABLESPOON GRATED, PEELED FRESH GINGER

1   CUP LOOSELY PACKED FRESH BASIL AND/OR MINT LEAVES, COARSELY CHOPPED

1 From limes, grate 1 teaspoon peel and squeeze ¼ cup juice.

2 In large saucepot, heat 3 quarts water to boiling over high heat; remove from heat. Place noodles in water; soak until softened, 6 to 8 minutes. Drain noodles; rinse under cold running water and drain again. Set aside.

3 Meanwhile, in deep nonstick 12-inch skillet, heat 1 tablespoon oil over medium-high heat until hot. Add broccoli, carrots, and **¼ cup water**; cover and cook, stirring once or twice, until vegetables are tender-crisp, about 7 minutes. Add bok choy to skillet and cook, uncovered, just until vegetables are tender, 3 to 4 minutes. Transfer vegetables to bowl.

4 In small bowl, combine **⅔ cup water**, coconut milk, sugar, soy sauce, fish sauce, crushed red pepper, and lime juice; stir until blended.

5 In same skillet, heat remaining 1 tablespoon oil over medium-high heat until hot. Add garlic, ginger, and lime peel; stir 30 seconds. Add coconut-milk mixture; heat to boiling. Stir in noodles and vegetables; heat through.

6 Transfer to warm serving bowl. Toss with basil and/or mint to serve.

EACH SERVING: ABOUT 420 CALORIES | 11G PROTEIN | 70G CARBOHYDRATE | 13G TOTAL FAT (4G SATURATED) | 0MG CHOLESTEROL | 1,215MG SODIUM

SESAME NOODLES

A peanut butter and sesame dressing spiked with orange juice makes this Chinese restaurant–style pasta a favorite with kids as well as adults.

ACTIVE TIME: 15 MIN · TOTAL TIME: 30 MIN
MAKES: 6 MAIN-DISH SERVINGS

1   PACKAGE (16 OUNCES) SPAGHETTI

1   CUP FRESH ORANGE JUICE

¼   CUP SEASONED RICE VINEGAR

¼   CUP SOY SAUCE

¼   CUP CREAMY PEANUT BUTTER

1   TABLESPOON ASIAN SESAME OIL

1   TABLESPOON GRATED, PEELED FRESH GINGER

2   TEASPOONS SUGAR

¼   TEASPOON CRUSHED RED PEPPER

1   BAG (10 OUNCES) SHREDDED CARROTS (ABOUT 3½ CUPS)

3   KIRBY CUCUMBERS (ABOUT 4 OUNCES EACH), UNPEELED AND CUT INTO 2" BY ¼" MATCHSTICK STRIPS

2   GREEN ONIONS, TRIMMED AND THINLY SLICED

2   TABLESPOONS SESAME SEEDS, TOASTED (OPTIONAL)

GREEN ONIONS FOR GARNISH

1   In large saucepot, cook pasta as label directs.
2   Meanwhile, in medium bowl, with wire whisk or fork, mix orange juice, vinegar, soy sauce, peanut butter, oil, ginger, sugar, and crushed red pepper until blended; set aside.
3   Place carrots in colander; drain pasta over carrots. In large warm serving bowl, toss pasta mixture, cucumbers, and sliced green onions with peanut sauce. If you like, sprinkle pasta with sesame seeds. Garnish with green onions.

EACH SERVING: ABOUT 445 CALORIES | 15G PROTEIN | 76G CARBOHYDRATE | 9G TOTAL FAT (2G SATURATED) | 0MG CHOLESTEROL | 1,135MG SODIUM

EGGPLANT PARMESAN

If making our weeknight recipe, Pasta with Eggplant Sauce (page 256), stash two cups of the tomato sauce and a quarter of the casserole in the fridge to use with that recipe.

ACTIVE TIME: 1 HR · TOTAL TIME: 2 HR PLUS STANDING
MAKES: 6 MAIN-DISH SERVINGS

TOMATO SAUCE

1   TABLESPOON OLIVE OIL

1   MEDIUM ONION, FINELY CHOPPED

4   GARLIC CLOVES, MINCED

2   CANS (28 OUNCES EACH) WHOLE TOMATOES IN PUREE

¼   CUP TOMATO PASTE

1   TEASPOON SALT

¼   TEASPOON COARSELY GROUND BLACK PEPPER

¼   CUP LOOSELY PACKED FRESH BASIL LEAVES, CHOPPED (OPTIONAL)

EGGPLANT

3   MEDIUM EGGPLANTS (ABOUT 3¼ POUNDS)

2   TABLESPOONS OLIVE OIL

½   TEASPOON SALT

BREAD-CRUMB TOPPING

2   TEASPOONS BUTTER OR MARGARINE

2   SLICES FIRM WHITE BREAD, COARSELY GRATED

1   GARLIC CLOVE, MINCED

2   OUNCES PART-SKIM MOZZARELLA CHEESE, SHREDDED (½ CUP)

2   TABLESPOONS FRESHLY GRATED PARMESAN CHEESE

CHEESE FILLING

1   CONTAINER (15 OUNCES) PART-SKIM RICOTTA CHEESE

2   OUNCES PART-SKIM MOZZARELLA CHEESE, SHREDDED (½ CUP)

2   TABLESPOONS GRATED PARMESAN CHEESE

¼   TEASPOON COARSELY GROUND BLACK PEPPER

1 Prepare tomato sauce: In 4-quart saucepan, heat oil over medium heat until hot. Add onion and cook, stirring occasionally, until tender, about 8 minutes. Add garlic and cook 1 minute longer, stirring frequently.

2 Stir in tomatoes with their puree, tomato paste, salt, and pepper, breaking up tomatoes with side of spoon; heat to boiling over high heat. Reduce heat to low and simmer, uncovered, until the sauce thickens slightly, about 25 minutes. Stir in basil, if using. Makes about 6 cups. (Cover and refrigerate 2 cups sauce to make Pasta with Eggplant Sauce, or save for another use).

3 While sauce is simmering, prepare eggplant: Preheat oven to 450°F. Grease 2 large cookie sheets. Trim ends from eggplants and discard. Cut eggplants lengthwise into ½-inch-thick slices. Arrange slices in single layer on cookie sheets. Brush top of eggplant slices with oil and sprinkle with salt.

4 Bake eggplant slices 25 to 30 minutes or until tender and golden, rotating sheets and turning slices over halfway through cooking; remove eggplant from oven and turn oven control to 350°F.

5 Prepare topping: In nonstick 10-inch skillet, melt butter over medium heat. Add grated bread and garlic, and cook, stirring occasionally, until lightly browned, about 7 minutes. Transfer to small bowl. Add mozzarella and Parmesan; toss until evenly mixed.

6 Prepare filling: In medium bowl, mix ricotta, mozzarella, Parmesan, and pepper until blended.

7 Assemble the casserole: Into 13" by 9" glass baking dish, evenly spoon 1 cup tomato sauce. Arrange half of eggplant, overlapping slices slightly, in baking dish. Top with 1 cup tomato sauce, then dollops of cheese filling. Top cheese with 1 cup tomato sauce, remaining eggplant, and remaining tomato sauce (about 1 cup). Sprinkle top with bread-crumb topping.

8 Cover baking dish with foil and bake 15 minutes. Remove cover and bake until hot and bubbly, about 15 minutes longer. Let stand 10 minutes for easier serving.

EACH SERVING: ABOUT 380 CALORIES | 21G PROTEIN | 35G CARBOHYDRATE | 21G TOTAL FAT (10G SATURATED) | 49MG CHOLESTEROL | 1,373MG SODIUM

SPINACH AND CORN QUESADILLAS

Fresh veggies, canned black beans, and spicy Jack cheese are layered between flour tortillas and then baked until deliciously crisp.

ACTIVE TIME: 30 MIN · TOTAL TIME: 40 MIN

MAKES: 4 MAIN-DISH SERVINGS

- 1 CAN (15 TO 19 OUNCES) BLACK BEANS, RINSED AND DRAINED
- 1 TABLESPOON OLIVE OIL
- 1 MEDIUM ONION, THINLY SLICED
- 1¼ CUPS CORN KERNELS CUT FROM COBS (2 EARS)
- 1 GARLIC CLOVE, CRUSHED WITH GARLIC PRESS
- 2 TEASPOONS CHILI POWDER
- 1 TEASPOON GROUND CUMIN
- ⅛ TEASPOON COARSELY GROUND BLACK PEPPER
- 1 BAG (6 OUNCES) BABY SPINACH LEAVES
- 8 (8-INCH) FLOUR TORTILLAS
- 4 OUNCES SHREDDED MONTEREY JACK CHEESE WITH JALAPEÑO CHILES (1 CUP)

1 Preheat oven to 400°F. In small bowl, with fork or potato masher, mash 1 cup black beans until almost smooth. Set aside mashed and whole beans, separately.

2 In nonstick 12-inch skillet, heat oil over medium heat until hot. Add onion and cook, stirring occasionally, until tender and golden, 15 to 20 minutes. Add corn, garlic, chili powder, cumin, pepper, and whole beans and cook, stirring frequently, 2 minutes.

3 Increase heat to medium-high. Gradually add spinach to skillet, stirring until spinach has wilted and water has evaporated, about 3 minutes.

4 Spread mashed beans on 1 side of 4 tortillas (mashed beans will be dry and pasty and will not cover the entire tortilla); place, bean side up, on large cookie sheet. Top with equal amounts of spinach mixture and sprinkle with cheese. Place remaining tortillas on top of filling.

5 Bake quesadillas until tortillas are crisp, cheese has melted, and filling is heated through, 8 to 10 minutes. Cut into wedges to serve.

EACH SERVING: ABOUT 665 CALORIES | 26G PROTEIN | 100G CARBOHYDRATE | 22G TOTAL FAT (9G SATURATED) | 30MG CHOLESTEROL | 1,180MG SODIUM

SAVORY TOMATO TART

A dramatically beautiful main dish. For more color, we included a yellow tomato, but it's equally delicious with all red.

ACTIVE TIME: 45 MIN · TOTAL TIME: 1 HR 15 MIN
MAKES: 6 MAIN-DISH SERVINGS

PASTRY FOR 11-INCH TART (PAGE 213)

1 TABLESPOON OLIVE OIL

3 MEDIUM ONIONS, THINLY SLICED

½ TEASPOON SALT

1 PACKAGE (3½ OUNCES) GOAT CHEESE

1 RIPE MEDIUM YELLOW TOMATO (8 OUNCES), CUT INTO ¼-INCH-THICK SLICES

2 RIPE MEDIUM RED TOMATOES (8 OUNCES EACH), CUT INTO ¼-INCH-THICK SLICES

½ TEASPOON COARSELY GROUND BLACK PEPPER

¼ CUP KALAMATA OLIVES, PITTED AND CHOPPED

1 Preheat oven to 425°F. Prepare Pastry for 11-Inch Tart as recipe directs. On lightly floured surface, with floured rolling pin, roll dough into 14-inch round. Ease dough into 11" by 1" round tart pan with removable bottom. Fold overhang in and press dough against side of pan so it extends ⅛ inch above rim. With fork, prick dough at 1-inch intervals. Line tart shell with foil; fill with pie weights or dry beans. Bake 15 minutes. Remove foil with weights. Bake until golden, 5 to 10 minutes longer. If the shell puffs up during baking, gently press it down with back of spoon.

2 Meanwhile, in nonstick 12-inch skillet, heat oil over medium heat until hot. Add onions and ¼ teaspoon salt; cook, stirring frequently, until very tender, about 20 minutes.

3 Turn oven control to Broil. Spread onions over bottom of tart shell and crumble half of goat cheese on top. Arrange yellow and red tomatoes, alternating colors, in concentric circles over onion-cheese mixture. Sprinkle with remaining ¼ teaspoon salt and pepper. Crumble remaining goat cheese on top of tart.

4 Place tart on rack in broiling pan. Place pan in broiler about 7 inches from heat source. Broil until cheese has melted and tomatoes are heated through, 6 to 8 minutes. Sprinkle with olives.

EACH SERVING: ABOUT 420 CALORIES | 8G PROTEIN | 33G CARBOHYDRATE | 29G TOTAL FAT (15G SATURATED) | 54MG CHOLESTEROL | 755MG SODIUM

TOFU AND VEGETABLE STIR-FRY

Choose extra-firm tofu so it won't fall apart during stir-frying. Spoon the saucy tofu-and-vegetable mixture over fragrant jasmine rice. Because the stir-fry takes only twenty minutes to cook, start the rice as soon as you step into the kitchen.

ACTIVE TIME: 15 MIN · TOTAL TIME: 35 MIN

MAKES: 4 MAIN-DISH SERVINGS

- 1 CUP JASMINE RICE
- 4 TEASPOONS VEGETABLE OIL
- 1 PACKAGE (16 OUNCES) EXTRA-FIRM TOFU, PATTED DRY AND CUT INTO 1" BY ½" PIECES
- 2 TABLESPOONS REDUCED-SODIUM SOY SAUCE
- 8 OUNCES (HALF 16-OUNCE BAG) BROCCOLI FLOWERETS
- 1 MEDIUM RED PEPPER, CUT INTO ½-INCH PIECES
- 1 CUP WATER
- 2 TABLESPOONS ASIAN FISH SAUCE (SEE TIP PAGE 199)
- 2 TABLESPOONS GRATED, PEELED FRESH GINGER
- 1 TABLESPOON BROWN SUGAR
- 1 TABLESPOON CORNSTARCH
- 1 LARGE GARLIC CLOVE, CRUSHED WITH GARLIC PRESS
- 1 BAG (10 OUNCES) SHREDDED CARROTS
- 3 TABLESPOONS FRESH LIME JUICE

1 Prepare jasmine rice as label directs; keep warm.

2 Meanwhile, in nonstick 12-inch skillet, heat 2 teaspoons oil over medium-high heat until hot. Add tofu and 1 tablespoon soy sauce and cook, stirring frequently (stir-frying) but gently, until heated through and golden, about 5 minutes. Transfer tofu to plate; set aside.

3 In same skillet, heat remaining 2 teaspoons oil. Add broccoli and red pepper and cook, covered, stirring occasionally, until vegetables are tender-crisp, about 6 minutes.

4 In small bowl, with fork, mix water with fish sauce, ginger, brown sugar, cornstarch, garlic, and remaining 1 tablespoon soy sauce.

5 Return tofu to skillet and add carrots. Stir soy-sauce mixture to blend and add to skillet; heat to boiling. Boil, gently stirring, 1 minute. Stir in lime juice. Serve over rice.

EACH SERVING: ABOUT 425 CALORIES | 19G PROTEIN | 61G CARBOHYDRATE | 11G TOTAL FAT (1G SATURATED) | 0MG CHOLESTEROL | 1,020MG SODIUM

GRILLED TOFU AND VEGGIES

Be sure to buy extrafirm tofu; other varieties will fall apart while cooking.

ACTIVE TIME: 25 MIN · TOTAL TIME: 37 MIN
MAKES: 4 MAIN-DISH SERVINGS

HOISIN GLAZE

⅓ CUP HOISIN SAUCE

2 GARLIC CLOVES, CRUSHED WITH GARLIC PRESS

1 TABLESPOON VEGETABLE OIL

1 TABLESPOON REDUCED-SODIUM SOY SAUCE

1 TABLESPOON GRATED, PEELED FRESH GINGER

1 TABLESPOON SEASONED RICE VINEGAR

⅛ TEASPOON GROUND RED PEPPER (CAYENNE)

TOFU AND VEGGIES

1 PACKAGE (15 OUNCES) EXTRA-FIRM TOFU

2 MEDIUM ZUCCHINI (ABOUT 10 OUNCES EACH), EACH CUT LENGTHWISE INTO QUARTERS, THEN CROSSWISE IN HALF

1 LARGE RED PEPPER, CUT LENGTHWISE INTO QUARTERS, STEM AND SEEDS DISCARDED

1 BUNCH GREEN ONIONS, TRIMMED

1 TEASPOON VEGETABLE OIL

1 Prepare glaze: In small bowl, with fork, mix hoisin sauce, garlic, oil, soy sauce, ginger, vinegar, and ground red pepper until well blended.

2 Prepare grill.

3 Prepare tofu and veggies: Cut tofu horizontally into 4 pieces, then cut each piece crosswise in half. Place tofu on paper towels; pat dry with additional paper towels. Spoon half of hoisin glaze into medium bowl; add zucchini and red pepper. Gently toss vegetables to coat with glaze. Arrange tofu on large plate and brush both sides of tofu with remaining glaze. On another plate, rub green onions with oil.

4 Place tofu, zucchini, and red pepper on hot grill rack over medium heat. Cook tofu, gently turning once with wide metal spatula, 6 minutes. Transfer tofu to platter; keep warm. Continue cooking vegetables until tender and browned, about 5 minutes longer, transferring them to platter with tofu as they are done. Add green onions to grill during last minute of cooking time; transfer to platter.

EACH SERVING: ABOUT 245 CALORIES | 15G PROTEIN | 22G CARBOHYDRATE | 11G TOTAL FAT (1G SATURATED) | 0MG CHOLESTEROL | 615MG SODIUM

GRILLED TOMATO AND BASIL PIZZAS

Garden tomatoes and basil make a wonderful topping for pizza cooked over the coals. For the crust, use frozen bread dough or fresh dough from the supermarket or pizzeria.

ACTIVE TIME: 30 MIN · TOTAL TIME: 36 TO 39 MIN PER PIZZA
MAKES: 4 PIZZAS OR 4 MAIN-DISH SERVINGS

1   POUND (1 PIECE) FROZEN BREAD DOUGH, THAWED (FROM 2- TO 3-POUND PACKAGE)

2   TABLESPOONS OLIVE OIL

4   RIPE MEDIUM TOMATOES (ABOUT 1½ POUNDS), SLICED

4   OUNCES FRESH MOZZARELLA CHEESE, SLICED, OR 1 CUP SHREDDED FONTINA CHEESE

½   TEASPOON SALT

½   TEASPOON GROUND BLACK PEPPER

1   CUP LOOSELY PACKED FRESH BASIL LEAVES, CHOPPED, PLUS ADDITIONAL LEAVES FOR GARNISH

1   Prepare grill.

2   Cut thawed bread dough into 4 pieces. On oiled cookie sheet, spread and flatten 1 piece of dough to ⅛-inch thickness. Lightly brush dough with some oil. On same cookie sheet, repeat with another piece of dough. Repeat with another oiled cookie sheet and remaining pieces of dough. For easiest handling, cover and refrigerate dough on cookie sheets until ready to use.

3   Place 1 piece of dough at a time, greased side down, on grill over medium-low heat. Grill until dough stiffens (dough may puff slightly) and grill marks appear on underside, 2 to 3 minutes. Brush top with some oil.

4   With tongs, turn crust over. Quickly top with one-fourth of tomatoes and one-fourth of cheese. Cook pizza until cheese melts and underside is evenly browned and cooked through, 4 to 6 minutes longer.

5   With tongs, transfer pizza to cutting board. Sprinkle pizza with ⅛ teaspoon salt and ⅛ teaspoon pepper. Scatter one-fourth of chopped basil on pizza and garnish with basil leaves. Drizzle with some oil, if you like. Serve immediately.

6   Repeat with remaining dough and toppings.

EACH SERVING: ABOUT 495 CALORIES | 18G PROTEIN | 63G CARBOHYDRATE | 20G TOTAL FAT (7G SATURATED) | 34MG CHOLESTEROL | 1,175MG SODIUM

WHOLE-WHEAT PITA PIZZAS WITH VEGETABLES

We topped whole-wheat pitas with ricotta cheese, garbanzo beans, and sautéed vegetables for a fast dinner the whole family will love.

ACTIVE TIME: 25 MIN · TOTAL TIME: 38 MIN

MAKES: 8 PIZZAS OR 4 MAIN-DISH SERVINGS

1   TEASPOON OLIVE OIL

1   MEDIUM RED ONION, SLICED

2   GARLIC CLOVES, CRUSHED
    WITH GARLIC PRESS

¼   TEASPOON CRUSHED RED PEPPER

8   OUNCES BROCCOLI FLOWERETS,
    CUT INTO 1½-INCH PIECES

½   TEASPOON SALT

¼   CUP WATER

1   CAN (15 TO 19 OUNCES) GARBANZO
    BEANS, RINSED AND DRAINED

1   CUP PART-SKIM RICOTTA CHEESE

4   (6-INCH) WHOLE-WHEAT PITAS,
    SPLIT HORIZONTALLY IN HALF

½   CUP FRESHLY GRATED PARMESAN
    CHEESE

2   MEDIUM PLUM TOMATOES,
    CUT INTO ½-INCH PIECES

1   Preheat oven to 450°F. In nonstick 12-inch skillet, heat oil over medium-high heat until hot. Add onion and cook, stirring occasionally, until golden, 7 to 10 minutes. Add garlic and crushed red pepper, and cook, stirring, 30 seconds. Add broccoli flowerets, ¼ teaspoon salt, and water; heat to boiling. Reduce heat to medium and cook, covered, until broccoli is tender-crisp, about 5 minutes.

2   Meanwhile, in small bowl, with potato masher or fork, mash beans with ricotta and remaining ¼ teaspoon salt until almost smooth.

3   Arrange pita halves on 2 large cookie sheets. Bake until lightly toasted, about 3 minutes. Spread bean mixture on toasted pitas. Top with broccoli mixture and sprinkle with Parmesan. Bake until heated through, 7 to 10 minutes longer. Sprinkle with tomatoes to serve. Serve 2 rounds per person.

EACH SERVING: ABOUT 510 CALORIES | 27G PROTEIN | 77G CARBOHYDRATE | 13G TOTAL FAT (6G SATURATED) | 27MG CHOLESTEROL | 1,155MG SODIUM

SOUTH-OF-THE-BORDER VEGETABLE HASH

A savory combination of classic hash ingredients (without the meat) gets a new flavor twist from kidney beans, cilantro, and fresh lime.

ACTIVE TIME: 20 MIN · TOTAL TIME: 50 MIN

MAKES: 8 CUPS OR 4 MAIN-DISH SERVINGS

3   LARGE YUKON GOLD POTATOES
    (ABOUT 1½ POUNDS),
    CUT INTO ¾-INCH PIECES

2   TABLESPOONS OLIVE OIL

1   LARGE ONION (12 OUNCES),
    CUT INTO ¼-INCH PIECES

1   MEDIUM RED PEPPER, CUT INTO
    ¼-INCH-WIDE STRIPS

3   GARLIC CLOVES, CRUSHED
    WITH GARLIC PRESS

2   TEASPOONS GROUND CUMIN

¾   TEASPOON SALT

1   CAN (15 TO 19 OUNCES) RED KIDNEY
    OR BLACK BEANS, RINSED AND DRAINED

2   TABLESPOONS CHOPPED FRESH
    CILANTRO

PLAIN YOGURT, LIME WEDGES, SALSA,
AND TOASTED CORN TORTILLAS
(OPTIONAL)

1 In 3-quart saucepan, combine potatoes and enough water to cover; heat to boiling over high heat. Reduce heat to low; cover and simmer until potatoes are almost tender, about 5 minutes. Drain well.

2 Meanwhile, in nonstick 12-inch skillet, heat oil over medium-high heat until hot. Add onion, red pepper, garlic, cumin, and salt and cook, stirring occasionally, 10 minutes. Add drained potatoes and cook until vegetables are lightly browned, 5 minutes longer. Stir in beans and cook until heated through, about 2 minutes longer. Sprinkle with chopped cilantro.

3 Serve vegetable hash with yogurt, lime wedges, salsa, and corn tortillas, if you like.

EACH SERVING WITHOUT ACCOMPANIMENTS: ABOUT 360 CALORIES | 12G PROTEIN | 63G CARBOHYDRATE | 8G TOTAL FAT (1G SATURATED) | 0MG CHOLESTEROL | 625MG SODIUM

SHORTCUT ASPARAGUS PIZZAS

You won't find this delicious pie—with shiitake mushrooms and asparagus topping—at your local pizzeria.

ACTIVE TIME: 30 MIN · TOTAL TIME: 50 MIN
MAKES: 2 PIZZAS OR 4 MAIN-DISH SERVINGS

1½ POUNDS ASPARAGUS, TRIMMED

1 TABLESPOON OLIVE OIL

1 LARGE ONION (12 OUNCES), CUT IN HALF AND THINLY SLICED

¼ POUND SHIITAKE MUSHROOMS, STEMS REMOVED AND CAPS THINLY SLICED

1 LARGE GARLIC CLOVE, MINCED

½ TEASPOON SALT

¼ TEASPOON GROUND BLACK PEPPER

¼ CUP WATER

1 POUND (1 PIECE) FROZEN BREAD DOUGH, THAWED (FROM 2- TO 3-POUND PACKAGE)

4 OUNCES FONTINA CHEESE, SHREDDED (1 CUP)

2 TABLESPOONS FRESHLY GRATED PARMESAN CHEESE

1 Preheat oven to 425°F.

2 If using thin asparagus, cut each stalk crosswise in half; if using medium asparagus, cut stalks into 1½-inch pieces. In nonstick 12-inch skillet, heat oil over medium-high heat until hot. Add onion and mushrooms and cook, stirring often, until vegetables are tender and golden, 8 to 10 minutes. Add asparagus, garlic, salt, pepper, and water; cover and cook until asparagus is tender-crisp, about 5 minutes longer. Remove skillet from heat.

3 Cut dough in half. On greased cookie sheet, spread and flatten 1 piece of dough to ⅛-inch thickness (about 10 inches in diameter). Pinch edges of dough to form rim. Repeat with another greased cookie sheet and remaining piece of dough. Sprinkle ½ cup Fontina over each piece of dough, then spread with equal amounts of vegetable mixture. Sprinkle each with 1 tablespoon Parmesan.

4 Bake pizzas on 2 oven racks until crust is lightly browned and cheese melts, 18 to 20 minutes, rotating cookie sheets between upper and lower racks halfway through baking.

EACH SERVING: ABOUT 505 CALORIES | 22G PROTEIN | 66G CARBOHYDRATE | 18G TOTAL FAT (7G SATURATED) | 36MG CHOLESTEROL | 1,230MG SODIUM

POLENTA WITH SPICY EGGPLANT SAUCE

A great dinner you can whip up after you get home from work: Polenta cooks in the microwave oven with minimal attention while you prepare a quick skillet sauce.

ACTIVE TIME: 15 MIN · TOTAL TIME: 40 MIN

MAKES: 4 MAIN-DISH SERVINGS

---

1 TABLESPOON OLIVE OIL

1 MEDIUM ONION, FINELY CHOPPED

2 SMALL EGGPLANTS (ABOUT 1 POUND EACH), CUT INTO 1-INCH PIECES

1 GARLIC CLOVE, CRUSHED WITH GARLIC PRESS

¼ TEASPOON CRUSHED RED PEPPER

1 CAN (28 OUNCES) CRUSHED TOMATOES

1½ TEASPOONS SALT

2 CUPS LOW-FAT (1%) MILK

1½ CUPS YELLOW CORNMEAL

PARMESAN-CHEESE WEDGE FOR GARNISH (OPTIONAL)

---

1 In nonstick 12-inch skillet, heat oil over medium heat until hot. Add onion and cook, stirring occasionally, 5 minutes. Increase heat to medium-high; add eggplant and cook, stirring occasionally, until golden and tender, about 8 minutes. Add garlic and crushed red pepper and cook, stirring, 1 minute. Add tomatoes, ½ teaspoon salt, and ½ cup water; heat to boiling. Reduce heat to low; cover and simmer, stirring occasionally, 10 minutes.

2 Meanwhile, in deep 4-quart microwave-safe bowl or casserole, combine milk, cornmeal, 1 teaspoon salt, and 4½ cups water. Cook in microwave oven on High until thickened, 15 to 20 minutes. After the first 5 minutes of cooking, whisk vigorously until smooth (mixture will be lumpy at first), and twice more during remaining cooking time.

3 While polenta is cooking, with vegetable peeler, remove long, thin strips from Parmesan wedge for garnish, if you like.

4 To serve, spoon polenta into 4 bowls; top with eggplant sauce. Garnish each serving with some Parmesan strips if using.

EACH SERVING: ABOUT 380 CALORIES | 13G PROTEIN | 71G CARBOHYDRATE | 6G TOTAL FAT (2G SATURATED) | 5MG CHOLESTEROL | 1,235MG SODIUM

POLENTA BAKE WITH BUTTERNUT SQUASH

Polenta with a creamy mix of butternut squash and Parmesan cheese.

ACTIVE TIME: 30 MIN · TOTAL TIME: 45 MIN

MAKES: 4 MAIN-DISH SERVINGS

1 LOG (24 OUNCES) PRECOOKED POLENTA

4 TEASPOONS OLIVE OIL

1 JUMBO ONION (1 POUND), CUT INTO ¼-INCH PIECES

2 GARLIC CLOVES, CRUSHED WITH GARLIC PRESS

1 BAG CUT-UP BUTTERNUT SQUASH (1¼ POUNDS)

1¼ CUPS LOW-FAT MILK (1%)

2 TEASPOONS CORNSTARCH

½ TEASPOON SALT

⅛ TEASPOON COARSELY GROUND BLACK PEPPER

6 TABLESPOONS FRESHLY GRATED PARMESAN CHEESE PLUS ADDITIONAL FOR SERVING

½ CUP LOOSELY PACKED FRESH BASIL LEAVES, CHOPPED

1 Preheat oven to 450°F. Cut polenta log crosswise in half, then cut each half lengthwise into 4 slices. In lightly greased 8" by 8" ceramic or glass baking dish, place 6 slices polenta. Cut remaining 2 slices into ¼-inch pieces; set aside.

2 In nonstick 12-inch skillet, heat oil over medium-high heat until hot. Add onion and garlic, and cook, stirring occasionally, 5 minutes. Add squash; cover and cook, stirring occasionally, until vegetables are tender and lightly browned, about 15 minutes longer.

3 Meanwhile, bake polenta slices in baking dish until heated through, about 10 minutes.

4 In small bowl with fork, stir milk, cornstarch, salt, pepper, and 4 tablespoons Parmesan until well combined. Add milk mixture to skillet; heat to boiling over medium-high heat. Reduce heat to low; cook, stirring occasionally, 2 minutes.

5 Spoon squash mixture over polenta slices; top with polenta pieces and remaining 2 tablespoons Parmesan. Bake until heated through, about 5 minutes. Sprinkle with basil before serving. Serve with additional Parmesan, if you like.

EACH SERVING: ABOUT 350 CALORIES | 12G PROTEIN | 60G CARBOHYDRATE | 8G TOTAL FAT (3G SATURATED) | 9MG CHOLESTEROL | 1,005MG SODIUM

MUSHROOM AND BARLEY PILAF

A mixture of fresh and dried mushrooms and hearty root vegetables are cooked with barley for a flavorful entrée—especially good on a crisp autumn day!

ACTIVE TIME: 20 MIN · TOTAL TIME: 1 HR 10 MIN PLUS STANDING

MAKES: 9 CUPS OR 4 MAIN-DISH SERVINGS

1 PACKAGE (ABOUT ½ OUNCE) DRIED PORCINI MUSHROOMS (ABOUT ½ CUP)

2 TABLESPOONS BUTTER OR MARGARINE

1 MEDIUM ONION, FINELY CHOPPED

2 MEDIUM CARROTS, PEELED AND EACH CUT LENGTHWISE IN HALF, THEN CROSSWISE INTO ¼-INCH-THICK SLICES

2 MEDIUM PARSNIPS (ABOUT 6 OUNCES EACH), PEELED AND EACH CUT LENGTHWISE IN HALF, THEN CROSSWISE INTO ¼-INCH-THICK SLICES

2 PACKAGES (ABOUT 4 OUNCES EACH) SLICED WILD MUSHROOM BLEND OR 8 OUNCES MIXED WILD MUSHROOMS, TOUGH STEMS REMOVED AND CAPS THINLY SLICED

1¼ TEASPOONS SALT

¼ TEASPOON COARSELY GROUND BLACK PEPPER

¼ TEASPOON DRIED THYME

1½ CUPS PEARL BARLEY (ABOUT 12 OUNCES)

½ CUP LOOSELY PACKED FRESH PARSLEY LEAVES, CHOPPED

1 In medium bowl, pour 3 cups boiling water over porcini mushrooms; let stand 10 minutes. With slotted spoon, remove porcini, reserving liquid. Rinse porcini to remove any grit, then coarsely chop and set aside. Strain mushroom liquid through sieve lined with paper towels into liquid measuring cup. Add enough water to liquid to equal 4½ cups total; set aside.

2 Meanwhile, in nonstick 5- to 6-quart Dutch oven or saucepot, melt butter over medium-high heat. Add onion, carrots, parsnips, wild mushrooms, salt, pepper, and thyme and cook, stirring occasionally, until vegetables are tender-crisp, about 10 minutes.

3 Add barley and porcini with soaking liquid; heat to boiling. Reduce heat to medium-low; cover and simmer, stirring occasionally, until barley and vegetables are tender, 35 to 40 minutes. Stir in parsley.

EACH SERVING: ABOUT 425 CALORIES | 12G PROTEIN | 82G CARBOHYDRATE | 10G TOTAL FAT (4G SATURATED) | 16MG CHOLESTEROL | 837MG SODIUM

EGGPLANT AND SPINACH STACKS

A fun new way to serveup eggplant.

ACTIVE TIME: 25 MIN · **TOTAL TIME:** 55 MIN

MAKES: 4 MAIN-DISH SERVINGS

1	MEDIUM EGGPLANT (ABOUT 1½ POUNDS)	1	BAG (6 OUNCES) BABY SPINACH LEAVES
1	TABLESPOON PLUS 3 TEASPOONS OLIVE OIL	1	CUP PART-SKIM RICOTTA CHEESE
1	TEASPOON SALT	¼	CUP FRESHLY GRATED PARMESAN CHEESE
2	GARLIC CLOVES, CRUSHED WITH GARLIC PRESS	2	PLUM TOMATOES, SEEDED AND CUT INTO PAPER-THIN STRIPS
⅛	TEASPOON CRUSHED RED PEPPER	⅛	TEASPOON CRACKED BLACK PEPPER
1	SMALL ZUCCHINI (ABOUT 6 OUNCES), TRIMMED AND COARSELY SHREDDED		

1 Preheat oven to 450°F. Trim ends from eggplant; discard. Cut eggplant crosswise into 8 rounds of equal thickness. Brush cut sides of slices with 1 tablespoon plus 2 teaspoons oil and sprinkle with ½ teaspoon salt.

2 In 15½" by 10½" jelly-roll pan, arrange slices in single layer. Roast, turning slices halfway through, until tender and golden, 20 to 25 minutes.

3 Meanwhile, in nonstick 12-inch skillet, heat remaining 1 teaspoon oil over medium-high heat until hot. Add garlic and red pepper and cook, stirring, 30 seconds. Add zucchini and ¼ teaspoon salt and cook, stirring, 2 minutes. Gradually add spinach to skillet, stirring until spinach has wilted and water has evaporated, about 3 minutes; set aside.

4 In small bowl, with fork, mix ricotta, Parmesan, and remaining ¼ teaspoon salt until blended.

5 Remove eggplant from oven. Mound spinach mixture on 4 of the larger eggplant slices; top with remaining eggplant slices. Mound equal amounts of cheese mixture on each eggplant stack. Return to oven and heat through, about 5 minutes (cheese will melt over side of stacks).

6 With wide metal spatula, transfer stacks to 4 dinner plates. Top with tomatoes and sprinkle with black pepper to serve.

EACH SERVING: ABOUT 230 CALORIES | 13G PROTEIN | 17G CARBOHYDRATE | 14G TOTAL FAT (5G SATURATED) | 23MG CHOLESTEROL | 795MG SODIUM

LIGHT & HEALTHY

Southwestern Black-Bean Burgers (page 451)

INTRODUCTION

Providing healthy, low-calorie meals that are satisfying and easy to prepare is a big concern for all of us today. As the relationship between diet and health hits the headlines repeatedly, we all want to do our best to produce meals for our families and ourselves that meet today's nutrition guidelines. But figuring out how to do it isn't always easy. The latest USDA Dietary Guidelines (www.health.gov/ Dietary Guidelines/) and My Pyramid Plan (www.MyPyramid.gov) have changed the rules, but the goal is the same. The specific suggestions have been revised based on current medical research and the presentation is different, but the intention is still to encourage us all to create a lifestyle that will lead to many years of good health.

Over the years, *Good Housekeeping* has been a trusted source for help in making the latest information on nutrition and health a part of your life. As the rules change, GH editors translate the underlying research and provide the tools you need to make it work for you. This book follows that tradition by bringing you this collection of delicious, thoroughly tested recipes that meet today's dietary guidelines. The recipes emphasize more whole grains, more fruits and vegetables, more variety in the vegetables served, fat-free or reduced-fat dairy products, less sodium, and less saturated fat (with fat coming from healthy sources such as nuts, fish, and vegetable oils). In addition, from enticing appetizers through decadent desserts, the percentage of calories from fat in each recipe is less than 30 percent.

CALORIES COUNT

We hear a lot about America's nationwide weight gain and about the "flavor-of-the-day" diets that everyone is trying—but very little about counting calories. Calories aren't an old-fashioned enemy; they are simply a way of measuring the amount of energy produced when food is used by the body, and keeping an eye on them is still the most successful way to ease into a lifetime of weight control. Weight maintenance is just a matter of balance: Food calories in must equal energy calories out.

For centuries our bodies have been stocking up during times of plenty to insure survival during times of scarcity, so we are naturally programmed to tuck away all excess food calories as those potential energy calories we know as fat. And that is not likely to change any time soon. You might try the latest diet fad and enjoy momentary success, but pretty soon your body will think the famine it has been planning for has arrived and will steadfastly hang on to those stored calories in case things get worse. Lifetime weight maintenance requires setting reasonable weight goals for yourself and enjoying just enough of today's bounty to provide the energy you need for all you do. The nutrition information at the end of each recipe in this book will help. Make balance a habit; go for healthy food that pleases you and exercise that is fun.

ALSO IMPORTANT

While controlling the nutrient content of the recipes you prepare is a primary concern, providing mealtime satisfaction is also essential. A diet of healthy, low-calorie foods that aren't delicious and satisfying will soon be abandoned. If everyone is foraging for their favorite snack an hour after dinner, the plan has failed. The recipes you'll find in this book have been tested and tasted in our kitchens with flavor and satiety in mind. We want you to discover how enjoyable healthy foods can be so you will want to make them a long-term part of your life.

And because we know there are many responsibilities competing for your time these days, as we developed recipes that are light and healthy, satisfying and delicious, we never forgot that quick and easy is also a plus when you have to get dinner on the table after a busy day. The recipes that made the cut require very little hands-on time. They can either be prepared quickly and served, or mind themselves in the oven while you do other things.

We think a collection of easy and nutritious recipes that your family loves is worth a place in your kitchen and the healthy eating patterns that it encourages will become a family tradition. You'll see: Light & Healthy can be habit forming.

ChooseMyPlate.gov

CREATE YOUR PLATE

Many of us remember the old food pyramid, but the USDA's latest nutritional recommendations are presented in a much more user-friendly format: a dinner plate. The most recent guidelines suggest that the ideal diet is rich in whole grains, vegetables, fruits, and fat-free or reduced-fat dairy products. Healthy meals include lean meat, fish, and poultry, as well as beans, eggs, and nuts. Saturated fats, trans fats, cholesterol, sodium, and added sugar are omitted or limited. The plate represents the ideal balance of food groups we should strive for at each meal: half full of fruits and vegetables, with the remaining half split between proteins and grains, plus a small amount of dairy. Whole grains are represented by the orange segment, vegetables are green, fruit is signified by red, protein is purple, and dairy is presented in the side, in blue.

On the website **choosemyplate.gov**, you can get an overview of each food group, learn about weight management and calories, find information about the importance of exercise and tips for incorporating more workouts into your daily routine, and explore online tools to help you eat healthier.

ORGANICS: HEALTH FOOD OR HYPE?

Organic food seems like a healthy choice—even if the price is tough to swallow. But until recently, it was anyone's guess what "organic" really meant (regulation was local and hodge-podge). Now national standards are taking effect, and with them comes a new crop of groceries: organic everything, from mac & cheese to vanilla wafers. Should you pay more for these products (often produced by the same companies that make the regular versions)? In our taste tests of organics versus old standbys, many people didn't have a preference (suggesting that your decision probably won't be based on flavor). One standout: Of those who had a preference, 75 percent liked the original Oreo cookie better than its organic cousin. Here, more food for thought.

Why you would eat organic:

- **To avoid artificial ingredients.** This includes synthetic colors and flavors, all prohibited by the new regulations.

- **To cut "bad" fats from your diet.** Artery-clogging partially hydrogenated oils are not allowed in organic food. Irradiated or genetically engineered ingredients also don't make the cut.

- **To limit exposure to pesticides.** Under the new rules, organic produce can't be treated with synthetic pesticides. But it's not pesticide free: There may be chemicals lingering in the soil or the air. A recent study found that organic foods contain a third of the residues present on conventional produce. Even so, the jury's still out on whether trace amounts of these substances are harmful to the consumer. Hormones, steroids, and antibiotics are also banned from organic meat, dairy, and poultry.

- **To protect the environment.** Organic farming reduces water contamination, improves soil quality, and protects wildlife habitats.

EASY CHANGES YOU CAN MAKE RIGHT NOW

Enjoying a healthy lifestyle might require some changes, but they don't have to be painful. In fact, giving up your favorites forever should never be part of the program. There are actually a lot of small changes that will make a big step in the right direction. Here are ten of our favorites:

- **Gradually switch to fat-free milk.** You'll be amazed how easy it is to downsize from whole to fat-free milk if you do it in stages. Go to 2% for a few weeks, 1% for a while, and you are there. We'll bet you don't ever want to go back.

- **Take control of salt.** Watch out for hidden salt in seasonings such as spice mixtures and the seasoning packets that come with packaged foods. Look for brands that don't include salt and add only as much as you need.

- **Break high-calorie combos.** Discover bread with a little olive oil (instead of butter), baked potatoes with herbs (hold the sour cream), dessert without whipped cream (or ice cream)— you'll enjoy the food's flavor even more.

- **Go whole grain.** There are now more whole-grain choices than ever. Choose brown rice, whole-wheat pasta, and whole-grain breads. Be sure to check bread labels to see how much of the rich brown color actually comes from whole grains rather than from coloring agents, cocoa, or molasses.

- **Snack from the produce department.** Even if you are in a hurry, there are a lot of ready-to-eat fruit and vegetable choices in the produce department these days. If you don't see anything prepackaged that you want, go to the salad bar and select your own, just skip the dressing or choose a fat-free dressing and use it as a veggie dip.

- **Always read the nutrition facts labels.** It doesn't take a lot of time and you can learn a lot. Sometimes those packages with the biggest fat-free, low-fat, or low-salt labels are very high in sugar and calories.

- **Remember, liquid calories count.** The number of calories in beverages might surprise you. Fruit juice, alcoholic drinks, milk, sweetened lemonade and iced tea, and soda all have more calories than you might expect. And, on a warm day, you might go ahead and have a refill. Just keep the calories in mind; you can always switch to water.

- **Select soup.** If you start a restaurant meal with even a cup of soup, you will feel satisfied faster and won't be tempted to order that high-calorie dessert. (Just make sure it's not a chowder or cream-based soup.) At home, a meal of soup makes a nutritious yet low-calorie dinner.

- **Explore reduced-fat, low-sodium options.** Many reduced-fat and low-sodium products that will work well in your favorite family recipes. Grandma's lasagna might be just as delicious with reduced-fat cheeses and low-sodium tomatoes. In fact, she probably would have used them if they had been in her local market when she wanted, most of all, to produce healthy meals for her family.

- **Walk to your local ice cream store** or drive if it is really too far to walk—just don't keep that half-gallon in the freezer. You don't need to deny yourself your favorite treat, but if enjoying a bowl of ice cream requires a trip, you have to think about it and it becomes a special occasion.

HEALTHY SHOPPING

Healthy lifestyle changes start in the supermarket; if you make the right selections there, your time in the kitchen will be easy. Here are some strategies for filling your cart and your cupboards with light, healthy, and natural choices.

- Select recipes and make a list of healthy items you will need for the week's meals.

- Discard high-fat items from your cupboards and add low-fat versions of your favorites to the list.

- Add one item from the snack aisle to the list so you won't feel deprived; make it the small size.

- Head for the market, but not until you have a healthy breakfast, lunch, or dinner. If you aren't hungry, you're not as likely to be tempted by unhealthy choices.

- Buy just what you need; the large size isn't a bargain if it is more than you need.

- Check sell-by dates of groceries and select produce that is the freshest, even if it means tweaking a recipe or changing your menu.

- Compare nutrition facts labels among similar products and select those that best meet your dietary goals.

- Buy only what's on your list; don't be tempted by the end-of-aisle specials.

- Select the candy-free checkout lane; treat yourself to a magazine.

APPETIZERS, SIDE DISHES & SALADS

There is a common misconception that if you're eating healthy, you have to give up appetizers and be sparing with side dishes. Not true! We've got recipes for starters and sides that are low in calories and easy to prepare. Some are twists on familiar favorites, like guacamole made from peas instead of avocado, a black bean dip to replace high-fat recipes with sour cream, and French fries that aren't fried at all, but baked in the oven. (We include plenty of other low-cal, low-fat ways to prepare the beloved potato.) And we've also tackled vegetables by adding irresistible flavors, like soy sauce, tarragon, and lemon. Some of our dishes, like chicken skewers or mussels, could even serve double duty as a light dinner.

Salad, in its most familiar guise, is composed of cool, crisp greens tossed with a piquant dressing. But a winning salad can be created from an endless array of ingredients. Our recipes include the most unexpected ingredients, such as peaches, melon, black-eyed peas, tabbouleh, and mint. And just like our apps and sides, you can stretch these recipes into a full lunch or dinner—just bolster the dish with chicken, meat, or seafood to create a delicious meal in a bowl.

Skewered Chicken with Papaya Salsa (page 337)
and Sweet Pea Guacamole (page 335)

BACKYARD BRUSCHETTA

Easy appetizers of grilled bread and your choice of two Italian-style toppings.

ACTIVE TIME: 15 MIN · **TOTAL TIME:** 25 MIN

MAKES: 16 BRUSCHETTA

TUSCAN WHITE BEAN TOPPING (BELOW)
OR TOMATO–GOAT CHEESE TOPPING
(PAGE 333)

1   LOAF (8 OUNCES) ITALIAN BREAD

2   GARLIC CLOVES,
    PEELED AND CUT IN HALF

1   TABLESPOON OLIVE OIL

1 Prepare one of the toppings; set aside.

2 Prepare grill. Cut off ends from bread; reserve for another use. Slice loaf diagonally into ½-inch-thick slices.

3 Place bread slices on grill over medium heat. Grill, turning occasionally, until lightly toasted, 8 to 10 minutes. Rub one side of each slice with cut side of garlic. Brush with oil.

4 Just before serving, assemble bruschetta by topping toast slices with either white bean topping, or goat cheese mixture and then tomato mixture.

TUSCAN WHITE BEAN TOPPING

1   CAN (15½ TO 19 OUNCES) WHITE
    KIDNEY BEANS, RINSED AND DRAINED

1   TABLESPOON MINCED FRESH
    PARSLEY LEAVES

1   TABLESPOON LEMON JUICE

1   TABLESPOON OLIVE OIL

1   TEASPOON MINCED FRESH
    SAGE LEAVES

2¼ TEASPOONS SALT

⅛   TEASPOON COARSELY GROUND
    BLACK PEPPER

In medium bowl, with fork, lightly mash beans, parsley, lemon juice, oil, sage, salt, and pepper until combined.

EACH BRUSCHETTA WITH WHITE BEAN TOPPING: ABOUT 80 CALORIES (23 PERCENT CALORIES FROM FAT) | 3G PROTEIN | 11G CARBOHYDRATE | 2G TOTAL FAT (0G SATURATED) | 0MG CHOLESTEROL | 175MG SODIUM

TOMATO–GOAT CHEESE TOPPING

1   PACKAGE (6 OUNCES) SOFT
    LOW-FAT GOAT CHEESE

1   TEASPOON MINCED FRESH
    OREGANO LEAVES

¼   TEASPOON COARSELY GROUND
    BLACK PEPPER

2   RIPE MEDIUM TOMATOES,
    SEEDED AND DICED

2   TEASPOONS MINCED FRESH
    PARSLEY LEAVES

1   TEASPOON OLIVE OIL

⅛   TEASPOON SALT

In small bowl, with fork, mix goat cheese, oregano, and pepper until blended. In medium bowl, mix tomatoes, parsley, oil, and salt.

EACH BRUSCHETTA WITH GOAT CHEESE TOPPING: ABOUT 70 CALORIES (13 PERCENT CALORIES FROM FAT) | 3G PROTEIN | 7G CARBOHYDRATE | 1G TOTAL FAT (0G SATURATED) | 2MG CHOLESTEROL | 100MG SODIUM

10 GUILT-FREE BEFORE-DINNER SNACKS

- Celery stuffed with nonfat bean dip
- Dried fruit (apple rings, strawberries, cherries, cranberries, apricots, or raisins)
- Fat-free cinnamon-raisin bagel chips
- Fresh tangerine or Clementine sections
- Low-fat caramel or Cheddar rice cakes or popcorn cakes
- 1% or skim milk with chocolate syrup
- Pretzel sticks or whole-grain pretzels
- Red- or green-pepper strips, cucumber spears, or peeled baby carrots with salsa
- Reduced-fat mozzarella string cheese
- Toasted pita wedges with shredded reduced-fat cheese melted on top

BLACK BEAN DIP

Simple to whip up, even when you're pressed for time. Serve with toasted pita points or crudités.

ACTIVE TIME: 5 MIN · **TOTAL TIME:** 10 MIN
MAKES: ABOUT 2 CUPS

4	GARLIC CLOVES, PEELED	1	TABLESPOON WATER
1	CAN (15 TO 19 OUNCES) BLACK BEANS, RINSED AND DRAINED	½	TEASPOON GROUND CUMIN
		½	TEASPOON GROUND CORIANDER
2	TABLESPOONS TOMATO PASTE	¼	TEASPOON SALT
2	TABLESPOONS OLIVE OIL	⅛	TEASPOON GROUND RED PEPPER (CAYENNE)
4½	TEASPOONS FRESH LIME JUICE		

1 In 1-quart saucepan, place garlic and enough **water** to cover; heat to boiling over high heat. Reduce heat to low; cover and simmer 3 minutes to blanch garlic; drain.

2 In food processor with knife blade attached, puree garlic, beans, tomato paste, oil, lime juice, water, cumin, coriander, salt, and ground red pepper until smooth. Spoon dip into serving bowl; cover and refrigerate up to 2 days.

EACH TABLESPOON: ABOUT 20 CALORIES (45 PERCENT CALORIES FROM FAT) | 1G PROTEIN | 3G CARBOHYDRATE | 1G TOTAL FAT (0G SATURATED) | 0MG CHOLESTEROL | 55MG SODIUM

TIP Beans are packed with protein and insoluble and soluble fiber. (Insoluble fiber helps promote regularity and may stave off such digestive disorders as diverticulosis. Soluble fiber can reduce blood cholesterol and help control blood-sugar levels in people with diabetes.) Beans are also high in saponin, a cancer-fighting plant compound.

SWEET PEA GUACAMOLE

The perfect impostor: all the flavor and none of the fat found in traditional guacamole. Serve with baked tortilla chips for the full effect. (See photo on page 330.)

TOTAL TIME: 10 MIN

MAKES: ABOUT 3 CUPS

2 PACKAGES (10 OUNCES EACH) FROZEN PEAS, THAWED

3 TABLESPOONS FAT-FREE CHICKEN OR VEGETABLE BROTH

2 TABLESPOONS LIGHT MAYONNAISE

2 TABLESPOONS FRESH LIME JUICE

2 TABLESPOONS CHOPPED FRESH CILANTRO LEAVES

2 TEASPOONS CHOPPED, SEEDED JALAPEÑO CHILE

¼ TEASPOON GROUND CUMIN

¼ TEASPOON CHILI POWDER

SALT TO TASTE

CHOPPED TOMATOES AND GREEN ONIONS FOR GARNISH

1 In food processor with knife blade attached, puree peas, broth, mayonnaise, lime juice, cilantro, jalapeño, cumin, chili powder, and salt until just smooth.

2 Spoon guacamole into serving bowl; garnish with tomatoes and green onions.

EACH TABLESPOON: ABOUT 10 CALORIES (0 CALORIES FROM FAT) | 1G PROTEIN | 2G CARBOHYDRATE | 0G TOTAL FAT, 0MG CHOLESTEROL | 30MG SODIUM

SKEWERED CHICKEN WITH PAPAYA SALSA

These make the perfect light treat at a cocktail party. The refreshing papaya salsa can be prepared several days in advance and refrigerated until ready to use.

ACTIVE TIME: 30 MIN · TOTAL TIME: 36 MIN PLUS MARINATING

MAKES: 10 APPETIZER SERVINGS

2 TABLESPOONS SEASONED RICE VINEGAR OR BALSAMIC VINEGAR

2 TABLESPOONS ASIAN SESAME OIL

1 TABLESPOON FRESH LEMON JUICE

1 TABLESPOON REDUCED-SODIUM SOY SAUCE

1 TABLESPOON HOISIN SAUCE

1 TEASPOON MINCED GARLIC

1 TEASPOON MINCED, PEELED FRESH GINGER

1 POUND SKINLESS, BONELESS CHICKEN BREAST HALVES, CUT INTO 1-INCH CUBES

6 (12-INCH) BAMBOO SKEWERS

PAPAYA SALSA

2 TEASPOONS OLIVE OIL

2 SHALLOTS, FINELY CHOPPED

2 TEASPOONS MINCED, PEELED FRESH GINGER

½ TEASPOON CURRY POWDER

1 LARGE RIPE PAPAYA, PEELED, SEEDED, AND FINELY CHOPPED

2 TABLESPOONS FRESH LIME JUICE

1 TABLESPOON FINELY CHOPPED FRESH CILANTRO LEAVES

SALT TO TASTE

LIME WEDGES FOR GARNISH

1 In large ziptight plastic bag, combine vinegar, sesame oil, lemon juice, soy sauce, hoisin sauce, garlic, and ginger; add chicken, turning to coat. Seal bag, pressing out as much air as possible. Place bag on plate and refrigerate 1 hour to marinate, turning occasionally. Soak skewers in water 20 minutes.

2 Meanwhile, prepare salsa: In nonstick 1-quart saucepan, heat olive oil over medium heat. Add shallots and ginger, and cook, stirring often, until softened, 6 to 7 minutes. Stir in curry powder; cook 1 minute. Transfer mixture to food processor with knife blade attached. Add papaya, lime juice, cilantro, and salt; pulse until just blended. Do not overprocess. Spoon salsa into bowl; serve at room temperature. If not serving right away, cover and refrigerate salsa up to 2 days. Bring to room temperature before serving. Makes about 2 cups.

3 Prepare grill. Thread chicken onto skewers without crowding. Place skewers on grill over medium heat and grill, turning occasionally, until chicken cubes lose their pink color throughout, 3 to 4 minutes a side. Arrange chicken skewers on platter; serve with salsa and lime wedges.

EACH SERVING, CHICKEN ONLY: ABOUT 70 CALORIES (26 CALORIES FROM FAT) | 11G PROTEIN | 1G CARBOHYDRATE | 2G TOTAL FAT (1G SATURATED) | 29MG CHOLESTEROL | 65MG SODIUM

EACH ¼ CUP SALSA: ABOUT 35 CALORIES (26 PERCENT CALORIES FROM FAT) | 1G PROTEIN | 6G CARBOHYDRATE | 1G TOTAL FAT (0G SATURATED) | 0MG CHOLESTEROL | 75MG SODIUM

TIP To get more juice from a lime, zap it whole in the microwave for 20 to 30 seconds. The juice flows more readily when the fruit is warm. Squeeze as you like, either with an electric citrus juicer for big jobs or an old-fashioned reamer for a few tablespoons.

MIXED PEA POD STIR-FRY

This sweet and tender-crisp medley celebrates the glorious flavor of fresh green vegetables.

ACTIVE TIME: 15 MIN · **TOTAL TIME:** 30 MIN
MAKES: 4 ACCOMPANIMENT SERVINGS

1   TEASPOON SALT

8   OUNCES GREEN BEANS, TRIMMED

2   TEASPOONS VEGETABLE OIL

4   OUNCES SNOW PEAS, TRIMMED AND STRINGS REMOVED

4   OUNCES SUGAR SNAP PEAS, TRIMMED AND STRINGS REMOVED

1   GARLIC CLOVE, FINELY CHOPPED

1   TABLESPOON SOY SAUCE

1 In 12-inch skillet, combine 4 cups water and salt; heat to boiling over high heat. Add green beans and cook 3 minutes. Drain; wipe skillet dry with paper towels.

2 In same skillet, heat oil over high heat. Add green beans and cook, stirring frequently (stir-frying), until they begin to brown, 2 to 3 minutes. Add snow peas, sugar snap peas, and garlic; stir-fry until snow peas and sugar snap peas are tender-crisp, about 1 minute longer. Stir in soy sauce and remove from heat.

EACH SERVING: ABOUT 63 CALORIES (29 PERCENT CALORIES FROM FAT) | 3G PROTEIN | 8G CARBOHYDRATE | 2G TOTAL FAT (0G SATURATED) | 0MG CHOLESTEROL | 844MG SODIUM

MUSSELS WITH TOMATOES AND WHITE WINE

This saucy dish should be served with plenty of good crusty bread for dipping.

ACTIVE TIME: 20 MIN · **TOTAL TIME:** 45 MIN

MAKES: 8 APPETIZER OR 4 MAIN-DISH SERVINGS

---

1   TABLESPOON OLIVE OR VEGETABLE OIL

1   SMALL ONION, CHOPPED

2   GARLIC CLOVES, FINELY CHOPPED

¼   TEASPOON CRUSHED RED PEPPER

1   CAN (14 TO 16 OUNCES) TOMATOES

¾   CUP DRY WHITE WINE

4   POUNDS LARGE MUSSELS, SCRUBBED AND DEBEARDED

2   TABLESPOONS CHOPPED FRESH PARSLEY

1 In nonreactive 5-quart Dutch oven, heat oil over medium heat. Add onion and cook until tender and golden, 6 to 8 minutes. Add garlic and crushed red pepper and cook 30 seconds longer. Stir in tomatoes with their juice and wine, breaking up tomatoes with side of spoon. Heat to boiling; boil 3 minutes.

2 Add mussels; heat to boiling. Reduce heat; cover and simmer until mussels open, about 5 minutes, transferring mussels to large bowl as they open. Discard any mussels that do not open. Pour broth over mussels and sprinkle with parsley.

EACH APPETIZER SERVING: ABOUT 104 CALORIES (26 PERCENT CALORIES FROM FAT) | 9G PROTEIN | 6G CARBOHYDRATE | 3G TOTAL FAT (1G SATURATED) | 18MG CHOLESTEROL | 277MG SODIUM

SUCCOTASH

Corn and lima beans, two staples of Native American cooking, are combined to make this simple dish. The name succotash comes from the Narraganset word for "ear of corn."

ACTIVE TIME: 10 MIN · **TOTAL TIME:** 35 MIN
MAKES: 10 ACCOMPANIMENT SERVINGS

---

5   SLICES BACON

3   STALKS CELERY,
    CUT INTO ¼-INCH-THICK SLICES

1   MEDIUM ONION, CHOPPED

2   CANS (15¼ TO 16 OUNCES EACH)
    WHOLE-KERNEL CORN, DRAINED

2   PACKAGES (10 OUNCES EACH)
    FROZEN BABY LIMA BEANS

½   CUP CHICKEN BROTH

¾   TEASPOON SALT

¼   TEASPOON COARSELY GROUND
    BLACK PEPPER

2   TABLESPOONS CHOPPED
    FRESH PARSLEY

1 In 12-inch skillet, cook bacon over medium-low heat until browned. With slotted spoon, transfer to paper towels to drain; crumble.

2 Discard all but 2 tablespoons bacon drippings from skillet. Add celery and onion and cook over medium heat, stirring, until vegetables are tender and golden, about 15 minutes. Stir in corn, frozen lima beans, broth, salt, and pepper; heat to boiling over high heat. Reduce heat; cover and simmer until heated through, 5 to 10 minutes longer. Stir in parsley and sprinkle with bacon.

EACH SERVING: ABOUT 171 CALORIES (26 PERCENT CALORIES FROM FAT) | 7G PROTEIN | 27G CARBOHYDRATE | 5G TOTAL FAT (1G SATURATED) | 5MG CHOLESTEROL | 458MG SODIUM

OVEN FRIES

A quick way to make crispy "fries" without frying.

ACTIVE TIME: 10 MIN · TOTAL TIME: 55 MIN
MAKES: 4 ACCOMPANIMENT SERVINGS

3   MEDIUM BAKING POTATOES OR
    SWEET POTATOES (8 OUNCES EACH),
    NOT PEELED

1   TABLESPOON VEGETABLE OIL

½   TEASPOON SALT

⅛   TEASPOON GROUND BLACK PEPPER

1 Preheat oven to 425°F. Cut each potato lengthwise into quarters, then cut each quarter lengthwise into 3 wedges.

2 In jelly-roll pan, toss potatoes, oil, salt, and pepper to coat. Bake, turning occasionally, until tender, about 45 minutes.

EACH SERVING: ABOUT 156 CALORIES (23 PERCENT CALORIES FROM FAT) | 4G PROTEIN | 28G CARBOHYDRATE | 4G TOTAL FAT (0G SATURATED) | 0MG CHOLESTEROL | 301MG SODIUM

TIP Select potatoes that are firm and smooth. Avoid any with wrinkled skins, bruises, discolorations, or sprouts. Store the potatoes in a cool, dark place—but not in the refrigerator, where the starch converts to sugar and the nutrient value is reduced. Also important: Do not store potatoes with onions. Each vegetable releases a gas that hastens the spoilage of the other. Gently scrub potatoes with a vegetable brush just before using; washing them in advance shortens their storage life. For even cooking, pick ones of uniform size. To prevent peeled potatoes from turning dark, toss with lemon juice.

HERBED PACKET POTATOES

Potato chunks tossed with parsley and butter cook into tender morsels when wrapped in foil and baked.

ACTIVE TIME: 15 MIN · **BAKE:** 45 MIN

MAKES: 6 ACCOMPANIMENT SERVINGS

2   TABLESPOONS BUTTER OR MARGARINE

1   TABLESPOON CHOPPED FRESH PARSLEY

½   TEASPOON FRESHLY GRATED LEMON PEEL

½   TEASPOON SALT

⅛   TEASPOON COARSELY GROUND BLACK PEPPER

1½ POUNDS SMALL RED POTATOES, CUT IN HALF

1 Preheat oven to 450°F. In 3-quart saucepan, melt butter with parsley, lemon peel, salt, and pepper over medium-low heat. Remove saucepan from heat; add potatoes and toss well to coat.

2 Place potato mixture in center of 24" by 18" sheet of heavy-duty foil. Fold edges over and pinch to seal tightly.

3 Place package in jelly-roll pan and bake until potatoes are tender when pierced (through foil) with knife, about 30 minutes.

EACH SERVING: ABOUT 126 CALORIES (29 PERCENT CALORIES FROM FAT) | 2G PROTEIN | 20G CARBOHYDRATE | 4G TOTAL FAT (2G SATURATED) | 10MG CHOLESTEROL | 241MG SODIUM

SAUTÉ OF POTATOES, TOMATOES, AND FRESH CORN

Accented with fresh tarragon and a lemony dressing, this simple side dish is perfect with steak.

ACTIVE TIME: 30 MIN · **TOTAL TIME:** 1 HR 10 MIN

MAKES: ABOUT 12 CUPS OR 12 ACCOMPANIMENT SERVINGS

---

4 TABLESPOONS OLIVE OIL	2 TEASPOONS CHOPPED FRESH TARRAGON LEAVES
2 POUNDS SMALL RED POTATOES, CUT INTO 1-INCH CHUNKS	2 TABLESPOONS FRESH LEMON JUICE
2 PINTS CHERRY TOMATOES	¾ TEASPOON SALT
4 CUPS CORN KERNELS CUT FROM COBS (ABOUT 8 EARS)	¼ TEASPOON COARSELY GROUND BLACK PEPPER

1 In nonstick 12-inch skillet, heat 1 tablespoon olive oil over medium heat. Add potato chunks and cook, stirring occasionally, until potatoes are browned on the outside and tender on the inside, about 35 minutes. Transfer potatoes to large bowl.

2 In same skillet, heat 1 more tablespoon oil; add whole cherry tomatoes and cook, stirring, 2 minutes. Add corn and tarragon, and cook 2 minutes longer. Transfer tomato mixture to bowl with potatoes.

3 In cup, mix lemon juice, salt, pepper, and remaining 2 tablespoons olive oil; pour over potato mixture and toss to combine.

EACH SERVING: ABOUT 165 CALORIES (27 PERCENT CALORIES FROM FAT) | 4G PROTEIN | 28G CARBOHYDRATE | 5G TOTAL FAT (1G SATURATED) | 0MG CHOLESTEROL | 150MG SODIUM

TIP Sweet corn is one of the tastiest sources of folic acid. It's often mistakenly dismissed as a dieter's foe, but one ear of fresh yellow or white corn has only 80 calories (if it's not slathered in butter, of course). Because its natural sugars start converting to starch as soon as it's picked, corn should be bought fresh and cooked the same day to preserve its sweetness.

CANDIED SWEET POTATOES

If there are marshmallow lovers in the family, top the already baked casserole with mini marshmallows and place in the oven for an extra 10 minutes. Do-ahead: This dish can be made through Step 1, covered, and refrigerated overnight. When ready to serve, continue with Steps 2 and 3.

ACTIVE TIME: 30 MIN · TOTAL TIME: 1 HR 10 MIN
MAKES: 12 ACCOMPANIMENT SERVINGS

4   POUNDS SWEET POTATOES (8 MEDIUM), PEELED AND SLICED INTO 1-INCH-THICK ROUNDS

½   CUP PACKED DARK BROWN SUGAR

¼   CUP WATER

4   TABLESPOONS BUTTER OR MARGARINE

¾   TEASPOON SALT

¼   TEASPOON COARSELY GROUND BLACK PEPPER

PINCH NUTMEG

1   In 6-quart saucepot, heat potatoes and enough water to cover to boiling over high heat. Reduce heat to low; cover and simmer until potatoes are barely fork-tender (slightly underdone), about 5 minutes. Drain well and place potatoes in shallow 2-quart casserole.

2   Preheat oven to 400°F. In 10-inch skillet, heat brown sugar, water, margarine, salt, pepper, and nutmeg over medium heat, stirring frequently, until margarine melts, about 3 minutes. Drizzle mixture evenly over potatoes.

3   Bake casserole, uncovered, basting potatoes occasionally with sugar mixture and turning slices over halfway through cooking, until potatoes are tender and lightly browned and sugar mixture thickens slightly, about 40 minutes.

EACH SERVING: ABOUT 205 CALORIES (18 PERCENT CALORIES FROM FAT) | 2G PROTEIN | 41G CARBOHYDRATE | 4G TOTAL FAT (3G SATURATED) | 10MG CHOLESTEROL | 193MG SODIUM

PEACHES AND GREENS

A cool, refreshing alternative to a classic green salad.

TOTAL TIME: 25 MIN

MAKES: 12 ACCOMPANIMENT SERVINGS

---

1   LARGE LIME

2   TABLESPOONS HONEY

1   TABLESPOON OLIVE OIL

1   TABLESPOON CHOPPED
    FRESH MINT LEAVES

½   TEASPOON DIJON MUSTARD

¼   TEASPOON SALT

¼   TEASPOON COARSELY GROUND
    BLACK PEPPER

2   BUNCHES WATERCRESS
    (4 OUNCES EACH), TOUGH STEMS
    DISCARDED

2   POUNDS RIPE PEACHES (6 MEDIUM),
    PEELED AND CUT INTO WEDGES

1   LARGE JICAMA (1¼ POUNDS), PEELED
    AND CUT INTO 1½" BY ¼" STICKS

1   From lime, grate ¼ teaspoon peel and squeeze 2 tablespoons juice.
Prepare dressing: In large bowl, with wire whisk, mix lime peel, lime juice,
honey, oil, mint, mustard, salt, and pepper.

2   Just before serving, add watercress, peaches, and jicama to dressing in
bowl; toss to coat.

EACH SERVING: ABOUT 55 CALORIES (16 PERCENT CALORIES FROM FAT) | 1G PROTEIN |
11G CARBOHYDRATE | 1G TOTAL FAT (0G SATURATED) | 0MG CHOLESTEROL | 55MG SODIUM

TOMATO AND MELON SALAD

TOTAL TIME: 15 MIN

MAKES: 8 ACCOMPANIMENT SERVINGS

1   PINT CHERRY TOMATOES

1   LARGE HONEYDEW MELON (4½ POUNDS)

1   LARGE CANTALOUPE (3 POUNDS)

¼   CUP RED CURRANT OR APPLE JELLY

½   TEASPOON SALT

1   TEASPOON COARSELY GROUND BLACK PEPPER

1   BUNCH SPINACH, TOUGH STEMS TRIMMED AND WASHED AND DRIED WELL

1   Cut small "x" in stem end of each cherry tomato. Add tomatoes to large saucepot of boiling water; cook 5 seconds. Drain; rinse tomatoes with cold running water to stop cooking. With fingers, slip tomatoes from their skins; place in colander to drain off excess liquid.

2   Cut each melon in half; discard seeds. With melon baller, scoop melons into balls; reserve any remaining melon for another use. Place melon balls in colander with cherry tomatoes. Cover colander, place on a plate to catch drips, and refrigerate if not serving right away.

3   To serve, in a large bowl, with wire whisk, stir jelly, salt, and pepper until smooth. Finely chop enough spinach to equal ¼ cup. Add chopped spinach and melon-tomato mixture to bowl with jelly mixture; toss to coat. Arrange remaining spinach leaves on platter; spoon melon-tomato mixture over spinach leaves. Toss to serve.

EACH SERVING: ABOUT 110 CALORIES (8 PERCENT CALORIES FROM FAT) | 2G PROTEIN | 27G CARBOHYDRATE | 1G TOTAL FAT (0G SATURATED) | 0MG CHOLESTEROL | 190MG SODIUM

TIP Tomatoes are an excellent source of vitamin C, which enhances the body's ability to absorb iron. They also contain lycopene and other substances associated with lowering the risk of certain cancers.

BLACK-EYED PEA SALAD

Black-eyed peas, also called cowpeas, are actually beans. Unlike most dried beans, they don't need to be soaked. Their short cooking time makes them a natural for summer salads. Cayenne pepper sauce is a milder variety of hot pepper sauce that adds tang and flavor, not just heat. It can be found in the condiment section of the supermarket.

ACTIVE TIME: 15 MIN · **TOTAL TIME:** 45 MIN

MAKES: 12 ACCOMPANIMENT SERVINGS

- 1 PACKAGE (16 OUNCES) DRY BLACK-EYED PEAS
- ⅓ CUP CIDER VINEGAR
- 2 TABLESPOONS OLIVE OIL
- 1 TABLESPOON CAYENNE PEPPER SAUCE
- 2 TEASPOONS SUGAR
- 1½ TEASPOONS SALT
- 2 MEDIUM STALKS CELERY, FINELY CHOPPED
- 1 MEDIUM RED ONION, FINELY CHOPPED
- 1 PACKAGE (10 OUNCES) FROZEN PEAS, THAWED

1 Rinse black-eyed peas with cold running water and discard any stones or shriveled peas. In 8-quart Dutch oven, heat black-eyed peas and 3 quarts water to boiling over high heat. Reduce heat to low; cover and simmer until peas are just tender, 25 to 30 minutes.

2 Meanwhile, prepare dressing: In large bowl, with wire whisk, mix vinegar, oil, pepper sauce, sugar, and salt until blended.

3 Drain black-eyed peas and rinse well. Add warm black-eyed peas to dressing in bowl and toss gently. Stir in celery, onion, and peas. Serve salad at room temperature or cover and refrigerate until ready to serve.

EACH SERVING: ABOUT 135 CALORIES (20 PERCENT CALORIES FROM FAT) | 8G PROTEIN | 21G CARBOHYDRATE | 3G TOTAL FAT (1G SATURATED) | 0MG CHOLESTEROL | 360MG SODIUM

SUMMER CORN SALAD

A colorful salad created from farmstand-fresh summer vegetables.

ACTIVE TIME: 30 MIN · **TOTAL TIME:** 40 MIN
MAKES: 12 ACCOMPANIMENT SERVINGS

---

12 EARS CORN, HUSKS AND
    SILK REMOVED

12 OUNCES GREEN BEANS, TRIMMED AND
    CUT INTO ¼-INCH PIECES

½ CUP CIDER VINEGAR

¼ CUP OLIVE OIL

¼ CUP CHOPPED FRESH PARSLEY

1 TEASPOON SALT

½ TEASPOON COARSELY GROUND
    BLACK PEPPER

1 RED PEPPER, FINELY CHOPPED

1 SMALL SWEET ONION, SUCH AS
    VIDALIA OR WALLA WALLA,
    FINELY CHOPPED

1 In 8-quart saucepot, heat 2 inches water to boiling over high heat; add corn. Heat to boiling. Reduce heat; cover and simmer 5 minutes. Drain. When cool enough to handle, cut kernels from corncobs.

2 Meanwhile, in 2-quart saucepan, heat 1 inch water to boiling over high heat; add green beans and heat to boiling. Reduce heat; simmer until tender-crisp, 3 to 5 minutes. Drain green beans. Rinse with cold running water; drain.

3 Prepare dressing: In large bowl, with wire whisk, mix vinegar, oil, parsley, salt, and black pepper until blended.

4 Add corn, green beans, red pepper, and onion to dressing in bowl; toss to coat. Serve at room temperature or cover and refrigerate up to 2 hours.

EACH SERVING: ABOUT 179 CALORIES (30 PERCENT CALORIES FROM FAT) | 5G PROTEIN | 31G CARBOHYDRATE | 6G TOTAL FAT (1G SATURATED) | 0MG CHOLESTEROL | 219MG SODIUM

ROASTED POTATO SALAD

Potatoes and shallots, roasted until tender and caramelized, become a spectacular salad when tossed with a lemon-Dijon dressing.

ACTIVE TIME: 25 MIN · TOTAL TIME: 1 HR 10 MIN
MAKES: 6 ACCOMPANIMENT SERVINGS

2 POUNDS RED POTATOES (12 MEDIUM), NOT PEELED, CUT INTO 1½-INCH PIECES	2 TABLESPOONS OLIVE OR VEGETABLE OIL
16 SMALL SHALLOTS, PEELED, OR 2 MEDIUM RED ONIONS, EACH CUT INTO 8 WEDGES	8 OUNCES FRENCH GREEN BEANS (HARICOTS VERTS) OR REGULAR GREEN BEANS, TRIMMED
1 TEASPOON SALT	1 TABLESPOON FRESH LEMON JUICE
¼ TEASPOON GROUND BLACK PEPPER	1 TEASPOON DIJON MUSTARD

1 Preheat oven to 425°F. In large roasting pan (17" by 11½"), sprinkle potatoes and shallots with salt and pepper. Drizzle with 1 tablespoon oil and toss. Roast 30 minutes.

2 After vegetables have roasted 30 minutes, stir in green beans. Roast, stirring occasionally, until all vegetables are tender, about 15 minutes longer.

3 Meanwhile, prepare dressing: In large bowl, with wire whisk, mix lemon juice, remaining 1 tablespoon oil, and mustard until blended and smooth.

4 Add vegetables to dressing in bowl and toss to coat. Serve warm or at room temperature.

EACH SERVING: ABOUT 212 CALORIES (21 PERCENT CALORIES FROM FAT) | 5G PROTEIN | 39G CARBOHYDRATE | 5G TOTAL FAT (1G SATURATED) | 0MG CHOLESTEROL | 428MG SODIUM

TOMATO AND MINT TABBOULEH

Tabbouleh, the popular bulgur wheat and vegetable salad, is one of the best ways to enjoy tomatoes, cucumbers, and herbs.

TOTAL TIME: 20 MIN PLUS STANDING AND CHILLING

MAKES: 12 ACCOMPANIMENT SERVINGS

1½ CUPS BOILING WATER

1½ CUPS BULGUR (CRACKED WHEAT)

¼ CUP FRESH LEMON JUICE

1 POUND RIPE TOMATOES (3 MEDIUM), CUT INTO ½-INCH PIECES

1 MEDIUM CUCUMBER (8 OUNCES), PEELED AND CUT INTO ½-INCH PIECES

3 GREEN ONIONS, CHOPPED

¾ CUP LOOSELY PACKED FRESH FLAT-LEAF PARSLEY LEAVES, CHOPPED

½ CUP LOOSELY PACKED FRESH MINT LEAVES, CHOPPED

1 TABLESPOON OLIVE OIL

¾ TEASPOON SALT

¼ TEASPOON COARSELY GROUND BLACK PEPPER

1 In medium bowl, combine water, bulgur, and lemon juice, stirring to mix. Let stand until liquid has been absorbed, about 30 minutes.

2 To bulgur mixture, add tomatoes, cucumber, green onions, parsley, mint, oil, salt, and pepper, stirring to mix. Cover and refrigerate to blend flavors, at least 1 hour or up to 4 hours.

EACH SERVING: ABOUT 87 CALORIES (21 PERCENT CALORIES FROM FAT) | 3G PROTEIN | 17G CARBOHYDRATE | 2G TOTAL FAT (0G SATURATED) | 0MG CHOLESTEROL | 157MG SODIUM

TUBETTI MACARONI SALAD

Carrots and celery add crunch to this lemon-scented salad. If the salad appears dry after chilling, stir in a touch of milk.

ACTIVE TIME: 25 MIN · **TOTAL TIME:** 50 MIN
MAKES: 12 ACCOMPANIMENT SERVINGS

1 PACKAGE (16 OUNCES) TUBETTI OR DITALINI PASTA

2¾ TEASPOONS SALT

4 CARROTS, PEELED AND CUT INTO 2" BY ¼" MATCHSTICK STRIPS

1 TO 2 LEMONS

⅔ CUP LIGHT MAYONNAISE

⅓ CUP MILK

2 STALKS CELERY, CUT INTO 2" BY ¼" MATCHSTICK STRIPS

2 GREEN ONIONS, THINLY SLICED

1 In large saucepot, cook pasta as label directs, using 2 teaspoons salt. After pasta has cooked 10 minutes, add carrots to pasta water and cook until carrots are just tender-crisp and pasta is done, 1 to 2 minutes longer.

2 Meanwhile, from lemon(s), grate 1 teaspoon peel and squeeze 3 tablespoons juice. Prepare dressing: In large bowl, with wire whisk, mix lemon peel, lemon juice, mayonnaise, milk, and remaining ¾ teaspoon salt until blended.

3 Drain pasta and carrots; add to dressing in bowl, along with celery and green onions; toss until mixed and coated with dressing. Serve at room temperature or cover and refrigerate up to 4 hours.

EACH SERVING: ABOUT 202 CALORIES (22 PERCENT CALORIES FROM FAT) | 5G PROTEIN | 33G CARBOHYDRATE | 5G TOTAL FAT (1G SATURATED) | 5MG CHOLESTEROL | 463MG SODIUM

SOUPS & SANDWICHES

Whether you favor a stockpot or a slow cooker, soups are one-pot cooking at its finest. Here you'll find wholesome recipes that'll ensure you're filling that pot with fiber-rich grains and beans, vitamin-packed veggies, and lean meat. If you want a light start to a meal, try the consommé. For a heartier dish, a recipe with white beans or lentils is just the ticket. And you don't have to kiss cream-based soups good-bye, as we have lower-fat versions with asparagus, lima beans, kale, cauliflower, corn, squash, and peas. You'll find familiar favorites like minestrone or beef and barley, as well as more exotic options such as an Asian spin on chicken noodle.

Sandwiches are not off-limits in a light and healthy meal plan. You just have to choose your bread and your fillings with care, and we offer satisfying low-cal options you can sink your teeth into without guilt. You'll find tasty options for a quick, healthy lunch, like roast beef club sandwiches. On hectic weeknights or lazy weekends, our turkey roll-ups or chicken pita pizzas will keep everybody happy. And for the hearty taste of the outdoors prepared right in your kitchen, try the barbecue pork sandwiches.

Turkey and Mango Roll-Ups (page 370)

CREAM OF ASPARAGUS SOUP

Start with a package of frozen vegetables, a can of broth, and seasonings—in twenty-five minutes you'll have a luscious, creamy, lower-fat soup.

ACTIVE TIME: 5 MIN · **TOTAL TIME:** 25 MIN

MAKES: ABOUT 3¾ CUPS OR 4 FIRST-COURSE SERVINGS

1   TABLESPOON BUTTER OR MARGARINE

1   MEDIUM ONION, FINELY CHOPPED

1   CAN (14½ OUNCES) FAT-FREE CHICKEN BROTH OR 1¾ CUPS HOMEMADE

1   PACKAGE (10 OUNCES) FROZEN ASPARAGUS CUTS OR SPEARS

¼   TEASPOON DRIED THYME

¼   TEASPOON DRIED TARRAGON

⅛   TEASPOON SALT

⅛   TEASPOON GROUND BLACK PEPPER

1½ CUPS FAT-FREE (SKIM) MILK

2   TEASPOONS FRESH LEMON JUICE

SNIPPED FRESH CHIVES FOR GARNISH (OPTIONAL)

1 In 2-quart saucepan, melt margarine over medium heat. Add onion and cook, stirring occasionally, until tender, 5 minutes. Add broth, asparagus, thyme, tarragon, salt, and pepper; heat to boiling over high heat. Reduce heat to low and simmer 10 minutes.

2 Spoon one-fourth of mixture into blender; cover, with center part of cover removed to let steam escape, and puree until smooth. Pour puree into bowl. Repeat with remaining mixture.

3 Return soup to saucepan; stir in milk. Heat through over medium heat, stirring often (do not boil, or soup may curdle). Remove saucepan from heat; stir in lemon juice. Garnish with snipped chives, if you like.

EACH SERVING: ABOUT 115 CALORIES (23 PERCENT CALORIES FROM FAT) | 8G PROTEIN | 11G CARBOHYDRATE | 3G TOTAL FAT (2G SATURATED) | 10MG CHOLESTEROL | 471MG SODIUM

CREAM OF LIMA BEAN SOUP

Prepare as directed but substitute **1 package (10 ounces) frozen lima beans** for the asparagus. Delete the dried tarragon. If you like, garnish with **chopped fresh thyme**.

EACH SERVING: ABOUT 155 CALORIES (17 PERCENT CALORIES FROM FAT) | 9G PROTEIN | 20G CARBOHYDRATE | 3G TOTAL FAT (2G SATURATED) | 10MG CHOLESTEROL | 506MG SODIUM

CREAM OF KALE SOUP

Prepare as directed but substitute **1 package (10 ounces) frozen chopped kale** for the asparagus. Add **1 garlic clove**, minced, to the onions at the end of cooking time and cook 30 seconds longer. Omit the dried tarragon. Add the milk to the soup before pureeing. If you like, garnish with **chopped fresh tomato**.

EACH SERVING: ABOUT 115 CALORIES (23 PERCENT CALORIES FROM FAT) | 8G PROTEIN | 11G CARBOHYDRATE | 3G TOTAL FAT (2G SATURATED) | 10MG CHOLESTEROL | 471MG SODIUM

CREAM OF CAULIFLOWER SOUP

Prepare as directed but substitute **1 package (10 ounces) frozen cauliflower florets** for the asparagus and **½ teaspoon curry powder** for the dried tarragon. If you like, garnish with **chopped fresh apple**.

EACH SERVING: ABOUT 115 CALORIES (23 PERCENT CALORIES FROM FAT) | 8G PROTEIN | 11G CARBOHYDRATE | 3G TOTAL FAT (2G SATURATED) | 10MG CHOLESTEROL | 471MG SODIUM

CREAM OF CORN SOUP

Prepare as directed but substitute **1 package (10 ounces) frozen whole-kernel corn** for the asparagus. Add **¾ teaspoon chili powder** to the onions at the end of cooking time and cook 30 seconds longer. Omit the dried tarragon. If you like, garnish with **chopped fresh cilantro**.

EACH SERVING: ABOUT 155 CALORIES (17 PERCENT CALORIES FROM FAT) | 9G PROTEIN | 20G CARBOHYDRATE | 3G TOTAL FAT (2G SATURATED) | 10MG CHOLESTEROL | 506MG SODIUM

CREAM OF SQUASH SOUP

Prepare as directed but substitute **1 package (10 ounces) frozen winter squash** for the asparagus. Add **¼ teaspoon pumpkin-pie spice** to the onions at the end of cooking time and cook 30 seconds longer. Omit the dried tarragon. If you like, garnish with **chopped tomato**.

EACH SERVING: ABOUT 115 CALORIES (23 PERCENT CALORIES FROM FAT) | 8G PROTEIN | 11G CARBOHYDRATE | 3G TOTAL FAT (2G SATURATED) | 10MG CHOLESTEROL | 471MG SODIUM

CREAM OF PEA SOUP

Prepare as directed but substitute **1 package (10 ounces) frozen peas** for the asparagus. Substitute **¼ teaspoon dried mint** for the dried tarragon. If you like, garnish with **nonfat yogurt**.

EACH SERVING: ABOUT 155 CALORIES (17 PERCENT CALORIES FROM FAT) | 9G PROTEIN | 20G CARBOHYDRATE | 3G TOTAL FAT (2G SATURATED) | 10MG CHOLESTEROL | 506MG SODIUM

LEEK CONSOMMÉ WITH HERBS

A simple yet elegant clear soup for a light start to a hearty meal.

ACTIVE TIME: 30 MIN · **TOTAL TIME:** 55 MIN

MAKES: ABOUT 10 CUPS OR 10 FIRST-COURSE SERVINGS

6	MEDIUM LEEKS (2 POUNDS)	3	CUPS WATER
2	MEDIUM STALKS CELERY	⅛	TEASPOON COARSELY GROUND BLACK PEPPER
4	MEDIUM CARROTS, PEELED	¼	CUP LOOSELY PACKED FRESH PARSLEY LEAVES, CHOPPED
1	LEMON		
3	CANS (14½ OUNCES EACH) CHICKEN OR VEGETABLE BROTH OR 5¼ CUPS HOMEMADE	1	TABLESPOON COARSELY CHOPPED FRESH DILL
			LEMON SLICES FOR GARNISH

1 Cut root ends from leeks. Cut each leek crosswise to separate green tops from white bottoms, removing any tough outer leaves. Cut green tops crosswise into 1-inch pieces; place in large bowl of cold water. Swish leeks around to remove any grit or sand; repeat process, changing water several times. Drain well and place in 4-quart saucepan. Slice leek bottoms crosswise into thin slices; rinse thoroughly and reserve separately.

2 Cut celery and 2 carrots crosswise into 1-inch chunks; thinly slice remaining 2 carrots crosswise on the diagonal. From lemon, with vegetable peeler, remove four 3" by 1" strips of peel; squeeze 1 tablespoon juice.

3 To saucepan with leek tops, add celery and carrot chunks, 2 strips lemon peel, broth, and water; heat to boiling over high heat. Reduce heat to low; cover and simmer 15 minutes.

4 Strain broth into 8-cup glass measuring cup or large bowl, pressing down on vegetables in strainer to extract as much broth as possible; discard vegetables. Return broth to saucepan.

5 Prepare consommé: Add pepper, lemon juice, leek bottoms, carrot slices, and remaining lemon peel to broth in saucepan; heat to boiling over high heat. Reduce heat to low; cover and simmer 10 minutes or just until vegetables are tender. Remove saucepan from heat; discard lemon peel. Stir in parsley and dill. Garnish each serving with a lemon slice.

EACH SERVING: ABOUT 45 CALORIES (20 PERCENT CALORIES FROM FAT) | 3G PROTEIN | 6G CARBOHYDRATE | 1G TOTAL FAT (0G SATURATED) | 1MG CHOLESTEROL | 405MG SODIUM

GERMAN LENTIL SOUP

German cooks like to add a meaty ham hock and some chopped bacon to their lentil soups to lend a smoky note.

ACTIVE TIME: 25 MIN · **TOTAL TIME:** 2 HR

MAKES: ABOUT 11 CUPS OR 6 MAIN-DISH SERVINGS

4   SLICES BACON, CUT INTO ½-INCH PIECES

2   MEDIUM ONIONS, CHOPPED

2   CARROTS, PEELED AND CHOPPED

1   LARGE STALK CELERY, CHOPPED

1   PACKAGE (16 OUNCES) LENTILS, RINSED AND PICKED THROUGH

1   SMOKED HAM HOCK (1 POUND)

8   CUPS WATER

1   BAY LEAF

1   TEASPOON SALT

½   TEASPOON DRIED THYME

½   TEASPOON GROUND BLACK PEPPER

2   TABLESPOONS FRESH LEMON JUICE

1 In 5-quart Dutch oven, cook bacon over medium-low heat until lightly browned. Add onions, carrots, and celery; cook over medium heat until vegetables are tender, 15 to 20 minutes. Add lentils, ham hock, water, bay leaf, salt, thyme, and pepper; heat to boiling over high heat. Reduce heat; cover and simmer until lentils are tender, 50 to 60 minutes. Remove and discard bay leaf.

2 Transfer ham hock to cutting board. Cut meat into bite-size pieces, discarding skin and bone. Return meat to soup. Heat through. Stir in lemon juice.

EACH SERVING: ABOUT 390 CALORIES (23 PERCENT CALORIES FROM FAT) | 25G PROTEIN | 52G CARBOHYDRATE | 10G TOTAL FAT (3G SATURATED) | 13MG CHOLESTEROL | 1,027MG SODIUM

TIP Looking to lose a few pounds? Indulge in soup. Research shows that the best way to start a meal may be water- or broth-based soup. It fills you up—even more so than other foods low in calorie density. You'll feel full faster and end up eating less at that sitting. Or make a soup a meal in itself; with vegetable-based soups, you'll get plenty of fiber to keep you feeling full longer.

ITALIAN WHITE BEAN AND SPINACH SOUP

A touch of fresh lemon juice, stirred in just before serving, gives this robust soup a light citrus note.

ACTIVE TIME: 20 MIN · **TOTAL TIME:** 50 MIN

MAKES: ABOUT 7 ½ CUPS OR 6 FIRST-COURSE SERVINGS

---

1   TABLESPOON VEGETABLE OIL

1   MEDIUM ONION, CHOPPED

1   STALK CELERY, CHOPPED

1   GARLIC CLOVE, FINELY CHOPPED

2   CANS (15 TO 19 OUNCES EACH) WHITE KIDNEY BEANS (CANNELLINI), RINSED AND DRAINED

2   CUPS WATER

1   CAN (14½ OUNCES) CHICKEN BROTH OR 1¾ CUPS HOMEMADE

¼   TEASPOON COARSELY GROUND BLACK PEPPER

⅛   TEASPOON DRIED THYME

1   BUNCH (10 TO 12 OUNCES) SPINACH, TOUGH STEMS TRIMMED

1   TABLESPOON FRESH LEMON JUICE

FRESHLY GRATED PARMESAN CHEESE (OPTIONAL)

1 In 3-quart saucepan, heat oil over medium heat. Add onion and celery; cook, stirring, until celery is tender, 5 to 8 minutes. Stir in garlic and cook 30 seconds. Add beans, water, broth, pepper, and thyme; heat to boiling over high heat. Reduce heat and simmer 15 minutes.

2 Roll up several spinach leaves together, cigar fashion, and thinly slice. Repeat with remaining spinach.

3 With slotted spoon, remove 2 cups beans from soup and reserve. Spoon one-fourth of remaining soup into blender; cover, with center part of cover removed to let steam escape, and puree until smooth. Pour into bowl. Repeat with remaining soup.

4 Return puree and reserved beans to saucepan; heat to boiling over medium-high heat. Stir in spinach and cook just until wilted, about 1 minute. Remove from heat and stir in lemon juice. Serve with Parmesan, if you like.

EACH SERVING: ABOUT 170 CALORIES (21 PERCENT CALORIES FROM FAT) | 11G PROTEIN | 24G CARBOHYDRATE | 4G TOTAL FAT (1G SATURATED) | 0MG CHOLESTEROL | 539MG SODIUM

MINESTRONE WITH PESTO

In Genoa, hearty minestrone is traditionally topped with a dollop of pesto.

ACTIVE TIME: 20 MIN · TOTAL TIME: 1 HR 20 MIN PLUS SOAKING BEANS
MAKES: 6 MAIN-DISH SERVINGS

8   OUNCES DRY GREAT NORTHERN BEANS (1 ⅓ CUPS)

2   TABLESPOONS OLIVE OIL

3   MEDIUM CARROTS, PEELED AND SLICED

2   STALKS CELERY, SLICED

1   LARGE ONION, FINELY CHOPPED

2   OUNCES SLICED PANCETTA OR BACON, FINELY CHOPPED

1   POUND ALL-PURPOSE POTATOES (2 LARGE), PEELED AND CUT INTO ½-INCH CUBES

1   POUND ZUCCHINI (2 MEDIUM), QUARTERED LENGTH-WISE THEN CUT CROSSWISE INTO ¼-INCH PIECES

4   CUPS SLICED SAVOY CABBAGE (½ MEDIUM HEAD)

1   LARGE GARLIC CLOVE, CRUSHED WITH GARLIC PRESS

2   CANS (14½ OUNCES EACH) CHICKEN BROTH OR 3½ CUPS HOMEMADE

1   CAN (14½ OUNCES) DICED TOMATOES

1   CUP WATER

½   TEASPOON SALT

2   TABLESPOONS PESTO, HOMEMADE OR STORE-BOUGHT

1 Rinse beans under cold running water and discard any stones or shriveled beans. In large bowl, place beans and enough water to cover by 2 inches. Cover and let stand at room temperature overnight. (Or, in 4-quart saucepan, place beans and enough water to cover by 2 inches. Heat to boiling over high heat; cook 2 minutes. Remove from heat; cover and let stand 1 hour.) Drain and rinse beans.

2 In 4-quart saucepan, combine beans and enough water to cover by 2 inches; heat to boiling over high heat. Reduce heat to low; cover and simmer, stirring occasionally, until beans are tender, 40 minutes to 1 hour. Drain beans.

3 Meanwhile, in 5-quart Dutch oven, heat olive oil over medium-high heat. Add carrots, celery, onion, and pancetta; cook, stirring occasionally, until onion begins to brown, 10 minutes. Add potatoes, zucchini, cabbage, and garlic; cook, stirring constantly, until cabbage wilts. Add broth, tomatoes with their juice, and water; heat to boiling over high heat. Reduce heat to low; cover and simmer until vegetables are tender, about 30 minutes.

4 Spoon ½ cup beans and 1 cup soup into blender; cover, with center part of cover removed to let steam escape, and puree until smooth. Stir bean puree, remaining beans, and salt into soup; heat to boiling. Reduce heat to low; cover and simmer 10 minutes. Spoon soup into six soup bowls. Top each serving of soup with 1 teaspoon pesto.

EACH SERVING: ABOUT 360 CALORIES (28 PERCENT CALORIES FROM FAT) | 16G PROTEIN | 52G CARBOHYDRATE | 11G TOTAL FAT (3G SATURATED) | 6MG CHOLESTEROL | 1,100MG SODIUM

ASIAN CHICKEN-NOODLE SOUP

Ours tastes just as good as, if not better than, any noodle-shop version. Use chopsticks or a fork to pick up the long noodles.

ACTIVE TIME: 15 MIN · **TOTAL TIME:** 50 MIN

MAKES: ABOUT 7 CUPS OR 4 MAIN-DISH SERVINGS

---

4   OUNCES RICE NOODLES OR LINGUINE

3   CANS (14½ OUNCES EACH) CHICKEN BROTH OR 5¼ CUPS HOMEMADE

¾   POUND SKINLESS BONELESS CHICKEN BREAST HALVES

4   OUNCES SHIITAKE MUSHROOMS, STEMS REMOVED AND CAPS THINLY SLICED

2   TABLESPOONS SOY SAUCE

1   TABLESPOON GRATED, PEELED FRESH GINGER

¾   TEASPOON SALT

⅛   TEASPOON CRUSHED RED PEPPER

¼   TEASPOON ASIAN SESAME OIL

1   CUP LOOSELY PACKED FRESH CILANTRO LEAVES

2   GREEN ONIONS, THINLY SLICED

1 Prepare noodles as label directs; drain.

2 Meanwhile, in 4-quart saucepan, heat broth to boiling over high heat. Add the chicken and reduce heat to low. Simmer until chicken is cooked through, about 15 minutes. Remove chicken with a slotted spoon and set aside to cool.

3 Stir mushrooms, soy sauce, ginger, salt, and crushed red pepper into broth. Simmer, uncovered, 10 minutes.

4 Cut chicken into thin strips. Add chicken, sesame oil, and noodles to broth and heat through. Stir in cilantro and green onions.

EACH SERVING: ABOUT 285 CALORIES (16 PERCENT CALORIES FROM FAT) | 25G PROTEIN | 30G CARBOHYDRATE | 5G TOTAL FAT (1G SATURATED) | 58MG CHOLESTEROL | 1,050MG SODIUM

TIP Looking to lose a few pounds? Indulge in soup. Research shows that the best way to start a meal may be water- or broth-based soup. It fills you up—even more so than other foods low in calorie density. You'll feel full faster and end up eating less at that sitting. Or make a soup a meal in itself; with vegetable-based soups, you'll get plenty of fiber to keep you feeling full longer.

BEEF AND BARLEY SOUP

One batch of this beef soup serves a party of eight. But we like to cook it over the weekend and freeze it in family-size portions for quick school-night dinners.

ACTIVE TIME: 45 MIN · **TOTAL TIME:** 3 HR 15 MIN

MAKES: ABOUT 16 CUPS OR 8 MAIN-DISH SERVINGS

1 TABLESPOON PLUS 4 TEASPOONS VEGETABLE OIL

3 MEDIUM STALKS CELERY, FINELY CHOPPED

1 LARGE ONION, FINELY CHOPPED

1½ POUNDS LEAN BONELESS BEEF CHUCK, TRIMMED AND CUT INTO ½-INCH PIECES

½ TEASPOON SALT

6 CUPS WATER

2 CANS (14½ OUNCES EACH) BEEF BROTH OR 3½ CUPS HOMEMADE

1 CAN (14½ OUNCES) DICED TOMATOES

1 CUP PEARL BARLEY

5 MEDIUM CARROTS (12 OUNCES), PEELED AND CUT CROSSWISE INTO ¼-INCH-THICK SLICES

5 MEDIUM PARSNIPS (12 OUNCES), PEELED AND CUT CROSSWISE INTO ¼-INCH-THICK SLICES

2 MEDIUM TURNIPS (8 OUNCES), PEELED AND FINELY CHOPPED

3 STRIPS (3" BY 1" EACH) ORANGE PEEL

PINCH GROUND CLOVES

1 In 8-quart Dutch oven, heat 1 tablespoon vegetable oil over medium-high heat. Add celery and onion and cook, stirring occasionally, until tender and golden, about 10 minutes; transfer vegetables to bowl.

2 Pat beef dry with paper towels. In same Dutch oven, heat 2 teaspoons oil over high heat until very hot. Add half of beef and cook until browned on all sides. Transfer to plate. Repeat with remaining 2 teaspoons oil and beef.

3 Return beef to Dutch oven. Stir in salt, celery mixture, water, broth and tomatoes with their juice; heat to boiling over high heat. Reduce heat to low; cover and simmer 1 hour.

4 Add barley, carrots, parsnips, turnips, orange peel, and cloves; heat to boiling over high heat. Reduce heat to low; cover and simmer until beef, barley, and vegetables are tender, 50 to 60 minutes.

EACH SERVING: ABOUT 320 CALORIES (25 PERCENT CALORIES FROM FAT) | 25G PROTEIN | 36G CARBOHYDRATE | 9G TOTAL FAT (3G SATURATED) | 41MG CHOLESTEROL | 740MG SODIUM

ROAST BEEF–WALDORF CLUB SANDWICHES

Horseradish dressing and a crunchy celery-and-apple mixture make rare roast beef taste even better. Soaking in ice water crisps the onion and tames its bite.

TOTAL TIME: 20 MIN PLUS STANDING

MAKES: 4 MAIN-DISH SERVINGS

---

4 VERY THIN SLICES RED ONION	1 TABLESPOON BOTTLED WHITE HORSERADISH
½ GOLDEN DELICIOUS APPLE, PEELED AND FINELY CHOPPED (½ CUP)	12 SLICES PUMPERNICKEL BREAD, LIGHTLY TOASTED IF DESIRED
2 STALKS CELERY, FINELY CHOPPED	8 OUNCES THINLY SLICED RARE ROAST BEEF
4 TABLESPOONS LIGHT MAYONNAISE	
2 TABLESPOONS SOUR CREAM	1 BUNCH WATERCRESS (4 OUNCES), TOUGH STEMS TRIMMED
½ TEASPOON FRESH LEMON JUICE	

1 In small bowl, combine onion with enough ice water to cover; let stand 15 minutes. Drain.

2 In separate small bowl, combine apple, celery, 2 tablespoons mayonnaise, 1 tablespoon sour cream, and lemon juice until well blended. In cup, combine remaining 2 tablespoons mayonnaise, remaining 1 tablespoon sour cream, and horseradish until blended.

3 Spread horseradish mixture evenly on 4 bread slices. Layer roast beef, onion, and watercress on top. Spread celery mixture evenly on 4 bread slices and place, celery mixture side up, over roast beef. Top with remaining bread slices. To serve, cut sandwiches in half.

EACH SERVING: ABOUT 451 CALORIES (30 PERCENT CALORIES FROM FAT) | 25G PROTEIN | 54G CARBOHYDRATE | 15G TOTAL FAT (5G SATURATED) | 50MG CHOLESTEROL | 842MG SODIUM

TURKEY AND MANGO ROLL-UPS

A lime-spiked curried chutney adds zip to this rolled sandwich. If you can't find lavash (an Armenian flatbread), divide the filling ingredients among four 8- to 10-inch flour tortillas.

TOTAL TIME: 25 MIN PLUS CHILLING

MAKES: 4 MAIN-DISH SERVINGS

1   LARGE LIME

¼   CUP LIGHT MAYONNAISE

3   TABLESPOONS MANGO CHUTNEY, CHOPPED

½   TEASPOON CURRY POWDER

⅛   TEASPOON PAPRIKA

1   LAVASH FLATBREAD (7 OUNCES)

1   MEDIUM CUCUMBER (8 OUNCES), PEELED AND THINLY SLICED

8   OUNCES THINLY SLICED SMOKED TURKEY BREAST

1   MEDIUM MANGO, PEELED AND FINELY CHOPPED

6   LARGE GREEN-LEAF LETTUCE LEAVES

1 From lime, grate ¼ teaspoon peel and squeeze 1 tablespoon juice. In bowl, combine lime peel, lime juice, mayonnaise, chutney, curry powder, and paprika until blended.

2 Unfold lavash; spread evenly with mayonnaise mixture. Arrange the cucumber slices over mayonnaise, then top with turkey, mango, and lettuce. From a short side, roll lavash up, jelly-roll fashion.

3 Wrap lavash roll in foil and refrigerate at least 2 hours or up to 4 hours to blend flavors and let bread soften. To serve, trim ends, then cut lavash roll into 4 pieces.

EACH SERVING: ABOUT 375 CALORIES (17 PERCENT CALORIES FROM FAT) | 18G PROTEIN | 55G CARBOHYDRATE | 7G TOTAL FAT (2G SATURATED) | 29MG CHOLESTEROL | 939MG SODIUM

BBQ PORK SANDWICHES

ACTIVE TIME: 10 MIN · **TOTAL TIME:** 25 MIN

MAKES: 6 MAIN-DISH SERVINGS

---

3 TABLESPOONS LIGHT MOLASSES

3 TABLESPOONS KETCHUP

1 TABLESPOON WORCESTERSHIRE SAUCE

1 TEASPOON MINCED, PEELED FRESH GINGER

½ TEASPOON GRATED LEMON PEEL

1 GARLIC CLOVE, CRUSHED WITH GARLIC PRESS

2 WHOLE PORK TENDERLOINS (¾ POUND EACH)

12 SMALL, SOFT DINNER ROLLS

---

1 Preheat broiler. In medium bowl, combine molasses, ketchup, Worcestershire, ginger, lemon peel, and garlic; add pork, turning to coat.

2 Place pork tenderloins on rack in broiling pan. Spoon any remaining molasses mixture over pork. Place pan in broiler 5 to 7 inches from heat source; broil pork, turning once, until meat is browned on the outside and still slightly pink in the center (internal temperature of tenderloins should be 160°F on meat thermometer), 15 to 20 minutes.

3 To serve, thinly slice pork. Serve on rolls with any juices from broiling pan.

EACH SERVING: ABOUT 390 CALORIES (30 PERCENT CALORIES FROM FAT) | 32G PROTEIN | 35G CARBOHYDRATE | 13G TOTAL FAT (4G SATURATED) | 70MG CHOLESTEROL | 360MG SODIUM

TIP Cutting a Mango: With a sharp knife, cut a lengthwise slice from each side of the long flat seed, as close to the seed as possible. Peel the seed section and cut off as much flesh as possible; discard the seed. Cut the mango pieces lengthwise into thick wedges. Use a knife to remove the peel from each wedge, cutting close to the peel.

CHICKEN-TOPPED PITA PIZZAS

ACTIVE TIME: 20 MIN **BROIL:** 22 MIN
MAKES: 6 MAIN-DISH SERVINGS

2	TEASPOONS VEGETABLE OIL	3	(6-INCH) PITAS
1	MEDIUM RED PEPPER, THINLY SLICED	6	OUNCES SMOKED CHICKEN, TORN INTO FINE SHREDS
1	MEDIUM GREEN PEPPER, THINLY SLICED	1	CUP SHREDDED PART-SKIM MOZZARELLA CHEESE (4 OUNCES)
1	MEDIUM ONION, THINLY SLICED	2	TABLESPOONS SLICED FRESH BASIL LEAVES
¾	CUP BOTTLED MARINARA SAUCE		
¼	TEASPOON CRUSHED RED PEPPER		

1 In nonstick 12-inch skillet, heat oil over medium-high heat. Add red pepper, green pepper, and onion and cook until vegetables are tender-crisp. Stir in marinara sauce and crushed red pepper; heat through.

2 Preheat broiler. Split each pita horizontally into 2 halves. Place pita halves, split-side up, on cookie sheet. Place cookie sheet in broiler at closest position to heat source; broil pitas until lightly browned.

3 Spoon sauce on pita halves; top with chicken and mozzarella. Broil until cheese melts. Sprinkle with basil.

EACH SERVING: ABOUT 215 CALORIES (29 PERCENT CALORIES FROM FAT) | 14G PROTEIN | 25G CARBOHYDRATE | 7G TOTAL FAT (3G SATURATED) | 26MG CHOLESTEROL | 735MG SODIUM

MAIN DISHES

A light and healthy main course is not an oxymoron: You can prepare a delicious and filling dish with low-fat, nutritious ingredients. Our main-dish salads are robust and hearty, and perfect to double (or triple) if you're feeding a crowd. And we have not forgotten the noodles. Most of our pasta is paired with veggies or lighter sauces so you don't break the calorie bank, and you'll also find fun variations on favorites like lasagna and linguine with clams.

If you're trying to cut back on red meat to lower your intake of saturated fat and cholesterol, you're not alone. The good news: You don't have to eliminate beef, pork, or even veal and lamb from your diet altogether (unless your doctor prescribes it). Simply focus on lean cuts of meat and explore low-fat cooking methods, from grilling to roasting. Poultry is simple to prepare in a multitude of satisfying ways. Better still, it's a lean and healthy option, especially if you prepare white meat or remove the skin from dark meat before serving. If you're eating light and healthy, fish and shellfish should make regular appearances on your dinner plate. Seafood is low in fat and a rich source of protein, vitamins, and minerals.

Looking to incorporate more grains and greens into your family's diet? We have the perfect solution: Go vegetarian a couple nights a week. Here, we provide so many tasty options, your kids will be looking forward to Meatless Mondays in no time.

Ziti with Roasted Asparagus (page 388)

TEX-MEX COBB SALAD

Warm Southwestern accents give this classic a new attitude.

TOTAL TIME: 30 MIN

MAKES: 4 MAIN-DISH SERVINGS

¼ CUP FRESH LIME JUICE

2 TABLESPOONS CHOPPED
FRESH CILANTRO LEAVES

4 TEASPOONS OLIVE OIL

1 TEASPOON SUGAR

¼ TEASPOON GROUND CUMIN

¼ TEASPOON SALT

¼ TEASPOON COARSELY GROUND
BLACK PEPPER

1 MEDIUM HEAD ROMAINE LETTUCE
(1 ¼ POUNDS), TRIMMED AND LEAVES
CUT INTO ½-INCH-WIDE STRIPS

1 PINT CHERRY TOMATOES,
EACH CUT INTO QUARTERS

12 OUNCES COOKED SKINLESS ROAST
TURKEY MEAT, CUT INTO ½-INCH
PIECES (2 CUPS)

1 CAN (15 TO 19 OUNCES)
BLACK BEANS, RINSED AND DRAINED

2 SMALL CUCUMBERS (6 OUNCES EACH),
PEELED, SEEDED, AND CUT INTO
½-INCH-THICK SLICES

1 Prepare dressing: In small bowl, with wire whisk, combine lime juice, cilantro, oil, sugar, cumin, salt, and pepper.

2 Place lettuce in large serving bowl. Arrange tomatoes, turkey, black beans, and cucumbers in rows over lettuce. Just before serving, toss salad with dressing.

EACH SERVING: ABOUT 310 CALORIES (20 PERCENT CALORIES FROM FAT) | 39G PROTEIN | 32G CARBOHYDRATE | 7G TOTAL FAT (1G SATURATED) | 71MG CHOLESTEROL | 505MG SODIUM

CURRIED CHICKEN-MANGO SALAD

Precooked chicken from the deli or supermarket makes our salad a cinch. The recipe can easily be doubled if you need to feed a crowd.

TOTAL TIME: 20 MIN

MAKES: 4 MAIN-DISH SERVINGS

1   STORE-BOUGHT ROTISSERIE CHICKEN (2 POUNDS)

¼   CUP PLAIN LOW-FAT YOGURT

¼   CUP LIGHT MAYONNAISE

2   TABLESPOONS MANGO CHUTNEY, CHOPPED

1   TABLESPOON FRESH LIME JUICE

1   TEASPOON CURRY POWDER

1   LARGE RIPE MANGO, PEELED AND FINELY CHOPPED

1   MEDIUM STALK CELERY, FINELY CHOPPED

1   MEDIUM GRANNY SMITH APPLE, CORED AND FINELY CHOPPED

½   CUP LOOSELY PACKED FRESH CILANTRO LEAVES, CHOPPED

1   HEAD LEAF LETTUCE, SEPARATED AND RINSED

1   Remove skin from chicken; discard. With fingers, pull chicken meat into 1-inch pieces.

2   In large bowl, with wire whisk, mix yogurt, mayonnaise, chutney, lime juice, and curry powder until combined. Stir in chicken, mango, celery, apple, and cilantro until well coated. Serve salad on bed of lettuce leaves.

EACH SERVING: ABOUT 310 CALORIES (26 PERCENT CALORIES FROM FAT) | 32G PROTEIN | 25G CARBOHYDRATE | 9G TOTAL FAT (2G SATURATED) | 95MG CHOLESTEROL | 255MG SODIUM

COUSCOUS AND SMOKED-TURKEY SALAD

If you see plums, peaches, or apricots at the farmers' market, try using them instead of the nectarines.

ACTIVE TIME: 10 MIN · **TOTAL TIME:** 15 MIN

MAKES: 6 MAIN-DISH SERVINGS

---

1   TEASPOON GROUND CUMIN

1   PACKAGE (10 OUNCES) COUSCOUS
    (MOROCCAN PASTA)

⅓   CUP DRIED TART CHERRIES

3   TABLESPOONS FRESH LEMON JUICE

2   TABLESPOONS OLIVE OIL

1   TABLESPOON DIJON MUSTARD

¾   TEASPOON SALT

¼   TEASPOON COARSELY GROUND
    BLACK PEPPER

3   RIPE MEDIUM NECTARINES,
    FINELY CHOPPED

4   OUNCES SMOKED TURKEY BREAST
    (IN 1 PIECE), CUT INTO ¼-INCH PIECES

BOSTON LETTUCE LEAVES

---

1   In 3-quart saucepan, heat cumin over medium-high heat until fragrant, 1 to 3 minutes. In saucepan with cumin, prepare couscous as label directs, adding cherries but no salt or butter.

2   Meanwhile, prepare dressing: In large bowl, with wire whisk or fork, mix lemon juice, oil, mustard, salt, and pepper until blended.

3   Stir warm couscous mixture, nectarines, and turkey into dressing in bowl. Spoon salad onto large platter lined with Boston lettuce leaves.

EACH SERVING: ABOUT 300 CALORIES (18 PERCENT CALORIES FROM FAT) | 11G PROTEIN | 51G CARBOHYDRATE | 6G TOTAL FAT (1G SATURATED) | 3MG CHOLESTEROL | 470MG SODIUM

TIP Originally from North Africa, couscous is a grainlike pasta is made from semolina wheat flour. The packaged, precooked version is ready to eat in just five minutes and is widely available in supermarkets. Look for whole-wheat couscous which is very similar in taste and texture to regular couscous, but packs a whopping 8 grams of fiber.

SESAME NOODLE AND CHICKEN SALAD

A great dish to make when you have leftover chicken.

ACTIVE TIME: 25 MIN · **TOTAL TIME:** 40 MIN
MAKES: 6 MAIN-DISH SERVINGS

---

12 OUNCES LINGUINE OR SPAGHETTI

6 OUNCES SNOW PEAS, STRINGS REMOVED AND CUT CROSSWISE INTO THIRDS

¾ CUP VERY HOT WATER

¼ CUP CREAMY PEANUT BUTTER

3 TABLESPOONS SEASONED RICE VINEGAR

3 TABLESPOONS SOY SAUCE

1 TABLESPOON LIGHT BROWN SUGAR

1 TABLESPOON MINCED, PEELED FRESH GINGER

1 TABLESPOON ASIAN SESAME OIL

¼ TEASPOON GROUND RED PEPPER (CAYENNE)

1 SMALL GARLIC CLOVE, CRUSHED WITH GARLIC PRESS

2 MEDIUM CARROTS, PEELED AND SHREDDED

3 CUPS THINLY SLICED RED CABBAGE (½ SMALL HEAD)

12 OUNCES BONELESS, ROASTED CHICKEN, PULLED INTO THIN STRIPS

1 In large saucepot, cook pasta as label directs. During last minute of pasta cooking, add snow peas. Continue cooking until pasta is done. Drain linguine and snow peas. Rinse under cold running water to cool; drain again and set aside.

2 Meanwhile, prepare dressing: In large bowl, with wire whisk, mix hot water, peanut butter, rice vinegar, soy sauce, brown sugar, ginger, sesame oil, ground red pepper, and garlic until blended.

3 Add pasta, snow peas, carrots, red cabbage, and chicken to dressing in bowl; toss to blend.

EACH SERVING: ABOUT 460 CALORIES (25 PERCENT CALORIES FROM FAT) | 28G PROTEIN | 58G CARBOHYDRATE | 13G TOTAL FAT (3G SATURATED) | 51MG CHOLESTEROL | 880MG SODIUM

WARM PORK TENDERLOIN SALAD WITH DIJON DRESSING

ACTIVE TIME: 20 MIN · **TOTAL TIME:** 25 MIN

MAKES: 4 MAIN-DISH SERVINGS

1 PORK TENDERLOIN (12 OUNCES), WELL TRIMMED

2 TABLESPOONS DRY SHERRY

1 TABLESPOON PLUS 1½ TEASPOONS SOY SAUCE

2 TEASPOONS GRATED, PEELED FRESH GINGER

2 TABLESPOONS LIGHT MAYONNAISE

2 TABLESPOONS BALSAMIC VINEGAR

1 TABLESPOON WATER

1 TABLESPOON DIJON MUSTARD WITH SEEDS

1 TEASPOON SUGAR

¼ TEASPOON COARSELY GROUND BLACK PEPPER

2 LARGE HEADS BELGIAN ENDIVE, CUT CROSSWISE INTO 1-INCH-THICK SLICES

1 SMALL HEAD RADICCHIO, THINLY SLICED

2 BUNCHES ARUGULA (8 OUNCES), STEMS TRIMMED

1 PACKAGE (10 OUNCES) FROZEN PEAS, THAWED

1 Holding knife almost parallel to the cutting surface, slice pork crosswise into very thin slices. In bowl, mix pork, sherry, soy sauce, and ginger; set aside.

2 In large bowl, with wire whisk, stir mayonnaise, vinegar, water, mustard, sugar, and pepper until blended. Add endive, radicchio, and arugula; toss well.

3 Spray nonstick 12-inch skillet lightly with nonstick cooking spray. Heat skillet over medium-high heat. Add pork mixture to skillet and cook, stirring quickly and constantly, until pork just loses its pink color, about 2 minutes.

4 Add pork and peas to salad; toss well.

EACH SERVING: ABOUT 230 CALORIES (27 PERCENT CALORIES FROM FAT) | 24G PROTEIN | 17G CARBOHYDRATE | 7G TOTAL FAT (2G SATURATED) | 45MG CHOLESTEROL | 270MG SODIUM

BOW TIES
WITH A TRIO OF PEAS

Snow peas, sugar snap peas, and green peas are combined in a lemon broth to make this a simple yet elegant pasta dish.

ACTIVE TIME: 15 MIN · **TOTAL TIME:** 40 MIN

MAKES: 4 MAIN-DISH SERVINGS

---

1 PACKAGE (16 OUNCES) BOW-TIE OR ROTINI PASTA

1 TABLESPOON BUTTER OR MARGARINE

1 TABLESPOON OLIVE OIL

4 OUNCES SNOW PEAS, STRINGS REMOVED

4 OUNCES SUGAR SNAP PEAS, STRINGS REMOVED

1 GARLIC CLOVE, CRUSHED WITH GARLIC PRESS

1 CUP FROZEN BABY PEAS

½ CUP LOW-SODIUM CHICKEN OR VEGETABLE BROTH

¾ TEASPOON SALT

¼ TEASPOON COARSELY GROUND BLACK PEPPER

½ TEASPOON FRESHLY GRATED LEMON PEEL

1 In large saucepot, cook pasta as label directs. Drain and keep warm.

2 Meanwhile, in 10-inch skillet, melt butter with oil over medium-high heat. Add snow peas and sugar snap peas and cook, stirring, until tender-crisp, 1 to 2 minutes. Stir in garlic and cook 30 seconds. Add frozen baby peas, broth, salt, and pepper; heat to boiling. Stir in lemon peel. In warm serving bowl, toss pasta with vegetable mixture until combined.

EACH SERVING: ABOUT 536 CALORIES (13 PERCENT CALORIES FROM FAT) | 19G PROTEIN | 95G CARBOHYDRATE | 8G TOTAL FAT (3G SATURATED) | 8MG CHOLESTEROL | 704MG SODIUM

ORZO "RISOTTO" WITH MUSHROOMS

ACTIVE TIME: 10 MIN · **TOTAL TIME:** 30 MIN
MAKES: 6 MAIN-DISH SERVINGS

1 PACKAGE (16 OUNCES) ORZO PASTA	½ TEASPOON SALT
1 TABLESPOON OLIVE OIL	¼ CUP DRY WHITE WINE
1 MEDIUM ONION, CHOPPED	2 TABLESPOONS CORNSTARCH
8 OUNCES MEDIUM SHIITAKE MUSHROOMS, STEMS REMOVED AND CAPS CUT INTO ¼-INCH-THICK SLICES	2½ CUPS LOW-FAT MILK (1%)
	⅓ CUP GRATED PARMESAN CHEESE
8 OUNCES MEDIUM WHITE MUSHROOMS, TRIMMED AND CUT INTO ¼-INCH-THICK SLICES	3 TABLESPOONS CHOPPED FRESH PARSLEY LEAVES
	1 TABLESPOON BUTTER OR MARGARINE

1 In 5-quart saucepot, cook orzo as label directs; drain and keep warm.

2 Meanwhile, in nonstick 12-inch skillet, heat oil over medium heat. Add onion and cook 5 minutes. Increase heat to medium-high. Add shiitake and white mushrooms and ¼ teaspoon salt; cook, stirring frequently, until mushrooms are tender and golden. Remove skillet from heat; stir in white wine.

3 In small bowl, mix cornstarch with milk. Add cornstarch mixture to same 5-quart saucepot. Heat to boiling over medium heat. Reduce heat to low; simmer 1 minute. Stir in orzo, mushroom mixture, grated Parmesan, parsley, margarine, and remaining ¼ teaspoon salt; heat through. Serve "risotto" immediately while still creamy.

EACH SERVING: ABOUT 425 CALORIES (17 PERCENT CALORIES FROM FAT) | 17G PROTEIN | 70G CARBOHYDRATE | 8G TOTAL FAT (3G SATURATED) | 13MG CHOLESTEROL | 609MG SODIUM

TIP Mushrooms contain two powerful antioxidants—the plant compound quercetin and the mineral selenium. Quercetin may reduce blood-clot formation, and selenium, in combination with vitamin E, protects cells from free-radical damage that may lead to heart disease and cancer.

LINGUINE WITH FRESH TOMATO SAUCE

If the ripe summer tomatoes you use taste a bit acidic, simply add one teaspoon sugar to the sauce. If using juicy beefsteak tomatoes instead of meaty plum tomatoes, simmer the sauce uncovered for about twenty minutes to allow the excess juices to evaporate.

ACTIVE TIME: 15 MIN · **TOTAL TIME:** 45 MIN
MAKES: 6 MAIN-DISH SERVINGS

- 1 TABLESPOON OLIVE OIL
- 1 SMALL ONION, CHOPPED
- 2 POUNDS RIPE PLUM TOMATOES OR BEEFSTEAK TOMATOES, PEELED AND COARSELY CHOPPED
- ½ TEASPOON SALT
- 3 TABLESPOONS BUTTER, CUT INTO PIECES, OR OLIVE OIL
- 2 TABLESPOONS CHOPPED FRESH SAGE OR ½ CUP CHOPPED FRESH BASIL
- 1 PACKAGE (16 OUNCES) LINGUINE OR PENNE

1 In nonstick 10-inch skillet, heat oil over medium heat. Add onion and cook until tender and golden, about 10 minutes. Add tomatoes and salt; heat to boiling over high heat. Reduce heat; cover and simmer, stirring and breaking up tomatoes with side of spoon, until sauce has thickened, 15 to 20 minutes. Stir in butter and sage.

2 Meanwhile, in large saucepot, cook pasta as label directs. Drain. In warm serving bowl, toss pasta with sauce.

EACH SERVING: ABOUT 388 CALORIES (23 PERCENT CALORIES FROM FAT) | 11G PROTEIN | 65G CARBOHYDRATE | 10G TOTAL FAT (4G SATURATED) | 16MG CHOLESTEROL | 334MG SODIUM

PENNE WITH TOMATO CREAM

This restaurant favorite is a cinch to prepare at home. Don't hesitate to add the vodka. You won't taste it: It just melds the flavors.

ACTIVE TIME: 15 MIN · **TOTAL TIME:** 45 MIN

MAKES: 6 MAIN-DISH SERVINGS

1 TABLESPOON OLIVE OIL	½ TEASPOON SALT
1 SMALL ONION, CHOPPED	½ CUP HEAVY OR WHIPPING CREAM
1 GARLIC CLOVE, FINELY CHOPPED	1 CUP FROZEN PEAS, THAWED
⅛ TO ¼ TEASPOON CRUSHED RED PEPPER	1 PACKAGE (16 OUNCES) PENNE OR ROTINI PASTA
1 CAN (28 OUNCES) TOMATOES IN PUREE, COARSELY CHOPPED	½ CUP LOOSELY PACKED FRESH BASIL LEAVES, THINLY SLICED
3 TABLESPOONS VODKA (OPTIONAL)	

1 In nonstick 12-inch skillet, heat oil over medium heat. Add onion and cook until tender, about 5 minutes. Add garlic and crushed red pepper; cook until garlic is golden, about 30 seconds longer. Stir in tomatoes with their puree, vodka if using, and salt; heat to boiling over high heat. Reduce heat and simmer until sauce has thickened, 15 to 20 minutes. Stir in cream and peas; heat to boiling.

2 Meanwhile, in large saucepot, cook pasta as label directs. Drain. In warm serving bowl, toss pasta with sauce and sprinkle with basil.

EACH SERVING: ABOUT 434 CALORIES (23 PERCENT CALORIES FROM FAT) | 13G PROTEIN | 71G CARBOHYDRATE | 11G TOTAL FAT (5G SATURATED) | 27MG CHOLESTEROL | 509MG SODIUM

TIP Enriched brands of whole-wheat pasta have more thiamin, riboflavin, and folic acid than regular pasta and contain about five times the amount of fiber. And the nutty taste of whole wheat makes it a great choice for fall and winter cooking. Whole wheat spaghetti, made with whole wheat flour, delivers more fiber per 2-ounce serving (5 grams versus 2 grams).

PASTA PRIMAVERA

This dish is traditionally made in spring, when the first tender young vegetables appear—thus the name *primavera*, which means spring in Italian. We used fresh asparagus and sugar snaps and cooked them along with the pasta to save time.

ACTIVE TIME: 15 MIN · **TOTAL TIME:** 40 MIN
MAKES: 6 MAIN-DISH SERVINGS

½ CUP HEAVY OR WHIPPING CREAM

3 TABLESPOONS BUTTER OR MARGARINE

4 OUNCES SHIITAKE MUSHROOMS, STEMS REMOVED AND CAPS THINLY SLICED

2 VERY SMALL YELLOW SQUASH OR ZUCCHINI (4 OUNCES EACH), CUT INTO 2" BY ¼" MATCHSTICK STRIPS

4 GREEN ONIONS, THINLY SLICED

1 TABLESPOON CHOPPED FRESH PARSELY

1 PACKAGE (16 OUNCES) FETTUCCINE

1 POUND ASPARAGUS, TRIMMED AND CUT ON DIAGONAL INTO 1½-INCH PIECES

4 OUNCES SUGAR SNAP PEAS, STRINGS REMOVED

¾ CUP FRESHLY GRATED PARMESAN CHEESE

¼ TEASPOON SALT

1 In 1-quart saucepan, heat cream to boiling and boil 1 minute. Remove saucepan from heat and set aside.

2 In nonstick 10-inch skillet, melt butter or margarine over medium heat. Add mushrooms and cook, stirring, 1 minute. Add squash and cook, stirring, until vegetables are tender, about 3 minutes. Remove from heat; stir in green onions and parsley. Keep warm.

3 Meanwhile, in large saucepot, cook pasta as label directs. After pasta has cooked 7 minutes, add asparagus and sugar snap peas to pasta water. Cook until pasta and vegetables are tender, 3 to 5 minutes longer. Drain pasta and vegetables, reserving ½ cup pasta cooking water.

4 In warm serving bowl, toss pasta and vegetables with reserved pasta water, Parmesan, and salt. Stir in cream and mushroom mixture.

EACH SERVING: ABOUT 368 CALORIES | 14G PROTEIN | 48G CARBOHYDRATE | 14G TOTAL FAT (8G SATURATED) | 39MG CHOLESTEROL | 347MG SODIUM

ZITI WITH ROASTED ASPARAGUS

Toasted pecans make this easy dish luxurious. (See photo on page 374.)

ACTIVE TIME: 15 MIN · **TOTAL TIME:** 45 MIN
MAKES: 6 MAIN-DISH SERVINGS

---

2   TABLESPOONS OLIVE OIL

¼   TEASPOON DRIED ROSEMARY

2   POUNDS ASPARAGUS, TRIMMED AND CUT INTO 1-INCH PIECES (6 CUPS)

1   PACKAGE (16 OUNCES) ZITI PASTA

1   CUP HALF-AND-HALF OR LIGHT CREAM

¾   TEASPOON FRESHLY GRATED LEMON PEEL

½   TEASPOON SALT

¼   TEASPOON GROUND BLACK PEPPER

⅓   CUP TOASTED PECANS, COARSELY CHOPPED

---

1   Preheat oven to 400°F. Combine oil and rosemary in 13" by 9" baking pan. Place pan in oven until oil is hot, about 4 minutes. Add asparagus; toss to coat with oil. Roast asparagus, tossing occasionally, until tender, about 15 minutes.

2   Meanwhile, in large saucepot, cook the pasta as label directs. Drain.

3   In 12-inch skillet, heat half-and-half to boiling over medium heat; cook 5 minutes. Stir in lemon peel, salt, and pepper. Add pasta and asparagus; toss to coat. Transfer to warm serving bowls and sprinkle with pecans.

EACH SERVING: ABOUT 410 CALORIES (26 PERCENT CALORIES FROM FAT) | 15G PROTEIN | 63G CARBOHYDRATE | 12G TOTAL FAT (4G SATURATED) | 15MG CHOLESTEROL | 282MG SODIUM

TIP Fresh asparagus is a springtime treat not to be missed. It's a great source of folic acid, which protects against birth defects (in women of childbearing years) and heart disease. Enjoy it with rich salmon, or steam up a big handful (it takes less than 10 minutes), sprinkle lightly with salt or a pinch of grated Parmesan cheese, and enjoy. At 3 calories a spear, you can afford to eat the whole bunch.

BOW TIES WITH SHRIMP AND FENNEL

The secrets to success here are a bag of frozen shrimp and a mixture of garlic and fennel seeds. If you don't have a mortar and pestle, crush garlic with a press and place the seeds in a sealed plastic bag, then mash with a rolling pin.

ACTIVE TIME: 10 MIN · **TOTAL TIME:** 25 MIN

MAKES: 6 MAIN-DISH SERVINGS

1 PACKAGE (16 OUNCES) BOW-TIE PASTA

1 BAG (16 OUNCES) FROZEN UNCOOKED EXTRA-LARGE SHRIMP, SHELLED AND DEVEINED

1 CUP FROZEN PEAS

1 SMALL GARLIC CLOVE

1 TEASPOON FENNEL SEEDS

½ TEASPOON SALT

¼ TEASPOON COARSELY GROUND BLACK PEPPER

4 RIPE MEDIUM TOMATOES, FINELY CHOPPED

2 TABLESPOONS OLIVE OIL

2 OUNCES FETA CHEESE, CRUMBLED (½ CUP)

1 In large saucepot, cook pasta as label directs. After pasta has cooked 12 minutes, add frozen shrimp and peas to pasta cooking water and continue cooking until pasta is done and shrimp turn opaque throughout, about 3 minutes. Drain pasta and shrimp; return to saucepot and keep warm.

2 Meanwhile, in mortar with pestle, crush garlic with fennel seeds, salt, and pepper. Transfer mixture to medium bowl and stir in tomatoes and olive oil.

3 Add tomato mixture and feta cheese to pasta and shrimp in saucepot; toss well.

EACH SERVING: ABOUT 465 CALORIES (17 PERCENT CALORIES FROM FAT) | 29G PROTEIN | 66G CARBOHYDRATE | 9G TOTAL FAT (3G SATURATED) | 125MG CHOLESTEROL | 520MG SODIUM

LASAGNA ROLL-UPS

ACTIVE TIME: 35 MIN · **TOTAL TIME:** 1 HR 10 MIN

MAKES: 6 MAIN-DISH SERVINGS

½ (16-OUNCE) PACKAGE CURLY LASAGNA NOODLES (9 NOODLES)

2 CANS (14½ OUNCES EACH) STEWED TOMATOES

1 CAN (8 OUNCES) TOMATO SAUCE

1 CONTAINER (15 OUNCES) PART-SKIM RICOTTA CHEESE

2 OUNCES PART-SKIM MOZZARELLA CHEESE, SHREDDED (½ CUP)

3 TABLESPOONS GRATED PARMESAN CHEESE

4 TABLESPOONS CHOPPED FRESH BASIL

½ TEASPOON COARSELY GROUND BLACK PEPPER

2 TEASPOONS OLIVE OIL

1 SMALL ONION, CHOPPED

1 SMALL ZUCCHINI (4 OUNCES), FINELY CHOPPED

1 SMALL TOMATO, FINELY CHOPPED

1 TABLESPOON CAPERS, DRAINED AND CHOPPED

1 In large saucepot, cook lasagna noodles as label directs. Drain and rinse with cold running water. Return noodles to saucepot with cold water to cover. Meanwhile, in 3-quart glass or ceramic baking dish, combine stewed tomatoes and tomato sauce; break up tomatoes with side of spoon.

2 Prepare filling: In large bowl, mix ricotta, mozzarella, Parmesan, 3 tablespoons basil, and pepper.

3 Preheat oven to 375°F. Place lasagna noodles on clean kitchen towels. Spread about ¼ cup filling on each lasagna noodle and roll up jelly-roll fashion. Slice each rolled noodle crosswise in half. Arrange lasagna rolls, cut side down, in sauce in baking dish; cover loosely with foil. Bake until heated through, 35 to 40 minutes.

4 Meanwhile, prepare topping: In nonstick 10-inch skillet, heat oil over medium heat. Add onion; cook until tender and browned. Stir in zucchini; cook until tender. Stir in finely chopped tomato, capers, and remaining 1 tablespoon basil; heat through.

5 To serve, place sauce and lasagna rolls on 6 plates; spoon topping over lasagna rolls.

EACH SERVING: ABOUT 335 CALORIES (30 PERCENT CALORIES FROM FAT) | 18G PROTEIN | 42G CARBOHYDRATE | 11G TOTAL FAT (6G SATURATED) | 30MG CHOLESTEROL | 725MG SODIUM

LINGUINE WITH BROCCOLI AND CLAMS

Our lightened version of classic linguine with clam sauce includes healthy broccoli flowerets.

ACTIVE TIME: 30 MIN · **TOTAL TIME:** 50 MIN

MAKES: 4 MAIN-DISH SERVINGS

SALT

15 OUNCES BROCCOLI FLOWERETS (6 CUPS)

1 PACKAGE (1 POUND) LINGUINE OR SPAGHETTI

½ CUP DRY WHITE WINE

2 DOZEN LITTLENECK OR SMALL CHERRYSTONE CLAMS, WELL SCRUBBED

1 TABLESPOON OLIVE OIL

2 GARLIC CLOVES, FINELY CHOPPED

½ TEASPOON COARSELY GROUND BLACK PEPPER

⅛ TO ¼ TEASPOON CRUSHED RED PEPPER

¼ CUP LOOSELY PACKED FRESH PARSLEY LEAVES, CHOPPED

1 In large saucepot of **boiling salted water**, cook broccoli until almost tender, 4 to 6 minutes. With slotted spoon or metal strainer, transfer broccoli to bowl; do not discard cooking water. Rinse broccoli with cold running water to stop cooking.

2 In same saucepot of boiling water, cook pasta as label directs. Drain.

3 Meanwhile, in deep 12-inch skillet, heat wine to boiling over high heat. Add clams and reduce heat to medium. Cover and simmer until clams open, 7 to 10 minutes, transferring clams to large bowl as they open. Discard any clams that do not open. Strain clam broth through sieve lined with paper towels; add enough water to clam broth to equal 1½ cups. When cool enough to handle, remove clams from shells and coarsely chop, adding any clam juices to reserved broth. (Reserve a few clams in the shell for garnish if you like.).

4 Clean skillet and wipe dry. Heat oil over medium heat. Add garlic and stir 30 seconds. Add broccoli flowerets, black pepper, red pepper, clams, and reserved broth to skillet; cook, stirring gently, until heated through.

5 In warm serving bowl, toss hot pasta with broccoli mixture. Add reserved clams in shells and sprinkle with parsley.

EACH SERVING: ABOUT 520 CALORIES (10 PERCENT CALORIES FROM FAT) | 24G PROTEIN | 91G CARBOHYDRATE | 6G TOTAL FAT (1G SATURATED) | 18MG CHOLESTEROL | 360MG SODIUM

SPAGHETTI WITH BACON AND PEAS

"The peas cook along with the pasta, and the sauce is really easy to make with ricotta and Romano cheese," says GH Food Director Susan Westmoreland of her speedy weeknight pasta dinner. Along with the spaghetti dish, she serves a side of sliced tomatoes, and fresh figs for dessert. To optimize the time it takes to prepare the meal, put water on to boil for the pasta, and while it heats, cook the bacon and onion. Then, as the pasta cooks, slice the tomatoes.

ACTIVE TIME: 10 MIN · **TOTAL TIME:** 20 MIN

MAKES: 8 MAIN-DISH SERVINGS

1   POUND THIN SPAGHETTI OR VERMICELLI

1   PACKAGE (10 OUNCES) FROZEN PEAS

4   SLICES BACON

1   MEDIUM ONION, FINELY CHOPPED

1   CONTAINER (15 OUNCES) PART-SKIM RICOTTA CHEESE

½   CUP GRATED PECORINO ROMANO OR PARMESAN CHEESE

½   TEASPOON SALT

¼   TEASPOON COARSELY GROUND BLACK PEPPER

1   In large saucepot, cook pasta as label directs. During last 2 minutes of pasta cooking, add frozen peas to pasta cooking water; continue cooking until pasta is done. Drain, reserving 1 cup pasta cooking water. Return pasta and peas to saucepot and keep warm.

2   Meanwhile, in 12-inch skillet, cook bacon over medium heat until browned. Transfer to paper towels to drain. Pour off all but 1 tablespoon bacon drippings from skillet. Add onion and cook until tender and golden, 8 to 10 minutes.

3   Add reserved pasta water, onion mixture, ricotta, Romano, salt, and pepper to pasta and peas in saucepot. Crumble in bacon and toss again.

EACH SERVING: ABOUT 372 CALORIES (24 PERCENT CALORIES FROM FAT) | 19G PROTEIN | 52G CARBOHYDRATE | 10G TOTAL FAT (6G SATURATED) | 27MG CHOLESTEROL | 440MG SODIUM

PAD THAI

Authentic Pad Thai is made with rice noodles (use the ⅛-inch-wide ones) that are available at Asian markets. If you can't find them, use angel hair pasta or linguine (cooked according to the package directions). It will still be delicious.

ACTIVE TIME: 25 MIN · **TOTAL TIME:** 30 MIN PLUS SOAKING NOODLES
MAKES: 4 MAIN-DISH SERVINGS

1 PACKAGE (7 TO 8 OUNCES) RICE STICK NOODLES (RICE VERMICELLI), OR 8 OUNCES ANGEL HAIR PASTA	2 GARLIC CLOVES, FINELY CHOPPED
¼ CUP FRESH LIME JUICE	¼ TEASPOON CRUSHED RED PEPPER
¼ CUP ASIAN FISH SAUCE (SEE TIP PAGE 199)	3 LARGE EGGS, LIGHTLY BEATEN
2 TABLESPOONS SUGAR	6 OUNCES BEAN SPROUTS (2 CUPS), RINSED AND DRAINED
1 TABLESPOON VEGETABLE OIL	⅓ CUP UNSALTED ROASTED PEANUTS, COARSELY CHOPPED
8 OUNCES MEDIUM SHRIMP, SHELLED AND DEVEINED, THEN CUT LENGTHWISE IN HALF	3 GREEN ONIONS, THINLY SLICED
	½ CUP LOOSELY PACKED FRESH CILANTRO LEAVES
	LIME WEDGES

1 In large bowl, soak rice stick noodles, if using, in enough **hot water** to cover for 20 minutes. Drain. With kitchen shears, cut noodles into 4-inch lengths. If using angel hair pasta, break in half, cook in large saucepot as label directs, drain, and rinse with cold running water.
2 Meanwhile, in small bowl, combine lime juice, fish sauce, and sugar. Assemble all remaining ingredients and place next to stove.
3 In 12-inch skillet, heat oil over high heat until hot. Add shrimp, garlic, and crushed red pepper; cook, stirring, 1 minute. Add eggs and cook, stirring, until just set, about 20 seconds. Add drained noodles and cook, stirring, 2 minutes. Add fish-sauce mixture, half of bean sprouts, half of peanuts, and half of green onions; cook, stirring, 1 minute.
4 Transfer Pad Thai to warm platter or serving bowl. Top with remaining bean sprouts and sprinkle with remaining peanuts, remaining green onions, and cilantro. Serve with lime wedges.

EACH SERVING: ABOUT 472 CALORIES (30 PERCENT CALORIES FROM FAT) | 21G PROTEIN | 63G CARBOHYDRATE | 16G TOTAL FAT (3G SATURATED) | 230MG CHOLESTEROL | 811MG SODIUM

SPAGHETTI AND MEATBALLS

A childhood favorite—with kids of all ages. We've baked the meatballs for leaner results. To further cut back on calories, reduce pasta portions.

ACTIVE TIME: 45 MIN · **TOTAL TIME:** 1 HR 30 MIN
MAKES: 6 MAIN-DISH SERVINGS

SPAGHETTI SAUCE

1   TABLESPOON OLIVE OIL

1   MEDIUM CARROT, PEELED AND FINELY CHOPPED

1   SMALL ONION, FINELY CHOPPED

1   GARLIC CLOVE, FINELY CHOPPED

1   CAN (28 OUNCES) ITALIAN-STYLE TOMATOES IN PUREE

1   SMALL BAY LEAF

¼   TEASPOON SALT

⅛   TEASPOON COARSELY GROUND BLACK PEPPER

MEATBALLS

2   SLICES FIRM WHITE BREAD, DICED

3   TABLESPOONS WATER

1   POUND LEAN GROUND BEEF OR LEAN GROUND TURKEY

1   LARGE EGG WHITE

2   TABLESPOONS GRATED PECORINO ROMANO OR PARMESAN CHEESE

1   TABLESPOON GRATED ONION

1   TABLESPOON FINELY CHOPPED FRESH PARSLEY LEAVES

1   SMALL GARLIC CLOVE, CRUSHED WITH GARLIC PRESS

½   TEASPOON SALT

1   PACKAGE (16 OUNCES) SPAGHETTI, COOKED AS LABEL DIRECTS

1   Prepare Spaghetti Sauce: In 3-quart saucepan, heat oil over medium heat. Add carrot and chopped onion and cook, stirring occasionally, until vegetables are very tender and golden, about 15 minutes. Add chopped garlic; cook, stirring, 1 minute.

2   Meanwhile, place tomatoes with their puree in bowl. With hands or slotted spoon, crush tomatoes well. Add tomatoes with their puree, bay leaf, salt and pepper to saucepan; heat to boiling over high heat. Reduce heat to low; cover and simmer 15 minutes. Uncover and simmer, stirring occasionally, 15 minutes longer. Discard bay leaf.

3   While sauce is cooking, prepare Meatballs: Preheat oven to 425°F. Line 13" by 9" metal baking pan with foil; spray foil with nonstick cooking spray.

4 In medium bowl, combine diced bread and water. With hand, mix until bread is evenly moistened. Add ground meat, egg white, Romano, grated onion, parsley, crushed garlic, and salt. With hand, mix until well combined.

5 Shape meat mixture into twelve 2-inch meatballs. (For easier shaping, use slightly wet hands.) Place meatballs in pan and bake until cooked through and lightly browned, 15 to 20 minutes. Add meatballs to sauce.

6 Place pasta in a large warm serving bowl; spoon meatballs and sauce over pasta.

EACH SERVING: ABOUT 430 CALORIES (17 PERCENT CALORIES FROM FAT) | 28G PROTEIN | 63G CARBOHYDRATE | 8G TOTAL FAT (2G SATURATED) | 144MG CHOLESTEROL | 520MG SODIUM

ORANGE-GLAZED STEAK

We marinate round steak in a soy-and-garlic mixture, then brush it with orange marmalade for a tasty finish.

ACTIVE TIME: 5 MIN · **TOTAL TIME:** 30 MIN PLUS MARINATING
MAKES: 6 MAIN-DISH SERVINGS

¼ CUP SOY SAUCE

2 GARLIC CLOVES, CRUSHED WITH GARLIC PRESS

1 TEASPOON COARSELY GROUND BLACK PEPPER

1 BEEF TOP ROUND STEAK, 1¼ INCHES THICK (2 POUNDS), WELL TRIMMED

⅓ CUP ORANGE MARMALADE

1 In 13" by 9" baking dish, combine soy sauce, garlic, and pepper. Add steak to soy-sauce mixture, turning to coat. Cover and refrigerate 30 minutes to marinate, turning once.

2 Prepare grill. Place steak on grill over medium heat and grill, brushing with orange marmalade during last 10 minutes of cooking and turning occasionally, 25 minutes for medium-rare or until desired doneness. Transfer steak to cutting board and let stand 10 minutes to set juices for easier slicing. Cut into thin slices across the grain.

EACH SERVING: ABOUT 202 CALORIES (18 PERCENT CALORIES FROM FAT) | 28G PROTEIN | 12G CARBOHYDRATE | 4G TOTAL FAT (1G SATURATED) | 72MG CHOLESTEROL | 419MG SODIUM

CHUNKY BEEF STEW

Lean beef, winter vegetables, and a richly flavored sauce make this a candidate for family suppers or casual entertaining.

ACTIVE TIME: 30 MIN · **TOTAL TIME:** 1 HR 30 MIN · **MAKES:** 6 MAIN-DISH SERVINGS

- 1 POUND LEAN BEEF FOR STEW, TRIMMED AND CUT INTO 1-INCH CUBES
- 1 TABLESPOON VEGETABLE OIL
- ½ TEASPOON SALT
- 2 LARGE STALKS CELERY, CHOPPED
- 1 LARGE ONION, CHOPPED
- 1 CAN (14 ½ OUNCES) STEWED TOMATOES
- 1 CAN (14 ½ OUNCES) BEEF BROTH OR 1¾ CUPS HOMEMADE
- 1 CUP PLUS 2 TABLESPOONS WATER
- 3 LARGE POTATOES (1½ POUNDS), PEELED AND CUT INTO 1½-INCH CHUNKS
- 3 MEDIUM CARROTS (½ POUND), PEELED AND CUT INTO ¾-INCH CHUNKS
- 3 MEDIUM TURNIPS (¾ POUND), PEELED AND CUT INTO 1½-INCH CHUNKS
- 1 TABLESPOON SOY SAUCE
- 1 TEASPOON SUGAR
- ¾ TEASPOON BROWNING AND SEASONING SAUCE (OPTIONAL)
- 2 TABLESPOONS ALL-PURPOSE FLOUR
- 1 PACKAGE (10 OUNCES) FROZEN PEAS
- 2 TABLESPOONS FRESHLY GRATED LEMON PEEL

1 Pat beef dry with paper towels. In 5-quart Dutch oven, heat vegetable oil over medium-high heat until very hot. Add beef, sprinkle with salt, and cook, turning occasionally, until browned on all sides. Transfer beef to bowl.

2 Add celery and onion to drippings in Dutch oven and cook, stirring, until lightly browned. Return beef to Dutch oven; stir in stewed tomatoes, broth, and 1 cup water. Heat to boiling over high heat. Reduce heat to low; cover and simmer 25 minutes.

3 Add potatoes, carrots, turnips, soy sauce, sugar, and the browning and seasoning sauce, if using; heat to boiling over high heat. Reduce heat to low; cover and simmer until meat and vegetables are fork-tender, about 20 minutes longer.

4 In cup, with fork, mix flour and remaining 2 tablespoons water until blended. Stir flour mixture into meat mixture; cook over medium-high heat until mixture boils and thickens slightly. Stir in frozen peas; heat through. Sprinkle with lemon peel.

EACH SERVING: ABOUT 330 CALORIES (19 PERCENT CALORIES FROM FAT) | 23G PROTEIN | 45G CARBOHYDRATE | 7G TOTAL FAT (2G SATURATED) | 53MG CHOLESTEROL | 905MG SODIUM

STEAK AND PEPPER FAJITAS

Arrange the meat and condiments in pretty dishes and let everyone make his or her own.

ACTIVE TIME: 10 MIN · **TOTAL TIME:** 30 MIN
MAKES: 4 MAIN-DISH SERVINGS

---

1 BEEF TOP ROUND STEAK, 1 INCH THICK (¾ POUND), WELL TRIMMED

1 BOTTLE (8 OUNCES) MEDIUM-HOT CHUNKY SALSA

1 TABLESPOON LIGHT CORN-OIL SPREAD (56% TO 60% FAT)

1 MEDIUM RED ONION, THINLY SLICED

1 MEDIUM GREEN PEPPER, THINLY SLICED

1 MEDIUM RED PEPPER, THINLY SLICED

2 TABLESPOONS CHOPPED FRESH CILANTRO LEAVES

8 (6-INCH) LOW-FAT FLOUR TORTILLAS, WARMED AS LABEL DIRECTS

1 CONTAINER (8 OUNCES) FAT-FREE SOUR CREAM

8 OUNCES FAT-FREE SHARP CHEDDAR CHEESE, SHREDDED

CHILE PEPPERS, LIME WEDGES, AND CILANTRO SPRIGS FOR GARNISH

1 Preheat broiler. Place steak on rack in broiling pan; spread ¼ cup salsa on top. Place pan in broiler at closest position to source of heat; broil steak 8 minutes. Turn steak over and spread ¼ cup salsa on top; broil 8 minutes longer for medium-rare or until desired doneness.

2 Meanwhile, in nonstick 12-inch skillet, melt corn-oil spread over medium-high heat. Add red onion, green pepper, and red pepper; cook until vegetables are tender-crisp. Stir in chopped cilantro. Spoon mixture into serving bowl.

3 To serve, place steak on cutting board; holding knife almost parallel to cutting surface, slice steak crosswise into thin slices. Serve sliced steak with pepper mixture, tortillas, sour cream, shredded cheese, and remaining salsa. Garnish with chile peppers, lime wedges, and cilantro.

EACH SERVING: ABOUT 450 CALORIES (14 PERCENT CALORIES FROM FAT) | 45G PROTEIN | 55G CARBOHYDRATE | 7G TOTAL FAT (1G SATURATED) | 51MG CHOLESTEROL | 1,060MG SODIUM

LEAN BEEF STROGANOFF

ACTIVE TIME: 20 MIN · **TOTAL TIME:** 50 MIN · **MAKES:** 6 MAIN-DISH SERVINGS

1 BONELESS BEEF TOP SIRLOIN STEAK, ¾ INCH THICK (1 POUND), WELL TRIMMED

3 TEASPOONS OLIVE OIL

1 POUND MEDIUM MUSHROOMS, TRIMMED AND THICKLY SLICED

1 MEDIUM ONION, CHOPPED

1 TEASPOON CORNSTARCH

1 CUP BEEF BROTH

½ CUP CHILI SAUCE

2 TABLESPOONS SPICY BROWN MUSTARD

2 TABLESPOONS PLUS ¼ CUP WATER

12 OUNCES SUGAR SNAP PEAS OR SNOW PEAS, STRINGS REMOVED

2 BAGS (6 OUNCES EACH) RADISHES, HALVED IF LARGE

½ TEASPOON SALT

1 PACKAGE (12 OUNCES) EXTRA-WIDE CURLY NOODLES, COOKED AS LABEL DIRECTS

6 TABLESPOONS NONFAT SOUR CREAM

2 TABLESPOONS CHOPPED FRESH PARSLEY LEAVES

1 Holding knife almost parallel to cutting surface, slice steak crosswise into very thin slices.

2 Spray nonstick 12-inch skillet lightly with olive oil nonstick cooking spray. Place skillet over medium-high heat and heat. Add half of meat and cook, stirring quickly and constantly, until meat loses its pink color, about 2 minutes. Transfer to bowl. Repeat with remaining meat but do not use nonstick spray again.

3 In same skillet, heat 2 teaspoons olive oil over medium-high heat. Add mushrooms and onion and cook, stirring, until tender. In cup, mix cornstarch and beef broth; stir into mushroom mixture with chili sauce and mustard. Cook, stirring, until mixture boils and thickens slightly. Return beef to skillet; heat through.

4 Meanwhile, in nonstick 10-inch skillet, heat remaining 1 teaspoon olive oil and 2 tablespoons water over medium-high heat until hot. Add sugar snap peas and cook until tender-crisp, 5 to 7 minutes. Transfer to bowl. In same skillet, cook radishes and remaining ¼ cup water over medium-high heat, until tender-crisp, 5 to 7 minutes. Add sugar snap peas and salt to radishes; heat through.

5 Spoon noodles onto 6 dinner plates. Spoon beef mixture over noodles; top each serving with 1 tablespoon sour cream and sprinkle with parsley. Serve with sugar snap peas and radishes.

EACH SERVING: ABOUT 430 CALORIES (19 PERCENT CALORIES FROM FAT) | 30G PROTEIN | 58G CARBOHYDRATE | 9G TOTAL FAT (2G SATURATED) | 90MG CHOLESTEROL | 740MG SODIUM

ORANGE BEEF AND PEPPERS

ACTIVE TIME: 20 MIN · **TOTAL TIME:** 40 MIN

MAKES: 4 MAIN-DISH SERVINGS

---

1 BEEF TOP ROUND STEAK, ¾ INCH THICK (1 POUND), WELL TRIMMED

2 TABLESPOONS SOY SAUCE

3 LARGE ORANGES

2 TABLESPOONS BUTTER OR MARGARINE

1 LARGE RED PEPPER, CUT INTO ¼-INCH-THICK SLICES

1 LARGE YELLOW PEPPER, CUT INTO ¼-INCH-THICK SLICES

1 BUNCH GREEN ONIONS, CUT INTO 2-INCH PIECES

1½ TEASPOONS GRATED, PEELED FRESH GINGER

¾ TEASPOON CORNSTARCH

2 BUNCHES ARUGULA (8 OUNCES), STEMS TRIMMED

---

1 Cut steak lengthwise in half. Holding knife almost parallel to cutting surface, slice steak crosswise into ⅛-inch-thick slices. In bowl, toss steak with soy sauce.

2 With a sharp paring knife, cut peel and white pith from 2 oranges; cut the oranges crosswise into ¼-inch-thick slices, then cut each slice in half. From remaining orange, grate 1 teaspoon peel and squeeze ½ cup juice.

3 In nonstick 12-inch skillet, melt 2 teaspoons margarine over medium-high heat. Add red pepper and yellow pepper and cook, stirring frequently, until tender-crisp; transfer to bowl.

4 In same skillet, melt 1 teaspoon margarine; add green onions and cook, stirring frequently, until tender-crisp; transfer to bowl with peppers.

5 In small bowl, mix grated orange peel, orange juice, ginger, and cornstarch until blended; set aside.

6 In same skillet, melt remaining 1 tablespoon margarine. Add half of beef mixture and cook, stirring quickly and constantly, just until beef loses its pink color; transfer to bowl with vegetables. In drippings in skillet, repeat with remaining beef mixture. Return vegetables and meat to skillet. Stir in orange-juice mixture and sliced oranges; cook until liquid boils and thickens slightly and mixture is heated through.

7 Serve beef mixture with arugula.

EACH SERVING: ABOUT 270 CALORIES (30 PERCENT CALORIES FROM FAT) | 29G PROTEIN | 19G CARBOHYDRATE | 9G TOTAL FAT (5G SATURATED) | 81MG CHOLESTEROL | 607MG SODIUM

CABBAGE-WRAPPED PORK ROAST

Pork and cabbage, a traditional pairing, is recast: The cabbage wrapping helps to keep today's leaner pork moist while it cooks.

ACTIVE TIME: 30 MIN · **TOTAL TIME:** 1 HR 30 MIN

MAKES: 12 MAIN-DISH SERVINGS

---

1 LARGE HEAD GREEN CABBAGE (3 POUNDS)	1 CUBE OR ENVELOPE CHICKEN-FLAVOR BOUILLON DISSOLVED IN 2 CUPS HOT WATER
1 BUNCH GREEN ONIONS	8 MEDIUM RED POTATOES (2½ POUNDS)
1 TABLESPOON FINELY CHOPPED FRESH THYME LEAVES OR ½ TEASPOON DRIED THYME	1 TABLESPOON VEGETABLE OIL
¼ TEASPOON GROUND BLACK PEPPER	1 TEASPOON CARAWAY SEEDS, CRUSHED
1½ TEASPOONS SALT	1 PINT CHERRY TOMATOES
1 BONELESS PORK LOIN ROAST (3 POUNDS), TRIMMED	2 TEASPOONS CORNSTARCH
	2 TABLESPOONS WATER

1 Remove 6 large outer leaves from cabbage; trim tough ribs from leaves. Reserve remaining cabbage. Cut off root ends of green onions.

2 In 5-quart Dutch oven or saucepot, heat 3 quarts water to boiling over high heat. Add cabbage leaves and cook, pressing leaves under water with tongs, until leaves are pliable, 3 to 5 minutes. With slotted spoon, transfer leaves to colander to drain. Add green onions to boiling water; blanch until just wilted, 10 seconds. Drain and pat dry with paper towels.

3 Preheat oven to 350°F. In cup, mix thyme, black pepper, and 1 teaspoon salt. Rub thyme mixture on pork roast. Wrap roast in wilted cabbage leaves; secure leaves with blanched green onions (you will probably have to tie 2 green onion leaves together so strand is long enough to wrap around the roast).

4 Place pork loin in 14" by 10" roasting pan. Pour bouillon mixture into pan. Roast pork, basting occasionally with pan juices, until meat thermometer inserted in center registers 155°F, about 1 hour (internal temperature will rise to about 160°F upon standing).

5 Meanwhile, in 4-quart saucepan, heat potatoes and enough water to cover to boiling over high heat. Reduce heat to low; cover and simmer until potatoes are tender, about 20 minutes. Drain well and cut into ½-inch cubes.

6 Coarsely slice remaining cabbage. In nonstick 5-quart Dutch oven, heat oil over medium-high heat. Add cabbage, caraway seeds, and remaining ½ teaspoon salt; cook, stirring frequently, until cabbage is tender-crisp. Add potato cubes; heat through. Spoon cabbage mixture onto large warm platter.

7 In same Dutch oven, heat cherry tomatoes over medium-high heat until heated through.

8 When pork loin is done, place on platter with cabbage mixture. In cup, mix the cornstarch with water. Stir cornstarch mixture into drippings in roasting pan. Place roasting pan over high heat; heat to boiling and boil 1 minute. Skim fat from pan sauce. Spoon sauce over pork and cabbage and serve with cherry tomatoes.

EACH SERVING: ABOUT 325 CALORIES (30 PERCENT CALORIES FROM FAT) | 30G PROTEIN | 24G CARBOHYDRATE | 11G TOTAL FAT (4G SATURATED) | 50MG CHOLESTEROL | 435MG SODIUM

GINGERED PORK AND VEGETABLE STIR-FRY

To store fresh ginger, peel it and place in a screw-top jar. Pour enough vodka or dry sherry on top to completely cover the root, then seal the jar and refrigerate for up to one year. Grate or chop the gingerroot as needed.

ACTIVE TIME: 15 MIN · **TOTAL TIME:** 30 MIN

MAKES: 4 MAIN-DISH SERVINGS

1 PORK TENDERLOIN (12 OUNCES), THINLY SLICED

2 TABLESPOONS GRATED, PEELED FRESH GINGER

1 CUP CHICKEN BROTH

2 TABLESPOONS TERIYAKI SAUCE

2 TEASPOONS CORNSTARCH

2 TEASPOONS VEGETABLE OIL

8 OUNCES SNOW PEAS, STRINGS REMOVED

1 MEDIUM ZUCCHINI (8 OUNCES), HALVED LENGTHWISE AND THINLY SLICED

3 GREEN ONIONS, CUT INTO 3-INCH PIECES

1 In medium bowl, toss pork and fresh ginger. In cup, mix broth, teriyaki sauce, and cornstarch.

2 In nonstick 12-inch skillet, heat 1 teaspoon oil over medium-high heat until hot. Add snow peas, zucchini, and green onions and cook, stirring frequently (stir-frying), until lightly browned and tender-crisp, about 5 minutes. Transfer to bowl.

3 In same skillet, heat remaining 1 teaspoon oil; add pork mixture and stir-fry until pork just loses its pink color. Transfer pork to bowl with vegetables. Stir cornstarch mixture; add to skillet and heat to boiling. Boil until sauce thickens, 1 minute. Stir in pork and vegetables; heat through.

EACH SERVING: ABOUT 170 CALORIES (26 PERCENT CALORIES FROM FAT) | 21G PROTEIN | 10G CARBOHYDRATE | 5G TOTAL FAT (1G SATURATED) | 51MG CHOLESTEROL | 550MG SODIUM

SMOKED PORK CHOP DINNER

A fruit compote, such as Spicy Plum Compote (page 459), is the perfect dessert for this hearty German favorite.

ACTIVE TIME: 10 MIN · **TOTAL TIME:** 1 HR 10 MIN
MAKES: 4 MAIN-DISH SERVINGS

---

4   SMOKED PORK LOIN OR RIB CHOPS, EACH ¾ INCH THICK (7 OUNCES EACH), WELL TRIMMED

1   TABLESPOON VEGETABLE OIL

1   MEDIUM GRANNY SMITH OR ROME BEAUTY APPLE, CUT IN HALF AND CORED

1   BAG (1 OUNCES) CARROTS, PEELED AND CUT INTO BITE-SIZE CHUNKS

1½ POUNDS SAUERKRAUT, RINSED AND DRAINED

1   CAN OR BOTTLE (12 OUNCES) BEER OR NONALCOHOLIC BEER

½   CUP WATER

¼   CUP PACKED LIGHT OR DARK BROWN SUGAR

2   TEASPOONS CARAWAY OR FENNEL SEEDS, CRUSHED

1   Pat pork chops dry with paper towels. In 12-inch skillet, heat oil over high heat until very hot. Add pork chops and cook until browned on both sides. Meanwhile, coarsely grate ½ of unpeeled apple.

2   To pork chops in skillet, add grated apple, carrots, sauerkraut, beer, water, brown sugar, and caraway seeds. Heat to boiling over high heat. Reduce heat to low; cover and simmer 35 minutes.

3   Cut remaining half apple into wedges; add to mixture in skillet. Cook, occasionally spooning liquid in skillet over pork chops, until carrots and pork chops are fork-tender, 10 minutes longer.

EACH SERVING: ABOUT 380 CALORIES (28 PERCENT CALORIES FROM FAT) | 32G PROTEIN | 36G CARBOHYDRATE | 12G TOTAL FAT (3G SATURATED) | 82MG CHOLESTEROL | 500MG SODIUM

BRAZILIAN PORK

Serve these bold chops with a mixed green salad.

ACTIVE TIME: 15 MIN · **TOTAL TIME:** 30 MIN
MAKES: 4 MAIN-DISH SERVINGS

---

4   BONELESS PORK LOIN CHOPS,
    ¾ INCH THICK (5 OUNCES EACH),
    WELL TRIMMED

½   TEASPOON GROUND CUMIN

½   TEASPOON GROUND CORIANDER

¼   TEASPOON DRIED THYME

⅛   TEASPOON GROUND ALLSPICE

½   TEASPOON SALT

1   TEASPOON OLIVE OIL

1   MEDIUM ONION, CHOPPED

3   GARLIC CLOVES, CRUSHED
    WITH GARLIC PRESS

1   CAN (15 TO 19 OUNCES)
    BLACK BEANS, RINSED AND DRAINED

½   CUP CHICKEN BROTH

1   TABLESPOON FRESH LIME JUICE

¼   TEASPOON COARSELY GROUND
    BLACK PEPPER

¼   CUP PACKED FRESH CILANTRO,
    CHOPPED

FRESH ORANGE WEDGES (OPTIONAL)

---

1   Pat pork chops dry with paper towels. In cup, mix cumin, coriander, thyme, allspice, and ¼ teaspoon salt. Rub spice mixture on pork chops.

2   Heat nonstick 12-inch skillet over medium-high heat until very hot. Add pork chops and cook 4 minutes; turn chops over and cook until lightly browned on the outside and still slightly pink on the inside, 3 to 4 minutes longer. Transfer pork to platter; cover with foil to keep warm.

3   In same skillet, heat oil over medium heat. Add onion and cook, stirring frequently, until golden, about 5 minutes. Add garlic and cook, stirring, 1 minute longer. Stir in beans, broth, lime juice, pepper, and remaining ¼ teaspoon salt; heat through.

4   To serve, spoon bean mixture over pork; sprinkle with cilantro. Serve with orange wedges if you like.

EACH SERVING: ABOUT 340 CALORIES (29 PERCENT CALORIES FROM FAT) | 42G PROTEIN | 25G CARBOHYDRATE | 11G TOTAL FAT (3G SATURATED) | 76MG CHOLESTEROL | 760MG SODIUM

PORK TENDERLOIN CUTLETS WITH PLUM GLAZE

The cutlets and glaze can be prepped in advance—up to several hours ahead. The grilling takes only minutes.

ACTIVE TIME: 10 MIN · **TOTAL TIME:** 16 MIN
MAKES: 4 MAIN-DISH SERVINGS

---

1   PORK TENDERLOIN (1 POUND), TRIMMED

¾   TEASPOON SALT

¼   TEASPOON COARSELY GROUND BLACK PEPPER

½   CUP PLUM JAM OR PRESERVES

1   TABLESPOON BROWN SUGAR

1   TABLESPOON GRATED, PEELED FRESH GINGER

2   GARLIC CLOVES, CRUSHED WITH GARLIC PRESS

1   TABLESPOON FRESH LEMON JUICE

½   TEASPOON GROUND CINNAMON

4   LARGE PLUMS (1 POUND), EACH PITTED AND CUT IN HALF

1   Prepare grill. Using sharp knife, cut tenderloin lengthwise almost in half, being careful not to cut all the way through. Open and spread flat like a book. With meat mallet or between two sheets of plastic wrap or waxed paper with rolling pin, pound meat to ¼-inch thickness. Cut crosswise into 4 equal pieces; sprinkle cutlets with salt and pepper.

2   In small bowl, combine plum jam, brown sugar, ginger, garlic, lemon juice, and cinnamon. Brush one side of each cutlet and cut side of each plum half with plum glaze. Place cutlets and plums on grill over medium heat, glaze side down, and grill 3 minutes. Brush cutlets and plums with remaining plum glaze; turn pork and plums over and grill until cutlets are lightly browned on both sides and just lose their pink color throughout and plums are hot, about 3 minutes longer.

EACH SERVING: ABOUT 333 CALORIES (16 PERCENT CALORIES FROM FAT) | 27G PROTEIN | 44G CARBOHYDRATE | 6G TOTAL FAT (2G SATURATED) | 80MG CHOLESTEROL | 509MG SODIUM

TIP Colorful plums are an excellent source of vitamin C, plus they offer fiber and potassium. Try them split, pitted, and grilled; their natural sugars caramelize, boosting their sweetness without adding extra calories.

CHINESE-STYLE PORK AND BABY PEAS

Serve this one-skillet dinner with basmati rice—a long-grain variety that cooks in twenty minutes—for a well-rounded meal.

ACTIVE TIME: 10 MIN · **TOTAL TIME:** 20 MIN

MAKES: 4 MAIN-DISH SERVINGS

2 TEASPOONS VEGETABLE OIL

1 PORK TENDERLOIN (1 POUND), TRIMMED AND CUT INTO ¼-INCH-THICK SLICES

2 GARLIC CLOVES, CRUSHED WITH GARLIC PRESS

1 PACKAGE (10 OUNCES) FROZEN BABY PEAS

3 TABLESPOONS REDUCED-SODIUM SOY SAUCE

2 TABLESPOONS SEASONED RICE VINEGAR

1 TABLESPOON GINGER

1 TABLESPOON LIGHT (MILD) MOLASSES

¼ TEASPOON CRUSHED RED PEPPER

1 In nonstick 12-inch skillet, heat oil over medium-high heat. Add pork slices and garlic and cook, stirring occasionally, until pork slices are browned on the outside and just lose their pink color on the inside, about 6 minutes. Transfer pork to plate.

2 To same skillet, add peas, soy sauce, rice vinegar, ginger, molasses, and crushed red pepper; cook until peas are heated through, about 4 minutes. Return pork to skillet; toss to coat. To serve, spoon over rice.

EACH SERVING: ABOUT 230 CALORIES (23 PERCENT CALORIES FROM FAT) | 28G PROTEIN | 19G CARBOHYDRATE | 6G TOTAL FAT (1G SATURATED) | 64MG CHOLESTEROL | 840MG SODIUM

THYME-ROASTED CHICKEN AND VEGETABLES

In just over an hour, you can have a one-dish meal of roasted chicken with fennel, potatoes, and onion ready to serve.

ACTIVE TIME: 20 MIN · **TOTAL TIME:** 1 HR 10 MIN
MAKES: 4 MAIN-DISH SERVINGS

1   CHICKEN (3½ POUNDS), CUT INTO 8 PIECES AND SKIN REMOVED FROM ALL BUT WINGS

1   POUND ALL-PURPOSE POTATOES (3 MEDIUM), NOT PEELED, CUT INTO 2-INCH PIECES

1   LARGE FENNEL BULB (1½ POUNDS), TRIMMED AND CUT INTO 8 WEDGES

1   LARGE RED ONION, CUT INTO 8 WEDGES

1   TABLESPOON CHOPPED FRESH THYME OR 1 TEASPOON DRIED THYME

1   TEASPOON SALT

½   TEASPOON GROUND BLACK PEPPER

2   TABLESPOONS OLIVE OIL

⅓   CUP WATER

1   Preheat oven to 450°F. In large roasting pan (17" by 11½"), arrange chicken pieces, skinned side up, and place potatoes, fennel, and onion around them. Sprinkle chicken with thyme, salt, and pepper. Drizzle oil over chicken and vegetables.

2   Roast chicken and vegetables 20 minutes; baste with drippings in pan. Roast, basting once more, until juices run clear when chicken breasts are pierced with tip of knife, about 20 minutes longer. Transfer chicken breasts to platter; keep warm.

3   Continue roasting remaining chicken pieces until juices run clear when thickest part of chicken is pierced with tip of knife and vegetables are fork-tender, about 10 minutes longer. Transfer chicken and vegetables to platter with breasts; keep warm.

4   Skim and discard fat from drippings in pan. To drippings, add water; heat to boiling over medium heat, stirring until brown bits are loosened from bottom. Spoon pan juices over chicken and vegetables.

EACH SERVING: ABOUT 401 CALORIES (29 PERCENT CALORIES FROM FAT) | 43G PROTEIN | 28G CARBOHYDRATE | 13G TOTAL FAT (2G SATURATED) | 124MG CHOLESTEROL | 870MG SODIUM

STICKY DRUMSTICKS

Have lots of napkins on hand for these delicious oven-barbecued drumsticks—guaranteed to be a favorite with the kids in your family.

ACTIVE TIME: 20 MIN · **TOTAL TIME:** 55 MIN
MAKES: 6 MAIN-DISH SERVINGS

½   CUP APRICOT PRESERVES

¼   CUP TERIYAKI SAUCE

1   TABLESPOON DARK BROWN SUGAR

1   TEASPOON CORNSTARCH

1   TEASPOON CIDER VINEGAR

¼   TEASPOON SALT

12   MEDIUM CHICKEN DRUMSTICKS
     (3 POUNDS), SKIN REMOVED

1   Preheat oven to 425°F. In large bowl, with wire whisk, mix apricot preserves, teriyaki sauce, brown sugar, cornstarch, vinegar, and salt until blended. Add chicken, tossing to coat.

2   Spoon chicken and sauce into 15½" by 10½" jelly-roll pan. Bake 15 minutes. Remove chicken from oven; with pastry brush, brush chicken with sauce in pan. Continue baking, brushing with sauce every 5 minutes, until juices run clear when drumsticks are pierced with tip of knife, 15 to 20 minutes longer.

3   Remove chicken from oven; brush with sauce. Let chicken cool on jelly-roll pan 10 minutes. Transfer chicken to serving dish and spoon sauce over chicken.

EACH SERVING: ABOUT 240 CALORIES (15 PERCENT CALORIES FROM FAT) | 26G PROTEIN | 24G CARBOHYDRATE | 4G TOTAL FAT (2G SATURATED) | 96MG CHOLESTEROL | 660MG SODIUM

HERBED SKILLET CHICKEN

Not only does this dish look yummy, it's simple to make!

ACTIVE TIME: 10 MIN · **TOTAL TIME:** 50 MIN

MAKES: 4 MAIN-DISH SERVINGS

---

1   POUND WHITE MUSHROOMS, HALVED

1   SMALL RED ONION, CUT INTO 8 WEDGES

1   TABLESPOON OLIVE OIL

1   TEASPOON FRESH THYME LEAVES

4   SMALL CHICKEN-LEG QUARTERS (6 OUNCES EACH), TRIMMED OF EXCESS FAT

1   TEASPOON SALT

½   TEASPOON COARSELY GROUND BLACK PEPPER

1   Preheat oven to 450°F.

2   Toss mushrooms, onion, and thyme with olive oil in 12-inch cast-iron or heavy skillet. Top with chicken and sprinkle with salt and pepper. Roast 35 to 40 minutes or until cooked through (165°F).

EACH SERVING: ABOUT 223 CALORIES (48 PERCENT CALORIES FROM FAT) | 25G PROTEIN | 6G CARBOHYDRATE | 12G TOTAL FAT (3G SATURATED) | 110MG CHOLESTEROL | 583MG SODIUM

TIP Cooking poultry with the skin on keeps the moisture in—so to slash the amount of fat and calories by almost half simply remove the skin before eating. The fat reduction is practically the same as if you removed the skin before cooking, but the resulting bird will be juicier and more flavorful.

BAKED "FRIED" CHICKEN

For this healthier version of fried chicken, skinless chicken pieces are dipped in a spicy bread-crumb coating and baked until crispy and golden brown. You won't miss the calories.

ACTIVE TIME: 15 MIN · **TOTAL TIME:** 50 MIN

MAKES: 6 MAIN-DISH SERVINGS

½ CUP PLAIN DRIED BREAD CRUMBS

¼ CUP FRESHLY GRATED PARMESAN CHEESE

2 TABLESPOONS CORNMEAL

½ TEASPOON GROUND RED PEPPER (CAYENNE)

1 LARGE EGG WHITE

½ TEASPOON SALT

1 CHICKEN (3½ POUNDS), CUT INTO 8 PIECES AND SKIN REMOVED FROM ALL BUT WINGS

1 Preheat oven to 425°F. Grease 15½" by 10½" jelly-roll pan with olive oil nonstick cooking spray.

2 On waxed paper, combine bread crumbs, Parmesan, cornmeal, and ground red pepper. In pie plate, beat egg white and salt.

3 Dip each piece of chicken in egg-white mixture, then coat with crumb mixture, firmly pressing so mixture adheres. Arrange chicken in prepared pan; lightly coat chicken with cooking spray.

4 Bake chicken until coating is crisp and golden brown and juices run clear when thickest part of chicken is pierced with tip of knife, about 35 minutes.

EACH SERVING: ABOUT 329 CALORIES (25 PERCENT CALORIES FROM FAT) | 46G PROTEIN | 14G CARBOHYDRATE | 9G FAT (3G SATURATED) | 137MG CHOLESTEROL | 660MG SODIUM

ROASTED TANDOORI-STYLE CHICKEN BREASTS

Plain yogurt tenderizes the chicken, while the exotic spices add plenty of flavor.

ACTIVE TIME: 10 MIN · **TOTAL TIME:** 40 MIN PLUS MARINATING
MAKES: 6 MAIN-DISH SERVINGS

2	LIMES	1	TEASPOON GROUND CORIANDER
1	CONTAINER (8 OUNCES) PLAIN LOW-FAT YOGURT	¾	TEASPOON SALT
½	SMALL ONION, CHOPPED	¼	TEASPOON GROUND RED PEPPER (CAYENNE)
1	TABLESPOON MINCED, PEELED FRESH GINGER		PINCH GROUND CLOVES
1	TABLESPOON PAPRIKA	6	MEDIUM BONE-IN CHICKEN BREAST HALVES (3 POUNDS), SKIN REMOVED
1	TEASPOON GROUND CUMIN		

1 From 1 lime, squeeze 2 tablespoons juice. Cut remaining lime into 6 wedges; set aside for garnish. In blender, puree lime juice, yogurt, onion, ginger, paprika, cumin, coriander, salt, ground red pepper, and cloves until smooth. Place chicken and yogurt marinade in medium bowl or in ziptight plastic bag, turning to coat chicken. Cover bowl or seal bag and refrigerate chicken 30 minutes to marinate.

2 Preheat oven to 450°F. Arrange chicken on rack in medium roasting pan (14" by 10"). Spoon half of marinade over chicken; discard remaining marinade.

3 Roast chicken until juices run clear when thickest part of chicken is pierced with tip of knife, about 30 minutes.

4 Transfer chicken to warm platter; garnish with lime wedges to serve.

EACH SERVING: ABOUT 197 CALORIES (14 PERCENT CALORIES FROM FAT) | 36G PROTEIN | 5G CARBOHYDRATE | 3G TOTAL FAT (1G SATURATED) | 88MG CHOLESTEROL | 415MG SODIUM

CHICKEN PROVENÇAL

A melt-in-your-mouth stew flavored with orange peel and fennel seed.

ACTIVE TIME: 30 MIN · **TOTAL TIME:** 1 HR 30 MIN
MAKES: 8 MAIN-DISH SERVINGS

2 TEASPOONS OLIVE OIL

2 POUNDS SKINLESS, BONELESS CHICKEN THIGHS, CUT INTO QUARTERS

¾ TEASPOON SALT

2 MEDIUM RED PEPPERS, CUT INTO ¼-INCH-THICK SLICES

1 MEDIUM YELLOW PEPPER, CUT INTO ¼-INCH-THICK SLICES

1 JUMBO ONION (1 POUND), THINLY SLICED

3 GARLIC CLOVES, CRUSHED WITH GARLIC PRESS

1 CAN (28 OUNCES) ITALIAN-STYLE PLUM TOMATOES

¼ TEASPOON DRIED THYME LEAVES

¼ TEASPOON FENNEL SEEDS, CRUSHED

3 STRIPS (3" BY 1" EACH) ORANGE PEEL

½ CUP LOOSELY PACKED FRESH BASIL LEAVES, CHOPPED

1 In nonstick 5-quart Dutch oven, heat 1 teaspoon oil over medium-high heat until very hot. Add half of chicken and ¼ teaspoon salt; cook, turning the pieces, until lightly browned on all sides, about 10 minutes. Transfer chicken to plate. Repeat with remaining oil, chicken, and ¼ teaspoon salt.
2 To drippings in Dutch oven, add red peppers, yellow peppers, onion, and remaining ¼ teaspoon salt; cook, stirring frequently, until vegetables are tender and lightly browned, about 20 minutes. Add garlic; cook 1 minute.
3 Return chicken to Dutch oven. Add tomatoes with their juice, thyme, fennel seeds, and orange peel, breaking up tomatoes with side of spoon; heat to boiling. Reduce heat to low; cover and simmer until chicken loses its pink color throughout, about 15 minutes. Sprinkle with basil to serve.

EACH SERVING: ABOUT 200 CALORIES (27 PERCENT CALORIES FROM FAT) | 25G PROTEIN | 13G CARBOHYDRATE | 6G TOTAL FAT (1G SATURATED) | 94MG CHOLESTEROL | 460MG SODIUM

BAKED HONEY-MUSTARD CHICKEN AND VEGETABLES

The beauty of this flavor-packed dinner? It all cooks in the oven at the same time.

ACTIVE TIME: 10 MIN · **TOTAL TIME:** 1 HR
MAKES: 4 MAIN-DISH SERVINGS

1½ POUNDS SMALL RED POTATOES, QUARTERED

1 JUMBO ONION (1 POUND), CUT INTO EIGHTHS

6 TEASPOONS OLIVE OIL

¾ TEASPOON SALT

¼ TEASPOON COARSELY GROUND BLACK PEPPER

4 MEDIUM BONE-IN CHICKEN BREAST HALVES (2½ POUNDS), SKIN REMOVED

2 TABLESPOONS HONEY MUSTARD

1 Preheat oven to 450°F. In 13" by 9" metal baking pan, toss potatoes and onion with 4 teaspoons oil, salt, and pepper. Place pan in oven on middle rack and bake 25 minutes.

2 Meanwhile, place chicken breasts in small roasting pan and coat with 1 teaspoon oil. In cup, mix remaining 1 teaspoon oil with honey mustard; set aside.

3 After vegetables have baked 25 minutes, remove pan from oven and carefully turn vegetables with metal spatula. Return vegetables to oven, placing pan on lower oven rack. Place chicken on upper rack. Bake 10 minutes.

4 Remove chicken from oven and brush with honey-mustard mixture. Return to oven and bake until juices run clear when thickest part of chicken is pierced with tip of knife and vegetables are golden, 12 to 15 minutes longer. Serve chicken with vegetables.

EACH SERVING: ABOUT 380 CALORIES (24 PERCENT CALORIES FROM FAT) | 31G PROTEIN | 44G CARBOHYDRATE | 10G TOTAL FAT (1G SATURATED) | 66MG CHOLESTEROL | 630MG SODIUM

CHICKEN BREASTS WITH VEGETABLE RIBBONS

A quick sprinkle of lemon peel, garlic, and parsley adds a burst of flavor and an elegant touch.

ACTIVE TIME: 15 MIN · **TOTAL TIME:** 40 MIN
MAKES: 4 MAIN-DISH SERVINGS

4 MEDIUM SKINLESS, BONELESS CHICKEN BREAST HALVES (1¼ POUNDS)	1 TABLESPOON OLIVE OIL
½ TEASPOON SALT	3 MEDIUM CARROTS, PEELED
¼ TEASPOON COARSELY GROUND BLACK PEPPER	2 MEDIUM ZUCCHINIS (1 POUND)
	¾ CUP CHICKEN BROTH
2 GARLIC CLOVES, FINELY CHOPPED	½ CUP WATER
2 TEASPOONS FRESHLY GRATED LEMON PEEL	1 CUP LOOSELY PACKED FRESH PARSLEY LEAVES, CHOPPED

1 Sprinkle chicken with ¼ teaspoon salt and the pepper. In cup, mix garlic, lemon peel, and remaining ¼ teaspoon salt; set aside.

2 In nonstick 12-inch skillet, heat oil over medium-high heat until very hot. Add chicken and cook 6 minutes. Reduce heat to medium; turn chicken over and cook until chicken is golden brown and loses its pink color throughout, 6 to 8 minutes longer. Transfer chicken to platter; sprinkle with garlic mixture and keep warm.

3 Meanwhile, with sharp vegetable peeler, peel carrots lengthwise into wide, thin strips. Repeat with zucchini.

4 In same skillet, heat broth and water to boiling over high heat. Reduce heat to medium-low and add carrots; cover and cook 3 minutes. Add zucchini; cover and cook until vegetables are just tender, 5 to 7 minutes longer. Stir in all but 1 tablespoon parsley.

5 To serve, spoon vegetable ribbons and broth onto 4 dinner plates; top with chicken. Sprinkle with remaining parsley.

EACH SERVING: ABOUT 240 CALORIES (23 PERCENT CALORIES FROM FAT) | 36G PROTEIN | 10G CARBOHYDRATE | 6G TOTAL FAT (1G SATURATED) | 82MG CHOLESTEROL | 530MG SODIUM

SKILLET LEMON CHICKEN

Impressive enough to serve to guests. Steam up a bunch of fresh spring asparagus to serve alongside.

ACTIVE TIME: 15 MIN · **TOTAL TIME:** 25 MIN

MAKES: 4 MAIN-DISH SERVINGS

- 4 MEDIUM SKINLESS, BONELESS CHICKEN BREAST HALVES (1¼ POUNDS)
- ½ TEASPOON SALT
- 2 TEASPOONS OLIVE OIL
- 3 GARLIC CLOVES, CRUSHED WITH SIDE OF CHEF'S KNIFE
- ½ CUP FAT-FREE CHICKEN BROTH
- ¼ CUP DRY WHITE WINE
- 2 TABLESPOONS FRESH LEMON JUICE
- 1½ TEASPOONS ALL-PURPOSE FLOUR
- 2 TEASPOONS BUTTER OR MARGARINE
- ½ LEMON, THINLY SLICED

1 With meat mallet, or between 2 sheets of plastic wrap or waxed paper with rolling pin, pound chicken breast halves to ¼-inch thickness. Sprinkle with salt.

2 In nonstick 12-inch skillet, heat oil over medium-high heat until very hot. Add chicken; cook 6 minutes. Reduce heat to medium; turn chicken over and cook until chicken is golden brown and loses its pink color throughout, 5 to 8 minutes longer. Transfer chicken to platter and keep warm.

3 Add garlic to skillet; cook until golden. In cup, with fork, mix broth, wine, lemon juice, and flour until smooth; stir into mixture in skillet and heat to boiling. Boil 1 minute. Stir in margarine. Discard garlic. Pour sauce over chicken and top with lemon slices.

EACH SERVING: ABOUT 205 CALORIES (26 PERCENT CALORIES FROM FAT) | 33G PROTEIN | 2G CARBOHYDRATE | 6G TOTAL FAT (4G SATURATED) | 98MG CHOLESTEROL | 462MG SODIUM

TIP Wine adds fat-free flavor and body to quick pan sauces, stews, and poached fruit desserts. Because the success of the dish is determined by the quality of its ingredients, it is important to cook with good wine. Avoid the cooking wines sold in supermarkets; they're high in salt and low in flavor.

ARROZ CON POLLO

From Santiago to Miami to Madrid, different versions of this comforting chicken-and-rice dish are served almost everywhere Spanish is spoken.

ACTIVE TIME: 15 MIN · **TOTAL TIME:** 55 MIN
MAKES: 4 MAIN-DISH SERVINGS

1	TABLESPOON VEGETABLE OIL	¼	CUP WATER
6	MEDIUM BONE-IN CHICKEN THIGHS (1½ POUNDS), SKIN AND FAT REMOVED	1	STRIP (3" BY ½") LEMON PEEL
		¼	TEASPOON DRIED OREGANO
1	MEDIUM ONION, FINELY CHOPPED	¼	TEASPOON SALT
1	RED PEPPER, CHOPPED	1	CUP FROZEN PEAS
1	GARLIC CLOVE, FINELY CHOPPED	¼	CUP CHOPPED PIMIENTO-STUFFED OLIVES (SALAD OLIVES)
⅛	TEASPOON GROUND RED PEPPER (CAYENNE)	¼	CUP CHOPPED FRESH CILANTRO
1	CUP REGULAR LONG-GRAIN RICE		LEMON WEDGES
1	CAN (14½ OUNCES) CHICKEN BROTH OR 1¾ CUPS HOMEMADE		

1 In 5-quart Dutch oven, heat oil over medium-high heat until very hot. Add chicken, in batches, and cook until golden brown, about 5 minutes per side. Transfer chicken pieces to bowl as they are browned.
2 Reduce heat to medium. Add onion and red pepper to Dutch oven and cook until tender, about 5 minutes. Stir in garlic and ground red pepper and cook 30 seconds. Add rice and cook, stirring, 1 minute. Stir in broth, water, lemon peel, oregano, salt, and chicken; heat to boiling. Reduce heat; cover and simmer until juices run clear when thickest part of chicken is pierced with tip of knife, about 20 minutes.
3 Stir in peas; cover and heat through. Remove from heat and let stand 5 minutes. Sprinkle with olives and cilantro; serve with lemon wedges.

EACH SERVING: ABOUT 387 CALORIES (21 PERCENT CALORIES FROM FAT) | 26G PROTEIN | 48G CARBOHYDRATE | 9G TOTAL FAT (2G SATURATED) | 81MG CHOLESTEROL | 927MG SODIUM

CHICKEN CORDON BLEU

An elegant entrée made more healthful—and easier. Sautéed chicken breasts are topped with sliced ham and mozzarella and served on a bed of baby spinach.

ACTIVE TIME: 10 MIN · **TOTAL TIME:** 25 MIN

MAKES: 4 MAIN-DISH SERVINGS

1   TEASPOON BUTTER OR MARGARINE

4   SMALL SKINLESS, BONELESS CHICKEN BREAST HALVES (1 POUND)

½   CUP FAT-FREE CHICKEN BROTH

2   TABLESPOONS BALSAMIC VINEGAR

⅛   TEASPOON COARSELY GROUND BLACK PEPPER

4   THIN SLICES COOKED HAM (2 OUNCES)

4   THIN SLICES PART-SKIM MOZZARELLA CHEESE (2 OUNCES)

1   BAG (5 TO 6 OUNCES) PREWASHED BABY SPINACH

1   In nonstick 12-inch skillet, melt magarine over medium-high heat until hot. Add chicken and cook 5 minutes. Reduce heat to medium and turn chicken over; cover and cook until chicken is golden brown and just loses its pink color throughout, about 5 minutes longer.

2   Increase heat to medium-high. Stir in broth, vinegar, and pepper; cook, uncovered, 1 minute. Remove skillet from heat; top each chicken breast with a slice of ham, then a slice of cheese. Cover skillet until cheese melts, about 3 minutes.

3   Arrange spinach on large platter; top with chicken breasts and drizzle with pan sauce.

EACH SERVING: ABOUT 210 CALORIES (26 PERCENT CALORIES FROM FAT) | 34G PROTEIN | 5G CARBOHYDRATE | 6G TOTAL FAT (4G SATURATED) | 91MG CHOLESTEROL | 551MG SODIUM

JAMAICAN JERK CHICKEN KABOBS

Originally, jerk seasoning was only used to season pork shoulder, which was "jerked" apart into shreds before serving. Nowadays, this very popular power-packed seasoning rub is enjoyed on fish and chicken as well.

ACTIVE TIME: 15 MIN · **TOTAL TIME:** 25 MIN PLUS MARINATING

MAKES: 4 MAIN-DISH SERVINGS

2 GREEN ONIONS, CHOPPED	1 TEASPOON GROUND ALLSPICE
1 JALAPEÑO CHILE, SEEDED AND FINELY CHOPPED	1 TEASPOON DRIED THYME
	½ TEASPOON PLUS ⅛ TEASPOON SALT
1 TABLESPOON MINCED, PEELED FRESH GINGER	1 POUND SKINLESS, BONELESS CHICKEN BREAST HALVES, CUT INTO 12 PIECES
2 TABLESPOONS WHITE WINE VINEGAR	1 RED PEPPER, CUT INTO 1-INCH PIECES
2 TABLESPOONS WORCESTERSHIRE SAUCE	1 GREEN PEPPER, CUT INTO 1-INCH PIECES
3 TEASPOONS VEGETABLE OIL	4 METAL SKEWERS

1 In blender or in food processor with knife blade attached, process green onions, jalapeño, ginger, vinegar, Worcestershire, 2 teaspoons oil, allspice, thyme, and ½ teaspoon salt until paste forms.

2 Place chicken in small bowl or in ziptight plastic bag and add green-onion mixture, turning to coat chicken. Cover bowl or seal bag and refrigerate chicken 1 hour to marinate.

3 Meanwhile, in small bowl, toss red and green peppers with remaining 1 teaspoon oil and remaining ⅛ teaspoon salt.

4 Preheat broiler. Alternately thread chicken and pepper pieces onto skewers.

5 Place kabobs on rack in broiling pan. Brush kabobs with any remaining marinade. Place pan in broiler at closest position to heat source. Broil kabobs 5 minutes; turn and broil until chicken loses its pink color throughout, about 5 minutes longer.

EACH SERVING: ABOUT 181 CALORIES (25 PERCENT CALORIES FROM FAT) | 27G PROTEIN | 6G CARBOHYDRATE | 5G TOTAL FAT (1G SATURATED) | 66MG CHOLESTEROL | 525MG SODIUM

THAI CHICKEN WITH BASIL

The essence of Thai cooking, the blending of cool and hot flavors, such as cilantro, basil, ginger, garlic, and chiles, lends an exotic touch to this stir-fry.

ACTIVE TIME: 20 MIN · **TOTAL TIME:** 30 MIN PLUS MARINATING

MAKES: 4 MAIN-DISH SERVINGS

1 POUND SKINLESS, BONELESS CHICKEN BREAST HALVES

3 TABLESPOONS ASIAN FISH SAUCE (SEE TIP PAGE 199)

1 TABLESPOON SOY SAUCE

1 TABLESPOON BROWN SUGAR

2 TEASPOONS VEGETABLE OIL

1 LARGE ONION (12 OUNCES), CUT INTO ¼-INCH-THICK SLICES

2 RED OR GREEN CHILES (SERRANO OR JALAPEÑO), SEEDED AND CUT INTO MATCHSTICK STRIPS

2 TEASPOONS MINCED, PEELED FRESH GINGER

2 GARLIC CLOVES, CRUSHED WITH GARLIC PRESS

1½ CUPS LOOSELY PACKED FRESH BASIL LEAVES

1 Holding knife almost parallel to cutting surface, cut each chicken breast half crosswise into ¼-inch-thick slices. In medium bowl, combine fish sauce, soy sauce, and brown sugar; add chicken slices, tossing to coat. Let marinate 5 minutes.

2 In nonstick 12-inch skillet, heat oil over medium-high heat until very hot. Add the chicken with marinade and cook, stirring frequently (stir-frying), until chicken loses its pink color throughout, 3 to 4 minutes. With slotted spoon, transfer chicken to bowl.

3 Add onion to marinade remaining in skillet and cook, stir-frying, until tender-crisp, about 4 minutes. Stir in chiles, ginger, and garlic; cook 1 minute longer.

4 Return chicken to skillet; heat through. Stir in basil leaves just before serving.

EACH SERVING: ABOUT 238 CALORIES (19 PERCENT CALORIES FROM FAT) | 3G PROTEIN | 16G CARBOHYDRATE | 5G TOTAL FAT (1G SATURATED) | 66MG CHOLESTEROL | 784MG SODIUM

GRILLED CHICKEN BREASTS WITH PLUM SALSA

Here's a quick dish that turns ordinary chicken into the specialty of the house. (The plum salsa can also be used to spice up plain fish and seafood dishes.)

ACTIVE TIME: 20 MIN · **TOTAL TIME:** 30 MIN PLUS MARINATING

MAKES: 4 MAIN-DISH SERVINGS

---

2 TABLESPOONS SEASONED RICE VINEGAR

½ TEASPOON SALT

⅛ TEASPOON COARSELY GROUND BLACK PEPPER

4 MEDIUM SKINLESS, BONELESS CHICKEN BREAST HALVES (1¼ POUNDS)

1 POUND RIPE PURPLE AND/OR GREEN PLUMS (4 MEDIUM), CHOPPED

¼ CUP FINELY CHOPPED RED ONION

¼ CUP FINELY CHOPPED YELLOW PEPPER

¼ CUP LOOSELY PACKED FRESH CILANTRO LEAVES, FINELY CHOPPED

1 JALAPEÑO CHILE, SEEDED AND FINELY CHOPPED

MIXED BABY GREENS (OPTIONAL)

1 In pie plate, with wire whisk or fork, combine vinegar, salt, and black pepper. Spoon half of vinegar mixture into medium bowl. Add chicken breasts to mixture in pie plate, turning to coat. Cover and refrigerate 30 minutes to marinate, turning occasionally.

2 Meanwhile, prepare grill and spray grill rack (away from heat source) with nonstick cooking spray. Prepare the plum salsa: Stir plums, red onion, yellow pepper, cilantro, and jalapeño into vinegar mixture in bowl. Set plum salsa aside.

3 Place chicken breasts on grill over medium heat; discard marinade in pie plate. Grill chicken, turning once, until chicken loses its pink color throughout, 10 to 12 minutes. (If using a grill pan, spray pan with nonstick cooking spray and heat over medium heat until hot but not smoking. Add chicken breasts and cook, turning once, until chicken loses its pink color throughout, 10 to 12 minutes.)

4 To serve, place chicken on a bed of mixed baby greens if you like, and spoon plum salsa on top.

EACH SERVING: ABOUT 245 CALORIES (15 PERCENT CALORIES FROM FAT) | 36G PROTEIN | 14G CARBOHYDRATE | 4G TOTAL FAT (1G SATURATED) | 96MG CHOLESTEROL | 550MG SODIUM

TORTILLA CHICKEN TENDERS WITH EASY CORN SALSA

ACTIVE TIME: 15 MIN · **TOTAL TIME:** 25 MIN

MAKES: 4 MAIN-DISH SERVINGS

2   OUNCES BAKED TORTILLA CHIPS

2   TEASPOONS CHILI POWDER

¼   TEASPOON SALT

OLIVE OIL NONSTICK COOKING SPRAY

1   POUND CHICKEN TENDERS

2   EARS CORN, HUSKS AND SILK REMOVED

1   JAR (11 TO 12 OUNCES) MILD SALSA

¼   CUP LOOSELY PACKED FRESH CILANTRO LEAVES, CHOPPED

LIME WEDGES

1   Place tortilla chips in ziptight plastic bag. Crush chips with rolling pin to fine crumbs (you should have about ½ cup crumbs). On waxed paper, combine tortilla-chip crumbs, chili powder, and salt; set aside.

2   Preheat oven to 450°F. Spray 15½" by 10½" jelly-roll pan with olive oil spray. Place chicken tenders in medium bowl; spray with olive oil spray, tossing to coat well. Roll chicken in tortilla crumbs to coat; place in jelly-roll pan and spray again.

3   Bake chicken until it loses its pink color throughout, about 10 minutes.

4   Meanwhile, prepare corn salsa: Cut corn kernels from cobs; place in small bowl. Stir in salsa and cilantro until blended.

5   Serve chicken with corn salsa and lime wedges.

EACH SERVING: ABOUT 245 CALORIES (11 PERCENT CALORIES FROM FAT) | 30G PROTEIN | 24G CARBOHYDRATE | 3G TOTAL FAT (0G SATURATED) | 66MG CHOLESTEROL | 685MG SODIUM

CHICKEN BREASTS WITH CUMIN, CORIANDER, AND LIME

An exotic blend of spices and lime juice adds instant flavor to boneless chicken breasts.

ACTIVE TIME: 10 MIN · **TOTAL TIME:** 20 MIN

MAKES: 4 MAIN-DISH SERVINGS

---

3   TABLESPOONS FRESH LIME JUICE (ABOUT 2 LIMES)

1   TEASPOON GROUND CUMIN

1   TEASPOON GROUND CORIANDER

1   TEASPOON SUGAR

1   TEASPOON SALT

⅛   TEASPOON GROUND RED PEPPER (CAYENNE)

4   SMALL SKINLESS, BONELESS CHICKEN BREAST HALVES (1 POUND)

1   TABLESPOON CHOPPED FRESH CILANTRO LEAVES

1 In large bowl, mix lime juice, cumin, coriander, sugar, salt, and ground red pepper; add chicken, tossing to coat.

2 Spray grill pan or cast-iron skillet with nonstick cooking spray; heat over medium-high heat until hot but not smoking. Add chicken and cook until chicken loses its pink color throughout, 5 to 6 minutes per side. Turn chicken once and brush with any remaining cumin mixture halfway through cooking. Place chicken breasts on platter; sprinkle with cilantro.

EACH SERVING: ABOUT 150 CALORIES (18 PERCENT CALORIES FROM FAT) | 27G PROTEIN | 3G CARBOHYDRATE | 3G TOTAL FAT (1G SATURATED) | 72MG CHOLESTEROL | 600MG SODIUM

MOULES À LA MARINIÈRE

This is the way French cooks like to serve mussels. Use a crisp white wine, such as sauvignon blanc, or a dry vermouth, which adds extra flavor because of the herbs used in the distillation process.

ACTIVE TIME: 20 MIN · **TOTAL TIME:** 35 MIN
MAKES: 4 MAIN-DISH SERVINGS

1½ CUPS DRY WHITE WINE OR DRY VERMOUTH

⅓ CUP FINELY CHOPPED SHALLOTS OR RED ONION

2 GARLIC CLOVES, FINELY CHOPPED

1 TABLESPOON BUTTER OR OLIVE OIL

½ TEASPOON SALT

PINCH GROUND BLACK PEPPER

4 POUNDS MUSSELS, PREFERABLY CULTIVATED, SCRUBBED AND DEBEARDED

¼ CUP CHOPPED FRESH PARSLEY

1 In nonreactive 5-quart Dutch oven, combine wine, shallots, garlic, butter, salt, and pepper; heat to boiling over high heat. Boil 2 minutes.
2 Add mussels; heat to boiling. Reduce heat; cover and simmer until mussels open, about 5 minutes, transferring mussels to large bowl as they open. Discard any mussels that do not open. Pour mussel broth over mussels and sprinkle with parsley.

EACH SERVING: ABOUT 212 CALORIES (25 PERCENT CALORIES FROM FAT) | 16G PROTEIN | 9G CARBOHYDRATE | 6G TOTAL FAT (2G SATURATED) | 45MG CHOLESTEROL | 703MG SODIUM

CRAB BOIL

A big pot of spiced boiled crabs, a Chesapeake Bay tradition, is a delicious but messy affair. Cover the table with newspaper and have lots of large napkins on hand. Serve with coleslaw and rolls. (If you want to cook crab so you can use the meat for another recipe, omit the crab boil seasoning and red pepper.)

ACTIVE TIME: 5 MIN · **TOTAL TIME:** 45 MIN
MAKES: 4 MAIN-DISH SERVINGS

2	MEDIUM ONIONS, COARSELY CHOPPED	1	TABLESPOON CRUSHED RED PEPPER
1	CARROT, PEELED AND COARSELY CHOPPED	1	TABLESPOON SALT
1	STALK CELERY, COARSELY CHOPPED	1	GALLON (16 CUPS) WATER
1	LEMON, SLICED	1	CAN OR BOTTLE (12 OUNCES) BEER
½	CUP CRAB BOIL SEASONING	2	DOZEN LIVE HARD-SHELL BLUE CRABS, RINSED

1 In 12-quart stockpot, combine onions, carrot, celery, lemon, crab boil seasoning, crushed red pepper, salt, water, and beer. Heat to boiling over high heat; cook 15 minutes.

2 Using tongs, transfer crabs to stockpot. Cover and heat to boiling. Boil 5 minutes (crabs will turn red). With tongs, transfer crabs to colander to drain, then place on platter.

3 To eat crab, twist off claws and legs, then crack shell to remove meat. Break off flat pointed apron from underside of crab; remove top shell. Discard feathery gills. With kitchen shears or hands, break body in half down center. With fingers or lobster pick, remove meat.

EACH SERVING: ABOUT 123 CALORIES (15 PERCENT CALORIES FROM FAT) | 24G PROTEIN | 0G CARBOHYDRATE | 2G TOTAL FAT (0G SATURATED) | 119MG CHOLESTEROL | 1,410MG SODIUM

JAMAICAN JERK SNAPPER WITH GRILLED PINEAPPLE

Other fish fillets like sole and flounder would also work well with these zesty flavors.

ACTIVE TIME: 15 MIN · **TOTAL TIME:** 25 MIN

MAKES: 4 MAIN-DISH SERVINGS

- 2 GREEN ONIONS, CHOPPED
- 1 JALAPEÑO CHILE, SEEDED AND CHOPPED
- 2 TABLESPOONS WHITE WINE VINEGAR
- 2 TABLESPOONS WORCESTERSHIRE SAUCE
- 1 TABLESPOON MINCED, PEELED FRESH GINGER
- 1 TABLESPOON VEGETABLE OIL
- 1¼ TEASPOONS DRIED THYME
- 1 TEASPOON GROUND ALLSPICE
- ¼ TEASPOON SALT
- 4 RED SNAPPER FILLETS (5 OUNCES EACH)
- 1 SMALL PINEAPPLE, CUT LENGTHWISE INTO 4 WEDGES OR CROSSWISE INTO ½-INCH-THICK SLICES
- 2 TABLESPOONS BROWN SUGAR

1 Prepare grill. In medium bowl, mix green onions, jalapeño chile, vinegar, Worcestershire, ginger, oil, thyme, allspice, and salt until combined. Add snapper fillets to bowl, turning to coat; let stand 5 minutes.

2 Meanwhile, rub pineapple wedges or slices with brown sugar.

3 Place pineapple and snapper on grill over medium heat. Spoon half of jerk mixture remaining in bowl on snapper. Grill pineapple and snapper 5 minutes, then turn over. Spoon remaining jerk mixture on fish and grill until fish is just opaque throughout and pineapple is golden brown, 5 to 7 minutes longer.

EACH SERVING: ABOUT 280 CALORIES (26 PERCENT CALORIES FROM FAT) | 24G PROTEIN | 25G CARBOHYDRATE | 8G TOTAL FAT (1G SATURATED) | 52MG CHOLESTEROL | 305MG SODIUM

SHRIMP AND SCALLOP KABOBS

One word of advice: Don't let the shellfish sit in the soy and rice vinegar mixture for more than a minute or two. The vinegar will firm and "cook" the flesh.

ACTIVE TIME: 20 MIN · **TOTAL TIME:** 26 MIN

MAKES: 6 MAIN-DISH SERVINGS

---

12 OUNCES LARGE SEA SCALLOPS

1 POUND LARGE SHRIMP, SHELLED AND DEVEINED, LEAVING TAIL PART OF SHELL ON, IF YOU LIKE

3 TABLESPOONS SOY SAUCE

3 TABLESPOONS SEASONED RICE VINEGAR

1 TABLESPOON ASIAN SESAME OIL

2 TABLESPOONS GRATED, PEELED FRESH GINGER

2 GARLIC CLOVES, CRUSHED WITH GARLIC PRESS

1 TABLESPOON BROWN SUGAR

1 BUNCH GREEN ONIONS, CUT ON DIAGONAL INTO 3-INCH PIECES

12 CHERRY TOMATOES

6 LONG METAL SKEWERS

1 Prepare grill. Pull off and discard tough crescent-shaped muscle from each scallop. Pat shrimp and scallops dry with paper towels.

2 In large bowl, combine soy sauce, vinegar, sesame oil, ginger, garlic, and brown sugar. Add shrimp and scallops, tossing to coat.

3 Alternately thread shrimp, scallops, green-onion pieces, and cherry tomatoes onto skewers. Place skewers on grill over medium heat and grill, turning skewers occasionally and brushing shrimp and scallops with any remaining soy-sauce mixture during first half of cooking, until shrimp and scallops are just opaque throughout, 6 to 8 minutes.

EACH SERVING: ABOUT 168 CALORIES (21 PERCENT CALORIES FROM FAT) | 23G PROTEIN | 9G CARBOHYDRATE | 4G TOTAL FAT (1G SATURATED) | 112MG CHOLESTEROL | 851MG SODIUM

GRILLED THAI SNAPPER PACKETS

Grilling snapper fillets in foil packets keeps the meat intact, and Thai seasonings give the fish a distinctive Asian flavor.

ACTIVE TIME: 25 MIN · **TOTAL TIME:** 33 MIN

MAKES: 4 MAIN-DISH SERVINGS

---

3 TABLESPOONS FRESH LIME JUICE

1 TABLESPOON ASIAN FISH SAUCE (SEE TIP PAGE 199)

1 TABLESPOON OLIVE OIL

1 TEASPOON GRATED, PEELED FRESH GINGER

1 SMALL GARLIC CLOVE, FINELY CHOPPED

½ TEASPOON SUGAR

4 RED SNAPPER FILLETS (6 OUNCES EACH)

1 LARGE CARROT, PEELED AND CUT INTO 2¼" BY ¼" MATCHSTICK STRIPS

1 LARGE GREEN ONION, THINLY SLICED

¼ CUP TIGHTLY PACKED FRESH CILANTRO

1 Prepare grill. In small bowl, with wire whisk, whisk lime juice, fish sauce, oil, ginger, garlic, and sugar. With tweezers, remove any bones from snapper fillets.

2 From roll of foil, cut four 16" by 12" sheets. Fold each sheet crosswise in half, then open up like a book.

3 Place 1 snapper fillet, skin side down, on one half of each piece of foil. Evenly sprinkle fillets with carrot, green onion, and cilantro; drizzle with lime-juice mixture. Fold unfilled half of foil over fish. To seal, fold and crimp edges of foil all around.

4 Place packets on grill over medium heat; grill 8 minutes. To serve, cut packets open.

EACH SERVING: ABOUT 228 CALORIES (24 PERCENT CALORIES FROM FAT) | 36G PROTEIN | 5G CARBOHYDRATE | 6G TOTAL FAT (1G SATURATED) | 63MG CHOLESTEROL | 268MG SODIUM

TIP One type of polyunsaturated fat, omega-3, is thought to combat heart disease. Omega-3s help inhibit the formation of blood clots and reduce the incidence of heartbeat abnormalities. You'll find omega-3s in fish—and the oilier the fish (like salmon, mackerel, and sardines), the more omega-3 it contains.

BAKED SCROD WITH FENNEL AND POTATOES

A simple dish that needs only a green salad to become a complete meal.

ACTIVE TIME: 15 MIN · **TOTAL TIME:** 1 HR 10 MIN
MAKES: 4 MAIN-DISH SERVINGS

1½ POUNDS RED POTATOES (4 LARGE), THINLY SLICED

1 MEDIUM FENNEL BULB (1 POUND), TRIMMED AND THINLY SLICED, FEATHERY TOPS RESERVED

1 GARLIC CLOVE, FINELY CHOPPED

2 TABLESPOONS OLIVE OIL

¾ PLUS ⅛ TEASPOON SALT

½ TEASPOON COARSELY GROUND BLACK PEPPER

4 PIECES SCROD FILLET (5 OUNCES EACH)

1 LARGE RIPE TOMATO (8 OUNCES), SEEDED AND CHOPPED

1 Preheat oven to 425°F. In shallow 2½-quart baking dish, toss potatoes, fennel, garlic, oil, ¾ teaspoon salt, and ¼ teaspoon pepper until well combined; spread evenly in baking dish. Bake, stirring once, until vegetables are tender and lightly browned, about 45 minutes.

2 With tweezers, remove any bones from scrod. Sprinkle scrod with remaining ⅛ teaspoon salt and remaining ¼ teaspoon pepper. Arrange on top of potato mixture. Bake until fish is just opaque throughout, 10 to 15 minutes. Sprinkle with tomato and garnish with reserved fennel tops.

EACH SERVING: ABOUT 335 CALORIES (21 PERCENT CALORIES FROM FAT) | 30G PROTEIN | 35G CARBOHYDRATE | 8G TOTAL FAT (1G SATURATED) | 61MG CHOLESTEROL | 679MG SODIUM

TIP Both fennel and anise are herbs of the carrot family, but anise has a sweeter, stronger licoricelike flavor. Fennel is cultivated for its bulb foliage, and its seeds. Look for pearly white fennel bulbs with no cracks or browning; you want them to be heavy for their size. The stalks should still be attached and have pale-green leaves.

MISO-GLAZED SALMON

Brian Hagiwara, one of *Good Housekeeping*'s favorite food photographers, shared this special recipe. We love the taste of the rich salmon with the sweet and savory glaze. Serve with a side of steamed rice.

ACTIVE TIME: 10 MIN · **TOTAL TIME:** 20 MIN
MAKES: 4 MAIN-DISH SERVINGS

¼ CUP WHITE MISO

5 TEASPOONS SUGAR

4 TEASPOONS SEASONED RICE VINEGAR

1 TABLESPOON WATER

2 TEASPOONS MINCED, PEELED FRESH GINGER

4 SALMON STEAKS, 1 INCH THICK (6 OUNCES EACH)

1 GREEN ONION, THINLY SLICED DIAGONALLY

1 Preheat broiler. Lightly spray rack in broiling pan with nonstick cooking spray.
2 In small bowl, mix miso, sugar, vinegar, water, and ginger; set aside.
3 Place salmon steaks on rack in broiling pan. Place pan in broiler at closest position to heat source; broil salmon 5 minutes. Remove pan from broiler and spread half of miso mixture on salmon; broil 1 minute longer.
4 Remove pan from broiler; turn salmon over and top with remaining miso mixture. Broil salmon until miso mixture is bubbly and salmon is opaque throughout, 3 to 4 minutes longer. Sprinkle with green onion before serving.

EACH SERVING: ABOUT 260 CALORIES (24 PERCENT CALORIES FROM FAT) | 35G PROTEIN | 13G CARBOHYDRATE | 7G TOTAL FAT (1G SATURATED) | 86MG CHOLESTEROL | 870MG SODIUM

EASY BARBECUED BEANS AND RICE

This vegetarian skillet dinner is especially good with a rich, smoky barbecue sauce.

ACTIVE TIME: 15 MIN · **TOTAL TIME:** 40 MIN

MAKES: 6 MAIN-DISH SERVINGS

¾ CUP REGULAR LONG-GRAIN RICE

1 TABLESPOON VEGETABLE OIL

1 MEDIUM GREEN PEPPER, CUT INTO ½-INCH PIECES

1 MEDIUM RED PEPPER, CUT INTO ½-INCH PIECES

1 MEDIUM ONION, CHOPPED

1 CAN (15 TO 19 OUNCES) BLACK BEANS, RINSED AND DRAINED

1 CAN (15 TO 19 OUNCES) RED KIDNEY BEANS, RINSED AND DRAINED

1 CAN (15 TO 19 OUNCES) GARBANZO BEANS, RINSED AND DRAINED

1 CAN (15 TO 16 OUNCES) PINK BEANS, RINSED AND DRAINED

1 CAN (14½ OUNCES) NO-SALT-ADDED STEWED TOMATOES

1 CUP WATER

½ CUP BOTTLED BARBECUE SAUCE

1 In 2-quart saucepan, prepare rice as label directs but do not add butter or margarine.

2 Meanwhile, in 12-inch skillet, heat oil over medium heat until hot. Add peppers and onion and cook, stirring, until tender. Add black beans, red kidney beans, garbanzo beans, pink beans, stewed tomatoes, water, and barbecue sauce; heat to boiling over high heat. Reduce heat to low; cover and simmer 15 minutes.

3 Spoon rice into center of beans. Before serving, stir to combine rice and bean mixture.

EACH SERVING: ABOUT 355 CALORIES (13 PERCENT CALORIES FROM FAT) | 16G PROTEIN | 61G CARBOHYDRATE | 5G TOTAL FAT (1G SATURATED) | 0MG CHOLESTEROL | 790MG SODIUM

CURRIED VEGETABLE STEW

Serve over brown rice for a healthful vegetarian meal.

ACTIVE TIME: 15 MIN · **TOTAL TIME:** 40 MIN

MAKES: 4 MAIN-DISH SERVINGS

2 TEASPOONS OLIVE OIL	1½ TEASPOONS CURRY POWDER
1 LARGE SWEET POTATO (12 OUNCES), PEELED AND CUT INTO ½-INCH PIECES	1 TEASPOON GROUND CUMIN
1 MEDIUM ONION, CUT INTO ½-INCH PIECES	1 CAN (15 TO 19 OUNCES) GARBANZO BEANS, RINSED AND DRAINED
1 MEDIUM ZUCCHINI (8 OUNCES), CUT INTO 1-INCH PIECES	1 CAN (14½ OUNCES) DICED TOMATOES
1 SMALL GREEN PEPPER, CUT INTO ¾-INCH PIECES	¾ CUP VEGETABLE BROTH
	½ TEASPOON SALT

1 In deep nonstick 12-inch skillet, heat oil over medium-high heat. Add sweet potato, onion, zucchini, and green pepper; cook, stirring, until vegetables are tender, 8 to 10 minutes. Add curry powder and cumin; cook 1 minute.

2 Add garbanzo beans, tomatoes with their juice, broth, and salt; heat to boiling over high heat. Reduce heat to medium-low; cover and simmer until vegetables are very tender but still hold their shape, about 10 minutes longer.

EACH SERVING: ABOUT 223 CALORIES (20 PERCENT CALORIES FROM FAT) | 8G PROTEIN | 39G CARBOHYDRATE | 5G TOTAL FAT (0G SATURATED) | 0MG CHOLESTEROL | 790MG SODIUM

WINTER VEGETABLE CHILI

Serve this black-bean chili with a stack of warmed tortillas.

ACTIVE TIME: 15 MIN · **TOTAL TIME:** 1 HR 30 MIN

MAKES: 6 MAIN-DISH SERVINGS

4 TEASPOONS OLIVE OIL	1 CAN (4 TO 4½ OUNCES) CHOPPED MILD GREEN CHILES
1 MEDIUM BUTTERNUT SQUASH (1¾ POUNDS), PEELED AND CUT INTO ¾-INCH PIECES	1 CUP VEGETABLE BROTH
2 CARROTS, PEELED AND CHOPPED	¼ TEASPOON SALT
1 MEDIUM ONION, CHOPPED	2 CANS (15 TO 19 OUNCES EACH) BLACK BEANS, RINSED AND DRAINED
3 TABLESPOONS CHILI POWDER	¼ CUP CHOPPED FRESH CILANTRO
1 CAN (28 OUNCES) PLUM TOMATOES	SOUR CREAM OR YOGURT (OPTIONAL)

1 In nonreactive 5-quart Dutch oven, heat 2 teaspoons oil over medium-high heat. Add squash; cook until golden. Transfer to bowl.

2 In same Dutch oven, heat remaining 2 teaspoons oil. Add carrots and onion; cook, stirring occasionally, until well browned. Stir in chili powder; cook, stirring, 1 minute. Add tomatoes with their juice, chiles with their liquid, broth, and salt. Heat to boiling over high heat, breaking up tomatoes with side of spoon. Reduce heat; cover and simmer 30 minutes.

3 Stir in beans and squash; heat to boiling over high heat. Reduce heat; cover and simmer until squash is tender and chili has thickened, about 15 minutes. Stir in cilantro. Serve with sour cream, if you like.

EACH SERVING: ABOUT 233 CALORIES (19 PERCENT CALORIES FROM FAT) | 9G PROTEIN | 42G CARBOHYDRATE | 5G TOTAL FAT (1G SATURATED) | 0MG CHOLESTEROL | 911MG SODIUM

VEGETABLE OMELET

More vegetables and fewer whole eggs make this a great healthy choice.

ACTIVE TIME: 30 MIN · **TOTAL TIME:** 42 MIN
MAKES: 4 MAIN-DISH SERVINGS

---

8 OUNCES RED POTATOES, CUT INTO ½-INCH PIECES

1 MEDIUM ONION, FINELY CHOPPED

1 MEDIUM RED PEPPER, CUT INTO ½-INCH PIECES

1 MEDIUM GREEN PEPPER, CUT INTO ½-INCH PIECES

1 SMALL ZUCCHINI (8 OUNCES), CUT INTO ½-INCH PIECES

1 TEASPOON SUGAR

¾ TEASPOON SALT

¼ TEASPOON COARSELY GROUND BLACK PEPPER

¼ CUP WATER

4 TABLESPOONS CHOPPED FRESH BASIL LEAVES

6 LARGE EGG WHITES

2 LARGE EGGS

½ CUP CRUMBLED FETA CHEESE (2 OUNCES)

1 In small saucepan, heat potatoes and enough water to cover to boiling over high heat. Reduce heat to low; cover and simmer until tender, about 10 minutes. Drain.

2 Spray nonstick 12-inch skillet with nonstick cooking spray. Add onion and cook over medium-high heat until golden. Add red pepper, green pepper, zucchini, sugar, salt, and black pepper and cook, stirring frequently, until vegetables are tender-crisp. Stir in water and heat to boiling. Reduce heat to low; cover and simmer until vegetables are tender, 10 minutes. Remove skillet from heat; stir in potatoes and 1 tablespoon basil.

3 Preheat oven to 375°F. In medium bowl, with wire whisk or fork, mix egg whites, eggs, ¼ cup crumbled feta, and remaining 3 tablespoons basil.

4 Spray oven-safe 10-inch skillet with nonstick cooking spray. (Wrap handle of skillet with double layer of foil if handle is not oven-safe.) Pour egg mixture into pan and cook over medium-high heat until egg mixture begins to set, 1 to 2 minutes. Remove skillet from heat. With slotted spoon, spread vegetable mixture over egg mixture in skillet; sprinkle with remaining ¼ cup crumbled feta. Bake omelet until set, 10 minutes. If you like, broil 1 to 2 minutes to brown top of omelet.

EACH SERVING: ABOUT 185 CALORIES (29 PERCENT CALORIES FROM FAT) | 13G PROTEIN | 20G CARBOHYDRATE | 6G TOTAL FAT (3G SATURATED) | 119MG CHOLESTEROL | 860MG SODIUM

CALIFORNIA FRITTATA

Mexican-style salsa, crisp jicama, and tortillas contribute a ton of California flavor. An egg substitute may be used instead of the eggs.

ACTIVE TIME: 30 MIN · **TOTAL TIME:** 1 HR 5 MIN

MAKES: 4 MAIN-DISH SERVINGS

- 2   TO 3 SMALL RED POTATOES (6½ OUNCES)
- 1   TABLESPOON OLIVE OIL
- 1½ CUPS THINLY SLICED ONIONS
- 1   ZUCCHINI (6 OUNCES), THINLY SLICED
- 1   CUP THINLY SLICED CREMINI MUSHROOMS
- 2   PLUM TOMATOES (6½ OUNCES), CORED, HALVED, AND THINLY SLICED
- ½   TEASPOON KOSHER SALT (OPTIONAL)
- ½   TEASPOON FRESHLY GROUND BLACK PEPPER
- 1   CUP SHREDDED SPINACH OR SWISS CHARD
- 1   TABLESPOON SLIVERED FRESH BASIL LEAVES (OPTIONAL)
- 2   LARGE EGGS
- 3   LARGE EGG WHITES
- 3   TABLESPOONS CRUMBLED FETA CHEESE (OPTIONAL)
- 2   TABLESPOONS CHOPPED FRESH FLAT-LEAF PARSLEY
- ¾   CUP BOTTLED SALSA
- 4   (6-INCH) CORN TORTILLAS
- ½   JICAMA (8 OUNCES), PEELED AND CUT INTO 2" BY ¼" MATCHSTICK STRIPS
- 2   TEASPOONS FRESH LIME JUICE

1 Preheat oven to 350°F. In saucepan, heat potatoes and enough water to cover to a boil over high heat. Reduce heat to low; cover and simmer until fork-tender, 15 to 20 minutes. Drain and cool. Cut into ¼-inch-thick slices.

2 In nonstick 10-inch oven-safe skillet, heat oil over medium heat. (Wrap handle of skillet with double layer of foil if handle is not oven-safe.) Add onions and cook until softened, about 5 minutes. Add potatoes, zucchini, mushrooms, and tomatoes; cook, stirring gently, until zucchini begins to soften, 2 to 3 minutes. Season with salt, if using, and pepper. Add spinach and basil, if using, and cook until spinach wilts, 1 to 2 minutes.

3 In medium bowl with wire whisk or fork, mix eggs and egg whites. With spatula, stir vegetables while pouring eggs into skillet. Transfer skillet to oven and bake until eggs are set, 3 to 5 minutes.

4 Sprinkle frittata with feta cheese, if using, and parsley. Cut frittata into 4 pieces and serve with salsa, tortillas, and jicama sticks sprinkled with lime juice.

EACH SERVING: ABOUT 265 CALORIES (24 PERCENT CALORIES FROM FAT) | 11G PROTEIN | 38G CARBOHYDRATE | 7G TOTAL FAT (1G SATURATED) | 106MG CHOLESTEROL | 140MG SODIUM

SOUTHWESTERN BLACK-BEAN BURGERS

To have handy for another meal, make a double batch and freeze the uncooked patties. Defrost for ten minutes, then cook burgers, turning once, until heated through, about twelve minutes.

ACTIVE TIME: 10 MIN · **TOTAL TIME:** 16 MIN

MAKES: 4 MAIN-DISH SERVINGS

---

1 CAN (15 TO 19 OUNCES) BLACK BEANS, RINSED AND DRAINED

2 TABLESPOONS LIGHT MAYONNAISE

¼ CUP PACKED FRESH CILANTRO LEAVES, CHOPPED

1 TABLESPOON PLAIN DRIED BREAD CRUMBS

½ TEASPOON GROUND CUMIN

½ TEASPOON HOT PEPPER SAUCE

NONSTICK COOKING SPRAY

1 CUP LOOSELY PACKED SLICED LETTUCE

4 MINI (4-INCH) WHOLE-WHEAT PITAS, WARMED

½ CUP BOTTLED MILD SALSA

1 In large bowl, with potato masher or fork, mash beans with mayonnaise until almost smooth (some lumps of beans should remain). Stir in cilantro, bread crumbs, cumin, and pepper sauce until combined. With lightly floured hands, shape bean mixture into four 3-inch round patties. Spray both sides of each patty lightly with nonstick cooking spray.

2 Heat nonstick 12-inch skillet over medium heat. Add patties and cook until lightly browned, about 3 minutes. With wide metal spatula, turn patties over and cook until heated through, 3 minutes longer.

3 Arrange lettuce on pitas; top with burgers, then salsa.

EACH SERVING: ABOUT 210 CALORIES (13 PERCENT CALORIES FROM FAT) | 13G PROTEIN | 42G CARBOHYDRATE | 3G TOTAL FAT (0G SATURATED) | 0MG CHOLESTEROL | 715MG SODIUM

DESSERTS

Everyone deserves to end a meal with a little something sweet—even those of us trying to keep things light. But you don't have to console yourself with a sweetened cup of tea or a sugar-free candy: You can eat healthy and still have dessert in style. You probably won't be surprised to find that our light and healthy desserts include plenty of fruit. It's the obvious way to end this type of meal, but that doesn't mean it has to be boring. Our recipes include a wide spectrum, including plums, apples, lemons, pears, peaches, raspberries, and dates, and you will be amazed at the variety of methods we use to prepare these delicious desserts.

We have chilly options, like pops and sherbet, and we walk you through several delicious varieties of granita and an unforgettable frozen chocolate mousse. We also cook up the fruit into streusel, cobbler, and compote, and work some magic at the stove with poaching.

If you're leaning toward something more decadent, you can bake up a batch of butterscotch blondies or fudgy brownies, or try something new with our tasty date bars. No matter what you choose, you'll enjoy digging into your dessert without an ounce of guilt.

Plum Yogurt Pops (page 460)

FAST BAKED APPLES WITH OATMEAL STREUSEL

Cooking apples in the microwave, rather than the regular oven, yields plumper, juicier, less shriveled fruit—and saves a big chunk of time!

ACTIVE TIME: 8 MIN · TOTAL TIME: 20 MIN
MAKES: 4 SERVINGS

---

4 LARGE ROME OR CORTLAND APPLES (10 OUNCES EACH)

¼ CUP PACKED BROWN SUGAR

¼ CUP QUICK-COOKING OATS, UNCOOKED

2 TABLESPOONS CHOPPED DATES

½ TEASPOON GROUND CINNAMON

2 TEASPOONS BUTTER OR MARGARINE

1 Core apples, cutting out a 1¼-inch-diameter cylinder from center of each, almost but not all the way through to bottom. Remove peel about one-third of the way down from top. Place apples in shallow 1½-quart ceramic casserole or 8" by 8" glass baking dish.

2 In small bowl, combine brown sugar, oats, dates, and cinnamon. Fill each cored apple with equal amounts of oat mixture. (Mixture will spill over top of apples.) Place ½ teaspoon margarine on top of filling in each apple.

3 Microwave apples, covered, on medium-high until tender, 12 to 14 minutes, turning each apple halfway through cooking time. Spoon cooking liquid from baking dish over apples to serve.

EACH SERVING: ABOUT 240 CALORIES (11 PERCENT CALORIES FROM FAT) | 2G PROTEIN | 54G CARBOHYDRATE | 3G TOTAL FAT (3G SATURATED) | 16MG CHOLESTEROL | 12MG SODIUM

LEMON-ANISE POACHED PEARS

Serve these tender pears and their bracing aromatic syrup in a large glass bowl, and garnish with glistening orange slices.

ACTIVE TIME: 20 MIN · TOTAL TIME: 1 HR 20 MIN PLUS CHILLING
MAKES: 8 SERVINGS

1 LEMON

8 FIRM-RIPE PEARS, SUCH AS BOSC OR ANJOU (8 TO 9 OUNCES EACH), PEELED AND CORED

6 CUPS WATER

1 CUP SUGAR

3 WHOLE STAR ANISE OR 1 TEASPOON ANISE SEEDS

1 SMALL ORANGE, THINLY SLICED

1 From lemon, with vegetable peeler, remove 3 strips (3" by ¾" each) peel; squeeze 2 tablespoons juice. In nonreactive 8-quart saucepot, combine lemon peel, pears, water, sugar, and star anise; heat to boiling over high heat. Reduce heat; cover and simmer until pears are tender, about 30 minutes. With slotted spoon, transfer pears to large bowl. Stir lemon juice into bowl with pears. Strain syrup through sieve into separate large bowl. Return syrup to saucepot.

2 Heat syrup to boiling over high heat; cook, uncovered, until reduced to 3 cups, about 15 minutes. Pour hot syrup over pears. Cover and refrigerate, turning occasionally, until pears are well chilled, at least 6 hours.

3 Serve pears with syrup, garnished with orange slices.

EACH SERVING: ABOUT 236 CALORIES (4 PERCENT CALORIES FROM FAT) | 1G PROTEIN | 61G CARBOHYDRATE | 1G TOTAL FAT (0G SATURATED) | 0MG CHOLESTEROL | 1MG SODIUM

TIP Bosc and Anjou pears are tops at holding their shape and texture when cooked. In a pinch, Bartletts and other varieties work fine too. Avoid Comice pears for cooking: their tender, juicy flesh tends to fall apart when baked whole or used in pies.

SPICY PLUM COMPOTE

Plum slices are simmered just long enough in a lemony allspice syrup to give them a hint of exotic flavor.

ACTIVE TIME: 10 MIN · TOTAL TIME: 16 MIN PLUS CHILLING

MAKES: 4 SERVINGS

½ CUP SUGAR

3 STRIPS LEMON PEEL (3" BY ½" EACH)

4 WHOLE ALLSPICE BERRIES

2 CUPS WATER

4 RIPE MEDIUM RED, PURPLE, AND/OR GREEN PLUMS (1 POUND), CUT INTO ½-INCH SLICES

½ TEASPOON VANILLA EXTRACT

LOW-FAT YOGURT (OPTIONAL)

1 In 2-quart saucepan, combine sugar, lemon peel, allspice, and water; heat to boiling over high heat. Boil 5 minutes.

2 Stir plums into syrup; heat to boiling over high heat. Reduce heat to low; simmer 1 minute or just until plums are tender.

3 Pour mixture into bowl; stir in vanilla. Cover and refrigerate until cold, about 2 hours. Serve with yogurt if you like.

EACH SERVING: ABOUT 135 CALORIES (0 CALORIES FROM FAT) | 1G PROTEIN | 34G CARBOHYDRATE | 0G TOTAL FAT | 0MG CHOLESTEROL | 0MG SODIUM

PLUM YOGURT POPS

Forget store-bought popsicles: This super-fruity refresher will be a cool hit with kids of all ages. Make a day in advance to allow enough time for freezing.

TOTAL TIME: 15 MIN PLUS FREEZING

MAKES: 16 POPS

---

1   POUND RIPE RED OR PURPLE PLUMS (4 MEDIUM), COARSELY CHOPPED

½   CUP SUGAR

1   TABLESPOON FRESH LEMON JUICE

2   CUPS VANILLA LOW-FAT YOGURT

1   In blender, at medium speed, puree plums, sugar, and lemon juice. Pour plum puree into medium-mesh sieve set over medium bowl. With spoon, press purée against sieve to push through pulp and juice. Discard solids in sieve.

2   With wire whisk, mix yogurt and plum mixture until well combined.

3   Spoon yogurt mixture into sixteen 3-ounce paper cups; freeze 4 hours or until partially frozen. Insert wooden ice-cream-bar sticks and freeze until completely frozen. (Or, spoon yogurt mixture into sixteen 2-ounce popsicle molds; seal and insert wooden sticks as manufacturer directs. Freeze overnight.)

EACH POP: ABOUT 60 CALORIES (15 PERCENT CALORIES FROM FAT) | 1G PROTEIN | 13G CARBOHYDRATE | 1G TOTAL FAT (0G SATURATED) | 2MG CHOLESTEROL | 20MG SODIUM

PEACH GRANITA

Be sure the peaches or nectarines are as ripe as possible.

TOTAL TIME: 20 MIN PLUS FREEZING

MAKES: ABOUT 8 CUPS OR 16 SERVINGS

---

1   CUP SUGAR

1¼ CUPS WATER

1¾ POUNDS PEACHES OR NECTARINES (5 MEDIUM), UNPEELED AND CUT INTO WEDGES

2   TABLESPOONS FRESH LEMON JUICE

1 In 1-quart saucepan, heat sugar and water to boiling over high heat, stirring occasionally. Reduce heat to medium; cook mixture about 1 minute or until sugar dissolves completely. Transfer to small bowl to cool.

2 In blender, at medium speed, blend unpeeled peach wedges until smooth. Pour puree into medium-mesh sieve set over medium bowl. With spoon, press puree against sieve to push through pulp and juice. You should have 3 cups puree; discard solids in sieve.

3 Stir sugar syrup and lemon juice into puree. Pour peach mixture into 9" by 9" metal baking pan.

4 Cover with foil or plastic wrap. Freeze until partially frozen, about 2 hours; stir with fork. Freeze until completely frozen, at least 3 hours or overnight.

5 To serve, let granita stand at room temperature until softened slightly, about 15 minutes. With spoon or fork, scrape across surface of granita to create pebbly texture.

EACH SERVING: ABOUT 65 CALORIES (0 CALORIES FROM FAT) | 0G PROTEIN | 17G CARBOHYDRATE | 0G TOTAL FAT | 0MG CHOLESTEROL | 0MG SODIUM

BLUEBERRY GRANITA

Prepare as directed but substitute **3 pints blueberries** for the peaches.

EACH SERVING: ABOUT 80 CALORIES (0 CALORIES FROM FAT) | 0G PROTEIN | 20G CARBOHYDRATE | 0G TOTAL FAT | 0MG CHOLESTEROL | 5MG SODIUM

RASPBERRY GRANITA

Prepare as directed but substitute **6 half-pints raspberries** for the peaches and **2 tablespoons lime juice** for the lemon juice.

EACH SERVING: ABOUT 70 CALORIES (0 CALORIES FROM FAT) | 0G PROTEIN | 18G CARBOHYDRATE | 0G TOTAL FAT | 0MG CHOLESTEROL | 0MG SODIUM

WATERMELON GRANITA

Prepare as directed but substitute **1 piece (5½ pounds) watermelon**, seeded and cut into chunks, for the peaches, **2 tablespoons lime juice** for the lemon juice, and decrease the water to ¾ cup.

EACH SERVING: ABOUT 70 CALORIES (0 CALORIES FROM FAT) | 1G PROTEIN | 17G CARBOHYDRATE | 0G TOTAL FAT | 0MG CHOLESTEROL | 2MG SODIUM

FROZEN CHOCOLATE KAHLÚA MOUSSE

When company's coming unexpectedly, or you need a special dessert at the last minute, this delicate, rich-tasting confection rises to the occasion—and it's fat-free to boot.

TOTAL TIME: 10 MIN PLUS FREEZING

MAKES: 6 SERVINGS

---

1   ENVELOPE UNFLAVORED GELATIN

1   CUP COLD WATER

½   CUP NONFAT RICOTTA CHEESE

½   CUP COLD FAT-FREE (SKIM) MILK

6   TABLESPOONS SUGAR

½   CUP KAHLÚA LIQUEUR

3   TABLESPOONS UNSWEETENED COCOA

PINCH SALT

1 In 1-quart saucepan, evenly sprinkle gelatin over cold water; let stand 2 minutes to soften gelatin slightly. Cook over medium heat, stirring frequently, until gelatin has completely dissolved (do not boil).
2 In blender, combine gelatin mixture, ricotta, milk, sugar, liqueur, and cocoa. Blend until smooth, about 1 minute. Pour into dessert glasses and freeze at least 2 hours.

EACH SERVING: ABOUT 100 CALORIES (0 CALORIES FROM FAT) | 5G PROTEIN | 16G CARBOHYDRATE | 0G TOTAL FAT | 3MG CHOLESTEROL | 80MG SODIUM

TIP The darker the chocolate, the better it is for you. Bittersweet chocolate is rich in flavonols that have been found to reduce blood pressure and LDL cholesterol (the "bad" kind).

BUTTERSCOTCH BLONDIES

These chewy treats are one of our test kitchen's favorites—it's hard to believe there are only three grams of fat in each one!

ACTIVE TIME: 15 MIN · TOTAL TIME: 50 MIN
MAKES: 16 BLONDIES

1   CUP ALL-PURPOSE FLOUR

½   TEASPOON BAKING POWDER

¼   TEASPOON SALT

3   TABLESPOONS BUTTER
    OR MARGARINE

¾   CUP PACKED DARK BROWN SUGAR

2   LARGE EGG WHITES

⅓   CUP DARK CORN SYRUP

2   TEASPOONS VANILLA EXTRACT

2   TABLESPOONS FINELY
    CHOPPED PECANS

1 Preheat oven to 350°F. Grease 8-inch square baking pan. In bowl, combine flour, baking powder, and salt.

2 In large bowl, with mixer at medium speed, beat butter and brown sugar until well blended, about 2 minutes. Reduce speed to low; beat in egg whites, corn syrup, and vanilla until smooth. Beat in flour mixture just until combined. Spread batter evenly in prepared pan. Sprinkle with pecans.

3 Bake until toothpick inserted in center comes out clean and edges are lightly browned, 35 to 40 minutes. Cool completely in pan on wire rack.

4 When cool, cut into 4 strips, then cut each strip crosswise into 4 pieces.

EACH BLONDIE: ABOUT 117 CALORIES (23 PERCENT CALORIES FROM FAT) | 1G PROTEIN | 21G CARBOHYDRATE | 3G TOTAL FAT (1G SATURATED) | 6MG CHOLESTEROL | 94MG SODIUM

FUDGY BROWNIES

Moist, chocolaty, and low-fat. Need we say more? Serve with cold skim milk for a healthful and delicious treat.

ACTIVE TIME: 15 MIN · **TOTAL TIME:** 33 MIN
MAKES: 16 BROWNIES

1 TEASPOON INSTANT ESPRESSO-
   COFFEE POWDER

1 TEASPOON HOT WATER

¾ CUP ALL-PURPOSE FLOUR

½ CUP UNSWEETENED COCOA

½ TEASPOON BAKING POWDER

¼ TEASPOON SALT

3 TABLESPOONS BUTTER
   OR MARGARINE

¾ CUP SUGAR

2 LARGE EGG WHITES

¼ CUP DARK CORN SYRUP

1 TEASPOON VANILLA EXTRACT

1 Preheat oven to 350°F. Grease 8-inch square baking pan. In cup, dissolve espresso powder in hot water; set aside. In large bowl, combine flour, cocoa, baking powder, and salt.

2 In 2-quart saucepan, melt butter over low heat. Remove from heat. With wooden spoon, stir in espresso, sugar, egg whites, corn syrup, and vanilla until blended. Stir sugar mixture into flour mixture just until blended (do not overmix). Pour batter into prepared pan.

3 Bake until toothpick inserted in center comes out almost clean, 18 to 22 minutes. Cool brownies completely in pan on wire rack.

4 When cool, cut brownies into 4 strips, then cut each strip crosswise into 4 pieces. If brownies are difficult to cut, use knife dipped in hot water and dried; repeat as necessary.

EACH BROWNIE: ABOUT 103 CALORIES (26 PERCENT CALORIES FROM FAT) | 2G PROTEIN | 19G CARBOHYDRATE | 3G TOTAL FAT (2G SATURATED) | 6MG CHOLESTEROL | 88MG SODIUM

DATE BARS

These beloved triple-layer sweets have a simple streusel topping.

ACTIVE TIME: 40 MIN · TOTAL TIME: 1 HR 25 MIN PLUS COOLING

MAKES: 12 BARS

OAT CRUST AND TOPPING

1¼ CUPS ALL-PURPOSE FLOUR

1 CUP OLD-FASHIONED OR QUICK-COOKING OATS, UNCOOKED

½ CUP PACKED LIGHT BROWN SUGAR

½ CUP BUTTER (1 STICK), SOFTENED

¼ TEASPOON BAKING SODA

¼ TEASPOON GROUND CINNAMON

¼ TEASPOON SALT

DATE FILLING

1 CONTAINER (10 OUNCES) PITTED DATES, CHOPPED

¾ CUP WATER

2 TABLESPOONS LIGHT BROWN SUGAR

1 Preheat oven to 375°F. Grease 9" by 9" metal baking pan. Line pan with foil; grease foil.

2 Prepare crust and topping: In large bowl, with hand, mix flour, oats, brown sugar, butter, baking soda, cinnamon, and salt until mixture comes together. Transfer 2 cups mixture to prepared baking pan; reserve remaining mixture for crumb topping. With hand, press mixture evenly onto bottom of pan to form a crust. Bake crust 10 minutes. Cool completely in pan on wire rack. Turn off oven.

3 While crust is cooling, prepare filling: In 2-quart saucepan, combine dates, water, and brown sugar. Cook over medium heat, stirring frequently, until mixture thickens and all liquid is absorbed, 6 to 8 minutes. Spoon filling into bowl and refrigerate until cool, about 30 minutes.

4 When filling is cool, preheat oven to 375°F. Spread filling over crust; top with reserved crumb mixture. Bake until topping is golden, 35 to 40 minutes. Cool completely in pan on wire rack.

5 When cool, transfer with foil to cutting board and remove foil. Cut into 4 strips, then cut each strip crosswise into 3 pieces.

EACH BAR: ABOUT 275 CALORIES (29 PERCENT CALORIES FROM FAT) | 4G PROTEIN | 47G CARBOHYDRATE | 9G TOTAL FAT (5G SATURATED) | 21MG CHOLESTEROL | 155MG SODIUM

METRIC EQUIVALENT CHARTS

The recipes that appear in this cookbook use the standard United States method for measuring liquid and dry or solid ingredients (teaspoons, tablespoons, and cups). The information on this chart is provided to help cooks outside the U.S. successfully use these recipes. All equivalents are approximate.

METRIC EQUIVALENTS FOR DIFFERENT TYPES OF INGREDIENTS

A standard cup measure of a dry or solid ingredient will vary in weight depending on the type of ingredient. A standard cup of liquid is the same volume for any type of liquid. Use the following chart when converting standard cup measures to grams (weight) or milliliters (volume).

Standard Cup	Fine Powder (e.g. flour)	Grain (e.g. rice)	Granular (e.g. sugar)	Liquid Solids (e.g. butter)	Liquid (e.g. milk)
1	140 g	150 g	190 g	200 g	240 ml
¾	105 g	113 g	143 g	150 g	180 ml
⅔	93 g	100 g	125 g	133 g	160 ml
½	70 g	75 g	95 g	100 g	120 ml
⅓	47 g	50 g	63 g	67 g	80 ml
¼	35 g	38 g	48 g	50 g	60 ml
⅛	18 g	19 g	24 g	25 g	30 ml

USEFUL EQUIVALENTS FOR LIQUID INGREDIENTS BY VOLUME

¼ tsp=					1 ml	
½ tsp=					2 ml	
1 tsp =					5 ml	
3 tsp =	1 tbls =		½ fl oz =	15 ml	
	2 tbls =	⅛ cup =	1 fl oz =	30 ml	
	4 tbls =	¼ cup =	2 fl oz =	60 ml	
	5⅓ tbls =	⅓ cup =	3 fl oz =	80 ml	
	8 tbls =	½ cup =	4 fl oz =	120 ml	
	10⅔ tbls =	⅔ cup =	5 fl oz =	160 ml	
	12 tbls =	¾ cup =	6 fl oz =	180 ml	
	16 tbls =	1 cup =	8 fl oz =	240 ml	
	1 pt =	2 cups =	16 fl oz =	480 ml	
	1 qt =	4 cups =	32 fl oz =	960 ml	
			33 fl oz =	1000 ml	= 1 L

USEFUL EQUIVALENTS FOR COOKING/OVEN TEMPERATURES

	Fahrenheit	Celsius	Gas Mark
Freeze Water	32° F	0° C	
Room Temperature	68° F	20° C	
Boil Water	212° F	100° C	
Bake	325° F	160° C	3
	350° F	180° C	4
	375° F	190° C	5
	400° F	200° C	6
	425° F	220° C	7
	450° F	230° C	8
Broil			Grill

USEFUL EQUIVALENTS FOR DRY INGREDIENTS BY WEIGHT
(To convert ounces to grams, multiply the number of ounces by 30.)

1 oz	=	¹⁄₁₆ lb	=	30g
2 oz	=	¼ lb	=	120g
4 oz	=	½ lb	=	240g
8 oz	=	¾ lb	=	360g
16 oz	=	1 lb	=	480g

USEFUL EQUIVALENTS LENGTH
(To convert inches to centimeters, multiply the number of inches by 2.5.)

1 in =		2.5cm
6 in = ½ ft =		15cm
12 in = 1 ft =		30cm
36 in = 3 ft = 1 yd =	90cm
40 in =		100cm = 1 m

PHOTOGRAPHY CREDITS

FRONT COVER
Mike Garten

BACK COVER
© Monica Buck, © Mary Ellen Bartley, © James Baigrie, © Ann Stratton,
© Alan Richardson, © James Baigrie (back clockwise from top left)

Antonis Achilleos: 150, 160
Quentin Bacon: 190
James Baigrie: 20, 27, 30, 32, 44, 100, 106, 116, 124, 133, 297
Mary Ellen Bartley: 277
Monica Buck: 17, 19,50, 56, 63, 67, 68, 80, 87, 95, 113,152, 153, 155
Beatrix Da Costa: 207, 226, 356
Tara Donne: 73
Mike Garten: 84
Brian Hagiwara: 8, 54, 58, 97, 118, 135, 210, 221, 243, 250, 254, 261, 267, 272, 274, 278, 282,
    293, 294, 317, 322, 330, 336, 341, 377, 390, 397, 412, 421, 427, 428, 431, 450, 437, 440, 452,
    455, 461, 463
Istockphoto: Eve Milla, 43; MistikaS, 127; Kevin Russ, 37
Rita Maas: 15, 16, 39, 121,131,158, 175, 345, 443
Steven Mark Needham: 444, 456
Ngoc Minh Ngo: 103, 105
Alan Richardson: 232, 245, 287, 288, 302, 312
Amy Kalyn Sims: 90
Ann Stratton: 138, 149, 168, 179, 182, 187, 193, 202, 229, 217, 222, 229, 367
Studio D: Chris Eckert, 7
Mark Thomas: 12, 46, 71, 83, 122, 141, 147, 258, 310, 350, 365, 374, 386, 394, 400, 408, 411
Jonelle Weaver: 162

INDEX

THE GOOD HOUSEKEEPING TRIPLE-TEST PROMISE

At Good Housekeeping, we want to make sure that every recipe we print works in any oven, with any brand of ingredient, no matter what. That's why, in our test kitchens at the **Good Housekeeping Research Institute**, we go all out: We test each recipe at least three times—and, often, several more times after that.

When a recipe is first developed, one member of our team prepares the dish and we judge it on these criteria: it must be **delicious, family-friendly, healthy**, and **easy to make**.

1. The recipe is then tested several more times to fine-tune the flavor and ease of preparation, always by the same team member, using the same equipment.

2. Next, another team member follows the recipe as written, **varying the brands of ingredients** and **kinds of equipment**. Even the types of stoves we use are changed.

3. A third team member repeats the whole process **using yet another set of equipment** and **alternative ingredients**.

By the time the recipes appear on these pages, they are guaranteed to work in any kitchen, including yours. WE PROMISE.